The Maastricht Treaty, signed in December 1991, set a timetable for the European Community's economic and monetary union (EMU) and clearly defined the institutional policy changes necessary for its achievement. Subsequent developments have demonstrated, however, the importance of many key issues in the transition to EMU that were largely neglected at the time.

This volume reports the proceedings of a joint CEPR conference with the Banco de Portugal, held in January 1992. In these papers, leading international experts address the instability of the transition to EMU, the long-run implications of monetary union, and the single market for growth and convergence in Europe. They also consider the prospects for inflation and fiscal convergence, regional policy and the integration of financial markets and fiscal systems. Attention focuses on adjustment mechanisms with differentiated shocks, region-specific business cycles and excessive industrial concentration, and the cases for a two-speed EMU and fiscal federalism.

T0312233

Adjustment and growth in the European Monetary Union

Centre for Economic Policy Research

The Centre for Economic Policy Research is a network of more than 180 Research Fellows, based primarily in European universities. The Centre coordinates its Fellows' research activities and communicates their results to the public and private sectors. CEPR is an entrepreneur, developing research initiatives with the producers, consumers and sponsors of research. Established in 1983, CEPR is already a European economics research organization with uniquely wide-ranging scope and activities.

CEPR is a registered educational charity. Grants from the Leverhulme Trust, the Esmée Fairbairn Charitable Trust, the Baring Foundation, the Bank of England and Citibank provide institutional finance. The ESRC supports the Centre's dissemination programme and, with the Nuffield Foundation, its programme of research workshops. None of these organizations gives prior review to the Centre's publications nor necessarily endorses the views expressed therein.

The Centre is pluralist and non-partisan, bringing economic research to bear on the analysis of medium- and long-run policy questions. CEPR research may include views on policy, but the Executive Committee of the Centre does not give prior review to its publications and the Centre takes no institutional policy positions. The opinions expressed in this volume are those of the authors and not those of the Centre for Economic Policy Research.

Executive Committee

Chairman
Anthony Loehnis

Vice-Chairmen
Guillermo de la Dehesa
Adam Ridley

Giorgio Basevi
Honor Chapman
Sheila Drew Smith
Jacob Frenkel
Otmar Issing

Mervyn King
Peter Middleton
Mario Sarcinelli
Alasdair Smith

Officers

Director
Richard Portes

Deputy Director
Stephen Yeo

Director of Finance and Research Administration
Wendy Thompson

8 February 1993

Adjustment and growth in the European Monetary Union

Edited by
FRANCISCO TORRES
and
FRANCESCO GIAVAZZI

CAMBRIDGE
UNIVERSITY PRESS

CAMBRIDGE UNIVERSITY PRESS
Cambridge, New York, Melbourne, Madrid, Cape Town, Singapore, São Paulo, Delhi

Cambridge University Press
The Edinburgh Building, Cambridge CB2 8RU, UK

Published in the United States of America by Cambridge University Press, New York

www.cambridge.org
Information on this title: www.cambridge.org/9780521440196

© Cambridge University Press 1993

First published 1993
Reprinted 1996
This digitally printed version 2008

A catalogue record for this publication is available from the British Library

Library of Congress Cataloguing in Publication data
Adjustment and growth in the European Monetary System / edited by
Francisco Torres and Francesco Giavazzi.
    p.   cm.
Includes index.
ISBN 0 521 44019 X
1. Monetary policy – European Economic Community countries – Congresses.
2. European Monetary System (Organization) – Congresses.
3. Monetary unions – Congresses.
I. Torres, Francisco S. II. Giavazzi, Francesco.
HG930.5.A65   1993
332.4′566′094 – dc20   93-19861   CIP

ISBN 978-0-521-44019-6 hardback
ISBN 978-0-521-10044-1 paperback

Contents

List of figures   *page* xiii
List of tables   xvi
Preface   xix
List of contributors   xxi
Foreword   xxiii

1 Introduction   1
Francisco Torres and Francesco Giavazzi
   1   Fiscal policy, geography and politics   2
   2   Inflation convergence in fixed exchange rate regimes   4
   3   Financial market integration and capital taxation   6
   4   The Maastricht Treaty   8

**2 Economic and monetary union: critical notes on the Maastricht
   Treaty revisions**   9
Niels Thygesen
   1   Introduction   9
   2   Stage II as agreed at Maastricht: commencement
       and content   11
   3   Stage II: how does it end?   15
   4   An interpretation of the monetary content of Stage II   20
   5   Conclusions   25
       Discussion
       Lorenzo Bini Smaghi   28
       Vitor Gaspar   37
       José Viñals   41

3 The design of optimal fiscal rules for Europe after 1992   46
Giancarlo Corsetti and Nouriel Roubini
   1   Introduction   46

2 Fiscal arithmetic at Maastricht   50
3 Tests of public sector solvency for the EC countries:
   the empirical evidence   53
4 Political determinants of budget deficits: a survey
   of the theory   63
5 Political determinants of fiscal deficits: the empirical
   evidence   67
6 A comparison of alternative fiscal rules   71
7 Concluding remarks: an evaluation of the EC fiscal
   guidelines   74
   Appendix: Alternative fiscal rules in a political equilibrium   76
   Discussion
   Axel A. Weber   83

**4 Contracts, credibility and common knowledge: their influence on
    inflation convergence**   93
Marcus Miller and Alan Sutherland
1 Introduction   93
2 Wage contracts and inflation persistence   95
3 Calvo contracts and lack of credibility   104
4 Lack of common knowledge   107
5 Conclusion   111
   Appendix 4A: The stable path with Taylor contracts   112
   Appendix 4B: Fischer contracts   113
   Appendix 4C: Bayesian learning about the realignment
   probability   113
   Discussion
   David Backus   116
   Michael Dooley   123

**5 Inflation in fixed exchange regimes: the recent Portuguese
    experience**   128
Sérgio Rebelo
1 Introduction   128
2 An economy with capital controls   130
3 Introducing free movement of capital   141
4 Explaining the nominal facts   142
5 Summary and conclusions   144
   Discussion
   Michael Moore   149
   Guido Tabellini   153

6 Models of economic integration and localized growth   159
   Giuseppe Bertola
   1 Introduction and overview   159
   2 Investment and macroeconomic growth   161
   3 Economic integration and endogenous growth   165
   4 Geographic linkages   167
   5 Labour mobility   170
   6 Europe, and directions for further research   176
   Discussion
   João César das Neves   179
   Charles Wyplosz   189

7 Shocking aspects of European monetary integration   193
   Tamim Bayoumi and Barry Eichengreen
   1 Introduction   193
   2 Optimum currency areas: theory and evidence   195
   3 Methodology   200
   4 Data   202
   5 Results   207
   6 Summary and implications   221
   Discussion
   Giorgio Basevi   230
   Patrick Minford   235

8 Lessons of Massachusetts for EMU   241
   Paul Krugman
   1 Introduction   241
   2 Integration, regional specialization and regional stability 243
   3 Evidence on integrated markets and monetary unions   249
   4 Integration, monetary union and stabilization policy   255
   5 Development and regional inequality   258
   6 Summary and conclusions   259
   Discussion
   Alessandra Casella   261
   Paul de Grauwe   266

9 Financial and currency integration in the European monetary
   system: the statistical record   270
   Jeffrey Frankel, Steven Phillips and Menzie Chinn
   1 Introduction   270
   2 How rapidly have country barriers diminished?   272
   3 Has the exchange risk premium diminished?   273

4 The EMS target zone 279
5 Have expected future exchange rates fallen inside
the bands since 1988? 283
6 Reassessing the performance of target zone models 286
7 Estimation of the realignment term 292
8 Conclusions 294
Appendix 9A: Interest rate differentials 300
Appendix 9B: EMS developments, 1986–91 302
Discussion
Rudiger Dornbusch 306
Paolo Onofri 312

10 **Currency substitution: from the policy questions to the theory and back** 318
Matthew Canzoneri, Behzad Diba and Alberto Giovannini
1 Introduction: from the policy questions to the theory 318
2 The case of a single currency 319
3 A two-currency economy 324
4 Relationship with previous results 329
5 Back to the policy questions 330
Discussion
Lucas Papademos 333
António S. Mello 338

11 **Coordination of capital income taxes in the economic and monetary union: what needs to be done?** 340
Peter B. Sørenson
1 The issues 340
2 The taxation of income from capital in the European
Community 341
3 Tax competition versus tax harmonization 360
4 Some proposals for coordination of capital income taxes
in the EC 365
5 The size and distribution of efficiency gains from tax
harmonization 372
6 Conclusions 377
Discussion
Alberto Giovannini 382

Index 385

Figures

page

D.3.1   Sustainability of German real public debt: recursive coefficient estimates and stability test results (1968, Q.1 – 1990, Q.4)   85

D.3.2   Sustainability of French real public debt: recursive coefficient estimates and stability test results (1968, Q.1 – 1990, Q.4)   86

D.3.3   Sustainability of Belgian real public debt: recursive coefficient estimates and stability test results (1968, Q.1 – 1990, Q.4)   88

D.3.4   EC fiscal guidelines and degree of fiscal convergence achieved in 1989 and 1990   89

4.1   Taylor contracts before and after entry   96
4.2   Fischer contracts before and after entry   101
4.3   Entry rates to avoid recession (N) or to end inflation (D) 102
4.4   Lack of credibility and learning   105
4.5   phi = 0.5   109
4.6   phi = 0.1   110
D.4.1   Rates of inflation: Germany, Netherlands, and France, 1960–90   117
D.4.2   Inflation rates, three US cities, 1976–90   117
D.4.3   Rates of inflation: USA and Canada, 1960–90   118
D.4.4   Rates of inflation: Germany, Italy, and Portugal, 1960–90 118
D.4.5   Real exchange rates: Netherlands and France in relation to Germany, 1960–90   119
D.4.6   Real exchange rates: Italy and Portugal in relation to Germany, 1960–90   120
D.4.7   Real exchange rates: Canada in relation to USA, 1960–90   120
D.4.8   Prices and nominal exchange rates   124
5.1   Exchange rates, interest rates and inflation in Portugal, 1980–92   129

5.2	Alternative shock paths	140
D.5.1	Labour share of income, manufacturing sector, Portugal relative to other OECD countries	155
D.5.2	Labour share of income, manufacturing sector, Italy relative to other OECD countries	156
D.5.3	Labour share of income, manufacturing sector, Spain relative to other OECD countries	156
D.5.4	Labour share of income, manufacturing sector, United Kingdom relative to other OECD countries	157
D.5.5	Labour share of income, manufacturing sector, average of Denmark, France, Germany, Belgium and the Netherlands relative to other OECD countries	157
6.1a	Private equilibrium	172
6.1b	Private equilibrium	173
6.2a	Planner's equilibrium	174
6.2n	Planner's equilibrium	175
D.6.1	Relative growth rate differentials, 1960–91, selected EC countries	183
D.6.2	Relative growth rate differentials, 1960–85, EC–USA, Canada–USA, Mexico–USA, Haiti–USA	184
D.6.3	Correlation between annual growth rates, selected EC countries	186
D.6.4	Correlation between annual growth rates, EC–USA, Canada–USA, Mexico–USA, Haiti–USA	187
7.1	The aggregate demand and supply model	199
7.2	Impulse-response functions for the European Community and the USA	208
7.3	Aggregate demand and supply shocks for the European Community and the USA	210
7.4	Correlation of demand and supply shocks with anchor areas	213
7.5	The size and correlation of the demand and supply disturbances	218
7.6	Impulse-response functions – supply shocks	220
7.7	Impulse-response functions to a demand shock	222
8.1	Geographical concentration	245
8.2	Annual rates of employment growth, Ohio and Belgium	252
8.3	Adjusted rates of employment growth, Ohio and Belgium	253
9.1	EMS currencies, March 1979 – December 1991	280
9.2	One-year expectations based on interest rate differentials, March 1979 – January 1987	282
9.3	EMS spot exchange rates, February 1988 – December 1991	284

9.4	Twelve-month expectations, using interest rate differentials, February 1988 – December 1991	285
9.5	One-month forecasts, February 1988 – December 1991	287
9.6	Three-month forecasts, February 1988 – December 1991	288
9.7	Twelve-month forecasts, February 1988 – December 1991	289
9.8	Five-year forecasts	290
9.9	q estimates: expected rate of realignment against the Deutschmark – 12-month horizon, annualized (Based on CFD survey)	295
9.10	q estimates: expected rate of realignment against the Deutschmark – 12-month horizon, annualized (Based on uncovered interest parity)	296
D.9.1	Three-month interest differential (Finland and Belgium relative to Germany)	310
D.9.2	Italy and France: value added per head in the service sector, 1980–89	315
D.9.3	Italy and France: relative price of service and industrial goods, 1980–91 (Q.1)	316
D.9.4	Italy and France: relative value added of service sector and industrial sector, 1980–91 (Q.1)	316
10.1	Organization and timing of markets and transactions	321

Tables

		page
2.1	An overall indicator of convergence	19
D.2.1	Use of monetary policy instruments	32
D.2.2	Selected features of inter-bank payment systems	35
3.1	Net debt to GDP ratio	54
3.2	Inflation-adjusted, seigniorage-adjusted deficit (overall and current)	58
3.3	Testing for solvency of the public sector in EC countries: test results for the series of discounted general government net interest-bearing liabilities	61
3.4	Panel data regression of deficit with political variables	69
D.3.1	Convergence judged by selected economic indicators, 1990	91
5.1	Rates of growth of selected economic variables and GDP ratios, Portugal 1980–91	131
5.2	Parameters used in baseline scenario	135
5.3	Alternative shock paths	138
5.4	Economy with capital controls: differences between inflation rates of tradables and non-tradables	139
5.5	Economy with free capital mobility: differences between inflation rates of tradables and non-tradables	142
D.6.1	Evolution of real gross domestic product ratio	181
D.6.2	Real gross domestic product ratio	182
D.6.3	Correlation coefficients of real GDP growth rates	185
7.1	Standard deviations and correlation coefficients with anchor areas	204
7.2	Percentage of variance explained by the first principal component across different groups of countries: raw data	205
7.3	Percentage of variance explained by the first principal component across different groups of US regions	206

7.4	Correlation coefficients between anchor areas and other regions: underlying shocks	211
7.5	Percentage of variance explained by the first principal component for geographic groupings	214
7.6	Standard deviations of aggregate supply and aggregate demand shocks	216
8.1	Indices of industrial specialization	250
8.2	Industrial specialization, 1985	251
8.3	Distribution of automobile production	251
8.4	Annual rates of employment growth, EC and USA, 1960–88	255
D.8.1	Divergences in regional and national growth rates of output	268
9.1	Average absolute interest rate differentials	271
9.2	Time trends in absolute covered interest rate differentials from September 1982	274
9.3	Time trends in absolute risk premium, February 1988 – December 1991	277
9.4	Mean 12-month expectations (from interest rates) as deviations from Deutschmark central rates	286
9.5	Correlation coefficients: spot position in band and expected change over 12-month horizon	291
9.6	Expected mean reversion within the band, estimates of β_1	293
9.7	Test of $\beta_2 = \beta_3 = 0$: marginal signfecance	294
9.8	Magnitude of expected rates of mean reversion	297
A.1	Trends in absolute interest rate differentials from September 1982	300
D.9.1	Euro-interest differentials relative to Germany, January 1987	310
11.1	Personal tax rates (all levels of government) on capital income in the European Community, 1991	346
11.2	Corporate tax rates and methods of double taxation relief in the European Community, 1991	348
11.3	Depreciation allowances and general investment reliefs in the European Community, 1991	350
11.4	The cost of capital in domestic and transnational direct investment in the European Community, 1991	357
11.5	Estimated effects on output levels of corporate tax harmonization in the European Community	374

Preface

This volume collects many of the contributions to a conference organized by Banco de Portugal and the Centre for Economic Policy Research on Economic and Monetary Union (EMU) held in Estoril on 16/18 January 1992, at the beginning of the first Portuguese presidency of the European Community.

The conference programme was carefully designed for more than a year, when I was on leave from Banco de Portugal and Universidade Católica Portuguesa at the Centre for European Policy Studies in Brussels. Its preparation benefited from a grant of Fundação Luso Americana para o Desenvolvimento to study the long-run implications of EMU cum the European Internal Market for a country such as Portugal. This volume constitutes certainly the most valuable outgrowth of that project. During that period I received inestimable advice from Daniel Gros, Paul de Grauwe, Niels Thygesen and, especially, from Francesco Giavazzi, who became an active co-organizer and enhanced the academic authority of the project.

The Board of Governors of Banco de Portugal agreed on co-organizing and sponsoring the conference. António Borges, who promptly welcomed the idea, followed the entire organization process with great enthusiasm, much institutional and personal commitment and excellent suggestions. The tireless dedication of Irene Lemos, head of conference staff, contributed much to the success of the conference.

CEPR joined in with its invaluable advice and prestige. In setting up the collaboration with Banco de Portugal and throughout the organization Richard Portes and Stephen Yeo provided high quality support. A timely overview of the conference by Clive Crook came out in April in a joint Banco de Portugal-CEPR report presented in Lisbon at the Centro de Estudos Europeus of Universidade Católica. It almost coincided with the official announcement, on the following day, of the escudo's entry into the ERM.

The production of this volume has benefited from the particularly good collaboration of all authors and discussants and Francesco Giavazzi's remarkable skills and experience as editor. David Guthrie and Kate Millward of CEPR and Thelma Liesner, with her work as Production Editor, have done an excellent job in guiding it to press.

Francisco Torres
February 1993

Contributors

David Backus *New York University*
Giorgio Basevi *Università di Bologna and CEPR*
Tamim Bayoumi *IMF*
Giuseppe Bertola *Princeton University and CEPR*
Lorenzo Bini Smaghi *Banca d'Italia*
Matthew Canzoneri *Georgetown University*
Alessandra Casella *University of California at Berkeley and CEPR*
Menzie Chinn *University of California at Santa Cruz*
Giancarlo Corsetti *Yale University*
Paul de Grauwe *Katholieke Universiteit Leuven and CEPR*
Behzad Diba *Georgetown University*
Michael Dooley *IMF*
Rudiger Dornbusch *MIT and CEPR*
Barry Eichengreen *University of California at Berkeley and CEPR*
Jeffrey Frankel *University of California at Berkeley*
Vítor Gaspar *Ministério das Finanças and Universidade Nova de Lisboa*
Francesco Giavazzi *Università Bocconi and CEPR*
Alberto Giovannini *Columbia University and CEPR*
Paul Krugman *MIT and CEPR*
António S Mello *Banco de Portugal and Universidade Católica Portuguesa*
Marcus Miller *University of Warwick and CEPR*
Patrick Minford *University of Liverpool and CEPR*
Michael Moore *Queen's University, Belfast*
João César das Neves *Universidade Católica Portuguesa*
Paolo Onofri *Universitá di Bologna*
Lucas Papademos *Bank of Greece*
Steven Phillips *IMF*
Sérgio Rebelo *Banco de Portugal and Universidade Católica Portuguesa*
Nouriel Roubini *Yale University and CEPR*
Peter Birch Sørenson *Copenhagen Business School*

Alan Sutherland *University of York and CEPR*
Guido Tabellini *Universitá di Brescia and CEPR*
Niels Thygesen *Kobenhaven Universitet*
Francisco Torres *Banco de Portugal and Universidade Católica Portuguesa*
José Viñals *Committee of Governors of the EC Central Banks, Basle, and CEPR*
Axel Weber *Universität Gesamthochschule Siegen and CEPR*
Charles Wyplosz *INSEAD, DELTA and CEPR*

Foreword

The approval by the European Council at Maastricht of the Treaty amendments leading to economic and political union represented the end of a long process of study and negotiation. This process generated enormous interest from both academics and central bankers. Many thoughtful and influential contributions took the form of papers presented at conferences, in which both groups of researchers cooperated.

As we have already seen, the Council's approval of the new Treaty does not resolve all the issues related to economic and monetary union (EMU). The ratification procedure has encountered unexpected obstacles, and the exchange rate mechanism of the European monetary system has been under great strain. We are convinced, however, that the political and economic forces that led to Maastricht are long-run tendencies that will continue to operate, and that the process of monetary unification in Europe will also continue. Nevertheless, the Treaty itself prescribes that EMU will take place only if the transition is successfully managed, so that a strong degree of convergence is achieved.

Economic policy over the next few years will determine the outcome. The management of national economies with independent policies in a context of an increasingly credible process of convergence raises new questions, which require new answers. For countries such as Portugal, which are furthest from the convergence objective, the challenge is especially ambitious. These issues have greatly stimulated interest in additional work on the implications of EMU, in particular for the real economy. New results should be expected and welcome in this area.

In January 1992, Portugal took over the Presidency of the European Community for the first time. To help stimulate intellectual input on key European matters related to EMU, the Banco de Portugal took the initiative in organizing a conference which, following the model of other previous meetings, gathered in Estoril some of the very best researchers from the academic world and the European central banks. The Centre for

Economic Policy Research has for some time been the market leader in the economics of European integration, and CEPR was happy to join in the initiative, as co-organizer of what became a highly successful conference.

Thanks to the enthusiastic response of all participants, the conference met the Banco de Portugal's initial objectives and CEPR's expectations. The papers and comments presented will certainly be judged as representing the 'state-of-the-art' in the area of European economic and monetary integration. Many insightful new ideas were debated, which should influence decision-making over the next few years.

The papers in this volume were commissioned and mainly written before Maastricht; it was especially timely to discuss them and the broader implications immediately after that historic meeting of the European Council. The excitement of bringing economic analysis to bear on a major process of institutional innovation was evident at the conference and shows through in these proceedings. The timing of the conference at Estoril made it a special occasion, and the quality of the participants and proceedings makes this clear.

Gradually, EMU will be based on a more and more solid body of research on the determinants of its success and on its ultimate implications. As in Estoril, academic researchers, central bankers and CEPR will continue to be key contributors to this indispensable intellectual effort.

We are very grateful to the Banco de Portugal's staff, who ensured that the conference ran so smoothly and enjoyably; for the efforts of CEPR's Deputy Director, Stephen Yeo, who collaborated in the conference organization; and to David Guthrie and Kate Millward of CEPR's publications staff.

António M.C.B. Borges
Richard Portes
8 February 1993

1 Introduction

FRANCISCO TORRES and
FRANCESCO GIAVAZZI

The inter-governmental conference convened to revise the Treaty of Rome, initiated at the end of 1990 and concluded at the Maastricht summit one year later, signalled the formal beginning of the process towards economic and monetary union (EMU). The Maastricht approach favoured gradualism over a rapid transition towards the adoption of a single currency. Gradualism was justified on the grounds that convergence of macroeconomic variables is a pre-condition of EMU and that time would be needed to set up new European monetary institutions.

The events that occurred during the summer of 1992 have cast a shadow over the Maastricht approach. The Treaty was first rejected by the Danish voters, and later won a wafer-thin majority in France. Meanwhile, the uncertainty about the outcome of these votes, and the lack of progress of some countries in implementing their convergence programmes, combined with the uncompromising attitude of the German monetary authorities, put pressure on the European monetary system. After 13 years of steady progress during which the system had expanded from eight to eleven members, and almost six years since the last realignment, the exchange rate mechanism eventually broke up. In September 1992, the United Kingdom and Italy withdrew from the exchange rate mechanism and Spain and Ireland resorted, albeit temporarily, to exchange controls. Most importantly, the Bundesbank indicated that it no longer felt obliged to comply with the rules of the system – i.e. the commitment to central bank intervention whenever a currency reached its fluctuation margin.

What happened is reminiscent of the events that 20 years ago brought about the abandonment of the Werner plan, the first attempt in the post-war period to create a European Monetary Union. At the time, in the early 1970s, what was left after the crisis was the 'snake-in-the-tunnel', essentially a Deutschmark-zone extending no further than Amsterdam and Brussels.

Both episodes raise doubts about gradualism as a way of achieving monetary union. The Maastricht approach, as the Werner plan 20 years earlier, is a product of the French vision of money being the driving force in politics and in economic fundamentals. But gradualism is inconsistent with that vision: if the *fait-accompli* of a single currency is deemed to provide sufficient discipline to force economic convergence, then waiting for fundamentals to converge is wrong. If the ability to use the same banknotes throughout Europe, and to understand foreign prices without having to undertake cumbersome computations, is enough to influence the median voter, then the adoption of a single currency should be accomplished swiftly rather than gradually.

Following the autumn crisis, the Maastricht process has now formally resumed, but the momentum seems to have been lost, and the doubts about the desirability of a single currency for Europe have come to the fore.

The essays in this volume provide excellent analyses of such doubts. When they were first presented at a conference in the weeks between the political agreement on Maastricht and the formal signing of the Treaty, they seemed to be out of step with current events in Europe. A year later their timing seems almost perfect.

The essays discuss the arguments for and against EMU from a long-run perspective. The contributions of both authors and discussants centre on two broad issues:

(i)   the rationale for 'convergence criteria' and the ability of a number of countries to meet these criteria as well as the desirability of their doing so; and (ii)   the effect of the adoption of a common currency together with the completion of the internal market upon the overall rate of economic growth in the EC and its convergence across countries.

1   Fiscal policy, geography and politics

A central question for these two issues and for the entire process of monetary union is the role of fiscal policy both at the national level and at the EC level. In Chapter 3, Corsetti and Roubini discuss the trade-off between the benefits of fiscal rules and the ability to use fiscal policy as a stabilization instrument.

Behind the idea of fiscal rules is the thought that they will provide an incentive to enable fiscally-weak countries to avoid 'excessive' or 'structural' deficits. These deficits may be politically motivated and may endanger, through the insolvency of the public sectors, the monetary stability of the entire union.

But rigid fiscal rules do not allow tax-smoothing in the presence of transitory shocks: they may thus prevent governments from running adequate deficits during recessions.

One of the most difficult issues in the management of economic policy in EMU is thus the ability of individual countries to respond to external shocks once they can no longer use the exchange rate as a means of adjustment. It is sometimes argued that fiscal policy must play a greater role in cushioning the impact of shocks, which seems difficult to reconcile with the Maastricht convergence criteria.

If shocks are distributed asymmetrically across countries and if national fiscal policies are constrained by binding rules, then there might be a case for either a two-speed EMU (core countries versus peripheral countries) or for an increase of fiscal funds at the federal level. The case for fiscal federalism (as in the US) and/or global tax incentives, may become stronger in the long-run, when there is no other available instrument to offset region-specific business cycles and/or excessive industry concentration.

Tamim Bayoumi and Barry Eichengreen describe and compare in Chapter 7 the underlying shocks to supply and demand in Europe and the USA since 1963. They find that shocks in Europe were significantly more differentiated among countries than shocks among regions of the USA, which suggests that Europe may find it harder to conduct a successful common monetary policy. For an 'inner core' of Germany and its closest neighbours, however, they found that shocks were notably more symmetric than for the Community as a whole.

As pointed out during the conference, however, the greater coherence of the shocks affecting the USA is not surprising – precisely because it is *already* a currency union. What matters is how the United States would have behaved if it had not been a currency union and how Europe will behave when it is. It may be that Europe will form a more natural common currency area than the USA: its countries are less specialized in production than US regions so shocks should be less idiosyncratic.

In Chapter 8 Paul Krugman examines how Europe might respond to a regional shock similar to the recent recession in New England. US regions are more specialized in production than European countries, so the specialization of the latter may increase as integration proceeds. Specialized regions are more vulnerable to shocks, especially those caused by shifts in tastes away from their exports. Moreover, capital movements in an integrated area may amplify shocks rather than attenuate them. A disturbing aspect of US growth is that regions appear to diverge over long periods, with no evident tendency to return to any historically 'normal' level of relative output or employment. This suggests that the EMU, together with the single internal market, will make US-style regional crises more common and more severe within Europe.

Krugman also argues that shocks will pose greater difficulties for Europe as labour mobility increases: as regions in recession lose labour more readily, temporary shocks will become permanent. Bayoumi and Eichengreen argue that it is precisely the lack of labour mobility that will make Europe's shocks harder to accommodate, as regions in recession suffer income reductions that further aggravate inter-regional disparities. One important difference between the two approaches is that, for Krugman, employment divergence is definitely more than a short-term phenomenon.

Although most of the economic integration that Europe could expect to achieve has already taken place, there are still obstacles to trade to be eliminated. Therefore it is argued that further European integration resulting from economic and monetary union will spur growth if, for example, specialization and geographic concentration of economic activities create beneficial externalities that promote faster growth. In Chapter 6 Giuseppe Bertola argues that such externalities need not imply that concentration is socially optimal. He distinguishes between the aggregate scale economies required to sustain endogenous growth, and local scale economies which may lead to privately optimal – but socially excessive – concentration. The ensuing policy conclusion is that both geographic and inter-temporal distortions must be considered in the planning of a unified European tax structure. While further integration may in theory lead to excessive specialization, there is a greater risk – it was argued during the conference – that attempts by governments to freeze existing production patterns will prevent the restructuring that is needed for EMU to deliver all its potential benefits.

2   Inflation convergence in fixed exchange rate regimes

Marcus Miller and Alan Sutherland, in Chapter 4, note the surprising persistence of inflation differentials in the countries belonging to the ERM, given the perceived lower likelihood of realignments in the period from January 1987 until 1992. They developed a model to assess the effects on inflation convergence of contract structures, speed of learning, shocks and perceived rules for realignments. They first found that with overlapping wage contracts and a fully credible exchange rate peg, there was some inflation inertia, but not enough to account for the sluggishness observed in practice. Second, overlapping contracts with a currency peg that is less than fully credible produced subdued inflation and protracted recessions after the adoption of the peg. Third, introducing informational asymmetry among agents increased the pace of adjustment.

If a large overvaluation is undermining the credibility of the peg, a devaluation may increase the credibility of the new rate provided the devaluation is perceived to be the last. A revaluation of the Deutschmark against the other ERM currencies at the moment of German unification might have met this criterion: German reunification is no everyday occurrence. Could this have prevented the crisis of 1992?

Sérgio Rebelo, in Chapter 5, examines, using data for Portugal, the extent to which the slow convergence of inflation could be the result of real forces that produce an appreciation in the relative price of non-tradables. Portugal's overall inflation rate fell by less than two percentage points towards the average of the exchange rate mechanism after the escudo began to shadow the ERM narrow band in 1990. Inflation in the traded-goods sector converged, while inflation in the non-traded-goods sector did not; so an essential part of the story was the persistent rise in the relative price of non-tradables to tradables.

The credibility story of Miller and Sutherland may partly explain the lack of inflation convergence in Portugal. The commitment to an exchange rate policy which provides for the ERM rate to be shadowed is by definition less credible than overt participation in the ERM, which Portugal joined only in April 1992.

Rebelo focuses on a different explanation: he suggests that the process of transition toward the steady state of an economy with low capital stock can also be responsible for an appreciation of the relative price of non-tradables.

It was pointed out during the conference that Japan's inflation rate had persistently remained five or more percentage points above that of the USA throughout the 1950–70 period, without any loss of competitiveness. In fact, consumer prices may not be a very good indicator of competitiveness; the prices of traded goods – or unit factor costs – may give a more accurate picture.

According to this explanation, the convergence of inflation of tradable goods should be a sufficient condition for membership of a fixed exchange regime such as the European monetary system. In other words, higher rates of inflation associated with movements in the relative price of non-tradables caused by real factors are compatible with a fixed exchange rate regime.

An economy with a high inflation rate will have a relatively low (or even negative) non-tradables real rate of interest while the tradables real interest rate will be the same in both countries. This real interest rate configuration does not in itself fuel the inflation process and undermine the fixed exchange rate regime.

3   Financial market integration and capital taxation

Recently many economists have drawn attention to the changing character of the exchange rate mechanism. Governments were, until the summer of 1992, evidently reluctant to seek realignments in circumstances that would earlier have prompted them to do so: the exchange rate mechanism, between 1987 and 1991, became more 'credible' than formerly.

In Chapter 9 Jeffrey Frankel, Steven Phillips and Menzie Chinn use both direct survey evidence of exchange rate forecasts and interest rate differentials to test how the credibility of the ERM's target zones has changed over time, and in particular whether the markets have regarded the currency bands as more credible since the last realignment of parities in the 1980s.

Their results indicate that the ERM was indeed more credible between 1987 and 1991 than before. Not surprisingly, the guilder's target exchange rate against the Deutschmark was the most credible. The credibility of other currencies was 'less than perfect' but had increased recently, and especially since the beginning of 1990. The failure of the simple target zone model to account for the behaviour of ERM members' exchange rates could not be attributed to errors in the measurement of expectations, as is often supposed, because the results which the authors obtained from survey data were no more supportive than those based on interest rates. The model's failure is more likely due to its implicit – and implausible – assumption that the credibility of exchange rates is constant.

It was pointed out during the conference that the main weakness of the simple target zone model was the assumption of rational expectations in the foreign exchange market, for which there is no evidence in favour and a great deal against.

As the internal market proceeds together with increased goods and financial market integration it may be possible that, even well before the introduction of a single currency, domestic money markets will not survive without perfectly syncronized national monetary policies. In fact, recent events within the European monetary system are a good illustration of that point. The current status of Stage II is therefore unlikely to remedy the present situation and may even further heighten exchange rate instability. The possibility of currency substitution may, on the other hand, be further aggravated by a vicious circle – countries trying to meet the convergence criteria will experience a higher degree of exchange rate instability making it harder for them to converge.

That possibility emphasizes the potential conflict between the gradualism envisaged at Maastricht and the stability of the entire EMU process. This instability in turn may affect all countries embarked on the

EMU course and not only the countries catching up with the convergence criteria. The latter already face the stringency of some of these criteria and therefore the trade-off between the need quickly to accomplish sufficient convergence and the aim to attain sustained economic growth during the convergence process and subsequently when full membership of the EMU has been accomplished.

Although typically consumers hold foreign as well as domestic currency, and a rise in the cost of holding one currency leads them to move smoothly to another, many commentators have asserted that currency substitution will jeopardize Europe's financial stability as EMU approaches. Conventional money demand equations do not permit an unambiguous definition of currency substitution. In Chapter 10 Matthew Canzoneri, Behzad Diba and Alberto Giovannini describe a model that explicitly accounts for money demand in terms of market organization and transactions imperfections. If goods and factor markets are integrated but governments continue to run divergent monetary policies, as is currently the case in Europe, the currencies that are relatively costly to carry will disappear, as will the corresponding financial intermediaries. Indeed, the corresponding firms will disappear as they will no longer be able to sell their output. The authors conclude by recommending that no effort be spared to ensure the convergence of monetary policies among the member countries during Stage II. Possible measures to achieve convergence include a narrowing of the ERM bands to secure the tighter synchronization of national discount rates and supplies of domestic credit.

Increased financial market integration may cause investment to flow to countries with the least demanding tax regimes. An example of competition forcing capital taxes to zero is Germany's experience in 1988–89 when an attempt to impose a withholding tax on interest income had to be abandoned to prevent further outflows of capital. The extent of this effect will depend on how far the existing tax systems distort investment, whether competition alone will achieve the necessary convergence in tax regimes or whether inter-governmental cooperation will be required, and how much harmonization of capital taxes is needed. The European Commission hopes to harmonize the tax base and set minimum tax rates in order to facilitate tax competition, reduce divergences in tax rates, and hence reduce the cost of distortions. In view of the difficulties in assessing the current situation, this looks like a reasonable approach. In Chapter 11 Peter Sørensen presents an exhaustive review of Europe's corporate tax systems, which indicates that intra-European tax distortions are now not very large and that most of the gains from Europe's economic and financial integration can be achieved without complete tax harmonization, although certain tax obstacles to cross-border investment should be removed. Tax competition among EC member countries is probably not strong enough to eliminate differences in corporate income tax; but the harmonization of personal taxes on capital income may be necessary to protect the integrity of the system of personal taxation.

4   The Maastricht Treaty

The European union envisaged in the new Treaty will adopt, at the latest by 1 January, 1999, a single central bank.

Countries wishing to participate in EMU have to satisfy some conditions (the convergence criteria) put forward in the Treaty. These are: the convergence of inflation and interest rates; the fluctuations of the respective currencies not exceeding the narrow ERM bands for at least two years without any central parity changes; a budget deficit not exceeding 3% of gross domestic product; and a gross public debt not exceeding, or converging to, 60% of gross domestic product.

Niels Thygesen examines the role of Stage II of EMU in the following chapter. The Treaty has unambiguously set 1 January 1994 as the starting date for Stage II and has relaxed the conditions to be met by that date. All 12 countries can now embark on Stage II, although this is to be 'less qualitatively different' from Stage I than initially envisaged. The European monetary institute (EMI) will oversee the exchange rate mechanism, promote the use of the Ecu during the transition and prepare for Stage III. The most important institutional innovation of the Treaty is to decree that the head of the EMI will be appointed, not elected by the governors of the national central banks; it cannot be judged in advance whether this will raise the public profile of the post.

Maastricht also resolved uncertainty about the end of Stage II: a majority of EC countries can move to Stage III if they meet the convergence criteria by the end of 1996; otherwise EMU will begin in January 1999 for those countries (whether a majority or not) that fulfil the criteria by mid-1998. Relaxing the requirements for Stage II and setting a binding terminal date will make it harder to make a straight move from something like the present voluntary and decentralized operations to the highly centralized system designed for Stage III, which will force the EMI's agenda beyond the tasks specified in the Maastricht texts.

It was suggested that the point of the Maastricht summit had been to provoke such instability; in other words, to threaten countries that were already unlikely to meet the convergence criteria.

These are the issues currently at the centre of the European policy debate. We hope that this volume will contribute to a better understanding of these problems.

2 Economic and Monetary Union: Critical notes on the Maastricht Treaty revisions

NIELS THYGESEN

1 Introduction

The inter-governmental conference (IGC) on economic and monetary union (EMU) which started in Rome in December 1990 and was concluded in Maastricht one year later had two main tasks. The first was to define, as precisely as possible, how collective authority over economic policy will be exercised in the final stage of EMU. This entailed setting out the legal and institutional framework for full monetary union and taking the necessary steps for the implementation of the non-monetary policies which will accompany the irrevocable locking of parities among the participating currencies and the subsequent introduction of a single currency. Preparations for the IGC, notably the draft statute proposed by the committee of EC central bank governors in November 1990, and early work in the IGC on EMU focused on this task. The institutional design which has emerged is the main achievement of the past year's negotiations. It has revealed a degree of support, which could not have been expected when the EMU debate started, among the policy-makers in the Community for entrusting joint monetary policy to a central banking institution which is (i) committed to the primary objective of price stability, and (ii) remarkably independent, through a number of safeguards, from short-term political pressures. It also revealed a readiness to go further than foreseen in giving the Council of Finance Ministers (ECOFIN) authority to monitor national budgetary deficits and government debt positions and to apply graduated pressures to member states with 'excessive deficits'.

This major accomplishment will not be analysed further in this chapter, although it has direct implications for the transition. The clear signposts regarding the final stage in the Treaty revision now submitted for ratification are of obvious significance. Clear rules and procedures for the final stage of EMU should ideally inspire national central banks and other policy-makers to behave voluntarily as if these provisions were already in place or imminent.

But the second task of the IGC was no less essential. It was to clarify how the EC member states can achieve transition to full EMU by a mixture of entry requirements and procedures for reaching decisions. For much of the second half of 1991 it seemed highly doubtful whether a sufficient degree of consensus could be achieved in the IGC to assure that the transition would not be of indefinite duration, hence making the accomplishments with respect to the content of the final stage rather academic. Most of the modifications (to the text prepared under the Luxembourg Presidency) introduced in the draft Treaty by the Dutch Presidency in September–October 1991 tended to enhance such concerns.

Particularly worrying was the prospect of a generally-worded clause which would allow individual countries to opt out of the commitment to EMU. This clause had the potential of quietly adjourning EMU *sine die*. Although originally inspired by the need to accommodate the difficulties of the United Kingdom in undertaking any such commitment at the time of signature of the revised Treaty, the opting-out clause turned out to hold attractions for politicians, particularly in national parliaments, in several other countries as well, including Germany. The clause was finally dropped in an ECOFIN meeting just before Maastricht when 10 out of 12 Finance Ministers declared that they did not want it. At Maastricht the United Kingdom and Denmark asked for, and were granted, separate protocols to retain the right to join the full EMU only if they obtained a positive decision in parliament (in the UK case) or in a referendum (in the Danish case).

A second source of concern was a continuing erosion of the institutional arrangements for the temporary central banking institution – the European monetary institute (EMI) – to be set up for the transition. This weakness was only partly remedied at Maastricht; it is discussed below.

A third concern was whether the member states were in the process of tightening the entry requirements to full EMU so much with respect to the consolidation of national budgetary policies, that only a few countries could hope to qualify within the present decade. This concern was also eased somewhat at Maastricht, both by the clarification of some flexibility in the interpretation of the formal criteria and by admitting that a smaller number of countries than originally envisaged – even a minority of member states – could move to full EMU including the adoption of a single currency.

Finally, some leading participants in the negotiations, notably the German Chancellor, linked their acceptance of EMU to significant progress in the parallel IGC on political union. It is not obvious on economic grounds why additional political unification should be required by EMU, though that view continues to be supported by German public opinion. Chancellor Kohl, however, settled for modest progress on political union and the promise of an additional Treaty revision to focus on political union in 1996.

All of these four concerns were eased by the decisions of the European Council at the Maastricht meeting. These decisions made it a virtual certainty that full EMU will be adopted by at least some member states, although possibly only a minority, before the end of the present decade.

The next two sections provide an examination of the provisions for the transition (Chapter 4 of the Maastricht Treaty). The discussion focuses on the duration of Stage II, the role of the EMI, the interpretation of the convergence criteria, and the prospect of variable speeds (or geometry) in the process. In the following section the outcome is interpreted in terms of the official and academic debate over the role of Stage II. Particular emphasis is given to the different approaches referred to in the Report of the Committee for the Study of Economic and Monetary Union (1989) – the Delors Report – and in the collection of papers annexed to this report. A short concluding section in which the author speculates on a bolder strategy for reaching EMU than that implied by the Maastricht Treaty completes the chapter.

2   Stage II as agreed at Maastricht: commencement and content

Three questions arise in relation to the transitional Stage II: (i) how and when does it start? (ii) what is its substantive content? (iii) how and when is it likely to end? The first two questions are taken up in the present section, the third in the next.

Stage II will begin on 1 January 1994. This date, 3 ½ years after Stage 1, was first set by the European Council when it met in Rome in October 1990. The wording of the Conclusions of the Presidency, however, left some ambiguity as to its definitive nature by adding entry conditions. The doubt has now been dispelled. Before the end of 1993 capital controls must be fully abolished, although Greece and Portugal retain the possibility of preserving derogations until the end of 1995. Each member state must have adopted a multi-annual programme to ensure lasting convergence, in particular with regard to price stability and sound public finances. Overdraft facilities in national central banks or the possibility of selling debt instruments directly to them will be closed to national government and other public authorities (except publicly-owned credit institutions). No bail-out arrangements for such bodies can be invoked after that date and member states will endeavour in Stage II to avoid 'excessive government deficits'. The reference values for defining the latter are indicated in a separate protocol as 3% for the ratio of the planned or actual government deficit to gross domestic product (GDP) and 60% for the ratio of government debt to GDP. We return to the likely effects of these requirements, and of the qualifications to them later. The ECOFIN will begin monitoring national government deficits, making first confidential then, if necessary, public and specific recommendations on their reduction, but stopping short of four graduated types of sanctions which are envisaged only for the final stage. Member states have to be ready to start the process leading to independence of their national central banks, which has to be completed before they can participate in the European system of central banks (ESCB), and in its operational part, the European central bank (ECB), to be set up at the start of Stage III.

None of these criteria are, however, definitive on 1 January 1994 and there is therefore no longer any doubt, as there was in October 1990, that all 12 current member states will embark on Stage II by the date set provided the Treaty has been ratified by all according to the timetable. In October 1990 additional and difficult prerequisites for entering Stage II had been envisaged: all member states should 'take the measures necessary to enable them to take part in the exchange-rate mechanism of the European monetary system', while 'satisfactory and durable progress towards real and monetary convergence, in particular price stability and the consolidation of public finances, should have been made'. The latter prerequisite would have offered considerable scope for procrastination, while the former, also stated in the Delors Report (para. 52), could hardly have avoided causing a major delay. At Maastricht, the Community finally clarified that it was not prepared to give any country a *de facto* capacity to veto the start of the transition.

The softening of the criteria for entering Stage II which occurred over the year prior to the Maastricht meeting is an indication, of course, that the substantive content of Stage II gradually became less qualitatively different from Stage I than originally intended. This is particularly evident in the provisions for the new and temporary framework for EC central bank cooperation which comes into being on 1 January 1994.

On that date, the European monetary institute (EMI) will be set up (Article 109 f of the Maastricht Treaty). It will have two types of tasks, as outlined in sub-paragraphs 2 and 3 of Article 109 and in the separate protocol containing the EMI statute, prepared by the Committee of central bank governors for the IGC in October 1991. These tasks are: (i) to take over the roles of that committee and of the board of the European fund for monetary cooperation (EMCF) in coordinating national monetary policies, monitoring the EMS and facilitating the use of the ECU; and (ii) to prepare for the final stage of EMU. Before the end of 1996 'the EMI has to specify the regulatory, organizational and logistical framework necessary for the European system of the central banks (ESCB) to perform its tasks in the third stage'. But this work will be preparatory only, to be submitted to the successor permanent institution at the date of its establishment at the beginning of Stage III. Since only some member states may initially take part in the final stage and hence in the decisions of the governing council of the ECB, while all will be involved in the work of the EMI Council, the preliminary nature of the latter's preparations is puzzling. Presumably adoption of the proposals prepared by the EMI in the early life of its successor will turn out to be largely a formality.

As regards the EMI's role in policy coordination it is difficult to see any significant changes relative to the performance of the committee of central bank governors set up in Stage I. The council of the EMI may formulate by qualified majority, opinions or recommendations on monetary and exchange-rate policy in the member states and convey these views confidentially. It may publish unanimously adopted opinions and recommendations. This does not go beyond what can be done by the present committee of central bank governors and its President. The role of the EMI in policy coordination closely reflects the concern of a majority of EC countries that monetary authority should remain in national hands until it can be fully transferred to the European level after the start of the final stage of EMU – the so-called 'indivisibility doctrine' discussed in the following section.

The one institutional innovation is that the European Council will appoint the President of the Council of the EMI on a recommendation from the committee of central bank governors, and after consulting ECOFIN and the European Parliament. The appointment will initially be for a period of three years, the likely life of the institute. This was a controversial point, since the governors had proposed in their draft statute to elect one of their colleagues to preside, as has been the practice in Stage I. They will now instead elect one such colleague as Vice-President, also for three years.

It is impossible to assess *a priori* to what extent the appointment of an external President – whether a senior political figure or a former central bank governor – will raise the profile of the EMI. The President will have one vote out of 13 votes initially although after a year the number may be increased to 16 or 18, if accession negotiations with Austria, Finland, Sweden and possibly other countries in the European Free Trade Area (EFTA) lead to these countries becoming members by 1 January 1995, as currently appears to be possible. That would give the President of the

EMI an influence similar to that of the Bundesbank President in the Council of that Bank. Being the only full-time member of the EMI Council will add further to the position, beyond what the special appointment procedure already confers. On the other hand, the in-built position of being the only outsider could make the President's position tricky, particularly if he has no prior central bank experience.

Certain pointers suggest that continuity with Stage I is likely to be the dominant trait of the EMI as far as its role in monetary policy coordination is concerned. For example, the Council has not been given any additional authority to coordinate monetary policy, and in preparing for the final stage its role will be advisory. Even more symbolic is the fact that the European Council did not reach a decision at Maastricht on where the EMI should be located, implying that the present practice of conducting all meetings and basing the secretariat in the Bank for International Settlements in Basle might have to be extended into Stage II.[1] It must be noted, however, that whether the individual national central banks have become independent or not, members of the EMI councils may not, in that capacity, 'seek or take any instructions from Community institutions or bodies or governments of member states' (EMI Statute, Article 8). This is a formulation similar to that in Article 107 or in the ESCB Statute dealing with the final stage. Collectively, at least, the members of the EMI council will begin to enjoy more independence from the beginning of Stage II.

The main new feature in the EMI provisions relates to its responsibility for preparing fully for the final stage. The preparation of instruments, procedures and operational rules, including the degree of centralization in the ECB to be aimed at in a full EMU, and finally of a more efficient system of cross-border payments, will provide the bulk of the agenda for the EMI Council and its staff. We return later to an interpretation of this mandate.

A final monetary provision for the transition is the decision to fix the currency composition of the ECU (Article 109 g). This implies that, once the Treaty proposals are ratified, there will be no more changes in the composition of the ECU basket; the shares of the 12 component national currencies will remain as agreed in September 1989. This removes one significant source of uncertainty for users of the unit, as the quinquennial review foreseen for 1994 (and possibly 1999) and the prospect of additional currencies of new EC members being added, is now excluded. On balance, the freezing of the basket implies a slight hardening of the ECU. This was a minimalist step, but one favoured by private users. Alternative and more radical formulas for hardening, including the so-called asymmetrical basket and the devaluation-proof 'hard ECU', originally proposed by the UK government in 1990, would have been more difficult for private market operators to assess during the transition period.

Another, more remote, source of uncertainty remains. From the start of Stage III the ECU will become the common currency of those member states ready for (and willing to join) the full EMU. While the external value of the ECU will not be modified at the time of this qualitative change, the subsequent evolution of the exchange rate of the ECU, and of the interest rate attached to it, will be determined by the joint monetary policy in Stage III and by the initial inflation and interest rates of the EMU participants. For someone entering into a long-term ECU-denominated contract to-day, an evaluation of this particular constellation of factors in 1997 or later (see below) cannot be made with any high degree of certainty.[2] This residual degree of uncertainty could not have been eliminated by any provision for the transition in the new Treaty, given that a qualitative change in the unit must take place at the start of Stage III. More important to the likely evolution of the ECU market than this residual and unavoidable uncertainty is the removal, by the Maastricht decisions on a firm timetable, of any doubt that full EMU will be achieved by at least some EC member states in this decade.

3 Stage II: how does it end?

This more definitive timetable is assured by Article 109 j–l. Article 109 j institutes a regular reporting procedure for the Commission and the EMI throughout the second stage. In their regular reports to ECOFIN the two bodies will monitor progress in the move towards independence for the national central banks and 'the achievement of a high degree of sustainable convergence' in terms of inflation, avoidance of 'excessive deficits', observance of normal fluctuation margins in the EMS and convergence of long term interest rates.

These four criteria are specified in quantitative detail in a separate protocol. Inflation (the consumer price index) has to be within 1½% of the, at most, three best performing members; long-term interest rates must not exceed those in the three same countries by more than two percentage points.[3] A country must have participated in the normal fluctuation margins of the EMS without devaluing, on its own initiative, its currency's bilateral central rate against any other EC currency over the preceding two years.[4] A governmental deficit is not excessive, as already noted, if the deficit/GDP ratio is below 3% and the debt/GDP ratio is, at most, 60%, or if substantial and continuous progress has been made in approaching a level close to these reference values (Article 104 c). The reports will, finally, 'take account of the development of the ECU, the results of the integration of markets, the situation and development of the balance of payments on current accounts and an examination of the developments of unit labour costs and other price indices'.

Not later than 31 December 1996 the Council, meeting in the com-position of the Heads of State or government, will decide by qualified majority how many member states fulfil the necessary conditions for the adoption of a single currency and subsequently decide 'whether it is appropriate for the Community to enter the third stage of EMU'. If the answer to both questions is affirmative, the date for the beginning of that stage must be set. While the locking of exchange rates will presumably take place immediately after the Council's decision the date for introduc-ing the single currency could, and is likely to be somewhat later, depend-ing upon the degree of technical preparedness which evolves through the EMI preparations in Stage II.[5]

The difficulty of evaluating the significance and the definitive nature of this commitment resides not only in the convergence criteria proposed, but also in guessing what will constitute a majority by end-1996. The United Kingdom, by a separate protocol, is not obliged or committed to move to the third stage, even if it meets the convergence criteria, without a separate decision by its government and parliament. Denmark, in another separate protocol, obtained recognition of its right to hold a referendum on its participation in the final stage. Unless these two countries notify the European Council, before the end of 1996, of their positive intention to participate in the third stage they will not be included among the member states from which a simple/qualified majority has to be found. On the other hand, the EC may, from 1995, have 2–4 additional member states; Austria, Finland and Sweden have already applied while Norway, and possibly Switzerland may do so in the near future. At least some of these new members are likely to fulfil the necessary conditions. Thus, expansion of membership could make it easier to find a majority qualified for full EMU in the second half of the decade; widening would in fact accelerate deepening.

While the two nominal conditions (inflation and interest rates) may be regarded as fairly lenient, particularly if the EMS continues to operate without realignments, the budgetary indicators, taken at face value, are more demanding even if inflation is sharply reduced, hence pushing the deficit down. It remains difficult to see how Italy could get close to meeting either criterion by 1995 which is the latest year for which actual budget and debt figures will be available at the time of the assessment. Similarly, Belgium with a debt/GDP ratio in excess of 120 per cent and Ireland with a ratio not much below 100 per cent at present, are highly unlikely to meet the debt criterion. But the Council has retained some discretion in its evaluation. Article 104 c which lists the more permanent criteria for monitoring budget deficits gives some scope for flexibility; these criteria will give guidance during the transition period. If the deficit ratio has declined substantially and continuously to a level close to the reference value, or if the ratio only exceeds this value exceptionally and temporarily, performance could still be regarded as acceptable. A similar formulation is found with respect to the debt ratio except that in this case there is no mention of the need to be close to the reference value. It is possible to see how such exceptions could be made to fit, say, Belgium in the process of substantial debt reduction by 1995, or Germany which has temporarily allowed the budget deficit to rise above 3% of its GDP. Interpreted in such a liberal manner, the budgetary criteria become less objectionable; in fact, they go a long way towards meeting the objections to mechanical criteria in CEPR (1991) and Corsetti and Roubini (1992) without running into the opposite danger of becoming devoid of any objective content and thus open to a purely political assessment. Their essential purpose, as here interpreted, is to give countries maximum incentives for restoring budgetary prudence in the transition period. Countries that have succeeded in this restoration will have regained budgetary autonomy.

The budgetary criteria remain tough even in this liberal interpretation and might still constitute the 'no-entry clause' advocated by some countries and analysed in the more academic literature, notably by Giovannini and Spaventa (1991). On the other hand, as argued above, they are unlikely to be applied mechanically to bar countries which have long observed the rigid discipline of the normal margins in the EMS, from entry into the final stage. The Maastricht criteria may have been set up primarily to create some uncertainty about participation and to set up strong incentives for countries with potentially 'excessive deficits' to undertake consolidation at a time when the more formal sanctions, which will replace them in the final stage, are not yet operative.

Supplementary criteria are also referred to in Article 109 j (current accounts and additional price and cost indices), which would permit a positive evaluation of a country if sufficient progress has been achieved over the 1992–95 period. At present only three member states (Luxembourg, France and Denmark) could be said to meet all the criteria individually; it is plausible that they will have been joined by Germany and the Netherlands by 1995 and by some of the new potential member states (Austria certainly, Finland, Norway and Sweden possibly). Belgium and Ireland will have to rely on a generous interpretation of the progress they have made in reducing the debt/GDP ratio. It is also

possible that Italy, Spain and Portugal could be judged ready to participate by the time the assessment has to be made in late 1996.

Rather than insisting on countries meeting all the entry requirements
separately it might be useful to consider an overall indicator of convergence that summarizes developments in all of the quantifiable areas in
which adjustment is required to qualify for full EMU. Such an indicator
has been proposed by de Grauwe and Gros (1991); here we follow the
updated and revised presentation in Gros and Thygesen (1992).

Convergence aims at the best performance; the overall indicator used
therefore measures the degree to which a country was close to becoming a
virtuous candidate for EMU in 1991, the last year for which figures are
available. It is characterized by stable consumer prices, a balanced public
budget, a debt-to-GDP ratio corresponding to the EC average of 60%
(also the reference value), no unemployment and current account equilibrium. In contrast to the Maastricht criteria the calculation of the
overall indicator rewards countries that have 'a better than virtuous'
performance in one or more respects. These five variables are simply
added up; they are all ratios or rates of change.[6] Obviously this simple
weighting is subjective; it gives a heavy weight to imbalances in the public
finances and to inflation. Table 2.1 shows how this overall assessment of
the need to converge would have worked out if performed on 1991 data.

The clustering of countries suggested by the overall indicator departs in
some respects from popular notions. A first and fairly homogeneous
group consists of the Netherlands, Denmark, France and Germany. The
United Kingdom, mainly because of its healthy public finances in 1991, is
close to this group. A second, somewhat less homogeneous tier is made up
of Portugal, Belgium, Ireland and Spain, with Italy not far behind. Greece
is in a situation of divergence all by herself. On the whole the ranking
appears reasonable; and it leaves the impression that qualification by 10
or 11 member states in 1996 seems to be a feasible ambition.

Whatever the correct interpretation of the criteria or the likelihood that
the two countries which have reserved their position on participation (the
United Kingdom and Denmark) will have lifted their reservations by
1996, the Maastricht Treaty has added, following a last-minute initiative
of France and Italy, a significant procedural innovation which makes it a
virtual certainty that some member states will enter the final stage of
EMU on 1 January 1999. Article 109 j (4) foresees automatic participation on that date for member states which are judged by a qualified
majority in the European Council to have met the necessary conditions –
provided, of course, that they have not explicitly reserved their position.
This decision will be taken before 1 July 1998 in order to ensure that the
ECB can be fully operational and take over from the EMI; the latter will

Table 2.1. *An overall indicator of convergence*

	Budget deficit	Debt indicator (a)	Inflation rate	Unemployment rate	Current account (b)	EMU indicator
Germany	3.2	− 2.3	4.5	6.0	1.4	12.8
France	1.5	− 2.2	3.0	9.5	0.7	12.5
Netherlands	4.4	0.9	3.2	7.2	− 4.1	11.6
Denmark	1.7	− 0.2	2.4	9.2	− 1.4	11.7
United Kingdom	1.9	− 2.5	6.5	8.4	2.1	16.4
Portugal	5.4	− 0.4	11.7	4.0	1.1	21.7
Belgium	6.4	6.0	3.2	8.6	− 1.0	23.2
Spain	3.9	− 2.3	5.8	15.8	3.1	26.2
Ireland	4.1	3.4	3.0	16.8	− 2.3	24.9
Italy	9.9	3.2	6.4	9.4	1.3	30.2
Greece	17.9	2.7	18.3	8.8	4.1	51.8

Notes: For Germany, the unemployment and inflation rates are for East and West Germany, weighted by GDP.
(a) National debt/GDP ratio minus the EC average divided by 10.
(b) A negative sign denotes a surplus.
Source: Commission of the European Communities Annual Report, Special Edition 1991.

then be liquidated from the first day of the final stage (Article 109 k). Countries that have still not met the necessary conditions for participation by mid-1998 will be given a derogation, to be reviewed subsequently at least every two years.

This modified procedure will ensure that full EMU starts, even if only a minority of member states are ready for it. That will provide an additional incentive for countries on the borderline for the 1996 (or 1998) decision to bring their credentials beyond argument. The procedure creates a powerful incentive: either a country looks like qualifying, hence triggering the favourable expectational effects associated with EMU on inflation and interest rates – themselves criteria for entry – or it risks additional divergence by looking unlikely to make it. By this procedure the help of the financial markets is enlisted; that is, the market will carry out some of the task of evaluation for ECOFIN.

The main concern about Stage II prior to Maastricht was its open-ended nature. The prospect that it might continue indefinitely, with successive reviews every two years failing to discover a majority ready to go to full EMU, would have proved deeply unsettling to any remaining confidence that the temporary institutional framework of Stage II could be relied upon to provide continuing stability. With the agreement at Maastricht on the modified procedure for 1998, an unforeseen degree of automaticity in moving to full EMU has been introduced. The adequacy of Stage II can no longer be evaluated purely or primarily in terms of its own qualities; the pull towards full EMU will itself be stabilizing through the incentives it sets up. The virtual certainty that it will be a reality for some at a definite date will also give added urgency to the preparations for Stage III.

Nevertheless it is necessary to discuss the monetary content of Stage II as agreed in Maastricht and its shortcomings relative to some of the ideas advanced for the transition. We also ask whether these shortcomings have been compensated by the upper bound to the length of Stage II and the proposed persistent monitoring of tough convergence criteria. The following section turns to this issue.

4   An interpretation of the monetary content of Stage II

Several approaches to Stage II can be identified in the discussion leading up to the IGC in December 1991. They are: (i) the gradual transition favoured by (some members of) the Delors Committee, (ii) the common, or parallel, currency approach, (iii) the extension (and intensification) of the voluntary coordination of Stage I, and (iv) the need to undertake detailed preparations for Stage III. Some observers have argued that the most likely outcome prior to Maastricht was (iii) – an extension of the main features of Stage I – with some elements of (iv). Without disagreeing with this evaluation I want to claim that the Maastricht outcome was also, to a modest extent, influenced by the first two, apparently discarded, approaches.

The most obvious interpretation of the present version of Stage II is, indeed, that there was little support for any gradual transfer of monetary authority in the transition period. The difficulties of sharing authority between, on the one hand, the national central banks (and their governments to the extent that the central banks are not yet independent) and, on the other hand, an emerging European institution, now the EMI, was evident from the discussions in the Delors Committee. These difficulties were also noted in a number of academic contributions, whether based on more theoretical analysis, for example, Wihlborg and Willett (1991), or on historical analogies, for example Eichengreen (1991) on the early and unsatisfactory Federal Reserve experience with inadequate centralization. The Delors Report paid some lip service to gradualism *within* Stage II, but that notion may be meaningful only if the transition period is longer than the 3–5 years now envisaged.[7] Gradualism may, however, still be a relevant notion for those member states which will have derogations from final EMU beyond 1 January 1999.

The Delors Committee grappled with the central issue of reconciling gradualism with indivisibility of monetary authority, but had to give up its drafting efforts. The argument that indivisibility of national monetary authority should in the end prevail during Stage II rests on the cumulative effect of two features: (i) exchange rate changes will still be possible, while (ii) national central banks are not yet independent of governments, or for other reasons are unable to commit themselves to joint actions. That combination of features makes it possible for temporary tensions in the EMS to escalate into exchange-rate crises and realignments, as illustrated by some episodes in the pre-1987 EMS experience. Though the possibility may seem remote after five years of considerable stability in the EMS it cannot be ruled out; and a divided authority for monetary policy might invite speculation in financial markets, hence increasing the risk of crises.

This view seems, however, too absolute when we examine more closely what sharing of monetary policy responsibilities between the national and the collective level would imply. In his contribution to the Delors Report, Lamfalussy (1989) referred to three possible approaches for strengthening the common element in monetary policy in the transition. The first was for the participating central banks to set up a jointly-owned subsidiary, whose facilities they would share in performing certain of their operations in domestic money and foreign-exchange markets; this would not require any formal transfer of authority. The second was to assign a small number of monetary instruments to the EMI for collective decisions while leaving others for national decisions or non-binding coordination. The third was to implement a gradual transfer of decision-making power from the national to the collective level. The three approaches may perhaps be labelled pooling of (i) operations, (ii) instruments and (iii) authority.

The three approaches have been presented by their respective proponents to be complementary rather than mutually exclusive. Indeed, (ii) and (iii) are difficult to distinguish, since both, in order to be effective, would require the introduction of some hierarchical order in the relations of the governing bodies at the European level and the constituent national monetary authorities. Pooling of operations is different in kind, however, as it requires no formal transfer of authority; in that sense it could well be experimented with while ultimate monetary authority is still in national hands as will be the case in Stage II (and, *a fortiori*, in the remainder of Stage I).

The pooling of operations would, in Lamfalussy's proposal, consist of the establishment of a common operations facility incorporating all of the foreign-exchange and domestic money market activities of participating national central banks in a jointly-owned subsidiary. Each central bank would staff its own operations; later the national staffs could be merged into a single unit. The use of common facilities would make the operations of each individual participant fully transparent to other participants; this is not the case today with respect to domestic money market operations or with respect to the management of foreign exchange reserves, apart from official interventions. Pooling of operations would at the same time present a common appearance in the markets. Private market participants would be unable to determine the source of the instructions to the jointly-owned agency. There could no longer be conflicting signals to the markets from the participating central banks. Centralization of operations would furthermore provide a more efficient training ground for national foreign exchange and money market operators than the *ad hoc* concertations by telephone in today's system. The approach would facilitate efforts to develop a more coherent framework for the design and implementation of monetary policy, including the domestic aspects of the latter. This would provide efficient preparation for full joint management in the final stage. Centralization may also offer some potential for cost savings.

The EMI Statute foresees that some centralization of foreign-exchange operations could take place on a voluntary basis in Stage II. Article 6.4 states:

> The EMI shall be entitled to hold and manage foreign exchange reserves as an agent for and at the request of national central banks. . . . The EMI shall perform this function on the basis of bilateral contracts. . . . Trans-

> actions with these reserves shall not interfere with the monetary policy
> and exchange rate policy of the competent authority of any member
> state . . .

This is a limited and strictly voluntary arrangement and it is currently not clear how many national central banks will wish to avail themselves of this opportunity for pooling of foreign-exchange operations, though it appears certain that the Bundesbank will not be one of them. Despite these severe limitations, the additional capacity of the EMI is at least a start along the lines suggested by Lamfalussy.

To those like myself who have advocated also some steps along the lines of approaches (ii) and (iii) above, limited pooling of operations is not sufficiently ambitious for a substantive Stage II, even in a short transition. It is clear, however, that any significant change towards pooling of decision-making over national policy instruments, notably short-term interest rates, or towards assigning any collective policy instruments to the EMI must now be regarded as virtually excluded. Yet a new case can be made, in the light of the present timetable for Stage II of 3–5 years, for joint experimentation with a policy instrument to influence aggregate money creation in the Community, namely, reserve requirements on bank deposits by EC residents. Gros and Thygesen (1992, Ch. 12), provide a restatement of the case for such an instrument.

The original proposals were made in some of the personal contributions to the collected papers attached to the Delors Report. These early proposals focused on enabling the joint monetary institution to set reserve requirements on either the increase in the monetary liabilities of each participating national central bank or on the credit extended by them to their respective domestic sectors. The requirement could be met only by holding reserves with the EMI (in ECU); and the supply of reserves would be controlled by the latter through allocations of official ECUs to each central bank corresponding to the demand for reserves which would arise if agreed targets for money creation were observed. Subsequent work on this proposal has, however, brought out that the incentives provided to central banks by both cost and availability considerations to stay close to collectively agreed objectives might be too weak to add much to monetary control in Stage II.

The case for using reserve requirements in Stage II must therefore rest on applying them directly to deposits with commercial banks – the so-called two-tier system outlined in Gros and Thygesen (1992). It must at the same time be based on more forward-looking arguments: to prepare for Stage III rather than mainly as a contribution to Stage II itself, particularly since the ESCB Statute explicitly authorizes the ECB, in Article 19, to impose reserve requirements on credit institutions in the final stage.

One of the central elements in the preparations for Stage III which, as emphasized above, must after Maastricht be regarded as the main task of the EMI, will be to evaluate carefully how such an instrument could be used after 1996 (or 1998). These reflections could hardly be pushed very far without both the considerable reductions foreseen in the present divergent national use of the instrument *and* some experimentation as to how collective use of the instrument – though in Stage II still formally decentralized – could contribute to the evolution of a Community-wide federal funds market in the future single currency. Reserve requirements in ECU might also usefully interact with the evolution of a cross-border payments system in Europe for which the EMI has been given explicit responsibility. For those who fear that there is a risk of monetary policy in Stage II drifting into a more inflationary stance than has marked most of the post-1983 EMS experience, it should also be reassuring that the instrument would be a convenient way of putting an upper limit on total monetary expansion; it could not be used for a policy that is more expansionary than that of the most stability-oriented participant. In short, the logic both of limiting the risk of instability and inflationary drift and of preparing as well as possible for the final stage suggests that use of reserve requirements, necessarily on the basis of voluntary and decentralized coordination, should re-appear on the EMI agenda.

This being said, it remains true that the strong emphasis on the indivisibility of national monetary authority in Stage II which is embodied in the Maastricht proposals implies that the transition will look primarily like an extension of Stage I. But the pull towards the final stage will tend to re-introduce other elements of more joint approaches than the limited operational pooling foreseen in the EMI.

The most difficult issue to evaluate for Stage II is how the limitation of its duration to 3–5 years for those countries ready and willing to enter full EMU will influence the penetration of the ECU into wider use in Europe. The definitive commitment to the single currency in the late 1990s will, in the view of private market operators, give a major impetus to the growth of the ECU markets for securities and other financial assets well beyond the primarily official encouragement offered through large government issues of ECU-denominated debt in recent years. The EMI – and before 1 January 1994 the committee of central bank governors – will be faced with challenges in the ECU market. These challenges are likely to emerge more quickly than was thought possible under a slower and less definite time-table for EMU than that agreed at Maastricht. As the future ECU becomes more visibly divorced from the present basket in the approach to full EMU, central banks will have to take a more explicit view on the fluctuations in the exchange rate and the interest rate on the ECU relative to the basket than the fairly detached attitude they have been able to permit themselves in 1990–91. The EMI will not issue ECU, as envisaged in some earlier suggestions for a common parallel currency approach to Stage II, yet this approach will not be totally absent from the transition. It will enter through the back door as market forces seize the major incentives to invest in the use of the ECU offered by the Maastricht timetable.

5   Conclusions

In conclusion, it is evident that Stage II will become more than Stage I. This will happen less as a result of conscious choice (few governments have been prepared for any explicit transfer of authority) than because of the new context in which the transition must now be seen. This will inevitably lead to more joint policies either in response to challenges in the market or because of the need to prepare for the full EMU in the near future. As the commitment to go to Stage III before the end of the decade has been given, national monetary authorities will be obliged to show more readiness to take that qualitative step by accumulating more experience than in Stage I on the formulation of objectives, on a common analytical framework for policy design and instrument use, and on common operations. The system that has been designed for Stage III is fairly centralized; it would hardly be possible to move straight from something not very different from the present voluntary and decentralized operations of Stage I to this ultimate model. Recognition of this difficulty will force the agenda of the EMI beyond the tasks readily visible in the Maastricht Treaty.

The Treaty revisions now submitted for ratification go as far as was politically possible to minimize the uncertainties surrounding the timetable for EMU and the steps to be taken in Stage II to get there. Attention has at the same time shifted from experimentation with provisional forms of joint decision-making in the monetary area towards individual country responsibility for achieving convergence, in particular in the budgetary area, to meet the entry requirements for EMU. This appears desirable, but in this chapter I have been critical of the limited monetary content of Stage II, although some consolation can be derived from the fact that the agenda for the EMI will expand because of the pressure from the markets and the initiatives of some participants anxious to use the newly available operational facilities.

Since Stage II is now going to be fairly short (3–5 years at most) its specific monetary features are less important than originally thought, and it may seem uncharitable to criticize them. Criticism is still justified, however, because in a Stage II that is primarily an extension of Stage I, there will be the risk of instabilities which can be definitively reduced only in a full EMU. With nominal convergence having already proceeded far, the removal of residual inflation differentials would take place more quickly once exchange rates were permanently locked than in even the best designed transition towards EMU.

The risk of instability is enhanced by one, otherwise desirable, feature of the Maastricht entry requirements for full EMU, namely that exchange rates must have been stable over at least a two-year period prior to the decision in 1996. Market participants now ask themselves two questions: (i) as devaluations can be made without impinging on a country's entry into EMU in the 'grace period' prior to mid-1994, when will the opportunity be seized and (ii) will any devaluation taking place between now and mid-1994 be the final one, or is there still scope for a final realignment at the start of full EMU, possibly in connection with the rounding-off of the present complicated central rates for the ECU in national currencies? The Maastricht Treaty unfortunately leaves doubt on this second point.

Both of these questions make for instability in the period up to the end of Stage II. It would be desirable, if a realignment is to be made, that it should be made early and that it should be accompanied by clear statements of the intention to make it the final one. Having a modest realignment in, say, 1992 without such accompanying statements could generate expectations that it will not be the final one. On the other hand, postponing a final and more substantial realignment to the eve of EMU would upset the nominal convergence achieved. There remains therefore an incentive for a bolder strategy, advocated by, for example, Dornbusch (1991) and CEPR (1991), of using the residual exchange-rate flexibility – if it is to be used at all – early rather than late and then proceeding to a declared policy of firm pegging of exchange rates among the candidates for EMU and to do so not later than the start of Stage II.

NOTES

The present chapter draws on a recently published book, *European Monetary Integration: From the EMS to EMU*, Longman, London 1992. I am indebted to my co-author of this volume, Daniel Gros, for close collaboration over the past six years. An earlier version of this chapter was given at a conference, organized by Banco de Portugal and the Centre for Economic Policy Research (CEPR) in Estoril, Portugal, 16–18 January 1992. Critical comments from the discussants of the conference paper, Lorenzo Bini Smaghi and José Viñals, as well as from the editors of the volume and Dr. Vítor Gaspar were helpful in the revision of the paper.
1 Article 13 of the EMI Statute stipulates, however, that a decision on the

location of the EMI should be taken before the end of 1992. Whether that will, in fact, be possible, depends on the resolution of the present conflicts over the seat of the European Parliament and of some new EC agencies. There is a similar provision in the ESCB Statute on the choice of location for the ECB; the realistic assumption is that this will be the same as for the EMI.

2 Presumably the hardening of the ECU which will occur sometime in the second half of this decade when the common currency takes over from the basket is the main explanation why the interest rate on 10-year ECU bonds is presently approximately 50 basis points lower than the basket formula would imply.

3 It is not clear whether the (at most) three best performers should be interpreted as the average, median or worst performance within this reference group.

4 It has not been easy in some past EMS realignments to determine who took the initiative to realign; it has also at times been difficult to agree on the balance between revaluations and devaluations in a realignment. This criterion is therefore less unambiguous than it may sound.

5 There may be a residual doubt whether a date for the beginning of Stage III could be set some distance into the future, possibly even later than 1 January 1999. Such a decision would not violate the letter of the Treaty, but certainly its spirit.

6 In the case of public debt the formulation chosen has been inspired by the prescription in the Treaty that 'substantial and continuous' reduction should be achieved; the contribution to the indicator is measured as the surplus which would be needed to bring the debt/GDP ratio to 60% over a ten-year period.

7 It is an indication that at least some members of the Delors Committee had a long and substantial Stage II in mind.

REFERENCES

Centre for Economic Policy Research (1991) *Monitoring European Integration: The Making of Monetary Union*, Annual Report, Centre for Economic Policy Research, London.

Committee for the Study of Economic and Monetary Union (1989) *Report on Economic and Monetary Union in the European Community* (Delors Report). Luxembourg: EC Official Publications Office.

Corsetti, Giancarlo and Nouriel Roubini, 'The Design of Optimal Fiscal Rules for Europe after 1992' Ch. 3, this volume.

de Grauwe, Paul and Daniel Gros (1991) 'Convergence and divergence in the Community's economy on the eve of economic and monetary union', in Peter W. Ludlow (ed.), *Setting EC Priorities*, London: Brassey's for CEPS.

Dornbusch, Rüdiger (1991) 'Problems of European Monetary Integration', in Alberto Giovannini and Colin Mayer (eds.), *European Financial Integration*, Cambridge: Cambridge University Press.

Eichengreen, Barry (1991) 'Designing a central bank for Europe: A cautionary tale from the early years of the Federal Reserve System', Discussion Paper Series No. 516, Centre for Economic Policy Research, London.

Gros, Daniel and Niels Thygesen (1992) *European Monetary Integration: From the EMS to EMU*, London: Longman.

Lamfalussy, Alexandre (1989) 'A Proposal for stage two under which monetary-policy operations would be centralized in a jointly-owned subsidiary', in Collection of Papers, annexed to the Delors Report, 213–19, op. cit.

Wihlborg, Clas and Thomas Willett (1991) 'The Instability of Half-way Measures in the Transition to a Common Currency', in Herbert Grubel (ed.), *EC 1992 – Perspectives from the Outside*, London: Macmillan.

Discussion

LORENZO BINI SMAGHI

In this short comment I would like to examine an issue which has been slightly overlooked in this chapter – i.e. the role of the European monetary institution (EMI) in Stage II of EMU. The new Treaty (Article 109 f) and the Statute in the annexed protocol attribute two basic responsibilities to the EMI: (i) to strengthen the coordination of the member states' monetary policies; (ii) to prepare the instruments and procedures necessary for the European central bank (ECB) to carry out a single monetary policy in the third stage.

Discussions at the inter-governmental conference mostly reflected the belief of many participants that the above tasks are not particularly demanding. According to this view, cooperation among central banks has already been strengthened in recent years and there is little scope for further steps without violating the constraint, to be in force until the last stage, requiring ultimate responsibility for the conduct of monetary policy to remain with national authorities. Moreover, since monetary policy will be implemented by the national central banks in the last stage, most of the instruments and procedures are already in place for running a single monetary policy and not much preparation is required.

When a second look is taken at the issue, however, the complexity of the tasks to be performed by the EMI becomes evident. The aim of this short note is to provide some indication of this complexity and to bring out the importance of the role that the EMI will play in the second stage.

D.2.1 The coordination of monetary policies in Stage II

Monetary policy coordination has substantially improved since the start of the first stage of EMU (Committee of Governors, 1992). Progress in achieving convergence of economic performance is generally thought to facilitate coordination. This is not entirely correct. I will examine two issues, the determination of the monetary policy of the system and currency substitution.

For most of its life the European monetary system (EMS) has been an asymmetric system, in which Germany's monetary policy played a dominant role. This was due mainly to four factors:

(i) Germany was the only large country, except for France, to participate in the system with narrow margins;
(ii) Germany's inflation rate was the lowest;
(iii) the Bundesbank enjoyed the greatest credibility in terms of anti-inflationary policy;
(iv) Germany's monetary conditions were the most stable and could be isolated from those of the other countries where exchange controls were in force.

This situation favoured an exchange rate system anchored to the Deutschmark, whereby the Bundesbank determined monetary policy, consistent with the requirement of price stability in Germany, while the other countries pegged their currency to the Deutschmark.

The situation has progressively changed and is bound to change even more during Stage II because:

(i) the other large countries of the Community have joined the European monetary system and are expected to adopt the narrow fluctuation margins, as Italy did in 1990;
(ii) Germany is no longer the best performer in the Community in terms of price performance, and it is not likely to recapture its primacy in the short term;
(iii) the Bundesbank's credibility is still the highest but that of the central banks of several other countries has improved;
(iv) with full capital mobility and German unification monetary conditions have become less stable in Germany.

The issue of the appropriateness of monetary policy can no longer be settled in the same systematic way as in the early period of the EMS, i.e. the monetary policy of the Bundesbank (oriented towards price stability) is no longer the one best suited to attain price stability in all the other countries.

In more general terms, as the performances of the member countries converge, the maintenance of price stability does not necessarily require all countries to adopt the same monetary policy stance all the time. Countries may temporarily experience different shocks, for instance in terms of wage dynamics or public finances. On the other hand, the constraint of exchange rate stability, which is already strongly felt and which will become binding during the two years preceding the decision to move to the final stage, does not allow even temporary differentiation of monetary policies. The question to be addressed is how exchange rate and price stability can be reconciled in this phase. Clearly, monetary policy alone will not be sufficient. Other policies, in particular fiscal and incomes policies, will have to complement monetary policy to achieve both domestic and external objectives. Moreover, the issue concerning the way the overall stance of the system's monetary policy is determined remains open.

The EMS does not provide a mechanism for adopting a more symmetric approach to the conduct of monetary policy in the system. At present, when tensions develop, countries whose currencies are near the top of the ban enjoy an advantage: when the exchange rate moves towards the margin, it is easier for the country whose currency appreciates to sterilize capital inflows than for the one at the other extreme to sterilize outflows, since foreign exchange reserves are limited. Countries that want to conduct a more restrictive monetary policy tend to have an advantage in being able to maintain their policy stance unchanged and thus influence the aggregate monetary policy of the system. Recent experience shows that countries whose currencies were near the bottom of the band could not relax monetary conditions, in spite of their lower inflation rate, because the restrictive stance adopted in other countries with higher inflation caused their currencies to rise to the top of the fluctuation band.[1] These situations are likely to create conflicts in the system.

The second issue which may make the coordination of monetary policies more difficult is the increased degree of currency substitution. If currency substitution is high within an area that extends beyond national boundaries, national monetary aggregates lose their informational content for the conduct of monetary policy. A broader approach is necessary. Evidence on currency substitution is difficult to assemble. Data on cross-border deposits, however, suggest that it increased significantly during the 1980s (Bini Smaghi and Vori, 1991). Econometric estimates also suggest that currency substitution is important because aggregate EMS demand for money is found to be more stable than national variables (Kremers and Lane, 1990). It is not clear whether currency substitution between European currencies will increase in the second stage of EMU. What is certain, however, is that the use of the ECU will increase, since agents will start getting accustomed to the future single currency. The financial use of the ECU is already quite widespread and increasing at a fast pace, in particular in the international banking and financial markets. Since the value of the ECU is closely related to that of the component currencies, its increasing use will *de facto* imply an increased substitutability between the component currencies. This will have an impact on monetary conditions in member countries and on the procedures underlying policy decisions. In particular, monetary aggregates will increasingly need to be examined at the system level to assess the appropriateness of monetary policy.

The two issues examined above do not raise problems for the conduct of monetary policy in the final phase, when the union will act as a single monetary entity. In the transition period, however, when national monetary conditions will be closely inter-related but decisions will still be taken at the national level, tensions may arise. It will be the role of the EMI to reduce these tensions and ensure a smooth transition towards a single monetary policy.

D.2.2 The preparation of the passage to the final stage

From the first day of the final stage, the ESCB governing council will need to have all the instruments and procedures required for the conduct of a single monetary policy. Two aspects of policy decisions can be distinguished: (i) the definition of targets and (ii) the use of instruments to achieve them. I will concentrate on the second issue. On the first, which I certainly do not consider to be a simple matter, progress on policy coordination in the second stage should provide the framework for setting intermediate aggregate targets in a way that will enable monetary policy to be used to pursue price stability effectively.

The preparation of the instruments for the implementation of a single monetary policy is a more complex issue since, paradoxically, these already exist in the national central banks. For monetary policy to be conducted in a unified way and distortionary financial flows avoided, national central banks can maintain an operational role only if their instruments are compatible. A further complication is that policy instruments cannot be changed overnight. They need to be adequately prepared and tried out so that market participants and national central banks can get accustomed to them. This implies that although during the second stage national central banks retain full control over the conduct of monetary policy, they will have to modify some of their operational procedures. Such adjustment takes a long time, as central bankers know.

I shall consider two categories of central bank activity – (i) monetary policy and (ii) the payments system – and briefly survey the main issues that will have to be addressed in the two areas, on the basis of the prevailing procedures in the member states. Tables D.2.1 and D.2.2 describe the different characteristics underlying the operational aspects of national monetary policies and payments systems.

I will deal first with monetary policy instruments. In Table D.2.1 four

Table D.2.1. *Use of monetary policy instruments*

	Belgium	Denmark	Germany	Greece	Spain	France	Ireland	Italy	Netherlands	Portugal	UK
Operations with/in											
Individual intermediaries											
– Degree of use	▨	■	■	▨	▨	□	▨	▨	■	▨	▨
– Relationships with market rates	▨	■	▨	□	▨	□	▨	■	■	□	□
Domestic market											
– Degree of use	■	▨	■	■	■	■	■	■	■	■	■
– Relationships with market rates	■	▨	■	■	■	■	▨	■	■	■	■
Treasury											
– Volume of credit line	▨	□	▨	▨	▨	▨	▨	■	▨	▨	□
– Purchase on primary market	□	□	□	■	▨	■	□	■	□	■	□
Reserve requirements											
– Volume	□	□	▨	▨	▨	▨	▨	■	□	■	□
– Mobilization[a]	□	□	□	□	□	□	□	□	□	■	□

Legend: ■ Yes/High ▨ Intermediate □ No/Non-existent

Note: [a] Computation as average of daily balances.

main types of central bank instrument for implementing domestic monetary policy are distinguished: (a) operations with individual intermediaries, (b) operations with the domestic market, (c) relations with the Treasury and (d) compulsory reserves. To begin with the latter, it is interesting to note that the reserve requirement is fairly small or non-existent in most countries; only two countries are out of line, Italy and Portugal. Imposing a reserve requirement, however, even at a low rate, might not be a simple decision for the four countries that do not have such an instrument at present. In any case, many other aspects of reserve holdings, in particular mobilization, will have to be harmonized.

The relationship with the Treasury should not pose a major problem since the Treaty bans direct access to central bank credit. National legislation will accordingly have to be adapted before 1994.

All central banks rely heavily on open market operations, which are an efficient and flexible instrument for controlling domestic liquidity. From Table D.2.1, it can be seen that these operations are largely of the same nature across countries and that they are used on a similar scale. In particular, most central banks rely on re-purchase agreements, which have a strong impact on domestic interest rates. Nevertheless, some of the characteristics of these operations will have to be made compatible, such as types of collateral, tender techniques and settlement conditions.

The monetary policy instruments that differ most are the transactions with single intermediaries. The differences concern not only the techniques adopted but also the objectives pursued, with the focus sometimes on monetary control and sometimes on support of the banking system. For instance in Germany, Italy and Denmark, the discount rate is an important monetary policy instrument which has a strong impact on market rates. In France this instrument is not used. In the UK and Spain it has little effect on market rates and is used more by the central bank in its operations as a lender of last resort than for monetary control. To conduct a single monetary policy in the union, conditions of access to central bank credit will have to be harmonized, in particular with respect to collateral and penalty rates (Banca d'Italia, 1990 and Padoa-Schioppa and F. Saccomanni, 1992).

Work in this area will probably have to start even before the EMI is created because sufficient time must be allowed to try out the new techniques after the main decisions described above are taken.

The second area where important preliminary work will have to be done is that of payments systems. The issue of payments systems has not been very fashionable in the academic literature. In view of the recent technological advances and the large volume of transactions undertaken daily, however, payments systems have become the main potential factor of the transmission of financial crises. For this reason all central banks in the Community need to be directly involved in ensuring the smooth operation of their payments system. This will be a crucial task for the ECB, since there can be no monetary union without a single payments system. At present there are 12 national payments systems plus the one for the ECU, the only Community-wide one. The creation of the Community payment system will result from the linkage of these systems.

National payments systems at present differ widely (see Table D.2.2). In particular, access to the system varies across countries and is highly regulated to ensure the ability of all participants to settle their net positions. The central banks supervise these participants, directly or indirectly, and in nearly all countries require them to hold an account with them. The methods of settling transactions also differ. In some countries gross rather than net settlement is undertaken instantaneously, which implies a large volume of transactions but also greater liquidity risks. This method requires direct involvement by the central bank in the form of daylight credit (extended for a period of less than one business day). In every country the central bank provides overnight credit facilities, but on different conditions, in particular with respect to collateral maturity and pricing. The use of settlement accounts also differs across countries, with respect to the degree of automation, the pricing of services and the settlement time. National payments systems cannot be linked unless these differences are eliminated.

In the absence of harmonization, undesirable competition among systems may arise, with the risk of operators carrying out their transactions in less protected systems. The EMI will therefore have an important role in linking national systems to create a single payments system for the Community. In fact, work has already started in the committee of governors since it is estimated it will take from 4–7 years to set up a new payments system.

The transition to EMU should take stock of the recent experience of the countries of Eastern Europe in the transition to a market economy. Moving from a controlled to a market economy proved to be much more complex than economists initially thought because of the need for a whole set of laws, regulations and practices (as well as human capital) that are often taken for granted by economists. Moving from 12 monetary systems to a single one also involves dealing with a wide range of issues that are often not considered in the academic literature because they concern basic institutional characteristics of monetary economies that are often taken for granted. In this short note I have tried to define some of these issues. It will be the task of the EMI to lay the foundations on which the whole future union will rest.

Table D.2.2. *Selected features of inter-bank payment systems*

	Belgium	Denmark	Germany	Greece	Spain	France
Membership	Banks, financial institutions, post office	Banks	Banks, financial institutions, post office	Banks, post office, financial institutions	Banks, financial institutions	Banks
Central bank services						
Gross settlement system	No	Yes	Yes	No	No	Yes
Net settlement system	No	Yes	Yes	No	No	Yes
Closing time of settlement services	17.00	15.30	13.30	15.00	16.00	17.30
Pricing of settlement services	Full cost	Running cost	Free of charge	Free of charge	Full cost	Full cost
Settlement accounts (use of compulsory reserves)	No	No	Yes	Yes	Yes	Yes
Degree of automation	Medium	High	High	High	Low	Low

Table D.2.2. (*continued*)

	Ireland	Italy	Luxembourg	Netherlands	Portugal	UK
Membership	Banks, Paymaster-General	Banks, post office	Banks, financial institutions, brokers	Banks, financial institutions, brokers	Banks	Banks
Central bank services						
Gross settlement system	No	Yes	No	Yes	Yes	No
Net settlement system	No	Yes	No	No	No	No
Closing time of settlement services	17.00	17.00	11.30	15.30	14.00	15.50
Pricing of settlement services	Free of charge	Running cost	Full cost	Full cost	Running cost	Free of charge
Settlement accounts (use of compulsory reserves)	Minimum balances	Yes	No	Yes	Yes	Minimum balances
Degree of automation	Low	High	Medium	High	Medium	High

NOTES

The author is solely responsible for the opinions expressed.
1 A rationalization of this problem can be found in Bini Smaghi (1992).

REFERENCES

Banca d'Italia (1990) 'Functions of the ECB in the second phase of EMU', mimeo, Rome.
Bini Smaghi, L. (1992) 'Waiting for EMU: Living with Monetary Policy Asymmetries in the EMS', *Temi di discussione*, Banca d'Italia, Rome.
Bini Smaghi, L. and S. Vori (1991) 'Currency substitution, monetary stability and European monetary unification', *Rivista Internazionale di Scienze Sociali*, Milan, January.
Committee of Governors of EC Central Banks (1992) *First Annual Report*, Basle.
Kremers, J. and T. Lane (1990) 'Economic and monetary integration and the aggregate demand for money in the EMS', *IMF Staff Papers*, 37, 4, Washington.
Padoa-Schioppa, T. and F. Saccomanni (1992) 'Agenda per la fase due: preparare la piattaforma monetaria', in S. Micossi and I. Visco (eds), *La posizione esterna dell'Italia*, Bologna: Il Mulino.

Discussion

VÍTOR GASPAR

This chapter is an important contribution to the understanding of the role of Stage II of economic and monetary union (EMU). It provides a clear presentation and interpretation of the final compromise of Maastricht. I will concentrate my comments on the non-monetary aspects of Stage II making my comments mostly complementary to the author's contribution.

As the author rightly stresses the most important news from Maastricht is the irreversibility of the process towards EMU. In fact, exchange rates will be irrevocably fixed no later than 1 January 1999. In any event, only the member states which fulfil the necessary conditions for the adoption of the single currency will participate fully in the final stage of EMU. It is this particular balance between credibility and irreversibility, on the one hand, and convergence requirements on the other, that was decisive in the final compromise and gives the Maastricht Treaty its distinctive character.

The importance of the necessary conditions for convergence, in particular in the area of budgetary discipline, may be illustrated by an example. Portugal, like most other European countries, adopted the gold standard during part of the nineteenth century. Specifically, the gold standard determined the monetary and exchange rate regime in Portugal from 1854 to 1891. It was the 1891 banking and financial crisis that marked the end of the gold standard in Portugal. According to Reis (1990), the doubts of financial markets on public sector solvency were important factors leading to the 1891 crisis. In 1891–92 public sector revenues only covered 70% of total expenditures. This happened after decades in which year after year deficits were followed by deficits (see Mata (1985)).

There are a number of strong arguments for fiscal prudence and the requirement of compliance with 'demanding budgetary indicators' to use the author's words. First the fiscal pre-requisites for an independent monetary policy. If the real interest rate exceeds the real growth rate and if there is an upper bound on the stock of public debt that the markets will absorb, a limit will be set on deficits or default. The second point follows from the impact of default or the likelihood of default on the stability of the financial system. Default by a highly indebted sovereign borrower could trigger successive bankruptcies by financial intermediaries and credit institutions thus fuelling a financial crisis. Third, there is the possibility that political pressure will be strong enough to ensure that a member state which risks insolvency will be 'bailed out'. If that is the case market discipline will be undermined and perverse incentives for budgetary profligacy will exist. In other words, and more generally, the avoidance of excessive deficits is a crucial component of a sound and stable macroeconomic environment which is a necessary condition for growth and development. Quoting from Feldstein (1991): 'There are many potential sources of economic crises and much that can be done to reduce future risks. But a low inflation, stable government policies, and an institutional environment that encourages sufficient diversification of risks can play a fundamental role in reducing the risk of future economic crises.'

There are, nevertheless, very strong arguments against mechanical rules which limit budget deficits, as the author stresses. Probably the most powerful point comes directly from the following remark by Kotlikoff (1986): '. . . the deficit is an inherently arbitrary accounting construct that provides no real guide to fiscal policy'.

Given these opposing arguments, a balance was sought in a procedure whereby a judgement by the Council of Finance Ministers (ECOFIN) has to be passed before a deficit is labelled excessive. Therefore the qualification of a deficit as excessive is a matter for judgement. Nevertheless this judgemental procedure will be initiated automatically by the violation of certain critieria ('triggers'). Given that it may be the case that budgetary difficulties may be identified rather late by using the criteria alone the Commission will have the right (and duty) to activate the procedure on its own initiative and responsibility.

Trigger mechanisms provide a constructive way to guarantee an effective starting point to an 'excessive deficit procedure' based on judgement. The criteria that were retained in Maastricht are basically the following:

(i) a gross debt-to-GDP ratio in excess of 60% and failure to reduce it;
(ii) a general government deficit in excess of 3% of GDP.

The first of the criteria is meant to be adequate as a sustainability criterion. Indicators of sustainability, should be based on the dynamic government budget constraint:

$$dB/ds = G + H - T + rB = P + rB,\tag{1}$$

where B is real debt, G is government spending on goods and services, H is transfers, T is taxes, P is the primary deficit and r is the real interest rate, and ds is used to identify the time trend.

Rewriting the budget constraint in terms of ratios to GDP (denoted by lower case letters):

$$db/ds = g + h - t + (r - y)b = p + (r - y)b\tag{2}$$

where y represents the rate of growth of GDP.

It is possible to integrate (2) to give:

$$b_t = b_0 \exp\int_0^t (r_v - y_v)\,dv - \int_0^t p_\tau\left[\exp\int_\tau^t (r_v - y_v)\,dv\right]d\tau\tag{3}$$

Assuming an asymptotic bound on public debt, which prevents it from growing faster than the discount factor $(r - y)$ it is possible to write:

$$b_0 \int_0^\infty p_\tau\left[\exp\left(-\int_0^\tau (r_v - y_v)\right)dv\right]d\tau\tag{4}$$

Equation (4) is the inter-temporal public sector budget constraint meaning that the present value of future tax collections should equal the present value of expenditures together with any obligations outstanding.

Substituting γ for $(p + (r - y)b)$ in (2) gives:

$$db/ds = \gamma\tag{5}$$

and integrating to give the debt to GDP ratio in t would give:

$$b_t = b_0 + \int_0^t \gamma_\tau d\tau \tag{6}$$

If we were to substitute b_t^* (a normative reference level for the debt to GDP ratio in any given particular country) for b_t in (4) or (6) we get an operational version of the public sector inter-temporal budget constraint that will be binding in a given and limited reference time frame.

In such case sustainability could be assessed on the basis of the following equivalent constraints:

$$b_t^* = b_0 \exp \int_0^t (r_v - y_v) dv - \int_0^t p_\tau \left[\exp \int_\tau^t (r_v - y_v) dv \right] d\tau \tag{7}$$

$$b_t^* = b_0 + \int_0^t \gamma_\tau d\tau$$

see also Blanchard (1990).

The first criterion is very closely related to (7). It can be motivated as follows:

   (a) $b_0 > 60\%$;   and
   (b) $\gamma_0 > 0$.

If (a) and (b) are met then the procedure will be triggered. It is clear from (7) that for any country with a ratio of debt to GDP in excess of 60% the procedure will fail to be triggered only if the debt to GDP ratio is projected to decrease *and* is, in fact, decreasing.

The second criterion may be rationalized first of all as an early warning indicator. Moreover, with a positive nominal growth rate, the upper limit on the deficit implies a ceiling on the public debt-to-GDP ratio. Therefore it acts jointly with the sustainability criterion to ensure a given convergence path to a level equal or below the reference debt-to-GDP ratio. In fact, the two criteria imply the same asymptotic debt-to-GDP ratio when nominal GDP growth equals 5%. If that is the case, a deficit-to-GDP ratio below 3% ensures that the primary gap will be negative for debt-to-GDP ratios in excess of 60%, i.e. compliance with the budget deficit to GDP ceiling will ensure automatic compliance with the sustainability criterion.

From 1891 to 1914 the monetary regime, following the collapse of the gold standard in Portugal, was regarded as provisional by the economic authorities. Nevertheless, high budget deficits were seen to exclude the gold standard option (see Reis, 1990). The example highlights the rationale for the application of budgetary discipline procedures from the second stage of EMU.

REFERENCES

Blanchard, O.J. (1990) 'Suggestions for a New Set of Fiscal Indicators', OECD Working Paper No. 79, Paris.

Feldstein, M. (1991) *The Risk of Economic Crisis*, Chicago and London: University of Chicago Press.

Kotlikoff, L. (1986) 'Deficit Delusion', *Public Interest*.

Mata, M.E. (1985) 'As Finanças Públicas da Regeneração à Primeira Guerra Mundial', Dissertação Apresentada no Instituto Superior de Economia, da Universidade Técnica de Lisboa, para a obtenção do grau de Doutor em Economia.

Reis, J. (1990) 'A Evolução da Oferta Monetária Portuguesa: 1854–1912', *História Económica*, Banco de Portugal, Lisbon.

Discussion

JOSÉ VIÑALS

The chapter by Niels Thygesen makes an important contribution towards our understanding of the institutional and economic contents of Stage II of EMU. I will focus my comments on three issues: (i) differences between Stages I and II; (ii) stability in Stage II, and (iii) convergence criteria for entering into Stage III.

D.2.3 Differences between Stage I and Stage II

I agree with the author that the Maastricht Treaty is a major step foward in the construction of EMU since it shows the political will to complete the process in a limited time horizon. I also share the view that at the heart of the compromise reached at Maastricht lies the principle of indivisibility; namely, that monetary sovereignty will remain firmly in the hands of the national authorities until the beginning of Stage III. This is critical to understanding why there will not be any gradual transfer of monetary sovereignty in Stage II from the national sphere towards the central monetary institution – the EMI – as originally envisaged by the Delors Report. As a result, Stage II will represent mainly an intensification of the process of monetary co-ordination already present in Stage I together with some elements of institutional preparation for Stage III.

Niels Thygesen would have liked to see a qualitiatively different Stage II with more monetary content and where the EMI had been empowered to use monetary instruments to regulate the overall monetary conditions in the Community. Yet, he is confident that market pressures and the need to prepare for Stage III will in practice lead the EMI to go beyond the tasks envisaged in the Treaty, even experimenting with policy instruments to influence overall monetary conditions in the Community. I remain, on the contrary, quite sceptical of this future scenario since I do not see how it squares with the fundamental principle of indivisibility.

While I agree with the author that the monetary content of Stage II is more limited than originally envisaged by the Delors Report and is less far-reaching than some member states would have liked, there are several features of Stage II that are going to make an important difference in the monetary domain. In particular, the process of monetary policy co-ordination could be greatly facilitated once monetary financing of deficits and financing at below market rates by national central banks are abolished from the start of Stage II. In addition, the initiation in Stage II of processes to establish the independence of central banks from their respective national governments could also help strengthen monetary policy co-ordination. Finally, the preparatory work of the EMI in establishing the regulatory, organizational and logistical framework which is needed for the ESCB to conduct effectively the single monetary policy from the beginning of Stage III may already in Stage II exert significant effects on financial markets and financial practices.

Still, the point raised by Thygesen regarding the need to devise procedures to avoid the drifting up of national inflation rates in the transition to Stage III is a crucial one. Indeed, the Treaty establishes only an inflation convergence criterion but not an absolute inflation criterion for entering into Stage III. While it is stated that the inflation rates of member states should be close enough to those of the best-performing countries, there is no explicit ceiling for the inflation rate of the latter. Given the importance of avoiding the creation of an EMU with a higher than desirable rate of inflation, it is thus of paramount importance to strengthen the process of monetary policy co-ordination in the run-up to Stage III. Nevertheless, because of the limits imposed on national monetary policies by the ERM in an environment of free capital mobility, it is also necessary that fiscal and other non-monetary policies significantly contribute to the anti-inflationary process, and particularly in the most divergent countries.

D.2.4 Stability in Stage II

Some attention is paid in the chapter to the issue of economic and financial stability in Stage II. In this respect, Thygesen makes a passing reference to the existence of expectational effects in Stage II which I believe is a most crucial issue. In particular, by allowing Stage III to start with only a sub-group of member states and by identifying the criteria for entering into Stage III, the Treaty provides markets with a rough and ready yardstick to assess the prospects of a particular country entering promptly into Stage III. Consequently, the Treaty opens the way for the existence of virtuous and vicious circles, where the expectations by markets of the likely prospects for entry into Stage III facilitates the convergence for well-behaved applicants and makes convergence more difficult for less-diligent candidates.

For instance, take the case of a country where inflation is relatively high as a result of excessive fiscal and/or wage pressures. In recent years, in an environment of increasingly credible central parities in the ERM, if the country experienced a fiscal slippage this would typically put upward pressures on prices, nominal interest rates and on the currency within the band. Nevertheless, between now and the beginning of Stage III, lack of sufficient progress by the country in reducing its fiscal deficit or inflation to comply with the Maastricht criteria could, at some point, lead markets to expect that it will not enter promptly into Stage III. In such an instance, there would be an erosion of exchange rate credibility, which would make interest rates and inflationary expectations go up, thus adversely affecting inflation, public finances and interest rate convergence. On the other hand, countries which make steady progress towards meeting the convergence criteria will benefit from enhanced exchange rate credibility and this will have favourable effects on convergence.

Evidently, the strength with which virtuous and vicious circles manifest themselves depends critically on the view markets take about the final success of the Treaty ratification process as well as on the degree of stringency which will be attached to the entry criteria at the time of the decision by the political authorities. The stricter the interpretation is expected to be the stronger will be these circles, and correspondingly the stronger will be the incentive for governments to benefit from favourable expectational effects by credibly committing themselves to implementing successful convergence strategies.

D.2.5 Convergence criteria

But are the entrance criteria into Stage III appropriate? Thygesen finds the criteria broadly acceptable as formulated in the Treaty. Although this contrasts with the more critical views often expressed in academic circles, I agree with the author for several reasons. First, the Maastricht Treaty criteria are necessary to give some guarantees to the traditionally lower inflation countries that their inflation performance would not be jeopardised in EMU. In particular, while it is true that achieving inflation convergence could be faster and thus less painful in Stage III, higher inflation countries have to demonstrate their resolve in lowering inflation in Stage II – where it is more costly – in order to give an unequivocal signal of their anti-inflationary commitment, and hence their 'fitness' to participate. Second, while some of the criteria may be debatable on purely economic grounds, they nevertheless provide some member states with a unique political opportunity to introduce sweeping policy measures which would have been desirable even in the absence of EMU. Finally, entering Stage III with lower inflation and healthier public finances will help the ESCB to conduct monetary policy with a higher degree of credibility from the very start.

I would nevertheless stress that it is not only important to satisfy the entrance criteria for Stage III but to make sure that countries have the necessary degree of structural flexibility to withstand asymmetric shocks without creating excessive tensions once they are in full EMU. This view, based on the traditional literature on optimal currency areas, implicitly assumes that differences in national inflation rates are not just the results of lack of full exchange rate credibility but rather reflect differences in the degree of structural flexibility in goods and factors markets. In this respect, evidence available on the functioning of goods and labour markets in Community economies suggests that in several countries structural rigidities in labour markets and lack of competition in non-traded goods markets are behind the downward rigidity of wage and price inflation. Of course, it could be argued that as the EMU process advances and market participants realise that exchange rate adjustment will no longer be available as an adjustment tool, they may endogenously adapt their wage and price setting behaviour. It seems to me, however, that this favourable change in private sector behaviour is all the more likely to occur and be stronger in those cases where the authorities introduce wide-ranging structural reforms designed to promote competition in goods and factors markets.

Increased structural flexibility will not only enhance the stability of full EMU by facilitating the macroeconomic adjustment process in the presence of large asymmetric shocks, but will also contribute to the stability of the transition. In particular, by increasing the speed with which prices and wages respond to contractionary fiscal and monetary policies it would reduce the short-run output costs of achieving nominal convergence. In addition, by improving the likelihood of achieving nominal convergence in time, an early introduction of supply-side reforms during the transition to Stage III will help countries to benefit from favourable expectational effects in financial, goods and factor markets which would further facilitate convergence. Consequently, a successful implementation of supply side reforms, alongside monetary and fiscal policy measures, is crucial both to avoid instabilities in Stage II and to deliver a good EMU.

To conclude, the chapter by Niels Thygesen greatly contributes to our understanding of the rationale behind the Maastricht Treaty as well as of the institutional and economic content of Stage II. In addition, it identifies a number of central issues and problems which need to be tackled to ensure the successful completion of the EMU process.

NOTE

The opinions expressed are solely those of the author and do not necessarily coincide with the views of the committee of central bank governors of the European Community.

3 The design of optimal fiscal rules for Europe after 1992

GIANCARLO COSETTI and
NOURIEL ROUBINI

1 Introduction

As the countries in the European Community are debating whether, when and how to move to a full economic and monetary union (EMU), the compatibility of such a move with independent and divergent fiscal policies of the member countries has become an important issue.[1] While the experience of the European monetary system (EMS) has shown that an exchange rate constraint might tie the hands of monetary authorities and lead to a convergence of monetary policies and inflation rates, a similar convergence of the fiscal policies of the EC countries has not been observed. On the contrary, the period from 1979–87 was characterized by a divergence of fiscal policies in the member countries, with large budget deficits in a number of them. In the cases of Italy, Belgium, Ireland, Greece, Portugal and the Netherlands, these deficits led to a significant increase in the public debt to gross domestic product (GDP) ratio (see Tables 3.1 and 3.2). Since 1987, the fiscal balances of a number of these countries have improved; significant primary surpluses in Belgium and Ireland have led to a reduction in their debt-to-GDP ratios. In Italy, Greece and the Netherlands, however, the fiscal adjustment in the last few years has not been sufficient to prevent further increases in this ratio.

The Committee for the Study of Economic and Monetary Union (1989) – the Delors Report – made a strong case that a monetary union without fiscal convergence might be unstable and therefore recommended the imposition of binding fiscal rules to limit the discretion of policy-makers in deciding the size and financing of fiscal deficits. More specifically, the report recommended that:

> In the budgetary field, binding rules are required that would: firstly, *impose effective upper limits on the budget deficits* of individual member countries of the Community, although in setting these limits the situ-

ation of each member country might have to be taken into consideration; secondly, exclude access to direct central bank credit and other forms of monetary financing while, however, permitting open market operations in government securities; thirdly, limit recourse to external borrowing in non-Community currencies. (Emphasis added.)

Following the publication of the Delors Report, there has been a very wide debate on the need for rigid fiscal rules in the EC and for a coordination of fiscal policies. There have been numerous proposals regarding specific fiscal rules and the nature of the 'fiscal conditionality' required for the participation of member countries in a monetary union. The debate on 'excessive' fiscal deficits, on the fiscal rules to impose on the member countries as well as on the sanctions to be imposed on deviant countries has been an important component of the discussion on the transition to full EMU.[2]

In the spirit of the Delors Report, serious consideration has been given at the EC level to proposals recommending a rigid *balanced budget* rule for the current fiscal budget and limits on borrowing for capital expenditure purposes. In particular, the draft treaty presented by the Dutch in September 1991 (as well as previous draft treaties by Germany and France) stressed the obligation of member states not to run 'excessive deficits' and the use of sanctions was suggested if this obligation was not met. One month later, a document by the Monetary Committee of the European Community set out threshold-values for 'excessive' debt and deficit. These reference values were:

  (i) a gross debt-to-GDP ratio in excess of 60%;
 (ii) fiscal deficits in excess of 3% of GDP;
(iii) budget deficits which exceed government investment expenditures.

The Monetary Committee also proposed a series of financial sanctions should the deficits deviate from the trigger guidelines; these included the imposition of fines and the suspension of payments from the EC budget. Some countries, for example Belgium, also suggested the use of 'political sanctions' such as a suspension of voting rights (see Woolley, 1991). Others, like Italy, expressed strong objections to a rigid and 'mechanical' application of the Monetary Committee guidelines and did not favour drastic financial sanctions. The terms of this debate may be found in the final version of the Maastricht Treaty, which on the one hand ratified the strict guidelines suggested by the Monetary Committee in October 1991, and on the other, established a set of rather mild sanctions against off-target countries to be decided according to 'political criteria'. The procedure will be as follows. The Commission will establish whether there is excessive debt or deficit in a member state and will convey its opinion to the Council. The latter, acting on a qualified majority, may make recommendations to the member state (not to be made public at first), establishing a deadline by which the necessary corrective steps have to be taken. If at the end of this time limit, no effective action has been taken, the recommendations are made public and the member state is required to submit periodic reports about its adjustment efforts. Finally, if the fiscal imbalance persists, the Council may decide: (a) to require the member state to publish additional information before issuing debt; (b) to invite the European investment bank to reconsider its lending poicy towards that state; (c) to require the member state to make a non-interest bearing deposit with the Community or (d) to impose a fine.

The rationale behind the recommendations of the Delors Report, and therefore behind the terms of the Treaty is that, in the absence of such binding fiscal rules, some of the EC governments might exhibit a systematic bias towards budget deficits and this bias might have serious negative external effects on other EC countries.

It is also clear that if such a 'structural deficit bias' exists, there must be an element of political distortion that leads some governments to follow systematic policies of fiscal deficits in excess of what can be considered economically optimal. If governments were benevolent optimizing agents, then binding fiscal rules might not be necessary. For example, fiscal deficits would occur as a result of tax-smoothing considerations and we would observe transitory fiscal deficits in the case of temporary decreases in output (as during recessions) or in periods of temporarily high fiscal spending.[3] Such fiscal deficits would be economically sound, and if governments were running deficits on the basis of such considerations, there should be no need for rigid and binding fiscal rules.[4] If political bias leads governments to follow fiscal policies that are not consistent with the long term solvency of the public sector, however, it might have serious negative effects on the stability of the monetary and economic union.[5]

This view of fiscal policy in Europe suggests a number of questions.

(i) Is the present trend of fiscal policies in some EC countries incompatible with the long term solvency of the public sector?

(ii) Is there evidence that these fiscal deficits (and unsustainable fiscal policies) are significantly determined by political distortions rather than by economic factors?

(iii) If there is evidence of an important political bias in fiscal deficits, what are the benefits and the costs of rigid fiscal rules such as an EC rule requiring a current balanced budget?

(iv) In particular, how would the benefits of a binding balanced budget rule (in terms of eliminating the political bias of discretionary fiscal policy-making) compare with the costs of not allowing tax-smoothing fiscal deficits in the presence of transitory output and spending shocks?

(v) Is there room for contingent and flexible rules that (a) solve the distortions of the discretionary political equilibrium by imposing the discipline of fiscal balance in normal times and (b) allow fiscal deficit financing in the presence of transitory real shocks?

(vi) Would such rules (both the rigid budget balance and the flexible fiscal rule) be credible? Should the EC have the role of monitoring their implementation and the power to enforce them? And would sanctions be necessary to make the enforcement credible and effective?

(vii) Should participation in the EMU or the real integration process be made conditional on the adherence of the member countries to particular fiscal behaviour?

(viii) What would be the consequence of 'no entry unless fiscally sound' rules for the process of real and monetary integration in Europe? What would be the implications of a 'two-speed' or 'three-speed' or a 'variable geometry' approach to integration?

In this chapter, we would like to address these points systematically. In Section 2, we start by looking at a simple accounting framework, constructing scenarios where countries which are currently off-target try to satisfy the fiscal guidelines established at Maastricht. Next, we will try to test whether the current fiscal policies of the EC countries are sustainable in the long run (Section 3). We perform formal tests of the solvency of the public sector for the EC countries. These tests suggest that problems of the sustainability of fiscal policies are present in Italy, Greece and, to a lesser extent, in Belgium, Ireland and the Netherlands. Given that there is some evidence of public sector insolvency in a number of EC countries, what can explain the large fiscal deficits and public debt accumulation observed in these countries? In Section 4 of the chapter, we argue that political factors matter and we present a survey of the theoretical literature on political biases in fiscal policy-making.

Next, in Section 5 we present some empirical evidence on the political determinants of budget deficits. In particular, we show that both government weakness and instability (measured by short-lived multi-party coalition governments) and electoral factors (pre-election fiscal expansions) help to explain the behaviour of fiscal deficits in a large number of countries in the Organisation for Economic Cooperation and Development (OECD).

In Section 6, we move to a comparison of alternative fiscal rules when political uncertainty and polarization leads to a deficit bias (see Alesina and Tabellini, 1990). In the presence of stochastic shocks to output, a discretionary political equilibrium leads to excessive deficits but allows governments to smooth tax rates in the presence of transitory output shocks. Compared with this discretionary political equilibrium, a binding balanced budget rule will avoid the political bias towards budget deficits. This rigid rule, however, would not allow the smoothing of taxes that could be optimal in the presence of transitory shocks and feasible in a discretionary equilibrium.

The optimal fiscal policy followed by a social planner would be one of full tax smoothing where fiscal deficits and surpluses are run in the face of transitory shocks. If such a first-best solution is not enforceable in a political equilibrium, a second best equilibrium might take the form of a 'fiscal rule with an escape clause'. Such a flexible rule would impose a fiscal balance whenever the real output shock is below a certain threshold and would allow for tax-smoothing fiscal deficits if the transitory disturbance is large enough.

We also argue that, in the presence of systematic uncertainty, reputational mechanisms might not be sufficient to enforce any of these alternative cooperative rules of fiscal discipline. We suggest that these rules should be monitored and enforced by an external agent (such as the European Commission). A credible enforcement mechanism, however, requires the use of explicit sanctions against undisciplined countries.

In the concluding remarks, in Section 7, we compare our flexible rules with the fiscal guidelines recently adopted by the Community. We argue that such guidelines are, in one sense, too rigid because they impose targets on the inflation-unadjusted and cyclically-unadjusted overall fiscal balances of the member countries. On the other hand, they are too loose because their implementation will be subject to a 'political' evaluation and will not be backed by effective sanctions.

We finally argue that political concerns about the negative consequences of a 'two-speed' EMU, from which countries like Italy would be excluded because of their deviant fiscal behaviour, explain the hybrid system of rigid but unrealistic fiscal guidelines backed by weak enforcement mechanisms and soft sanctions that appears to have been adopted by the EC.

2   Fiscal arithmetic at Maastricht

The set of fiscal guidelines established by the Treaty of Maastricht is defined in terms of performance indicators: the overall public deficit should not exceed 3% of GDP, and, if the debt-to-GDP ratio is above 0.6, the country should not fail to reduce it over time. Why these particular numbers? A 60% debt-to-GDP ratio happened to be the average value for the 12 Community members in 1990. If it is considered desirable that Europe should have a steady state growth rate of nominal income equal to 5% – say 3% real growth and 2% inflation – then the value of the deficit to GDP ratio which is consistent with this long run stationary equilibrium is exactly 3%. Nonetheless, it would be more satisfactory if some theoretical justification could be given or historical arguments used to support the choice of these numbers, as short run strict guidelines for national fiscal policy. In this section, we by-pass this set of issues and concentrate on a very simple, but important, exercise. By using the dynamic budget constraint of the government, we will construct simple scenarios where off-target countries will try to adjust their fiscal stance.

First, we will have a quick look at the government budget identity using the same definitions as they appear in the documents of the European Community. Consider

$$D_t = D_{t-1} + DEF_t \tag{1}$$

where D is gross nominal debt (gross means that it includes both monetary debt and public financial assets) valued at par; DEF is the overall deficit in nominal terms, which is the sum of the primary deficit (including investment expenditure) and interest payments. Subscripts refer to time.

Dividing both sides of the identity by nominal GDP, and using lower case letters for expressing variables as a ratio to GDP, we can write

$$d_t = \frac{d_{t-1}}{(1 + g_t)(1 + \pi_t)} + def_t \equiv \frac{d_{t-1}}{\phi_t} + def_t \tag{2}$$

where g and π denote the growth and the inflation rate respectively and $\phi_t \equiv (1 + g_t)(1 + \pi_t)$ is the rate of growth of nominal GDP.

Consider any country that is not currently meeting the Community's fiscal standards. As a starting point, a debt to GDP ratio equal to 1 is assumed, as well as a constant ϕ equal to 7.5% (say, 5% inflation and 2.5% real growth). These figures are close to the cases of Italy, Belgium and Ireland.

The first experiment builds upon a rather mechanical implementation of fiscal rules agreed at Maastricht: we will trace the evolution of public debt over time under the hypothesis of lowering the deficit to 3% of GDP by 1992 and keeping it at this level in the years to come. The striking point in this exercise is that, even under the assumption of an immediate and complete adjustment of the government budgetary process, simple calculations show that the debt-to-GDP ratio will not hit the target of 60% before the year 2007. This date is obviously delayed if the growth of nominal income slows down, as an effect of the fiscal contraction on either inflation or real output growth, or both. In particular, if φ decreased too much (under 4.8%) the debt target will never be reached.

On the other hand, we may not expect a complete adjustment right away. For example, the deficit to GDP ratio may increase over time according to some auto-regressive process

$$def_{t+1} = \Psi def_t + C \qquad (3)$$

If $\Psi = 0.8$ this ratio would decrease by approximately 20% a year.[6] Let us take Italy as our reference country, positing an initial deficit to GDP ratio equal to 1. In this case, even if nominal output kept growing at 7.5%, it would now take until the year 2014 to meet the Community standards.

A striking point in these calculations is that nothing has been said about interest rates. This follows from the terms in which the fiscal targets are defined in the Maastricht Treaty, i.e., targets for the total deficit and total debt. If we break down the total deficit into the sum of the primary deficit (spending minus revenue) and interest payments, simple algebra shows that our identity can be written as

$$def_t = pdef_t + \frac{i_t}{(1 + \pi)(1 + g)} d_{t-1} \qquad (4)$$

where $pdef_t$ is the ratio of primary deficit to GDP and i_t denotes the nominal interest rate. For a nominal interest rate averaging around 9% (4% real, 5% inflation), we can trace the path of the primary deficit to GDP ratio during the adjustment process.[7] Primary surpluses are quite large during the first few years (4.11% of GDP in 1992, 3.42% of GDP in 1993). Thus, high debt countries, where a large share of the fiscal balances consists of interest payments, would have to run large and persistent primary surpluses well beyond, in most cases, their historical experience. It will be recalled that the primary surplus includes expenditure on capital formation, which in 1991 averaged 3% of GDP in EC countries. If this pattern persists over time, a 3% upper limit to the overall deficit to GDP ratio would be equivalent to a rigid balanced budget in terms of the current deficit.

To sum up, our simple exercise shows that it is extremely unlikely that countries such as Italy, Ireland and Belgium will meet the fiscal prerequisites to enable them to join the European monetary union by the deadline agreed in the Maastricht Treaty. Nonetheless, the terms in which fiscal standards were defined at Maastricht suggest a number of additional considerations, which we will discuss in the final section of this chapter.

3   Tests of public sector solvency for the EC countries: the empirical evidence

In this section we will consider tests of the solvency of the public sector in the EC countries. The objective is to verify whether, and which, EC countries might be on an unsustainable fiscal path. We will draw on the empirical work of Hamilton and Flavin (1986), Trehan and Walsh (1989), Wilcox (1989), Buiter and Patel (1990) and Corsetti and Roubini (1991). Under the hypothesis that a government solvency constraint must be imposed, the class of tests in this literature attempt to verify whether the present value budget constraint of the public sector would be satisfied: (a) had the fiscal and financial policy in a given time period been pursued indefinitely, and (b) if the relevant features of the macroeconomic environment characterizing the sample period, were stable over time.[8] According to this approach, if solvency is not supported by empirical evidence, a change either in the policy or in the relevant macroeconomic variables (growth, inflation, interest rate, demographic factors) must occur at some point in the future. Note that these tests refer to the feasibility rather than the optimality of the fiscal and financial policy. Moreover, they give no information about the time in which the necessary changes should occur.

The empirical implications of the solvency constraint can be obtained as follows. The public sector is solvent when the present discounted value of future primary surpluses minus seigniorage revenue is at least equal to the value of the outstanding stock of net financial debt. Starting from the definition of the inter-temporal budget constraint of the government, it is easy to show that solvency implies the following condition:

$$\lim_{i \to \infty} E_t \prod_{j=0}^{i} (1 + \xi_{t+j})^{-1} D_{t+1+i} = 0. \tag{5}$$

where D_t now denotes the real value of total financial liabilities less foreign reserves evaluated in domestic currency and ξ_{t-1} is the real (*cum capital gains*) implicit interest rate on the net liabilities outstanding at the beginning of the period. This condition says that the public sector cannot be a net debtor in present-value terms, so that, ultimately, the stock of debt cannot grow at a rate higher than the interest rate on the debt. The crucial point is that Ponzi schemes, in the form of systematic financing of interest payments with additional borrowing, are ruled out.

Our test (following Wilcox) builds on the fact that the present-value budget constraint requires the expected value of discounted debt to be zero. Thus, if we discount the series of net debt back to some base period, we can test whether the Data Generating Process (DGP) describing the

Table 3.1. *Net debt[a] to GDP ratio*

	Germany	France	United Kingdom	Italy	Belgium	Greece[b]	Ireland[b]	Netherlands[b]	Spain	Denmark	Portugal[b]
1960	− 24.82	14.56	116.17	NA	59.17	NA	NA	NA	NA	NA	NA
1961	− 26.37	10.81	109.96	NA	57.17	NA	NA	NA	NA	NA	NA
1962	− 26.16	7.09	104.91	NA	54.47	NA	NA	NA	NA	NA	NA
1963	− 24.10	4.79	98.44	NA	51.91	NA	NA	NA	NA	NA	NA
1964	− 25.69	3.49	91.91	5.63	47.54	NA	NA	NA	NA	NA	NA
1965	− 23.55	1.68	85.39	8.18	45.79	NA	NA	NA	NA	NA	NA
1966	− 22.57	1.13	81.72	11.95	45.21	NA	NA	NA	NA	NA	NA
1967	− 20.36	0.84	82.16	11.84	44.35	NA	NA	NA	NA	NA	NA
1968	− 18.92	1.22	77.20	14.76	44.13	NA	NA	NA	NA	NA	NA
1969	− 18.18	1.64	72.30	14.51	42.83	NA	NA	NA	NA	NA	NA
1970	− 18.17	0.44	64.83	17.36	40.31	5.37	NA	42.68	− 9.10	− 9.24	NA
1971	− 17.42	0.06	62.00	20.54	39.87	4.51	NA	41.22	− 10.30	− 11.48	NA
1972	− 17.65	− 3.68	55.95	24.98	37.54	4.97	45.47	38.83	− 10.99	− 14.56	NA
1973	− 18.16	− 3.69	47.43	24.85	36.10	2.52	42.05	36.19	− 11.27	− 17.14	NA
1974	− 15.29	− 3.10	45.70	23.05	34.28	2.66	47.26	34.70	− 11.61	− 18.22	NA
1975	− 9.51	2.80	49.65	31.96	37.06	4.44	55.95	34.29	− 11.64	− 15.82	25.5
1976	− 5.94	− 3.23	48.85	33.96	38.11	4.46	63.20	33.55	− 11.66	− 12.84	31.4
1977	− 3.71	2.72	48.64	34.53	41.58	4.02	61.90	33.10	− 9.82	− 9.03	33.2
1978	− 1.83	2.84	46.51	36.26	45.53	11.00	64.67	34.27	− 9.08	− 6.03	36.3
1979	0.57	2.83	41.76	37.51	50.39	10.96	70.48	35.99	− 8.92	− 2.10	41.0
1980	4.42	2.05	42.63	37.71	58.53	9.95	73.56	39.10	− 6.72	3.39	37.1
1981	8.08	3.32	42.08	42.83	71.13	11.28	82.82	43.70	− 3.40	12.73	46.6
1982	10.27	4.57	41.45	48.74	80.31	14.18	93.47	48.73	− 0.65	22.89	50.0
1983	11.80	6.86	42.16	54.07	90.82	21.16	99.22	54.52	− 5.83	30.81	56.0
1984	12.15	8.57	44.35	59.72	95.86	28.30	103.04	58.61	0.90	34.19	61.4

1985	12.78	9.51	43.17	65.89	103.44	39.41	107.50	61.92	6.80	27.55	69.5
1986	12.20	11.71	41.83	70.69	108.59	40.38	123.24	66.21	10.01	23.77	68.4
1987	13.00	11.53	38.42	74.47	113.71	44.62	125.30	66.69	7.66	18.83	71.6
1988	13.18	12.02	32.98	76.88	116.01	50.00	122.85	68.66	8.60	17.68	74.0
1989	11.51	12.47	28.64	NA	115.10	57.88	115.80	NA	NA	NA	71.2

Notes:

[a] Net debt is equal to gross debt minus the financial assets of the government. The debt figures are also net of base money.

[b] Gross debt (rather than net debt) figures have been used in these cases.

Sources: OECD *Economic Outlook*, various issues, 1987–91; OECD *National Accounts 1961–88*, Organisation for Economic Cooperation and Development, Paris.

behaviour of this series over the sample period is covariance stationary and the unconditional mean of the process is zero (or non-positive). Either a positive drift or a time trend will eventually imply insolvency.

If non-stationarity of the process cannot be rejected, we have to consider two cases, depending on whether or not deterministic components also belong in the DGP of the series. A process with a unit root, but no drift or time trend is, in principle, compatible with both insolvency and a sort of supersolvency (i.e., in the limit, the government becomes a net creditor). When the unit root coexists with positive deterministic components in the DGP of the series, however, this will provide some evidence against solvency.

Following a conservative (albeit arbitrary) approach to the interpretation of the test results, we consider the case of a non-deterministic but non-stationary process as inconclusive. We will reject solvency only when a positive drift or time trend exists in addition to a unit root.[9] As far as the interpretation of the test is concerned, therefore, insolvency will follow from positive deterministic components in the DGP of the series of the discounted debt – but only in the absence of structural changes in the process at some point in the future.

The test concerns stationarity of the DGP of the series as well as the presence of deterministic components in it; the Phillips–Perron approach (Phillips and Perron, 1987; Phillips, 1987; Perron, 1988) has been used. The details of the testing approach are described in a technical appendix to the chapter but the approach basically relies on three different statistics $(Z(t_{a_i})$, $Z(\Phi_2)$ and $Z(\Phi_3))$ to test for the presence of a unit root, a deterministic trend and a drift in the series for the discounted debt.

The sample consists of ten EC countries.[10] The available OECD debt series are evaluated at par (rather than market) value, so that our analysis will reflect at least an important error of approximation. Results for the test which show the probability value at which each null hypothesis can be rejected are given in Table 3.3. A brief scheme containing the corresponding null hypotheses is reported at the end of this table. Tables 3.1 and 3.2 show, respectively, the debt to GDP ratio and the seigniorage-adjusted, inflation-adjusted deficit (overall and current).[11] The measure of the deficit in Table 3.2 is obtained by taking the first difference of the end of period stocks of net (in some instances, gross) debt in real terms and subtracting seigniorage revenue from the differentiated series. Note that this definition of the real deficit has the advantage of purging the government interest bill of its inflation-related component. Our set of tests in Table 3.3 are based on a measure of discounted debt.

We will begin with the cases in which the results of the test are against solvency: Italy, Belgium, Greece and Ireland. The test provides strong evidence against the sustainability of current policies in Italy.[12] While $Z(t_{a_3})$ does not reject the null hypothesis of a unit root, both $Z(\Phi_2)$ and $Z(\Phi_3)$ reject the joint null of a unit root and a zero time trend (and a zero drift for the second statistic). In the case of Italy, the estimated time trend is positive (the trend of the discounted debt is clearly upwards) suggesting a rejection of solvency.

Belgium's discounted debt follows a non-stationary, non-trended process; both the statistics $Z(t_{a_3})$ and $Z(\Phi_3)$ accept the corresponding null hypotheses. The statistic $Z(\Phi_2)$, however, suggests the presence of a deterministic drift, which is positive in the estimation. This is evidence against solvency.

In principle, it is possible that the necessary steps towards a correction of the fiscal stance had already been taken within the sample period, but the test failed to detect their effects on the series of the discounted debt. Italy never achieved primary surpluses in the 1980s, however, so that the series of discounted debt was monotonically increasing. Real overall deficits were around 4% of GDP at the end of the sample and even the current fiscal balance (i.e. net of public investment) showed deficits throughout the 1980s (see Table 3.2).

It should also be observed that both Italy and Belgium show large and often increasing current real fiscal deficits in the 1980s. In these two countries, despite the high public investment to GDP ratio, even the current balance of the general government was negative in that period. (See Table 3.2.)

Given the large and persistent current fiscal deficit and a debt-to-GDP ratio of around 100% in Italy, long term fiscal insolvency is likely in the absence of a major shift in fiscal policy. The case of Belgium is, however, slightly different. In the late 1980s, this country undertook a programme of fiscal adjustment which led to significant primary surpluses. While the formal test suggested insolvency, it is likely that the test did not detect the structural change in Belgium's fiscal policy that has occurred in the last few years.

Test results for Greece and Ireland provide evidence for the presence of deterministic components in the DGP of discounted debt series. Evidence against solvency is available in the case of Greece and Ireland, where the $Z(\Phi_2)$ supports the presence of a non zero drift. Moreover, the statistic $Z(\Phi_3)$ rejects the null hypothesis suggesting the presence of a non-zero time trend in the DGP of the series, which results in this trend being positive in the estimation. These two countries, however, differ significantly in their present fiscal outlook. Ireland started a major programme of fiscal adjustment and deficit reduction in the late 1980s, achieving significant primary surpluses and a reduction in the ratio of

Table 3.2. *Inflation-adjusted, seigniorage-adjusted deficit (overall and current) (percent of GDP)*

	Germany	France	United Kingdom	Italy	Belgium	Denmark	Greece	Ireland	Netherlands	Spain	Portugal
Overall deficit											
1961	−3.11	−3.58	−3.61	NA	0.20	NA	NA	NA	NA	NA	NA
1962	−1.41	−3.80	−2.89	NA	−0.83	NA	NA	NA	NA	NA	NA
1963	1.00	−2.55	−3.45	NA	−1.56	NA	NA	NA	NA	NA	NA
1964	−3.30	−1.44	−2.89	NA	−2.11	NA	NA	NA	NA	NA	NA
1965	0.42	−2.02	−4.43	2.18	−0.73	NA	NA	NA	NA	NA	NA
1966	−0.15	−0.86	−1.79	3.70	0.33	NA	NA	NA	NA	NA	NA
1967	2.11	−0.72	1.63	0.31	0.40	NA	NA	NA	NA	NA	NA
1968	0.19	−0.29	−3.05	2.92	0.70	NA	NA	NA	NA	NA	NA
1969	−0.80	−0.20	−4.66	−0.60	0.60	NA	NA	NA	NA	NA	NA
1970	−1.49	−1.71	−6.70	2.24	−0.84	NA	NA	NA	NA	NA	NA
1971	−0.63	−1.01	−2.07	2.27	−0.02	−2.78	−1.19	NA	−0.64	−2.46	NA
1972	−1.43	−4.43	−4.23	2.20	−1.38	−3.91	−1.49	NA	−1.61	−2.42	NA
1973	−1.94	−1.25	−6.59	−2.83	−1.68	−3.29	−4.80	−0.90	−1.50	−2.38	NA
1974	1.99	−0.82	−6.18	−4.01	−1.79	−1.44	−2.26	1.13	−0.87	−2.62	NA
1975	5.25	4.52	4.17	3.64	1.74	1.64	−0.39	6.67	−0.83	−1.94	NA
1976	2.66	−0.16	−0.36	−0.17	2.13	1.51	−1.81	7.10	0.77	−2.14	NA
1977	1.64	−1.05	0.22	−1.02	3.39	3.06	−2.31	2.52	0.12	−0.88	NA
1978	1.30	−0.45	−1.86	−0.37	4.42	2.36	4.03	4.07	1.87	−1.45	NA
1979	1.83	−0.61	−4.90	−0.69	5.28	3.31	−2.27	5.10	1.87	−1.70	NA
1980	3.37	−1.39	0.45	−0.92	8.80	4.93	−3.56	2.00	2.99	0.31	NA
1981	3.19	0.54	−0.78	2.69	10.09	8.47	−2.76	9.77	3.73	1.57	NA
1982	1.78	0.68	0.21	3.81	9.24	10.02	−0.86	12.25	5.01	0.95	NA
1983	1.54	1.76	2.11	4.58	10.00	8.25	2.88	6.26	6.28	−6.90	NA
1984	0.52	1.38	2.51	6.29	6.15	4.58	4.10	7.40	5.59	4.26	NA

Year											
1985	0.56	0.72	0.51	6.80	8.76	−5.46	8.17	5.75	5.13	3.69	NA
1986	−0.45	2.24	−0.56	5.74	7.75	−3.19	−0.71	16.34	5.94	1.96	NA
1987	0.89	−0.13	−2.37	5.01	7.24	−5.17	1.37	5.84	0.38	−2.87	NA
1988	0.40	0.66	−3.93	3.96	NA	−1.39	4.10	3.58	3.87	−0.05	NA
1989	−1.33	0.64	−2.42	4.07	NA	NA	NA	NA	NA	NA	NA

Current deficit

1961	−6.04	−5.93	−5.83	NA	−1.35	NA	NA	NA	NA	NA	NA
1962	−4.79	−6.40	−5.38	NA	−2.53	NA	NA	NA	NA	NA	NA
1963	−2.87	−5.34	−6.00	NA	−3.45	NA	NA	NA	NA	NA	NA
1964	−7.64	−4.49	−6.02	NA	−4.44	NA	NA	NA	NA	NA	NA
1965	−3.48	−5.23	−7.54	−0.21	−2.44	NA	NA	NA	NA	NA	NA
1966	−3.88	−3.93	−5.15	1.34	−1.65	NA	NA	NA	NA	NA	NA
1967	−1.02	−3.83	−2.21	−1.84	−1.91	NA	NA	NA	NA	NA	NA
1968	−3.02	−3.22	−6.98	0.46	−1.94	NA	NA	NA	NA	NA	NA
1969	−4.11	−2.99	−8.37	−2.92	−2.03	NA	NA	NA	NA	NA	NA
1970	−5.40	−4.41	−10.36	−0.46	−3.69	NA	NA	NA	NA	NA	NA
1971	−4.40	−3.49	−5.44	−0.26	−3.34	−7.00	NA	NA	−4.85	−5.02	NA
1972	−4.82	−6.72	−7.33	−0.44	−4.65	−7.76	NA	NA	−5.27	−4.64	NA
1973	−5.05	−3.45	−10.30	−5.18	−4.34	−6.48	NA	−4.23	−4.68	−4.44	NA
1974	−1.29	−3.01	−10.08	−6.55	−4.25	−4.60	NA	−2.95	−3.86	−4.60	NA
1975	2.17	2.13	0.77	0.70	−0.87	−1.43	NA	3.14	−4.03	−4.14	NA
1976	−0.08	−2.44	−3.38	−2.99	−0.55	−1.43	NA	4.32	−2.29	−4.00	NA
1977	−0.87	−2.84	−1.81	−3.75	0.83	0.04	NA	−0.29	−2.59	−3.08	NA
1978	−1.26	−1.97	−3.39	−2.86	2.03	−0.74	NA	1.16	−0.68	−3.13	NA
1979	−0.81	−2.09	−6.25	−3.15	2.86	0.11	NA	1.82	−0.55	−2.99	NA
1980	0.61	−2.89	−0.59	−3.87	6.22	2.26	NA	−1.46	0.44	−1.00	NA
1981	0.79	−0.95	−1.21	−0.73	7.66	6.29	NA	6.04	1.31	−0.05	NA
1982	−0.22	−0.81	−0.07	0.31	7.02	8.22	NA	8.31	2.79	−1.45	NA
1983	−0.14	0.48	1.43	1.09	8.17	6.91	NA	2.59	4.21	−9.06	NA

Table 3.2. (cont.)

1984	−1.05	0.23	1.68	2.92	4.65	3.25	NA	4.10	3.45	1.98	NA
1985	−0.95	−0.59	−0.20	3.32	7.49	−6.94	NA	2.42	3.17	0.73	NA
1986	−2.07	0.97	−1.25	2.44	6.66	−4.46	NA	13.42	4.12	−0.98	NA
1987	−0.69	−1.39	−2.92	1.79	6.19	−6.56	NA	3.69	−1.30	NA	NA
1988	−1.18	−0.67	NA	0.80	NA	−3.04	NA	NA	2.23	NA	NA

Note: The 'overall' inflation-adjusted, seigniorage-adjusted deficit is the first difference of the end-of-period stock of net (gross) debt in real terms minus seigniorage. The 'current' deficit is the 'overall' deficit minus government net investment.
Source: Basic data as for Table 3.1.

Table 3.3. *Testing for solvency of the public sector in EC countries: test results for the series of discounted general government net interest-bearing liabilities*

	$Z(a_3)$	$Z(t_{a_3})$	$Z(\Phi_2)$	$Z(\Phi_3)$
Belgium	< 90	< 90	> 99	< 90
France	< 90	< 90	< 90	< 90
Germany	< 90	< 90	< 90	< 90
Italy	< 90	< 90	> 99	> 99
United Kingdom	< 90	< 90	< 90	< 90
Denmark	< 90	< 90	< 90	< 90
Greece	< 90	< 90	> 99	> 99
Ireland	< 90	< 90	> 99	> 99
Netherlands	< 90	< 90	< 90	< 90
Spain	< 90	< 90	< 90	< 90

Note:

Regression Model: $y_t = \mu_3 + \beta\left(t - \dfrac{T}{2}\right) + a_3 y_{t-1} + u_t^3$

Null hypotheses:
H_0: $a = 1$ for $Z(a)$ and $Z(t_a)$
H_0: $a = 1$ and $\beta = 0$ and $\mu = ?$ for $Z(\Phi_3)$
H_0: $a = 1$ and $\beta = 0$ and $\mu = 0$ for $Z(\Phi_2)$

debt to GDP. Conversely, significant primary deficits persist in Greece; these suggest a serious solvency problem in that country.

The case of the Netherlands is interesting from the point of view of assessing the behaviour of the test in the presence of within-sample structural changes. The statistics in Table 3.3 suggest the presence of a non-zero deterministic drift if we exclude the last two years in the sample (1987 and 1988), when the government started a programme of fiscal adjustment. When the full sample span is considered, however, the test statistics support a non-deterministic, non-stationary process.

For the other two countries (Denmark and Spain) discounted debt appears to follow a drift-less and trend-less non-stationary process, providing no clear evidence either against or in favour of solvency. In the case of Denmark, years of severe fiscal imbalances in the 1979–84 period were followed by a serious fiscal retrenchment and surpluses in current fiscal balances from 1985. After peaking to 34% of GDP in 1984 the net debt to GDP ratio rapidly fell to 17.7% of GDP in 1988. The data for Spain also show current fiscal surpluses for all years except 1984 and 1985. Until 1983, the net financial public debt was negative (i.e. the government was a net financial creditor). Net debt has been very small since then (8.6% of

GDP in 1988). Therefore the sustainability of public debt does not appear to be an issue in the Spanish case.

For the three major EC countries (Germany, France and the UK), the discounted debt also appears to follow a drift-less and trend-less non-stationary process. In this case, super-solvency and insolvency are equally likely. Evidence for these countries should be interpreted as inconclusive. Additional information about the fiscal balances of these countries, however, allows us to make some inferences.

For Germany, the data in Table 3.2 for the current fiscal balance show surpluses in most years in the sample, with the exception of 1975, 1980 and 1981. Moreover, while the German government became a net financial debtor in 1978, the debt-to-GDP ratio has stabilized around 10–13% since 1982 (see Table 3.1). This additional evidence would suggest that public sector solvency might not be an issue in the German case. It should be noted, however, that our analysis is based on past trends and is not able to capture the potential implications of the recent German unification for the future fiscal balances of a united Germany.

In the case of the United Kingdom, the net debt to GDP ratio systematically fell from 116% in 1960 to 28.6% in 1989. The current fiscal balance was in surplus in all years between 1960 and 1989, with the exception of 1975, 1983 and 1984. The overall evidence is therefore quite consistent with public sector solvency in the UK.

In the case of France, additional tests provide evidence in favour of the stationarity of the processes followed by the adjusted current balance (this is the test suggested by Trehan and Walsh, 1988). Moreover, Tables 3.1 and 3.2 show that France had current fiscal surpluses in all but four years in the last three decades, plus stable and low levels of debt-to-GDP ratio in the 1980s (around 10–12%). The overall evidence would therefore suggest that the French public sector is solvent.

Finally, while the lack of data does not permit formal testing of public sector solvency in Portugal, the evidence based on alternative indicators of sustainability such as those used by Blanchard (1990) and Giovannini and Spaventa (1991) suggest that a fiscal problem might have also been present in Portugal until 1988. A pattern of persistent primary deficits and rising debt-to-GDP ratios, however, seem to have been reversed recently (the debt-to-GDP ratio has been decreasing since 1989).

To summarize, among the EC countries, problems of sustainability of the present paths of fiscal policy appear to exist in Italy, Belgium, Ireland, the Netherlands and Greece.[13] These countries have in common a large debt to GDP ratio (close to or above 100% in Italy, Belgium and Ireland). Only two of them, Ireland and Belgium, started a process of fiscal adjustment in the mid-1980s which has led to the achievement of significant primary surpluses and, in the case of Ireland, to a reduction of the debt to GDP ratio. Conversely, primary deficits still persist in the other three countries (their size is larger in Greece than in the Netherlands and Italy); this appears to be inconsistent with long term solvency.

4   Political determinants of budget deficits: a survey of the theory

In the previous section, it was shown that the path of fiscal policy followed by many EC countries might not be consistent with long term solvency of their public sector. Since the tests referred to the feasibility rather than the optimality of fiscal and financial policy, however, evidence in favour of solvency does not necessarily imply that the solvent countries have followed optimal fiscal policies. For instance, the evidence in Roubini and Sachs (1989a, 1989b), Roubini (1991), Cukierman, Edwards and Tabellini (1991) suggests that the tax smoothing view of fiscal policy-making and the optimal seigniorage model of the inflation tax are both rejected for developed as well as developing countries. In particular, transitory shocks to output and government spending fail to explain the movements of public debt in a large number of countries and inflation rates do not appear to be correlated (or co-integrated) with tax rates.

Given that optimizing theories of fiscal policy tend to be rejected, while there is some evidence of public sector insolvency for a number of EC countries, what can explain the large fiscal deficits and public debt accumulation observed in these countries? Recent theoretical and empirical literature suggest that the political determinants of fiscal deficits should be examined. In this section we present a brief survey of the theoretical literature on political biases in fiscal policy making while in the next section we present the empirical evidence on this issue.

From a theoretical point of view, there are at least four classes of political explanations of politically motivated fiscal deficits: (i) 'public choice' models of deficits biases in democracy; (ii) models of political instability and decentralized government; (iii) models of strategic debt; (iv) 'political business cycle' models.

4.1   Public choice models

The idea that fiscal spending and budget deficits might be affected by political institutions is not new. The 'public choice' school of James Buchanan has been the leading proponent of the idea that, in the absence of constitutional constraints, governments in modern democracies have a bias towards over-spending and fiscal deficits.[14] These traditional theories of a fiscal deficit bias in democratic societies have been criticized for the weakness of some of their assumptions. In particular, in these models private agents (the electorate) are assumed to be backward looking and systematically unable to recognize the motivations of the policy-makers. On the other hand, governments and policy-makers are not representing the preferences of private agents but are assumed to be malevolent Leviathans attempting to maximize revenues or deficit spending. Moreover, from an empirical point of view, the implications of this theory do not seem to be borne out by the data. This approach implies that all democracies have a bias towards budget deficits but the evidence shows that only a sub-set of democracies appears to have a systematic tendency to run fiscal deficits. Moreover, fiscal deficits appear to be as widespread among non-democratic regimes as in democratic ones.

4.2   Political instability and decentralized government models

A number of authors have suggested that political instability and a decentralization of government spending decisions may be a source of sub-optimal fiscal policy behaviour and an important cause of fiscal deficits.

Roubini and Sachs (1989a, 1989b) have suggested that short duration multi-party coalition governments lead to fiscal deficits because it is difficult to enforce cooperation, in the presence of negative economic shocks, in a coalition setting. In fact, game theory suggests that cooperation is harder when the number of players is large (multi-party coalition governments) and when the horizon of the players is short and not repeated (short duration governments). The reasons why parliamentary multi-party coalition governments will have a hard time eliminating budget deficits after adverse shocks is that the individual parties in the coalition will each veto spending cuts or tax increases that would impinge on their narrow constituencies, thereby frustrating the attempts of the executive branch to implement deficit reduction measures.

Tabellini (1991) stressed the importance of the decentralization of government fiscal decisions. When the decisions to spend and tax are decentralized among different agents (such as the ministers of a coalition government or between central, regional and local fiscal authorities), there may be an incentive to excessive government spending which is deficit financed.

Along similar lines, stressing the lack of political cohesion, Alesina and Drazen (1991) explained the delay in fiscal adjustment in the presence of an unsustainable fiscal deficits as the result of a 'war of attrition' between two different social classes. Here the conflict is about which social class will bear the tax burden of stabilization. The model implies that a greater dispersion in the income distribution and a lower degree of political cohesion will cause a delay in the expected rate of stabilization and will therefore imply a greater and prolonged pre-stabilization period of fiscal imbalance and inflation.

From an empirical point of view, by using panel data on a sample of 15 OECD countries, Robuini and Sachs (1989a, 1989b) found that political instability as proxied by a number of variables such as the type of government (single party majority, presidential, presidential with divided government, multi-party coalition, minority) or low average duration of the government, leads to higher real (inflation-adjusted) budget deficits. More recently, Grilli, Masciandaro and Tabellini (1991) have found similar evidence showing the effects of weak government and short duration coalition governments on fiscal deficits.

4.3   Strategic debt models

In a number of recent papers, the relationship between political variables and budget deficits has been explained by looking at the role of partisan factors in economic policy-making. The origin of this literature is in Alesina's (1987) work on partisan effects in monetary policy but the same methodological approach has been applied to the issue of fiscal policy, domestic and foreign debt accumulation. These recent studies share a common theoretical background in that they assume heterogeneous agents (usually two types of agents) with different preferences about types of government spending or the inflation-unemployment trade-off. The political distortion is introduced by assuming that different political parties represent the preferences of these agents and that these parties come to power according to stochastic probabilities of re-election. The probability of the current government/party not being re-elected affects the discount rate of the party by effectively shrinking the horizon of the policy-maker (it increases the effective rate of time preference). In this political equilibrium, variables such as budget deficits or the inflation rate diverge from the optimal value that would obtain in the absence of the political distortion (i.e. if a benevolent social planner were to supplant the two parties).

Alesina and Tabellini (1990) and Tabellini and Alesina (1990) showed that the greater the probability of not being re-elected and the degree of political/ideological polarization (the difference in preferences) of the two parties, the larger the budget deficit will be in a model where the optimal policy is to run a budget balance in every period. The current government uses the level of public debt strategically, with the goal of tying the hands of successive governments with different fiscal policy objectives.[15]

Alesina and Tabellini (1989) considered the effects of political distortions on external debt and capital flight. They showed that, in a model in which two types of government with conflicting distributional goals randomly alternate in office, 'uncertainty over the fiscal policies of future governments generates private capital flight and small domestic investment. This political uncertainty also provides the incentives for current governments to over-accumulate external debt'.

4.4   Political business cycle models

A last group of models stresses the electoral motivations of policy-makers and suggests that fiscal policy might be too expansionary before elections. In particular, the 'political business cycle' (PBC) theory of Nordhaus (1975) suggests that office-motivated politicians will tend to follow expansionary monetary and fiscal policies before elections in order to maximize their re-election probabilities. This implies that excessive government spending, tax reductions, delays in tax increases and therefore fiscal deficits will be observed in electoral years.

This traditional PBC theory of a pre-electoral fiscal deficit bias in democratic societies has been criticized for the weakness of some of its assumptions. In particular, in this model also private agents (the electorate) are assumed to be backward looking and unable to recognize the motivations of the policy makers.

More recently, several authors have re-formulated the 'political business cycle' hypothesis of a pre-electoral fiscal deficit bias in models with rational agents. The rational political business cycle models of Rogoff (1990) and Rogoff and Sibert (1989) are recent examples of this approach. In these models, governments have the same utility function as private agents (i.e. they care about government spending in the same way as private agents do), but they are also 'opportunistic'. That is, governments care about winning elections, get welfare from being in power, and do not have 'partisan' motivations. These approaches share two basic ingredients: (i) different governments are characterized by different degrees of competency; and (ii) the government is more informed than the voters about its own level of competency.[16] In all of these models, the incumbent government has an incentive to 'signal' its competence by engaging in pre-electoral manipulations of policy instruments.

In the Rogoff and Sibert (1989) paper, an equilibrium with signalling appeared as follows: incumbents reduce taxes and/or increase spending before elections in order to appear 'competent', i.e. able to reduce waste in the budget process. Needless to say, voters prefer competent governments to less competent ones. Pre-electoral deficits are monetised, but the effects of monetisation on inflation and seigniorage are perceived by the voters only with a lag, i.e. after the election. Although voters are rational and aware of the policy-makers' incentives, pre-electoral deficits for signalling purposes still occur.[17]

Rogoff (1990) presented a non-monetary model in which he focused upon government spending on 'consumption' (or transfers) and 'investments'. Signalling, in this model, took the form of pre-electoral surges in immediately visible expenditures for 'consumption' or transfers and cuts in 'investment' expenditure. Although the decrease in investment is harmful for both productivity and efficiency, these results are observable by voters only with lags. Thus, budget cycles take the form of distortions in the allocation of resources across public spending programmes.

5   Political determinants of fiscal benefits: the empirical evidence

In this section we will consider empirically the effects of elections and political instability on fiscal deficits.[18] The theoretical literature surveyed in the previous section suggests several political determinants of fiscal deficits. On the one hand, both traditional and recent 'rational' PBC models imply that we should observe fiscal deficits before elections. On the other hand, both strategic models of public debt and models of political instability and decentralized governments suggest that political instability and polarization (to be duly defined) may lead to high budget deficits.

In analysing the effects of elections and political instability on fiscal deficits, a structural model of budget deficits is needed, in order to control for their economic determinants. We rely upon the structural model used by Roubini and Sachs (1989a) to study the effects of political instability on budget deficits. The specification of the model is consistent both with elements of optimizing approaches to fiscal deficits (such as the 'tax smoothing' model of Barro (1979)) and with traditional Keynesian models of fiscal deficits. In fact, both theories imply that fiscal deficits are counter-cyclical: i.e. fiscal deficits will emerge during periods of recession and growth slowdown.

In addition to the tax-smoothing considerations stressed by Barro (1979), the tendency towards deficits after a slowdown in growth, is exacerbated for two additional reasons. First, many major areas of public spending (e.g. unemployment compensation, social welfare expenditure, early retirement benefits, job retraining and subsidies for ailing firms) are inherently counter-cyclical, so that some elements of government spending actually tend to rise automatically when growth slows down and unemployment increases. The second reason is the intentional implementation in some countries of Keynesian aggregate demand policies in the face of a growth slowdown: right or wrong, many governments reduce taxes or increase government spending during recessions.

As in Roubini and Sachs (1989a), we estimate a pooled cross-section time-series regression where the left-hand side variable is the annual deficit, measured as the change in the debt to GDP ratio, $d(b_{it})$.[19] The basic explanatory variables are:

(i) the lagged deficit, $d(b_{it-1})$;
(ii) the change in the unemployment rate, $d(U_{it})$;
(iii) the change in the GDP growth rate, denoted $d(y_{it})$;
(iv) the change in the real interest rate minus the growth rate, multiplied by the lagged debt–GDP ratio, $b_{it-1} * d(r_t - n_t)$;[20]
(v) a dummy for political instability, pol_{it} first used in Roubini and Sachs (1989a); and
(vi) an electoral dummy ele_{it} both to be defined below.

The basic structure of the pooled regression model is the following (i denotes country, t denotes time, and $d(x)$ denotes the change in variable x):

$$d(b_{it}) = a_0 - a_1^* d(b_{i,t-1}) + a_2^* d(U_{it}) + a_3^* d(n_{it})$$
$$+ a_4^* b_{it-1} * f(r_t - n_t) + a_5^* pol_{it} + a_6^* ele_{it} + v_{it} \qquad (6)$$

where v_{it} is an error term. We expect the following: $0 < a_1 < 1$ (to allow for any slow adjustment and persistence of budget deficits); $a_2 > 0$ (since a rise in the unemployment rate raises government spending above its permanent value in the short term); $a_3 < 0$ (since a rise in GDP growth lowers government spending below its permanent value in the short term and may raise tax revenues); $a_4 > 0$ (since a rise in the real interest rate directly raises the real deficit, which if transitory should be accommodated by a temporary rise in the budget deficit).

Before introducing and discussing the political and electoral determinants of budget deficits, we present, in column (1) of Table 3.4, the results of the regression when only the economic variables are included. This specification provides a rather successful account of the role of economic shocks in inducing budget deficits in the industrial countries. In particular, a rise in unemployment (denoted by DUB) raises the budget deficit; a rise in the debt-servicing cost (denoted by DRB) raises the budget deficit; and an acceleration of GDP growth denoted by GDR) lowers the budget deficit, indicating that the deceleration of GDP growth after 1973 contributed to the rise in budget deficits. Note that the variable measuring this slowdown in growth is highly significant.[21] Finally, the lagged deficit (DBYL) enters with a coefficient of about 0.70, suggesting that about 70% of the lagged budget deficit persists to the next period.

Table 3.4. *Panel data regression of deficit with political variables (dependent variable: DBY)*

Regressors:	Equation (1)	Equation (2)	Equation (3)	Equation (4)	Equation (5)
Constant	− 0.002	− 0.006	− 0.007	− 0.004	− 0.0037
	(− 1.19)	(− 2.73)	(− 3.28)	(− 1.97)	(− 1.98)
DBYL	0.74	0.71	0.72	0.74	0.70
	(17.0)	(16.0)	(16.2)	(17.2)	(14.0)
DUB	0.23	0.18	0.19	0.24	0.24
	(2.98)	(2.32)	(2.51)	(3.15)	(3.17)
DRB	0.56	0.61	0.56	0.51	0.50
	(2.66)	(2.91)	(2.71)	(2.46)	(2.38)
DGR	− 0.47	− 0.45	− 0.46	− 0.48	− 0.47
	(− 8.49)	(− 8.31)	(− 8.50)	(− 8.69)	(− 8.49)
DUJAP[a]	1.82	2.75	2.62	1.76	1.70
	(1.46)	(2.16)	(2.07)	(1.42)	(1.38)
ELE	−	−	0.0065	0.0072	0.0063
			(2.17)	(2.41)	(2.04)
POL	−	0.0042	0.0039	−	−
		(2.77)	(2.57)		
DBYLELE	−	−	−	−	0.13
					(1.55)
R^2	0.65	0.66	0.67	0.66	0.66

Notes: *T*-statistics in parentheses.
[a] The regressor DUJAP is a country-specific dummy for DUB for Japan. This is the only country for which a country-specific effect was found in the data: its positive estimate implies that an increase in Japanese unemployment has a much stronger effect on budget deficits than in any other country. This results, however, do not depend in any way on the inclusion of this variable.
Source: See text.

In considering the effects of political variables on fiscal deficits we will consider both the role of elections and the effects of political instability and weak governments.

In order to test the hypothesis that governments manipulate fiscal policies before elections in order to maximize their re-election probabilities, a dummy *ele*, that takes value 1 in election years and zero otherwise, is added to the basic regression (columns (3)–(5). In constructing the variable *ele* we need to consider that, since our data on deficits are on a yearly basis, the exact time of an election during a year might be important for assessing the effects of elections on fiscal deficits. More specifically, if an election occurs towards the end of the year t, we can expect that an opportunistic government would run a fiscal deficit during that year. If, however, the election occurs towards the beginning of year t, it is more reasonable to assume that the fiscal expansion will occur in year $t - 1$ so as to be timed with the early election time in year t. In practice, in constructing the variable *ele* we assign value 1 to the dummy in the pre-electoral year $t - 1$ if the election will occur in the first and second quarters of year t; while we assign value 1 in the electoral year t if the election occurs in the third or fourth quarter of year t. As an additional check on the model we also run regressions using a slightly different electoral dummy (*elx* instead of *ele*). *elx* takes value 1 in the election year regardless of whether the election occurs in the first half of the year or the second half.

In order to consider the role of political instability and government weakness, we also add to the regression, in addition to the electoral variable, the political variable successfully used by Roubini and Sachs (1989a) to study the effect of government fragmentation on budget deficits. The hypothesis in that paper was that multi-party coalition governments, especially those with a short expected tenure, are poor at reducing budget deficits. We therefore add to the regression the Roubini-Sachs index (denoted pol_{it} for country i at time t) which measures the degree of political cohesion of the national government.[22]

The results of the estimations are shown in columns (2)-(4) in Table 3.4. Several different versions of the regression are shown, involving different ways of including the variables *ele* and *pol*, either jointly or separately. In column (2), we introduce the political instability variable and, as in Roubini and Sachs (1989a), we find that (after controlling for the economic determinants of deficits) a greater degree of political instability (as proxied by the index *pol*) leads to higher budget deficits.[23] In column (3), we add our electoral dummy *ele* to the regressors used in column (2); we find that, after controlling for the economic determinants, both *pol* and the electoral dummy, *ele*, have the right sign and are statistically significant at the 5% confidence level. In other words, real fiscal deficits are higher in the year leading to an election. In column (4), we drop the *pol* variable and consider the effects of *ele* only; we again find a statistically significant coefficient.

The effect of elections on budget deficits is significant both statistically and economically; the estimated coefficients on *ele* in column (3) and (4) imply that, after controlling for other determinants of fiscal balances, real fiscal deficits will be higher in election years by more than 0.6% of GDP. We also ran the panel regressions in Table 3.4 using the electoral dummy *elx* instead of *ele*. As expected, *elx* does not work as well as *ele*, since this dummy variable does not correspond to the timing of elections. In these regressions, however, *elx* has the right sign and is statistically significant at the 10% confidence level.

We also investigated the inter-action of the electoral variable with the lagged deficit (termed DBYLELE), on the premise that the speed of adjusting to an inherited level of the deficit, $d(bit - 1)$ might be lower in election years. We found that the sign of the inter-action variable DBYLELE (column (5) in Table 3.4), was the expected positive one (deficits are more persistent in election years, i.e. the fiscal adjustment to past deficits is slower during election periods) but it was only borderline significant (the t-statistic is equal to 1.55).

To sum up, the above evidence suggests that, after controlling for the economic determinants of budget deficits, political factors significantly account for the fiscal policies of a large number of OECD countries: budget deficits are larger in election years and in countries characterized by weak, short-duration multi-party coalition governments.[24]

6   A comparison of alternative fiscal rules

In the previous sections, we have shown that a number of EC countries appear to be following unsustainable fiscal policies and that political factors might explain part of the bias toward budget deficits. Given the evidence on political biases in fiscal policy, what are the potential benefits and costs of rigid fiscal rules such as the imposition of a balanced budget rule for the EC countries? In particular, how would the benefits of a binding balanced budget rule (in terms of eliminating the political bias of discretionary fiscal policy choices) compare with the costs of not allowing tax-smoothing fiscal deficits in the presence of transitory output and spending shocks?

In this section, we will compare alternative fiscal rules by presenting some preliminary results of an analysis (Corsetti and Roubini (1991b)) that extended the model by Alesina and Tabellini (1990) to the case of productivity shocks, thus providing a rationale for tax-smoothing fiscal deficits (see Appendix I). In the model of Alesina and Tabellini (1990), agents have preferences over different types of public goods and the parties representing them alternate in power according to given re-election probabilities. In the discretionary political equilibrium, there will be a fiscal deficit bias: the government in power will spend only on the good preferred by the agent it represents and it will run a budget deficit even if it would be socially optimal to have a balanced budget in every period. The current government will use the level of public debt strategically, in order to tie the hands of successive governments which will have different preferences for fiscal spending. The greater the probability of not being re-elected and the greater the degree of political/ideological polarization of the two parties, the larger the budget deficit will be. In the above set-up, the first-best policy followed by a benevolent social planner would be to spend in every period on both types of public goods and run a balanced budget in every period. Since Alesina and Tabellini (1990) did not introduce shocks to productivity, a balanced budget was optimal in every period.[25] Suppose now that the productivity of labour is subject to shocks; how would the behaviour of a benevolent social planner differ? Optimal taxation principles suggest that, as long as agents' utility is separable between consumption and leisure and the supply elasticity of labour is constant, a benevolent planner will follow a tax-smoothing rule with uniform tax rates over time. As pointed out by Barro (1979), transitory negative productivity shocks will lead to budget deficits and a build-up of public debt that will be repaid in periods of transitory positive productivity shocks. Therefore, in the presence of productivity shocks, the first best-policy rule which would be followed by a social planner would be one of a fully state contingent fiscal rule that allows tax-smoothing fiscal deficits and surpluses rather than a balanced budget.

The imposition of a rigid and binding balanced-budget rule in this framework would lower welfare: a transitory negative output shock will lead to a revenue loss at unchanged tax rates; the increase in tax rates required to balance the budget will distort the inter-temporal labour and consumption decision of the agents and lead to a welfare loss. This loss will increase the size of the transitory shock (or its variance in a stochastic set-up). Compared to a discretionary political equilibrium, however, a binding balanced budget rule will avoid the political bias towards budget deficits that would occur in a discretionary political equilibrium where parties use the deficits for strategic purposes.

While fiscal policy discretion leads to a deficit bias, it also has some advantages. In particular, it allows the government in power to smooth tax rates in the presence of real transitory shocks, something that is ruled out by the balanced budget rule. A welfare comparison between the discretionary political equilibrium and a rigid balanced budget rule would therefore not deliver unambiguous rankings: depending on the size of the productivity shock relative to the political biases in the system, a balanced budget rule (that avoids politically biased deficits) might be superior or inferior to a discretionary political equilibrium (that allows tax-smoothing deficits).

A fully contingent tax-smoothing rule implemented by a benevolent social planner would support a first-best allocation dominating both a discretionary political equilibrium and the balanced budget rule. If there is no social planner and political parties alternate in power stochastically, this first-best equilibrium might be sustained by a reputational mechanism only under quite unrealistic conditions. In fact, the real disturbance to labour productivity is usually not observed with certainty by agents: output is measured with delay and errors occur. Moreover, it is often hard to assess whether the shock is transitory, in which case a fiscal imbalance would be appropriate, or whether the shock is permanent, in which case a real tax adjustment would be required. Uncertainty about the size and nature of the shock implies that the incumbent government has a strong incentive to cheat by announcing that negative output shocks are large and transitory so that it can run large deficits. Therefore the first-best cooperative equilibrium might not be enforceable in a political equilibrium when the realization of the shock is subject to observational errors and potential cheating on the part of the ruling governments.

Given that a first-best, fully state contingent fiscal rule is impractical, a second best 'fiscal rule with an escape clause' (a flexible rule) should be considered. Such a rule would impose a fiscal balance whenever the real shock was below a certain threshold level and would allow for tax-smoothing fiscal deficits if the transitory disturbance was large enough. In other words, under this rule only large recessions would trigger budget deficits while minor movements in economic activity would be matched by tax adjustments that would maintain a budget balance. Such a rule with an escape clause might be superior both to a rigid balanced budget rule which does not allow tax smoothing and to a discretionary political equilibrium that results in excessive budget deficits. Moreover, compared with a fully state contingent rule, the rule with an escape clause could be easier to monitor and enforce.

The discussion above regarding alternative fiscal rules leaves open a serious issue. Regardless of whether a balanced budget rule or a flexible rule with escape clauses is jointly chosen by the EC countries, what is the enforcement mechanism that will guarantee that this rule is actually implemented. Are reputational forces enough to support such cooperative rules in a democratic institutional framework where different governments and parties alternate in power? Alternatively, is it necessary that an external agent (for example, the European Commission) be given the surveillance authority to monitor the implementation of these rules? Moreover, would such external monitoring be enough or are explicit sanctions against fiscally deviant countries necessary to enforce fiscal discipline? Finally, should the threat of sanctions go as far as making the participation of a member country to the third stage of the EMU conditional on the attainment of fiscal balance?[26]

Game theory suggests that, in some circumstances, reputational forces might be enough to sustain a cooperative rule. If discount rates are not too large, if the benefits of cooperation are large and the additional short term benefits of cheating small, the above fiscal rules could be sustained without the use of an external agent to enforce them.

In reality the presence of systematic and unavoidable uncertainty is likely to weaken seriously these reputational forces for the following reasons:[27]

(i) as discussed above, there are likely to be delays in observing output shocks as well as errors in their measurement;

(ii) there might be legitimate disagreements about the transitory or permanent nature of output and spending disturbances;

(iii) the distinction between current and capital expenditure (important for any rule regarding the current fiscal balance) or the size of the future liabilities of the public sector (as in the case of the liabilities of the social security system) is similarly subject to ambiguities;

(iv) as the experience of the USA with Gramm-Rudman targets has shown, rigid fiscal targets can be circumvented by putting off-budget certain spending items (see for example the savings and loan bail-out and the Federal Deposit Insurance Corporation re-financing cases).

(v) any general rule is by definition an incomplete contract that cannot cover the myriad of unanticipated contingencies that occur in reality.

In the presence of such a systematic uncertainty, the reputational mechanisms for a fiscal discipline break down and institutions become necessary to monitor agreements, interpret rules, adjudicate controversies, and enforce the agreed rules through sanctions against deviant agents.[28]

The European Commission could undertake the enforcement role, providing external surveillance and monitoring of the fiscal balances of the member countries. The constant monitoring would strengthen the domestic incentives for fiscal discipline. Such a surveillance, however, would be toothless without the presence of explicit sanctions aimed at punishing deviant countries.

In this regard, the argument made against strong sanctions, i.e. that the discipline of the market will be enough to ensure fiscal discipline in the deviant countries, seems based more on wishful thinking than on an assessment of the incentives faced by the member countries. The market discipline in the form of high interest rates did not prevent members of the Community from pursuing unsustainable fiscal policies throughout the 1980s.

7   Concluding remarks: an evaluation of the EC fiscal guidelines

In this chapter we have argued that a number of EC countries appear to be following unsustainable fiscal policies and that the divergence of fiscal policies in the EC might not be compatible in the long run with the process of monetary unification. We have argued that these 'excessive' fiscal deficits appear to be partly explained by political factors and that this 'deficit bias' might be corrected by fiscal rules monitored and enforced by the Community.

In the presence of political biases towards deficits, we compared alternative fiscal rules. Binding balanced budget fiscal rules, while avoiding the political biases of discretionary fiscal policy-making, have serious disadvantages in that they do not allow for beneficial tax smoothing in the presence of transitory output shocks (recessions). Flexible rules that set balanced budget targets for normal cyclical conditions and allow deficit financing in the case of recessions appear to be superior both to rigid balanced budget rules and to 'deficit biased' discretionary (political) equilibria. We have argued, however, that these rules are not likely to be supported by reputational mechanisms or market discipline alone. Rather, they should be supported by a system of clear and effective sanctions against deviant countries.

How do the fiscal guidelines recently proposed by the European Community match up with the flexible rule cum-effective sanctions recommended in this chapter? The fiscal guidelines recommended by the Monetary Committee appear to be very rigid and unrealistic as will be indicated below.

First, one of the guidelines refers to the nominal interest deficits of governments. A large component of interest payments in several EC countries, however, represents a purely nominal interest burden. A fiscal guideline based on nominal interest deficits does not make sense as long as inflation rates among the EC countries are not equalized. Second, the component of interest payments that is real represents a very different fiscal burden for high debt versus low debt countries. Even assuming equal real interest rates across the Community, this burden is twice as large for a country with debt-to-GDP ratio of 100% as for one with a 50% ratio. Therefore, this particular guideline requires a much heavier fiscal adjustment for countries with a large inherited public debt.

Third, no consideration is given to the fact that the impact of the budget balance rule would very different for countries with different growth rates of real output.

Fourth, the guidelines do not make any allowance for the cyclical component of fiscal deficits, i.e. they do not leave any room for the tax-smoothing fiscal deficits suggested by the flexible rules discussed above.

Finally, since the guidelines include both the current and capital account, they would force the member countries to run substantial primary surpluses (in the order of 5% of GDP for a highly indebted country such as Italy).

The realization that the present guidelines are unrealistic has led the EC countries to agree that they should be interpreted in a 'political' way and that strong sanctions should be avoided. Such 'political' flexibility is, however, quite murky and far from the clearly defined flexible rules advocated above. The latter rules suggest the use of targets for the primary balances rather than for the overall balances; they explicitly allow for clearly defined tax-smoothing deficits in case of recessions and they would be enforced by a clear set of credible sanctions. The European Community, however, appears to have opted for unrealistic targets based on nominal, non-cyclically-adjusted, overall deficits only to allow for an ex-post 'political' flexible evaluation supported by soft and ineffective sanctions.

The decision to follow a political criterion in the evaluation of the fiscal guidelines is clearly motivated by the concern that a rigid application of fiscal rules would result in a 'two-speed' process of monetary unification. The concern of the French and of the Commission is that a 'two-speed' EMU, that would leave out Italy because of its fiscal imbalances, would be seriously flawed. In fact, the exclusion of Italy and the likely refusal of the United Kingdom to join a fully unified monetary union could imply that the EMU might turn out to be a 'Deutschmark area' enlarged to France. It might also mean that fiscally divergent countries like Italy could face weakened incentives to correct their fiscal balances.

In conclusion, the political concerns about the negative consequences of a 'two-speed' EMU seems to explain the hybrid system of rigid but unrealistic fiscal guidelines backed by weak enforcement mechanisms and soft sanctions that appears to have been adopted by the European Community.

Appendix: Alternative fiscal rules in a political equilibrium

This appendix sketches the model underlying the discussion in Section 6. Consider a small open economy populated by N individuals with different preferences over two types of public goods, g and f, each maximizing

$$\varphi^i = U(c_0) + V(x_0) + a^i H(g_0) + (1 - a^i) H(f_0)$$

$$+ \frac{1}{R} U(c_1) + V(x_1) + a^i H(g_1) + (1 - a^i) H(f_1) \tag{A.1}$$

subject to

$$c_0 = (1 - x_0 + \epsilon)(1 - \tau_0) - b_0 + b_0^*$$

$$c_1 = (1 - x_1 - R\epsilon)(1 - \tau_1) + R(b_0 + b_0^*) \tag{A.2}$$

where, for period 0 and 1, C is consumption, x is leisure, g and f are levels of spending on the two types of public goods, a^i is a parameter characterizing individual-specific preferences for good g, τ is a tax on labour income, b and b^* are public domestic debt and foreign private debt respectively. R is the world gross interest rate, $U(\cdot)$, $V(\cdot)$ and $H(\cdot)$ are concave functions. Endowment is higher in period 0 by ϵ and lower in period 1 by $R\epsilon$, so that the present value of these two components is zero from a social point of view. In other words, the resource constraint for this economy is

$$c_0 + g_0 + f_0 + \frac{1}{R}(c_1 + g_1 + f_1) = (1 - x_0) + \frac{1}{R}(1 - x_1) \qquad (A.3)$$

where we have assumed that the private and the public goods are produced with the same technology. A social welfare function can be built by specifying a set of exogenously given, non-negative welfare weights ω_i, with $\Sigma_i^N \omega_i = 1$, such that $\phi = \Sigma_i^N \omega_i \varphi^i$. Thus, the social planner problem will be that of maximizing ϕ subject to the first order conditions for problem (A1)–(A2) and the resource constraint (A3). Conditional on the specifications of the welfare weights ω_i, the solution to this problem will lead us to a traditional tax-smoothing result, where borrowing will offset a non-smooth income profile.

The construction of a political equilibrium follows Alesina and Tabellini (1990) in assuming the existence of a party in power which does not derive utility from spending on f and faces an exogenously given probability of re-election (P). By the same token, the second party does not derive utility from g. The party in office will maximize

$$E_0 \left\{ U(c_0) + V(x_0) + a^i H(g_0) + \frac{1}{R}[U(c_1) + V(x_1) + a^i H(g_1)P] \right\} \qquad (A.4)$$

once again, subject to the first order conditions for problem (A1)–(A2) and the resource constraint for the economy. For the sake of simplicity, suppose that the probability of re-election is zero. While in power, the party will have an incentive to increase the amount of resources spent on the public good g. Given the inter-temporal budget constraint, debt accumulated in the first period will be re-paid in the future, thus reducing spending on the public good f. Nonetheless, in the presence of a temporary shock, the party in power will also have an incentive to smooth tax revenue, thus borrowing instead of changing tax rates. The total deficit will therefore be affected by two factors, one reflecting the political bias and the other tax smoothing. This second factor supports the argument in favour of discretionary fiscal policy.

A balanced-budget rule would add a constraint to the above problem, in

78 Giancarlo Cosetti and Nouriel Roubini

the form: $b = 0$. From a social point of view, overspending on g will be avoided. It will now be impossible to smooth tax rates.

NOTES

This paper was written while Nouriel Roubini was a National Fellow at the Hoover Institution. We thank Wilhelm Buiter, Ken Judd, Jim Leitzel and our two discussants, Francisco Torres and Axel Weber for helpful comments and suggestions. Financial support from the Council for West European Studies at Yale University is gratefully acknowledged.
  1 Some of the recent contributions to the debate on fiscal convergence and EMU include Buiter and Kletzer (1990), Bovenberg *et al.* (1990), Giovannini and Spaventa (1991), Glick and Hutchison (1990), Padoa Schioppa (1990), Van der Ploeg (1990) and Wyplosz (1990).
  2 For a detailed overview of this debate, see Woolley (1991).
  3 Of course, deficits might be optimal also for many other reasons that are not related to tax smoothing (see Buiter and Kletzer (1991) on this). In this chapter, however, we will concentrate on tax-smoothing arguments in favour of fiscal imbalances.
  4 A second class of arguments suggesting the benefits of fiscal coordination and/or fiscal discipline rules is based on 'economic' rather than 'political' externalities. Since government spending and fiscal deficits might spillover to other countries, discretionary fiscal policy might lead to 'excessive' fiscal spending and/or deficits. We agree with Buiter and Kletzer (1991) and Giovannini and Spaventa (1991) that too much attention has been given in the literature to these arguments suggesting the need for fiscal coordination on the basis of the economic externalities and international spillovers of non-cooperative fiscal policies. We believe that a much stronger case for fiscal discipline can be made by considering that excessive deficits caused by political and structural biases might threaten the stability of the monetary union in the long run.
  5 The nature of these negative effects is varied but one of the main concerns of a number of EC countries is that an unsustainable fiscal policy by a member country leading to a fiscal crisis will force the others to 'bail-out' the deviant country. Alternatively, a fiscal and financial crisis in one EC country could quickly spread to other countries and force the future central bank to inject excessive liquidity in the EC area and therefore create monetary and price instability. Germany has been especially concerned about this bail-out risk and it introduced language in its draft of the treaty stressing that the Community has no obligation to bail out the member states. Many observers, however, are concerned that, regardless of formal or informal statements about a 'no bail-out' rule, the Community would be hard pressed to intervene and support a member country because of the possibility that excessive deficits would lead to a financial crisis and a risk of default.
  6 The parameter C is chosen in such a way as to make the process consistent with the desired long run value of d. In other words, the value of C is found by solving the dynamic equation of the debt to GDP ratio for the steady state,

$$def = \frac{C}{1 - \Psi}$$

and positing $def = 0.03$. For example, setting $\psi = 0.8$ will make $\mathbb{C}$ equal to 0.006.

7   In this simulation, we correct the debt figure to take into account that gross debt includes liabilities towards the central bank.

8   The stability of the data generating process describing the series is really the key point in the construction of this class of tests. In our empirical analysis, the stability of the DGP will be taken as a maintained assumption. (For a discussion of the conceptual as well as technical aspects of this issue, see Corsetti and Roubini, 1991.) Weber carries out similar econometric work including an endogenous procedure to test for 'within sample' structural breaks. For example, he shows that the series of net debt in Belgium does exhibit a break, so that there is no evidence of insolvency for this country.

9   Since non-stationarity *per se* rules out (5) for a non-zero debt, other contributions to the literature consider it sufficient to rule out the hypothesis of solvency regardless of the presence of a deterministic components in the DGP (Wilcox 1989, Buiter and Patel 1990). This approach, however, magnifies the power-related problems in the actual implementation of the test. In fact, given a small sample size, available tests for non-stationarity tend to accept the null hypothesis of a unit root too often.

10   In the case of Portugal, the published time series for the stock of public debt is not long enough to permit us to test for solvency of the public sector.

11   Net investment refers to general government gross capital formation minus depreciation.

12   See also Corsetti (1991).

13   It can also be observed that the results obtained in this section are broadly consistent with those obtained by using alternative indicators of fiscal sustainability such as those used by Blanchard (1990) and Giovannini and Spaventa (1991).

14   See Buchanan, Rowley and Tollison (1986) for a recent synthesis of this approach.

15   See Persson and Svensson (1989) for a model with similar implications.

16   In Cukierman and Meltzer (1987), different governments are characterized by differing abilities to forecast. In Rogoff and Sibert (1989) and Rogoff (1990) 'competency' is referred to as the government's efficiency in reducing 'waste' in the budget process. That is, more competent governments can produce more public goods for given fiscal revenues.

17   To be precise, in Rogoff and Sibert (1988) the budget is always balanced, in the sense that the difference between spending and taxes is covered by seignorage.

18   The results in this section partly draw on Roubini and Sachs (1989a) and Alesina, Cohen and Roubini (1991a) who present a more systematic analysis of the political determinants of budget deficits. Other recent empirical tests of political factors in fiscal policy-making include Roubini and Sachs (1989b), Roubini (1991), Cukierman, Edwards and Tabellini (1991), Alesina, Cohen and Roubini (1991b) and Grilli Masciandaro and Tabellini (1991).

19   The size of the sample in this section is limited by the availability of consistent OECD data on public debt (see Roubini and Sachs (1989)). The countries (and sample periods) included are as follows: Austria (1970–1985), Belgium (1960–

1985), Canada (1961–1985), Denmark (1971–1985), France (1960–1985), Finland (1970–1985), Germany (1960–1985), Italy (1964–1985), the Netherlands (1970–1985), Norway (1970–1985), Sweden (1970–1985), the United Kingdom (1960–1985), the United States (1960–1985).

20 This variable is included to capture the effects of real interest rate shocks. For example, after 1979 the increase in world real interest rates, significantly and unexpectedly raised the costs of debt servicing of most governments. One useful measure of the budgetary costs of higher interest rates is given by the debt to GDP ratio multiplied by the change in the differential between real interest rates and growth rates.

21 Its magnitude suggests that each one percentage point slowdown in GDP growth initially raises the budget deficit relative to GDP by 0.45 percentage points. Since the average slowdown in growth was of the order of three percentage points, the impact of this effect was a growth of the budget deficit relative to GDP by more than one percent of GDP.

22 The index is constructed as follows. It takes values of zero in a one-party majority parliamentary government or a presidential government, with the same party in the majority in the executive and legislative branches; one in a coalition parliamentary government with two coalition partners or in a presidential government, with different parties in control of the executive and legislative branches; two in a coalition parliamentary government with three or more coalition partners; three in a minority parliamentary government. Details on the construction of the index for each particular country can be found in Roubini and Sachs (1989a).

23 The magnitude of the coefficient of the *pol* variable, 0.004, signifies that the difference, *ceteris paribus*, between a majority government and a minority government ($p = 0$ versus $p = 3$), is 0.012, or 1.2 percentage points of added budget deficit per year.

24 Alesina, Cohen and Roubini (1991a, 1991b) present a more systematic analysis of electoral effects on budget deficits.

25 In the conclusions to the paper, Alesina and Tabellini (1990) outline the implications of their model for the case of output shocks.

26 This 'no entry clause' (unless fiscally sound) has been suggested by Giovannini and Spaventa (1991) as a fiscal discipline incentive.

27 On this point see the discussion in Weingast and Garrett (1991).

28 Weingast and Garrett (1991) and Milgrom, North and Weingast (1990) stress the important role of institutions as a means of enforcing cooperation.

REFERENCES

Alesina, A. (1987) 'Macroeconomic Policy in a Two-Party System as a Repeated Game', *Quarterly Journal of Economics*, **102**, 651–78.

Alesina, A., G. and N. Roubini (1991a) 'Macroeconomic Policy and Elections in OECD Economies', National Bureau of Economic Research Working Paper No. 3830.

(1991b) 'Political Business Cycles in Industrial Economies', mimeo, Yale University, August.

(1991) 'Political Cycles in OECD Economies', *Review of Economic Studies*.

Alesina, A. and A. Drazen (1991) 'Why Are Stabilizations Delayed? A Political-Economic Model', *American Economic Review*, 1170–88.

Alesina, A. and G. Tabellini (1989) 'External Debt, Capital Flight and Political Risk', *Journal of International Economics*, November, 199–220.

(1990) 'A Political Theory of Fiscal Deficits and Debt in a Democracy', *Review of Economic Studies*, July, 403–14.

Barro, R. (1979) 'On the Determination of Public Debt', *Journal of Political Economy*, October, **87**, 940–71.

Blanchard, O. (1990) 'Suggestions for a New Set of Fiscal Indicators', Organisation for Economic Cooperation and Development, Department of Economics and Statistics Working Papers, No. 79, April.

Bovenberg, A.L., J.J.M. Kremers and P.R. Masson (1990) 'Economic and Monetary Union in Europe and Constraints on National Budget Policies', International Monetary Fund Working Paper 90/60, July.

Buchanan, J.M., C.K. Rowley and R.D. Tollison (1986) *Deficits*, New York: Basil Blackwell.

Buiter, W. and K. Kletzer (1990) 'Reflections on the Fiscal Implications of a Common Currency', Centre for Economic Policy Research Discussion Paper No. 418, May.

Buiter, W.H. and U.R. Patel (1990), 'Debt, Deficits and Inflation: An Application to the Public Finances of India', National Bureau of Economic Research Working Paper No. 3287.

Committee for the Study of Economic and Monetary Union (1989), *Report on Economic and Monetary Union in the European Community* (Delors Report). Luxembourg: EC Official Publications Office.

Corsetti, G. (1991) 'Testing for Solvency of the Public Sector: An Application to Italy', *Economic Notes*, 3, 581–99.

Corsetti, G. and N. Roubini (1991b) 'The Design of Optimal Fiscal Rules in a Political Equilibrium, in progress, Yale University.

(1991a) 'Fiscal Deficits, Public Debt and Government Solvency: Evidence from OECD Countries', *Journal of Japanese and International Economies*, 5, 354–80.

Cukierman, A. and Meltzer (1989) 'A Political Theory of Government Debt and Deficits in a Neo-Ricardian Framework', *American Economic Review*, **4**, 713–32.

Dickey, D.A. and W.A. Fuller (1981) 'Likelihood Ratio Statistics for Autoregressive Time Series with a Unit Root', *Econometrica*, **49**, 1057–72.

Garrett, J. and B. Weingast (1991) 'Ideas, Interests and Institutions: Constructing the EC's Internal Market', unpublished working paper, Stanford University.

Giovannini, A. and L. Spaventa (1991) 'Fiscal Rules in the European Monetary Union: A No-Entry Clause', Centre for Economic Policy Research Discussion Paper No. 516, January.

Glick, R. and M. Hutchison (1990) 'Fiscal Constraints and Incentives with Monetary Coordination: Implications for Europe 1992', mimeo, May.

Grilli, V., D. Masciandaro and G. Tabellini (1991) 'Political and Monetary Institutions and Public Finance Policies in the Industrial Democracies', *Economic Policy*, **13**, 342–92.

Hamilton, J.D. and M.A. Flavin (1986), 'On the Limitations of Government Borrowing: A Framework for Empirical Testing', *American Economic Review*, 76, 808–19.

Milgrom, P., D. North and B. Weingast (1990) 'The Role of Institutions in the Revival of Trade: The Medieval Law Merchant, Private Judges, and the Champagne Fairs', *Economics and Politics*, 1.

Nordhaus, W. (1975) 'The Political Business Cycle', *Review of Economic Studies*, **42**, 169–90.

Padoa Schioppa, T. (1990) 'Fiscal Prerequisites of a European Monetary Union', mimeo, January.

Perron, P. (1988) 'Trend and Random Walks in Macroeconomic Time Series', *Journal of Economic Dynamics and Control*, **12**, 297–332.

Perron, P. and P.C.B. Phillips (1987), 'Does GNP have a Unit Root?', *Economic Letters*, **23**, 139–45.

Persson, T. and L. Svensson (1989) 'Why a Stubborn Conservative Would Run a Deficit: Policy with Time Inconsistent Preferences, *Quarterly Journal of Economics*, Masy, 325–46.

Phillips, P.C.B. (1987) 'Time Series Regression with a Unit Root', *Econometrica*, **55**, 277–301.

Rogoff, K. (1989) 'Equilibrium Political Budget Cycles', *American Economic Review*, **80**, 21–36.

Rogoff, K. and A. Sibert (1989) 'Elections and Macroeconomic Policy Cycles', *Review of Economic Studies*, **55**, 1–16.

Roubini, N. (1991) 'Economic and Political Determinants of Budget Deficits in Developing Countries', *Journal of International Money and Finance*, **10**, 549–72.

Roubini, N. and J. Sachs (1989a) 'Political and Economic Determinants of Budget Deficits in the Industrial Democracies', *European Economic Review*, May, 903–33.

(1989b) 'Government Spending and Budget Deficits in the Industrial Countries', *Economic Policy*, **8**, 99–132.

Tabellini, G. (1991) 'Instituzioni Politiche e Debito Pubblico', presented at the meeting of the Societa' Italiana degli Economisti, October.

Tabellini, G. and A. Alesina (1990) 'Voting on the Budget Deficit', *American Economic Review*, **80**, 37–52.

Trehan, B. and C.E. Walsh (1988), 'Common Trends, the Government Budget Constraint, and Revenue Smoothing', *Journal of Economic Dynamics and Control*, **12**, 425–44.

Van der Ploeg, F. (1990) 'Macroeconomic Policy Coordination during the Various Phases of Economic and Monetary Integration in Europe', *European Economy*.

Wilcox, D.W. (1989) 'The Sustainability of Government Deficits: Implications of the Present Value Borrowing Constraint', *Journal of Money Credit and Banking*, **21**, 291–306.

Woolley, J.T. (1991) 'Creating a European Central Bank: Negotiating EMU and the ESCB', mimeo, University of California, Santa Barbara, November.

Wyplosz, C. (1991) 'Monetary Union and Fiscal Policy Discipline', Centre for Economic Policy Research Discussion Paper No. 488, January.

Discussion

AXEL A. WEBER

To begin with, let me say that I have enjoyed reading this chapter and I have learned a lot about current issues in the fiscal strand of the 'political economy' literature. The three fiscal policy issues surveyed in the chapter concern (i) solvency tests for government debt, (ii) the political determinants of budget deficits, both in theory and practice, and (iii) the controversy over tax smoothing versus balanced budget rules. The insights from this discussion of the literature are then combined in a critical evaluation of the fiscal convergence criteria written into the draft treaty for a European economic and monetary union (EMU). I will start my discussion of the chapter with the three issues above before commenting in more detail on the authors' principle policy recommendations and conclusions for Europe after 1992.

Section 3 of the chapter deals with the sustainability of public debt. Fiscal rules, so it is argued, may have to be enforced if fiscal policies imply unsustainable time-paths for public debt in EC member countries. Sustainability of public debt thereby implies that the present-value budget constraint of the public sector is not violated. This solvency condition is satisfied if the time series of discounted debt is covariance stationary with zero expectation. In order to check empirically for the solvency of the public sector and the sustainability of debt dynamics the authors perform unit root tests of the Phillips-Perron variety with annual discounted debt data (1961–1988). The authors are well aware of the limitations of these tests, which arise from: (a) their reliance on asymptotic distributions (only 18–30 observations are used); (b) their low power with respect to distinguishing a unit root from one close to unity; (c) their dependence on the structural stability of the data generating process (DGP). The problem is that the authors do not take these limitations seriously, in particular the last one and I am inclined to argue that in the present application this is fatal. To see this, it is important to recall that their solvency tests are based on regressions over samples of 18 (Ireland) to 30 years, and such long-term policy evaluation is bound to be subject to the 'Lucas critique'. In Germany, probably one of the more stable fiscal policy environments in Europe, several changes in fiscal policy stances have occurred, three exchange rate regimes have been in place, government has passed from the Conservatives to Social Democrats and back, the economy was hit by two oil-shocks and recently German unification has had a strong fiscal impact. Can we really expect to find that the history of fiscal policy outcomes constitutes a structurally stable data generating process which is immune to changes in the policy environment? I think the answer clearly is no, as will be demonstrated below by selectively reconsidering (with slightly different data definitions) the empirical evidence given in the chapter, which may be summarized by the finding that insolvency is found for Italy, Belgium, Greece and Ireland, and indeterminate results for the remaining EC countries.

For Germany, the authors find a drift-less and trend-less non-stationary (unit root) process, which they consider to be inconclusive, but point out that additional evidence (the absolute level of both the debt to GDP ratio and the current fiscal balance) suggests that solvency might not be an issue in the German case. The recursive estimates reported in Figure D.3.1 establish German solvency formally: by using quarterly data for real central government debt, defined as nominal debt (*International Financial Statistics, IFS*, line 88) deflated by the consumer price index (*IFS* line 64), it is indicated by all four parametric stability tests in the four lower panels of Figure D.3.1 that a significant structural break exists in the data generating process (DGP) of the German debt data; adjusting the estimates for this break by estimating two separate regressions, one up to the 1975 break point (first two panels) and one after this breakpoint (second two panels) confirms solvency in both sub-samples. Interestingly, the DGP in both sub-samples is given by a stationary positive deterministic drift, but for the overall sample the significant structural break biases the results towards indeterminancy in the form of a unit root process with no deterministic drift.

A similar result is obtained for the case of France, which the authors also judge as being inconclusive on the grounds of the formal evidence, but state that both additional formal tests and the absolute size of the current fiscal balance suggest solvency. Again, the formal evidence reported in Figure D.3.2 brings these solvency results out more clearly: in the case of France two significant structural breaks, the first in 1975 and the second in 1982/83, are indicated by three of the stability test statistics. The solvency estimates adjusted for these breaks then confirm solvency for the post-1983 period, but indeterminate results for the pre-1983 period.

The above finding, that structural breaks in the DGPs bias the results towards rejecting solvency has important implications for those countries which have been found to have unsustainable public debt paths. This is illustrated in Figure D.3.3 for Belgium, the country for which the authors find clear evidence rejecting solvency. As stressed in the paper, '. . . in the late 1980s, this country (Belgium) undertook a programme of fiscal adjustment which led to significant primary surpluses. While the formal

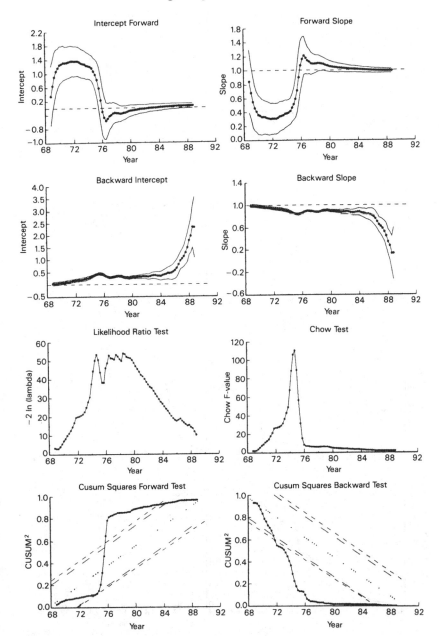

Figure D.3.1 Sustainability of German real public debt: recursive coefficient estimates and stability test results (1968 Q1 – 1990 Q4)
Source: Estimates from Weber (1992)

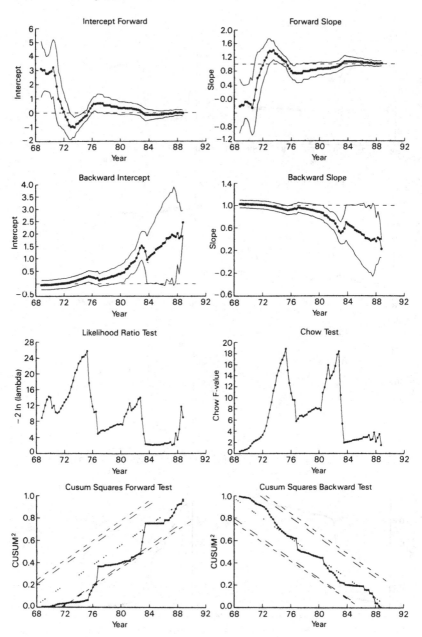

Figure D.3.2 Sustainability of French real public debt: recursive coefficient estimates and stability test results (1968 Q1 – 1990 Q4)
Source: Estimates from Weber (1992)

test suggests insolvency, it is likely that the test did not detect the structural change in Belgium's fiscal policy that has occurred in the last few years.' I think that this structural change in fiscal policies has not been detected simply because it was not tested for. The flexible estimation procedure proposed in Figure D.3.3 detects a significant structural break in the DGP of Belgium's public debt in 1984/85, and the significance of this break is indicated by all four stability test statistics. The coefficient estimates further suggest indeterminate results for the pre-1984/85 period, but clearly point towards sustainability in the time-path of the post-1984/85 public debt in Belgium. To summarize, I think much more care has to be exercised in analysing the data if the aim is an econometric policy evaluation in samples as long as 30 years. I would argue that, in particular, in the field of fiscal policies the 'Lucas critique' has to be taken very seriously and that the assumption of structural stability of the fiscal DGPs in the face of frequently changing democratically elected governments is quite an heroic one to make.

Let me now turn to Sections 4 and 5 of the chapter which deal with the political determinants of government deficits and debt. I think the stylized facts and the cross-section estimates presented here are fairly uncontroversial: it is claimed that fiscal deficits (a) rise before elections, (b) are counter-cyclical and (c) in part are caused by political instability. These hypotheses are not rejected by the cross-country evidence with all coefficients being significant with the correct sign. I have no critical remarks to make on this section, except perhaps that I would have liked to see some country-specific single-equation regression estimates, since the necessity to estimate the model in cross-section rather than time space is not obvious.

In Section 6 of the chapter the authors discuss the potential costs and benefits of rigid balanced budget rules relative to tax smoothing discretion. In analogy to the Barro and Gordon framework for monetary policy, fiscal discretion typically results in a deficit bias. Is there any fiscal rule which may eliminate this deficit bias in the presence of strictly temporary shocks to labour productivity?

Tax-smoothing discretion with uniform tax rates across the business cycle results in deficits during a recession which are repaid during a boom. Balanced budget rules distort the inter-temporal allocation of labour and reduce welfare. Based on their model, the authors then advocate rules with an escape clause, which allow tax smoothing within a certain threshold, beyond which tax adjustments are called for. Basically, the variance of the productivity shock translates into a variance band for tolerable deficits, beyond which tax adjustments are triggered. I would argue, not having seen the model, that this result is almost self-evident given the

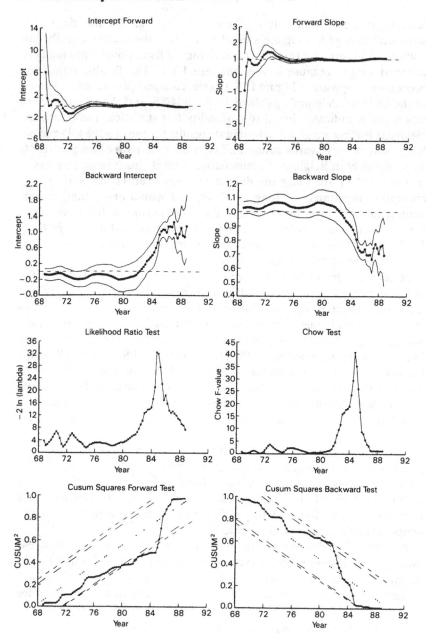

Figure D.3.3 Sustainability of Belgian real public debt: recursive coefficient estimates and stability test results (1968 Q1 – 1990 Q4)
Source: Estimates from Weber (1992)

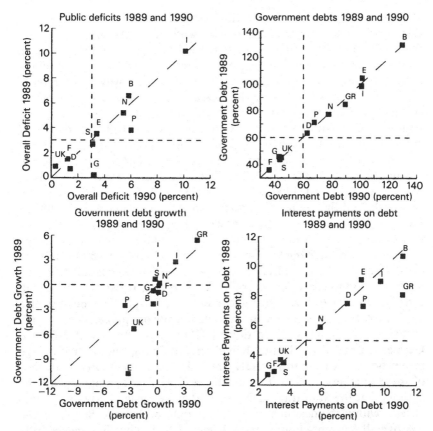

Figure D.3.4 EC fiscal guidelines and degree of fiscal convergence achieved in 1989 and 1990
Source: Weber (1991)

purely transitory nature of the disturbances, and that in order to analyse an interesting issue the introduction of a Cukierman-Meltzer type of confusion between transitory and permanent shocks is needed. Clearly, under purely permanent productivity shocks instantaneous tax adjustments are optimal, whilst tax-smoothing rules or rules with escape clauses trigger debt that is never recovered. The transitory-permanent confusion advocated above would further add much empirical realism to the model without necessarily assuming that governments use deficits strategically: they may simply not always be well informed, and may learn about the permanence of shocks only after some time, having accumulated some debt in the meanwhile.

Let me now turn to the final section of the chapter, in which the authors take stock and move into the murky world of real-world policy recommendations. The authors state that the fiscal guidelines recommended by the Monetary Committee are 'both unrealistic and too rigid'. I totally agree with this statement, and in order to demonstrate why, let me refer to Figure D.3.4 which displays the actual degree of fiscal convergence achieved in 1989 and 1990 together with the fiscal convergence criteria written into the draft treaty. This treaty explicitly spells out two fiscal convergence criteria, both in terms of ceilings: budget deficits should not exceed 3% of gross domestic product (GDP), and public debt should not amount to more than 60% of GDP. But according to Figure D.3.4, fiscal deficits in 1989 and 1990 were below 3% of GDP only in France, Denmark, and the United Kingdom, and extremely high (above 10% of GDP) in Italy and Greece (not shown). Government debt, on the other hand, was in 1989 and 1990, below 60% of GDP only in Germany, France, the United Kingdom and Spain, and relatively high (above 80% of GDP) in Greece, Italy, Ireland and Belgium. This ratio is still diverging for Italy and Greece, but converging for Portugal, Belgium and Ireland. Finally, in order to highlight the dynamics of EC public debts it is also instructive to compare the interest payments on public debt, which absorbed only a small proportion of GDP (less than 4% of GDP) in Germany, France, the United Kingdom and Spain, but relatively large proportions (8% or more) in Italy, Ireland, Belgium and Greece. In view of these numbers I think it would be very hard not to agree with the authors that the Maastricht debt to GDP guideline is utterly unrealistic, at least within the deadline of the Maastricht agreement. Similarly, the 3% overall (current-cum-interest) deficit to GDP guideline makes little sense for two main reasons. First, as indicated in Table D.3.1, both inflation and interest rates have not yet fully converged between EC countries, so part of the asymmetries in the dynamics of debt and hence the interest inclusive fiscal deficit are caused purely by monetary factors and not just differentials in debt levels. Second, as the real interest burden on debt differs drastically between low-debt and high-debt EC countries, the 3% interest inclusive deficit to GDP guideline requires drastic fiscal adjustments in the latter countries, and in some cases even substantial primary surpluses. This is economically undesirable. The authors therefore propose the use of a primary fiscal balance target, ideally in the form of flexible rules which allow tax smoothing and which should be enforceable by a clear set of credible sanctions. It may be argued that an important drawback of such tax-smoothing fiscal balance rules is that whilst they may prevent further fiscal divergence, they will not enhance fiscal convergence, and that such convergence is politically desirable as a

Table D.3.1. *Convergence judged by selected economic indicators, 1990*

Variable	GER	FRA	ITA	NDL	BEL	DNK	IRE	UK	ESP	PRT	GRC
Inflation rate* (*IMF*)	2.7	3.4	6.5	2.6	3.4	2.6	3.3	9.5	6.7	13.3	20.4
ECU rate*	−0.9	−1.6	0.7	−0.7	−22	−24	−12	−60	−6.0	46	127
Short term interest	8.1	10.2	12.4	8.5	9.6	10.8	10.9	14.1	14.2	13.4	18.5
Long-term interest	8.9	10.0	11.5	8.9	10.1	10.7	10.1	11.1	14.7	15.2	18.5
Narrow money* (*IMF*)	7.0	3.3	7.9	5.5	0.7	5.2	7.5	9.9	20.5	27.6	24.0
Broad money* (*IMF*)	11.8	2.1	9.9	7.0	4.0	6.5	8.9	10.9	13.9	18.3	14.3
Deficit/GDP	−3.2	−1.2	−10.1	−5.4	−5.8	−1.4	−3.4	−0.3	−3.1	−6.0	−18.8
Debt/GDP	43.7	36.1	100.9	77.8	129.4	62.8	101.4	43.0	44.7	67.8	89.5
Interest on debt/GDP	2.6	3.0	9.7	5.9	11.1	7.6	8.5	3.4	3.6	8.6	11.1

Note: All entries refer to the levels (in % or % p.a.), except for those marked with *, which are annual growth rates.
Source: Weber (1992), with data from *IMF International Financial Statistics*, various issues (where explicitly stated) and *European Economy*, Statistical Annex, July 1991.

safeguard against the possible financial spillovers of a debt crisis in countries with structural fiscal imbalances. The necessity of such fiscal convergence as a prerequisite for the creation and viability of a European monetary union is, however, a completely different issue, and, in my view, highly contestable.

REFERENCES

Weber, Axel A., 1991, 'EMU and Who to Leave Behind: Some Answers from Discriminant and Clustering Analysis', paper presented at a Workshop organised by the Centre for Economic Policy Research on German Unification and European Integration, Bonn, November 1991.
1992, 'Government Solvency and European Monetary Integration', mimeo, Siegen University, April 1992.

4 Contracts, credibility and common knowledge: their influence on inflation convergence

MARCUS MILLER and
ALAN SUTHERLAND

1 Introduction

In recent years, countries in the European monetary system (EMS) have pegged their exchange rates to the Deutschmark in an attempt to reduce their inflation to German levels. Although there have been no realignments since 1987, inflation rates have been slow to adjust. Indeed, from the evidence of European inflation indices over the period 1987–91, the authors of the report on monitoring European integration (CEPR 1991) concluded: 'There is no doubt . . . that inflation convergence has not occurred and it is not occurring. The differential between higher-inflation countries and Germany has recently fallen; but this has been almost entirely due to a surge in the German inflation rate which is believed to be temporary'. We examine three possible reasons for the sluggish inflation response observed in the EMS.

Some observers have stressed the role of staggered wage setting in perpetuating inflation and have recommended synchronizing pay settlements as an institutional solution, see for example Layard (1990). This chapter begins, therefore, with an investigation of the link between inflation persistence and overlapping contracts in the rational expectations models of John Taylor and Stanley Fischer (where wage settlements are for two periods, but two groups alternate in making settlements). We do find some inflation persistence, but only for one period. Upward inflation pressure from high settlements made in the past is soon overwhelmed by the downward pressure from transitory unemployment and from expectations of a non-inflationary future within the exchange rate mechanism (ERM). The graphical methods used to illustrate the transition readily admit alternative strategies for setting the exchange rate on entry to be contemplated. We consider in particular the options of devaluing to avoid the initial recession and of revaluing so as to stop inflation in its tracks. In a related model of staggered contracts, that of

93

Guillermo Calvo, where the price level is an average of contracts of random length, neither of these options proves necessary, however, as there is no inflation persistence despite the contracts.

It should be stressed that two assumptions play a key role in the demonstration that overlapping contracts are consistent with low or no inflation persistence. The first of these is that the change of policy is *fully credible*: wage setters know what the new policy is and do not anticipate any reversal. The second is the assumption of rational expectations: forecasts are made with a model of the inflation process which is assumed to be *common knowledge* so wage setters know, and know that others are also aware of how the policy will work. If there has been a major shift of policy regime, however, these assumptions are not appropriate.

The commitment to a fixed exchange rate pegged to the Deutschmark may not therefore be fully credible, at least for a while. Until Stage III, realignments will always be possible; and European interest rate differentials suggest that market-makers do give some credence to the prospect of a revaluation of the Deutschmark against its more inflationary partners in the ERM. (Indeed, the CEPR report earlier cited discusses the case for a last, competitiveness-correcting realignment prior to the irrevocable locking of parities.) So there could be a period – possibly quite prolonged – in which the members of the ERM gradually acquire credibility for their policy of pegging against a hard currency. And even if individual wage setters are persuaded of the determination of the authorities to pursue such a policy, they may be unsure of what others believe, and will be tempted to keep wage claims up as a consequence. Frydman and Phelps (1983) argue that this lack of 'common knowledge' may explain the failure of Latin American stabilization policies. Could it also be relevant for the delay in stabilizing inflation in Europe?

These two features of the situation are examined in turn. To allow for the lack of full credibility in the peg we assume that the private sector expects random realignments of the exchange rate. For convenience, we use the model with Calvo contracts, which implies that the inflation adjustment depends only on the speed with which people come to believe the exchange rate peg. If it takes some time for the peg to become credible, the inflation generated in the meantime will cause the price level to 'overshoot'. When inflation does finally fall to German levels, the economy will be uncompetitive and this will only be corrected by a period in which price increases are less than the German rate of inflation. If the price level is sticky, because of overlapping, this disinflation will be associated with a prolonged contraction of output, triggered by the lack of competitiveness itself. By combining overlapping contracts with lack of credibility in this way, we can explain the emergence of stagflation after a regime change.

To investigate the effects of a lack of 'common knowledge' on inflation inertia we weaken the usual rational expectations assumption by supposing that each agent fully believes in the peg but assumes that other agents do not and will take time to learn. While inflation inertia may arise from this lack of common knowledge, it is less than that implied by the lack of credibility discussed before.

We conclude that the rapid convergence of inflation in the presence of overlapping contracts can be significantly reduced when the policy shift is not seen as fully credible. Our analysis is conducted with reference to three popular macroeconomic models of wage contracts. An alternative approach to explaining inflation inertia might be to explore the role of near-rational behaviour by imperfectly competitive firms along the lines suggested by Akerlof and Yellen (1985).

2 Wage contracts and inflation persistence

In this section we analyse the extent to which wage contract structures induce persistence in the inflation rate. We consider the models proposed by Taylor (1979) and Fischer (1977) where wage contracts have an exogenous fixed term and the model of Calvo (1983a, b) where wage contracts are of random length.

2.1 Taylor contracts

A model with Taylor-type two period overlapping contracts takes the following form

$$p_t = \tfrac{1}{2}(x_{t-1} + x_t) \tag{1}$$

$$x_t = \tfrac{1}{2}(\hat{p}_t + \beta\hat{y}_t + \hat{p}_{t+1} + \beta\hat{y}_{t+1}) \tag{2}$$

$$y_t = \eta(s - p_t + p_t^*) \tag{3}$$

where p = log of the price level
x = log of the current new contract
y = log of output
s = log of the exchange rate (price of foreign currency)
* indicates a foreign variable

There are two equal sized groups of workers which negotiate their nominal wage rates in alternate periods. So, for instance, the group which settles in period $t - 1$ receives x_{t-1} in period $t - 1$ and period t while the group which settles in period t receives x_t in period t and period $t + 1$. Thus, as shown in equation (1), the price level is a mark-up over the

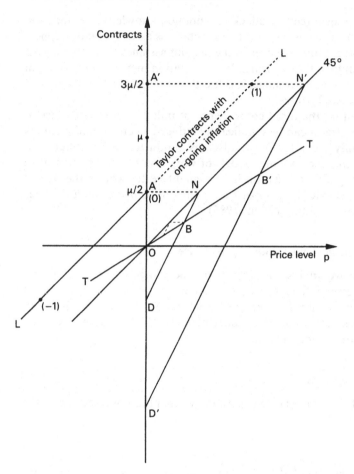

Figure 4.1 Taylor contracts before and after entry

average of the contract wage set last period, x_{t-1}, and the contract wage set this period, x_t (the mark-up is set to zero for simplicity). The current contract, defined in equation (2), is the average of prices and demand pressure over the two periods of the contract (a hat over a variable indicates expectations conditional on information available at the time of settling the contract). Equation (3) is the IS relationship, where, for simplicity, we assume that aggregate demand depends only on the level of competitiveness. For convenience in what follows we set $p^* = 0$.

Appendix 4A shows that when the exchange rate is fixed at $\bar{s}$ the equilibrium level of contracts and the price level is also $\bar{s}$. Thus, in Figure 4.1, where $\bar{s} = 0$, the equilibrium point is at the origin. Appendix 4A also shows that, when expectations are rational, adjustment to this long run equilibrium takes place along a stable path. This is given by the expression

$$x_t = \theta p_t + \bar{s} \tag{4}$$

where $\theta = 1 - \sqrt{\beta\eta}$. The slope can be either positive or negative depending on the parameters β and η. In Figure 4.1 the stable path is shown as the positively sloped schedule TT.

Prior to joining a fixed rate regime we assume that the money supply is growing and the exchange rate is depreciating at rate μ. The resulting (inflationary) equilibrium is as follows

$$p_t = s_t \tag{5}$$

$$x_t = \tfrac{1}{2}(\hat{p}_t + \hat{p}_{t+1}) = \hat{p}_t = \frac{\mu}{2} = p_t + \frac{\mu}{2} \tag{6}$$

Thus, the price level tracks the exchange rate while each new contract is set above the current (expected and actual) price level to allow for future anticipated inflation. Note that this allowance for inflation between the two periods of the contract only needs to be $\mu/2$ because the current contract is an average of the price level in the two periods. In Figure 4.1 the inflationary equilibrium is illustrated by a series of steps along the 45° line marked LAL.

We now consider the transitional effects of a switch from the inflationary steady-state just described to a fixed exchange rate regime. We assume that the announcement of the peg is made at the start of period 1 and that the exchange rate is pegged at the level ruling in the market in period 0. Initially in our analysis we assume that the group setting its wage in period 1 is aware of the regime change before x_1 is settled. (We consider the alternative assumption below.) For convenience we set $\bar{s} = 0$ so, from equation (5), it follows that the price level in period 0 is 0, and from equation (6), it can be seen that the value of the contract which was set in period 0 is $\mu/2$. The position at the end of period 0, immediately before the announcement of the regime switch, is therefore given by point A in Figure 4.1, where the distance OA is $\mu/2$.

With $\bar{s} = 0$ the post-entry equilibrium is at the origin and the stable path is given by the line TT. The impact effect of the regime change must therefore be a jump from point A in period 0 to some point on TT in period 1. The correct point on TT is determined by the requirement that equation (1) be satisfied, i.e. by the requirement that the price level in period 1 should be the average of x_0 and x_1. By rearranging equation (1) it is found that

$$x_t = 2p_t - x_{t-1} \qquad\qquad\qquad (7)$$

This relationship is illustrated in Figure 4.1 by the schedule DN which intersects the vertical axis at $-x_{t-1}$ (the distance OD in Figure 4.1 is $-x_0 = -\mu/2$). In period 1 the contract and price level are therefore given by point B where TT and DN intersect, i.e. by the point on the stable path at which equation (1) is satisfied. In subsequent periods the contract and price level converge towards equilibrium by a series of steps down TT.

The implications of this solution path for inflation inertia are immediately apparent. The jump from point A in period 0 to point B in period 1 implies a rise in the price level of $\mu/(2 + 2\sqrt{\beta\eta})$ but in subsequent periods the price level falls towards equilibrium. Thus, the inflation rate falls in the first period after the regime switch to less than half its pre-entry value, and then turns negative in following periods. There is therefore only a very limited degree of inflation inertia.

The period of positive inflation following the switch of regime is somewhat understated in this analysis because of the assumption that wage negotiators know about the new regime before wages are set in period 1. It is simple to show the effects of the alternative assumption, that wages are set before the announcement, with reference to Figure 4.1. If wage negotiators in period 1 are unaware of the new regime they will continue to forecast depreciation and inflation at rate μ and will set the contract in period 1 to be above the contract in period 0 by the amount μ. The contract is therefore given by the distance OA' in Figure 4.1 where the distance AA' is μ. The price level will consequently rise by μ between period 0 and period 1. There is thus no immediate impact on the inflation rate.

The negotiators who settle in period 2, however, know about the new regime and will therefore set a contract on the stable path TT. But because of the higher value of the contract set in the previous period, the schedule DN moves out to D'N' (where the distance OD' is $-x_1 = -3\mu/2$) and the contract and price level in period 2 are set at point B'. In subsequent periods the contract and price level move towards equilibrium along TT. The effect of changing the timing of the announcement of the peg is, therefore, to increase by one the number of periods of positive inflation.

Even though there is little persistence of inflation in this model, regardless of the timing of the announcement of the regime change, there is a long recession. Output has to be below capacity in order to drive prices down to their equilibrium level.

This analysis has concentrated on two-period contracts. More generally, Taylor-type contracts which are longer than two periods will cause more persistence of inflation. The period of positive inflation after a switch to a fixed exchange rate, however, is never longer than the length of the contract. Thus, for instance, n period contracts will generate (depending on the timing of the announcement of the switch) either $n - 1$ or n periods of positive inflation after a regime change.

2.2   Fischer contracts

The important difference between the Fischer model of two period overlapping contracts and the Taylor model is that in the former model the wage rate need not be equal in the two periods of the contract. The contract set in period t therefore consists of a wage rate for the first period of the contract, denoted $x_{t,1}$ and a wage rate for the second period of the contract, denoted $x_{t,2}$. Equation (1) and (2) of the Taylor model are replaced by the following

$$p_t = \tfrac{1}{2}(x_{t-1,2} + x_{t,1}) \tag{8}$$

$$x_{t,1} = \hat{p}_t + \beta \hat{y}_t \tag{9}$$

$$x_{t,2} = \hat{p}_{t+1} + \beta \hat{y}_{t+1} \tag{10}$$

Equation (8) defines the price level as the average of the wage set for period t by the group which settled in period $t - 1$ and the wage set for period t by the group which settles in period t. Equations (9) and (10) show that the two wage rates embodied in the period t contract depend on the expected price level and demand pressure in the respective periods of the contract. The determination of demand is identical to that of the Taylor model, i.e. equation (3) still applies.

The long-run equilibrium with a fixed exchange rate at $\bar{s}$ is also identical to that of the Taylor model, specifically

$$p_t = x_{t,1} = x_{t,2} = \bar{s} \tag{11}$$

In Figure 4.2, where contracts are plotted on the vertical axis and $\bar{s} = 0$, the equilibrium point is at the origin.

Again we assume that the pre-entry regime is one of constant money growth and exchange rate depreciation at rate μ. The resulting inflationary equilibrium is characterized as follows

$$p_t = x_{t,1} = x_{t-1,2} = \bar{s}_t \tag{12}$$

$$p_{t+1} = x_{t+1,1} = x_{t,2} = s_{t+1} \tag{13}$$

The price level and the wage rate track the (actual and expected) exchange rate. In particular, the wage rate in the first period of a contract is set equal to the exchange rate in the first period and the wage rate in the second period of a contract is set equal to the exchange rate in the second period.

The transition from this inflationary regime to a fixed rate regime is now analysed. Again it is assumed that the exchange rate is fixed at $\bar{s} = 0$ in period 1. And at first we assume that the announcement is made before the period 1 contract is settled. The solution is determined in two stages. The first stage, which is illustrated here, is to determine the wage rate set in period 1 for period 1 (i.e. $x_{1,1}$). The second stage, which is outlined in Appendix 4B, is to determine the wage rate set in period 1 for period 2 (i.e. $x_{1,2}$) and the wages set thereafter.

The determination of $x_{1,1}$ can be illustrated as follows. By rearranging equation (8) it is found that

$$x_{t,1} = 2p_t - x_{t-1,2} \tag{14}$$

This relationship can be illustrated in Figure 4.2 by noting that in period 1 the outstanding contract from period 0, $x_{0,2}$, will have been set at level μ. This implies that equation (14) defines line DN (where the distance OD is $-\mu$). This schedule shows combinations of $x_{t,1}$ and p_t which satisfy equation (8) in period 1. The other equations which must be satisfied in period 1 are equation (3), the demand equation, and equation (9), the contract equation. If equation (3) is substituted into equation (9) the following is found

$$x_{t,1} = (1 - \beta\eta)p_t + \beta\eta\bar{s} \tag{15}$$

In Figure 4.2 this defines the line FF (which passes through the origin since $\bar{s} = 0$). For $\beta\eta < 1$ the slope of FF is positive (but less than θ, the slope of the stable path of the Taylor model). The equilibrium value of $x_{1,1}$ is given at point B where FF and DN cross. This completes the first part of the solution.

The second part of the solution is derived in Appendix 4B. It is shown there that the second wage rate of the period 1 contract is set to the long run equilibrium value defined by equation (11) and that the economy moves straight to the long run equilibrium from period 2 onwards.

The implications of this model for inflation inertia are now clear. As with the Taylor model, positive inflation continues for only one period after the change in regime. In this model inflation in that period is given by $\mu/(1 + \beta\eta)$ (which is higher than in the Taylor model if $\beta\eta < 3 + 2\sqrt{2}$). But unlike the Taylor model there is an immediate return to equilibrium in the second and subsequent periods after the regime switch. There is therefore only a short recession.

This analysis has been carried out with the assumption that the announcement of the regime switch takes place before the period 1

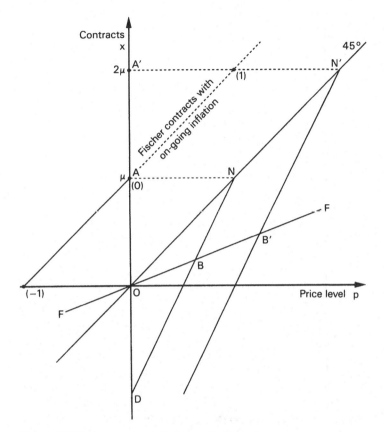

Figure 4.2 Fischer contracts before and after entry

contract is settled. As with the Taylor model, if the announcement is delayed until after this contract is settled, positive inflation persists for one further period as shown by the points labelled A' and B' in Figure 4.2.

In models like this the entry rate can in principle be set so as to eliminate inflation immediately, though the revaluation this will require deepens the recession. Conversely the entry rate can be set so as to avoid the recession at a cost of higher initial inflation. Choosing an entry rate to maintain output is what Taylor (1984) has described as an 'efficient' disinflationary policy as it leads (one period later) to price stability without any loss of output. This strategy is shown in Figure 4.3, where the outcomes shown in Figure 4.1 for an entry rate of $\bar{s} = 0$ is represented by the point B_T on $N_T D_T$. Observe that an entry rate of $\bar{s} = \mu/2$ (which involves a devaluation of $\mu/2$) would raise the contract schedule to $T^* T^*$ and shift

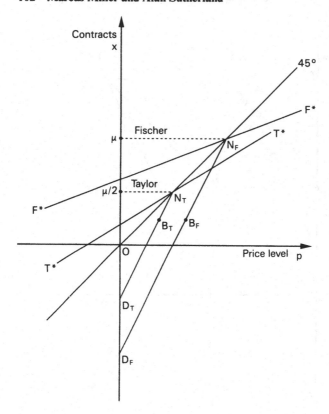

Figure 4.3 Entry rates to avoid recession (N) or to end inflation (D)

the initial equilibrium to N_T. This increases inflation in period 1 (to $\mu/2$); but is consistent with price stability thereafter as N_T is now the long run equilibrium. (The same logic applies to Fischer contracts where setting an entry rate of $\bar{s} = \mu$ shifts the line showing the out-turn for Fischer contracts up to $F^* F^*$ and moves the initial and final equilibrium up to the point shown as N_F.)

The act of devaluing as a prelude to curbing inflation doubtless requires that the exchange rate policy is underpinned by some 'precommitment', as Backus and Driffill (1986) point out. Joining the exchange rate mechanism of the EMS is, of course, intended to be just such a precommitment. It may not, however, be fully convincing, as exchange rates can be realigned. So the alternative policy of revaluing the entry rate to achieve an immediate reduction of inflation to zero may be considered. The out-turn in period 1 for such a 'cold turkey' policy towards inflation is also shown in Figure 4.3. Revaluing the currency sufficiently so as to shift the Taylor contract locus to give a first period equilibrium of D_T will stop inflation in its tracks in period 1. Prices would fall thereafter, as the long run equilibrium price level with this entry rate would necessarily be on the 45° line at a lower price level. (In similar fashion a bigger revaluation would shift the initial equilibrium for Fischer contracts to point D_F where inflation also falls to zero.) Setting $\bar{s} = 0$ as in Figures 4.1 and 4.2 can be thought of as something of a compromise between this very deflationary 'cold turkey' policy and the more inflationary 'full employment' policy.

2.3 Calvo contracts

In later sections of this chapter, where other sources of inflation inertia are considered, it proves more convenient to use the alternative (continuous-time) model of contracts proposed by Calvo (1983a, b). A model with Calvo contracts consists of the following equations

$$p(t) = \delta \int_{-\infty}^{t} x(\tau) e^{-\delta(t-\tau)} d\tau \qquad \text{or } Dp = \delta(x - p) \qquad (16)$$

$$x(t) = \delta \int_{t}^{\infty} [\hat{p}(\tau) + \beta \hat{y}(\tau)] e^{-\delta(\tau-t)} d\tau \text{ or } Dx = \delta(x - p - \beta y) \quad (17)$$

$$y = \eta(\bar{s} - p + p^*) \qquad (18)$$

where D = time differential operator.

In equation (16) the current price level is given as an average of all outstanding contracts, while the current new contract is a forward looking integral of expected future prices and demand pressure as shown in equation (17). The aggregate demand relationship [equation (18)] is unchanged from the previous models.

The model can be rewritten as

$$\begin{bmatrix} Dp \\ Dx \end{bmatrix} = A \begin{bmatrix} p \\ x \end{bmatrix} + \begin{bmatrix} 0 \\ -\delta\beta\eta\bar{s} \end{bmatrix} \qquad (19)$$

where

$$A = \begin{bmatrix} -\delta & \delta \\ -\delta(1 - \beta\eta) & \delta \end{bmatrix}$$

Again it is assumed that prior to joining the fixed rate system the economy was in equilibrium with constant money growth at rate μ. This inflationary equilibrium implies a constant depreciation of the exchange rate at rate μ and constant growth in the price level at rate μ. It can be seen from equation (16) that the current contract must therefore be given by $x = p + \mu/\delta$. Clearly, the currently negotiated contract must be set higher than the current price level to compensate for anticipated inflation during the expected term of the contract. From equation (17) it can be seen that, in inflationary equilibrium, output is at its natural rate and that $p = s$ (with $p^* = 0$).

It is once more assumed that the government chooses to peg the exchange rate at its market level on the joining date. Thus, if the regime switch takes place when $p = 0$ then $\bar{s}$ is set to zero and immediately prior to joining the fixed rate system the current contract, x, is given by μ/δ. We assume that the pre-entry position is at point A in Figure 4.4 where the distance OA is μ/δ.

With $\bar{s}$ the post-entry equilibrium point is again at the origin in Figure 4.4 and, if the peg is *fully credible*, the post-entry solution for the contract lies on the stable path marked CC. It is easily shown that the slope of the stable path in this model has the same value as in the Taylor model, that is $1 - \sqrt{\beta\eta}$. (In what follows this slope is denoted θ.) The impact effect of the change of regime must therefore be a jump in the contract from point A onto CC. Unlike the previous model, however, this is achieved by a vertical jump from point A straight to the long run equilibrium point at the origin. Thus, the inflation rate drops from μ to zero as soon as the peg is announced. There is, therefore, no persistence of inflation when the fixed exchange rate is fully credible and contracts are of the Calvo form.

3   Calvo contracts and lack of credibility

To capture the lack of full credibility in a model with Calvo contracts, it is assumed that there is a perceived constant probability of a devaluation of size J in financial labour markets: so the exchange rate peg suffers from a 'peso problem'. The perceived probability of devaluation (per unit of time) is denoted π.

In the labour market the expectation of realignments affects the forward-looking contract (defined in integral (7)) by modifying expected future prices and demand levels. Denote the rate of change of x con*ditional on the current value of* $\bar{s}$ by Dx. In the case where there are no expected realignments Dx is as defined in equation (17). When realignments are expected, however, the expression for Dx is

$$Dx = \delta(x - p - \beta y) - (1 - \theta)\pi J$$
$$= \delta(x - p - \beta y) - \sqrt{\beta\eta}\,\pi J \tag{20}$$

where $\theta < 1$ is the slope of the stable path. But when this is combined with the equation for price adjustment and the variables are measured from the

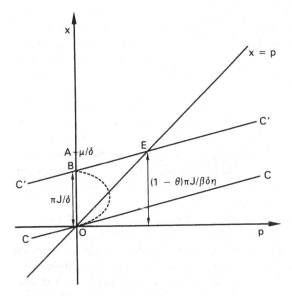

Figure 4.4 Lack of credibility and learning

current parity we find that the system has an additional constant term. Specifically

$$\begin{bmatrix} Dp \\ Dx \end{bmatrix} = A \begin{bmatrix} p \\ x \end{bmatrix} + \begin{bmatrix} 0 \\ b - \delta\beta\eta\bar{s} \end{bmatrix} \tag{21}$$

where A is as before and $b = (\theta - 1)\pi J$. Thus the effect of the expected realignments is to shift the 'equilibrium' of the model to the north-east along the 45° line. In Figure 4.4 the new equilibrium is marked E with associated path $C'C'$ which has the same slope as CC and has a vertical intercept at $\pi J/\delta$. Because the equilibrium point E is associated with expectations of realignments which never occur it is referred to as a 'quasi-equilibrium'.

At this quasi-equilibrium $Dp = Dx = 0$, and $x - \bar{s} = p - \bar{s} \equiv q$ where

$$q = \frac{(1 - \theta)}{\beta\delta\eta}\pi J \tag{22}$$

measures the difference between quasi-equilibrium and true equilibrium. Hence $q > 0$ so long as $\pi J > 0$.

Now consider a switch to a fixed exchange rate from a downwards float at rate μ which takes place when point A is reached. The contract jumps from point A onto the path $C'C'$ at point B. At point B the rate of inflation is πJ so, in contrast to the fully credible case, inflation does not fall to zero on impact. As time proceeds, prices rise and the contract move along $C'C'$ towards point E. The rise in prices erodes competitiveness (because the nominal exchange rate is fixed) and this causes inflation to slow. But this is at the cost of a recession which continues for as long as the expectations of realignment persist.

The assumption that the private sector permanently expects realignments at average rate πJ, despite the fact that no realignments actually occur, is obviously unsatisfactory. There is likely to be some form of learning which leads to a convergence of private sector expectations towards the true value of πJ (which is zero). Thus as time passes the quasi-equilibrium point would also move towards the long run equilibrium (as q is proportional to π).

In Appendix 4C we indicate how a process of Bayesian updating will lead to just this sort of result where the unknown value of π (assumed by the public to be either π_H or π_L) is approximated by an estimate $\hat{\pi}$ which exponentially converges on π_L as time proceeds without any realignments being observed. (For present purposes $\pi_L = 0$.) In particular it is shown that for large values of t (the time since the peg was fixed) the process implies that $D\hat{\pi} = -\phi\hat{\pi}$, where $\phi = \pi_H$, the high realignment probability. But since q is proportional to $\hat{\pi}$ it follows that

$$Dq = -\phi q. \tag{23}$$

In addition $x - q = \theta(p - q)$ on the stable path and $Dp = \delta(x - p)$ as in equation (16). This implies that

$$Dp = \delta(1 - \theta)(q - p) \tag{24}$$

(where, for convenience, we are continuing to assume that $\bar{s} = 0$). So the dynamics of adjustment under Bayesian learning may, in the neighbourhood of equilibrium, be written

$$\begin{bmatrix} Dp \\ Dq \end{bmatrix} = \begin{bmatrix} -\delta(1-\theta) & \delta(1-\theta) \\ 0 & -\phi \end{bmatrix} \begin{bmatrix} p \\ q \end{bmatrix} \tag{25}$$

where $\phi = -\pi_H$. So the adjustment of prices and contracts will follow a curved path such as that shown in Figure 4.4. The inflation that persists after the switch of regime causes a recession which dies away as the private sector learns that there are to be no realignments.

The effect of rational learning in bringing down inflation will not of course be foreseeable in advance; so the authorities may be tempted by the 'cold turkey' policy of revaluing to achieve prompt inflation reduction. If the entry rate is chosen so that the current price level is the quasi-equilibrium then the inflation rate will be zero on entry and will fall later as learning takes place. Formally

$$\bar{s} = p_0 - q_0 = p_0 - \frac{1-\theta}{\delta\beta\eta}\bar{p}_0 J \tag{26}$$

The idea of using the exchange rate as a signal of a new policy stance is analysed by Winckler (1991) using a game-theoretic framework.

4   Lack of common knowledge

In the previous section, it was demonstrated that, if a switch in policy regime is *not* fully credible at the time it is implemented and announced, then the intended effects on private sector inflationary expectations are delayed until credibility is acquired, essentially by the government 'sticking to its guns'. The assumption made was that agents did not believe in the government's commitment and were learning from the observations of government policy *and* that each individual agent regarded his or her own beliefs as being held by all other agents.

In this section, however, we examine not the lack of credibility but rather the 'lack of common knowledge', along the lines suggested by Frydman and Phelps (1983, Ch. 1). They emphasize that, even where agents know the true parameters of the model and the intended change of policy is announced

> 'The agent's forecasting problem is further complicated when government policy alters the parameters of the process governing the behaviour of exogenous variables [. . . by] the problem that although an individual agent may know and believe the government's announcement *he does not know if other agents also know and believe in the change in policy.'. . . .* Where the rational expectations approach predicts instantaneous movement to a new equilibrium, the difficulties faced by agents in their expectations formation lead to a protracted period of disequilibrium.' (p. 6, emphasis added.)

In the Calvo model it was indeed found that rational expectations and policy credibility ensured *instantaneous* adjustment to a new non-inflationary equilibrium despite the presence of overlapping contracts. To capture the issues discussed in Frydman and Phelps we continue to assume that the model parameters are known to all agents and also that the policy shift is announced and is believed by every agent. But, because agents do not know about the beliefs of others, they are assumed to incorporate a model of learning in their forecasts of wage settlements – and the model they use for this purpose is that suggested in equation (19) of Section 2!

This does, of course, imply that during the period of transition from one policy rule to another, agents misperceive the expectations of other agents: after all, everyone knows what the policy is, so what is going on is not learning about policy but eliminating errors in forecasting the behaviour of others. This view of the world is rather asymmetric (everyone is inwardly sure but is not sure about others) but may be appropriate in circumstances where the credible policy commitment made by the government involves a considerable change of regime whose consequences for collective behaviour have not been fully spelt out. That this may be true of monetary disinflations was argued by Phelps and Di Tata in Frydman and Phelps (1983, Ch. 2 and Ch. 3); and it may also be applied to a change of exchange rate regime.

To see what happens under our somewhat stylized account of the lack of common knowledge, we proceed at first to see how forecasting the learning of others affects current contracts. The result obtained is that the time path of the price level mimics what would have been true with genuine learning; but because agents do here anticipate what cannot be forecast if everyone was really learning, the price level is always closer to equilibrium.

As in Section 2 we continue to assume that prices are an (infinite) moving average of past contracts, see equation (16), and that contracts are weighted forecasts of future prices and output levels, see equation (17). But we reject the rational expectations assumption that the forecasts will be generated by the model itself (including the credibly fixed exchange rate peg), and assume instead that the forecast for prices is given by the learning model in equation (25).

The expected values of p and y, denoted $\hat{p}$ and $\hat{y} = -\eta\hat{p}$, now involve forecasting the forecasts of others. From equations (23) and (24) the following autonomous system is obtained describing the evolution of the expected price level and quasi-equilibrium

$$D\hat{p} = \delta(1 - \theta)(\hat{q} - \hat{p}) \tag{27}$$

$$D\hat{q} = -\phi\hat{q} \tag{28}$$

For convenience we combine this with the equations that describe actual prices in the following matrix system

$$\begin{bmatrix} D\hat{q} \\ D\hat{p} \\ Dp \\ Dx \end{bmatrix} = \begin{bmatrix} -\phi & 0 & 0 & 0 \\ (1-\theta)\delta & -(1-\theta)\delta & 0 & 0 \\ 0 & 0 & -\delta & \delta \\ 0 & -\delta(1-\beta\eta) & 0 & \delta \end{bmatrix} \begin{bmatrix} \hat{q} \\ \hat{p} \\ p \\ x \end{bmatrix} \tag{29}$$

The roots of this system are conveniently displayed on the diagonal; there are three stable roots and one unstable root (δ). We assume that the contract will jump as necessary to remain on the stable path to ensure stability. This allows us to write

$$x = v_1 \hat{q} + v_2 \hat{p} + v_3 p \tag{30}$$

where

$$[v_1 \quad v_2 \quad v_3 \quad -1][\delta I - A] = [0 \quad 0 \quad 0 \quad 0] \tag{31}$$

$[v_1 \quad v_2 \quad v_3 \quad -1]$ being the *LHS* row eigenvector associated with the unstable root and A is the matrix appearing in (29) (see Dixit (1980)).

In this case we find specifically that the parameters entering the determination of the current contract are

$$v_1 = \frac{1 - \beta\eta}{2 - \theta} \quad v_2 = \theta \quad v_3 = 0$$

where $\theta = 1 - \sqrt{\beta\eta}$, as in Section 2. With contracts determined in this way equation (29) can be reduced to a third order system, namely

$$\begin{bmatrix} D\hat{q} \\ D\hat{p} \\ Dp \end{bmatrix} = \begin{bmatrix} -\phi & 0 & 0 \\ (1-\theta)\delta & -(1-\theta)\delta & 0 \\ -\dfrac{(1-\beta\eta)\delta}{2-\theta} & -\theta\delta & -\delta \end{bmatrix} \begin{bmatrix} \hat{q} \\ \hat{p} \\ p \end{bmatrix} \tag{32}$$

The term θ could have either sign: but in simulating these equations we assumed it to be positive. Specifically we assume $\beta = \eta = 1/2$ so $\theta = 1/2$, setting $\delta = \phi = 1/2$ also generates the results shown in Figure 4.5. It is assumed that both the price level and the forecast begin at equilibrium but $\hat{q}$ is positive, specifically $\hat{q}(0) = 1$. Consequently both p and $\hat{p}$ rise for three periods before falling back towards equilibrium. (Note that in this case p and $\hat{p}$ are perfectly correlated, specifically $p = 0.25\hat{p}$.)

Note that the initial conditions are those in which a rational expectations solution of this model would have led to *instant* price stabilization; no realignments are expected by any individual and the price is at

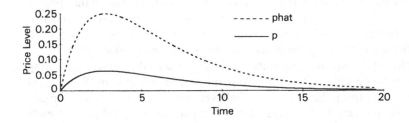

Figure 4.5 phi = 0.5

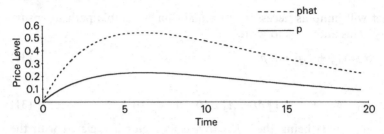

Figure 4.6 phi = 0.1

equilibrium. But we assume here that each agent thinks that *others* expect devaluation ($\hat{q} > 0$) and that they will only gradually learn that they are mistaken. So each person forecasts high settlements and this leads to the price level rising, and to unemployment. The forecast inflation falls because of the 'learning' that is postulated for others and because of unemployment. Note that y is proportional to p, ($y = -\eta p = -0.5p$).

If the speed of learning postulated for others is much slower, then the phase of rising prices will be that much more prolonged, as will be the period of slack demand. For the second simulation, shown in Figure 4.6, ϕ has been much reduced ($\phi = 0.1$) and this means that inflation lasts twice as long, with prices peaking in period 6. In this case the actual price level moves more closely in line with the forecast price level as $p = 0.417\hat{p}$.

The example we have worked through is one in which agents *can* correctly forecast government policy, but do not correctly forecast the forecast of others. For an open economy with a pegged exchange rate it illustrates the point made by Phelps that 'in order to reduce the price level (in relation to the accustomed trend) it is not sufficient that the central bank persuades each agent to reduce his private expectations of the money supply (in relation to past trend) by the warranted amount. The prevalence of this knowledge must be public knowledge – an accepted fact,'. (For the open economy the money supply needs to be replaced by the exchange rate in the quotation.)

Like other examples of this genre, it is subject to the criticism that people could work out that they are wrong about the forecasts of others; and also that the central bank would surely in the circumstances do its best to publicize the private credibility that its policies enjoy (by conducting a poll for example). But the learning process may take some time – long enough to be judged a failure. And the task of persuading the general public that the policy is widely believed may well in practice include 'convincing them that groups that they regard as powerful have already bought it. Appealing over the heads of these groups to the people will not work unless you can simultaneously persuade them that traditionally powerful groups are no longer so strong as to be able to deflect you from your policy.' (Bull (1983), comment on Di Tata in Frydman and Phelps.)

Our example is not meant to demonstrate the impossibility of securing convergent beliefs; rather to illustrate how policy-makers need to work actively to secure this end rather than simply leaving it to 'rational expectations'.

5   Conclusion

In this chapter, we have considered various possible explanations for a protracted process of inflation convergence after a switch to a hard currency peg. When a fully credible peg and rational expectations are assumed, it appears that nominal stickiness in the form of Taylor or Fischer contracts does not account for much inflation sluggishness. Giovannini (1990), however, concluded that 'This is not to say that nominal inertia is irrelevant, but only that additional explanations may be useful.' To focus clearly on these additional explanations we proceeded by working with Calvo contracts, for which nominal inertia implies no sluggishness for inflation whatsoever.

First we assumed that agents anticipate random realignments, so the hard peg is less than fully credible. This devaluation prospect does, of course, impart an inflationary bias to the economy – but the inflation gets converted into economic slack if no realignments actually take place. As it seems implausible that agents would *permanently* expect realignments in these circumstances, we allowed for Bayesian learning about the policy shift. This combination of nominal inertia and credibility which is slow to build generates sluggish inflation and a protracted recession after a peg is adopted. The roots of the process depend essentially on the expected life of contracts and on the speed of learning.

Then we followed the lead of Frydman and Phelps by relaxing the common knowledge assumption implicit in the usual rational expectations hypothesis. The way this is done is for each agent to postulate that others are learning about the policy switch while he or she knows it to have happened for sure. Since no one is, in fact, learning the speed of adjustment is faster than in the case where genuine learning takes place. But if the intensity of realignments is not expected to be very high (i.e. π_H is not high) then this process can be protracted.

If indeed the problem is simply one of learning, either about the policy shift, or about the views of others, then there is presumably a good case for the authorities trying to signal the change of policy in a way that will speed up the learning process. Alternatively the inertia might be due to interactions between imperfectly competitive firms and unions. This calls for a more strategic analysis than the staggered contract models used here.

Appendix 4A   The stable path with Taylor contracts

With the exchange rate fixed at $\bar{s}$ and by assuming rational expectations, equations (1), (2) and (3) in the text can be used to derive the following difference equation for the contract, x_t:

$$-\tfrac{1}{4}(1 - \beta\eta)x_{t+1} + \tfrac{1}{2}(1 + \beta\eta)x_t - \tfrac{1}{4}(1 - \beta\eta)x_{t-1} = \beta\eta\bar{s} \tag{A1}$$

From this it is simple to check that the equilibrium level of x is $\bar{s}$. The solution for the contract will take the following form

$$x_t = \bar{s} + K\rho^t \tag{A2}$$

where K is a constant which is determined by an initial condition for x_{t-1} and ρ is the stable root (i.e. the root which has an absolute value less than unity) of the characteristic equation

$$-\tfrac{1}{4}(1 - \beta\eta)\rho^2 + \tfrac{1}{2}(1 + \beta\eta)\rho - \tfrac{1}{4}(1 - \beta\eta) = 0 \tag{A3}$$

It is simple (but tedious) to check that ρ takes the following value

$$\rho = \frac{1 - \sqrt{\beta\eta}}{1 - \sqrt{\beta\eta}} \tag{A4}$$

To obtain an expression for the stable path observe that, while on the stable path, equation A2 implies that the contract in period $t - 1$ is related to the contract in period t by the following expression

$$x_{t-1} = \frac{x_t - \bar{s}}{\rho} + \bar{s} \tag{A5}$$

This can be used to eliminate x_{t-1} from equation (1), and, after some rearrangement, the following expression is found relating the current contract to the current price level

$$x_t = \frac{2\rho}{1 + \rho}p_t + \bar{s} = \theta p_t + \bar{s} \tag{A6}$$

where θ is the slope of the stable path. Using equation (A4) it follows that

$$\theta = 1 - \sqrt{\beta\eta} \tag{A7}$$

which is the value of θ used in the text.

Appendix 4B Fischer contracts

This appendix derives the solution for the wage rate set for period 2 by the group which settles in period 1. From equation (10) in the main text it can be seen that this must involve a forecast of the wage to be set for period 2 by the group which settles in period 2, i.e. a forecast of $x_{2,1}$. By combining equation (14) and (15) in the text it is simple to work out that, in general, $x_{t,1}$ is given by the expression

$$x_{t,1} = \frac{1 - \beta\eta}{1 + \beta\eta} x_{t-1,2} + \frac{2\beta\eta}{1 + \beta\eta} \bar{s} \tag{A8}$$

(This is the algebraic equivalent of deriving point B in Figure 2). This expression can be used to generate the required forecast. It is effectively a reaction function which shows the behaviour of the group settling in period t as a function of the wage set by the group settling in period $t - 1$. In particular it shows that

$$x_{2,1} = \frac{1 - \beta\eta}{1 + \beta\eta} x_{1,2} + \frac{2\beta\eta}{1 + \beta\eta} \bar{s} \tag{A9}$$

If this is substituted into the price equation [equation (8)] it provides a forecast of the price level in period 2 as a function of the wage set by the group settling in period 1 as follows

$$p_2 = \frac{1}{1 + \beta\eta} x_{1,2} + \frac{\beta\eta}{1 + \beta\eta} \bar{s} \tag{A10}$$

Meanwhile, if the demand equation [equation (3)] is substituted into the second contract equation [equation (10)] the following is found

$$x_{1,2} = (1 - \beta\eta)p_2 + \beta\eta\bar{s} \tag{A11}$$

Finally substituting equation (A10) into this equation yields the result

$$x_{1,2} = \bar{s} \tag{A12}$$

Thus, the wage set in period 1 for period 2 is the long run equilibrium level. It follows that all subsequent wage settlements are also at the equilibrium level.

Appendix 4C Bayesian learning about the realignment probability

The realignment expectations discussed in the text can be derived from a model of Bayesian learning, as shown in Driffill and Miller (1991). The argument may be summarized briefly as follows.

After the exchange rate is pegged the public still believes that realignments of size J may occur as a Poisson process but they are not sure of the intensity, π. Assume specifically that their uncertainty is simply whether this intensity is high (π_H) or low (π_L) and suppose they start out immediately after the end of floating with initial probability $P_H(0)$ and $P_L(0) = 1 - P_H(0)$ attached to each of these intensities, i.e. $\hat{\pi}(0) = P_H(0)(\pi_H - \pi_L) + \pi_L$. If these probabilities are then updated in a Bayesian fashion, then, as long as no realignments take place, P_H declines exponentially towards zero. Specifically

$$P_H(t) = \frac{1}{1 + \exp\{(\pi_H - \pi_L)t\}(1 - P_H(0))/P_H(0)} \tag{A13}$$

where time t is measured from the date at which the rate was first pegged.

If a realignment occurs at time t then this causes a discrete jump in $P_H(t)$ so

$$P_H(t^+) - P_H(t^-) = \frac{(1 - P_H(t^-))\dfrac{\pi_L}{\pi_H}}{1 + \dfrac{(1 - P_H(t^-))\pi_L}{P_H(t^-)\pi_H}} \tag{A14}$$

Thereafter P_H will decline exponentially from its new high value just as in equation (A13), but measuring time from the date of the realignment.

Note that for large values of t,

$$P_H(t) \approx e^{-(\pi_H - \pi_L)}\left(\frac{P_H(0)}{1 - P_H(0)}\right) \tag{A15}$$

and so, if $\pi_L = 0$, then for large t

$$\hat{\pi}(t) = P_H(t)\pi_H \approx e^{-\pi_H t}\hat{\pi}(0) \tag{A16}$$

so

$$D\hat{\pi} = -\pi_H\hat{\pi} \tag{A17}$$

the result we use in the text.

NOTE

We would like to thank David Backus, Juan Carlos Di Tata and the editors for comments and suggestions. For financial support we are indebted to the Economic and Social Research Council of the United Kingdom.

REFERENCES

Akerlof, George and Janet Yellen (1985) 'A Near-Rational Model of the Business Cycle with Wage and Price Inertia', *Quarterly Journal of Economics*, **100** (Supplement), 823–38.

Backus, David and John Driffill (1986) 'Credible Disinflation in Closed and Open Economies', mimeo, University of Southampton.

Calvo, Guillermo (1983a) 'Staggered Prices in a Utility-Maximising Framework', *Journal of Monetary Economics*, 12, 383–98.

(1983b) 'Staggered Contracts and Exchange Rate Policy', in Jacob Frenkel (ed.), *Exchange Rates and International Macroeconomics*, Chicago: University of Chicago Press.

Calvo, Guillermo and Carlos Vegh (1991) 'Exchange-Rate-Based Stabilisation under Imperfect Credibility', Research Department Working Paper 91/77, Washington, DC, International Monetary Fund.

Centre for Economic Policy Research (1991) *Monitoring European Integration: The Making of Monetary Union*, Annual Report, Centre for Economic Policy Research, London.

Di Tata, Juan Carlos (1983) 'Expectations of Others' Expectations and the Transitional Non-neutrality of Fully Believed Systematic Monetary Policy', in R. Frydman and E. Phelps, *Individual Forecasting and Aggregate Outcomes*, Cambridge: Cambridge University Press.

Dixit, Avinash (1980) 'A Solution Technique for Rational Expectations Models with Applications to Exchange Rate and Interest Rate Determination', University of Warwick, November.

Driffill, John and Marcus Miller (1991) 'Learning About a Shift in Exchange Rate Regime', mimeo presented to Workshop on Exchange Rate Target Zones, Centre for Economic Policy Resarch, London, October.

Fischer, Stanley (1977) 'Long Term Contracts, Rational Expectations and the Optimal Money Supply Rule', *Journal of Political Economy*, 85, 163–90.

Frydman, Roman and Edmund Phelps (1983) *Individual Forecasting and Aggregate Outcomes*, Cambridge: Cambridge University Press.

Giavazzi, Francesco and Luigi Spaventa (1990) 'The "New" EMS', in Paul De Grauwe and Lucas Papademos (eds.), *The European Monetary System in the 1990's*, London: Longman.

Giovannini, Alberto (1990) 'European Monetary Reform' Progress and Prospects', *Brookings Papers on Economic Activity*, 2, pp. 217–91.

Layard, Richard (1990) 'Wage Bargaining and EMU', in Pöhl, Karl *et al.*, *Britain and EMU*, London School of Economics.

Miller, Marcus and Alan Sutherland (1991) 'The "Walters Critique" of the EMS – A Case of Inconsistent Expectations?', *The Manchester School*, 59 (Supplement), June, 23–37.

Phelps, Edmund (1983) 'The Trouble with "Rational Expectations" and the Problem of Inflation Stabilisation', in R. Frydman and E. Phelps, *Individual Forecasting and Aggregate Outcomes*, Cambridge: Cambridge University Press.

Taylor, John (1979) 'Staggered Wage Setting in a Macro Model', *American Economic Review*, 69, pp. 108–13.

(1984) 'Union Wage Settlements During a Disinflation', *American Economic Review*, 74, 206–10.

Winckler, George (1991) 'Exchange Rate Appreciation as a Signal of a New Policy Stance', Research Department Working Paper No. 91/32, Washington, DC, International Monetary Fund.

Discussion

DAVID BACKUS

This is an interesting chapter and I am pleased to discuss it. Before I read it my guess was that, given the success of the European monetary system (EMS) so far, moving to a common currency would probably not be that big a deal. If we were talking about, say, what is left of the USSR, monetary factors may be very important. But for the European Community, I would guess that a common currency is probably a good idea, but much less important than harmonizing the standards and procedures that tend to make trade difficult. That is a topic, though, for other sessions. What I would like to do now is to use the chapter as motivation for exploring the issue of monetary credibility in the EMS in general terms. I should say, however, that my comments are not constrained by much previous knowledge of the EMS or its continuing evolution.

D.4.1 Convergence in the data?

The issue is inflation convergence, and I think some data will lend concreteness to the discussion. From Figure D.4.1, it can be seen that for France and especially the Netherlands, the difference in inflation rates relative to Germany has been fairly small, and declining. Given the state of macroeconomic data, I view this as a success for the EMS. But would a common currency improve the situation further?

In Figure D.4.2 similar inflation differentials are shown, on the same scale, for different cities in the USA. Although there are unavoidable measurement errors in small samples, the figure indicates that we are not likely to see identical inflation rates across countries any time soon, since they do not exist even within the US currency area. (Not to mention that the differences in definition and data collection methods that arise in international comparisons do not apply within the USA.) On the other hand, 'convergence' is shown in Figure D.4.3 for the USA and Canada even though they do not yet use a common currency, or even one with a fixed parity. The US and Canada do not seem to find the absence of a common currency a major impediment to trade, which is why I say that a common currency may not be the most important issue for European integration.

The problem for the EMS, of course, is with the 'other' countries like Italy and Portugal (see Figure D.4.4). They, too, have exhibited some

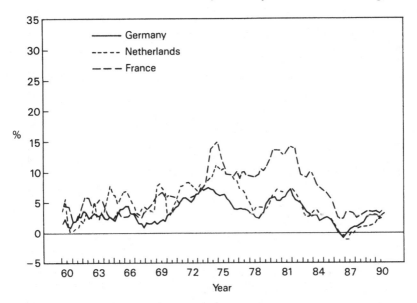

Figure D.4.1 Rates of inflation: Germany, Netherlands, and France 1960–90
Source: International Financial Statistics, International Monetary Fund, Washington D.C.

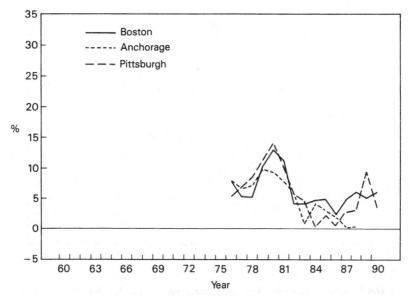

Figure D.4.2 Inflation rates, three US cities, 1976–90
Source: Bureau of Labor Statistics, Washington D.C.

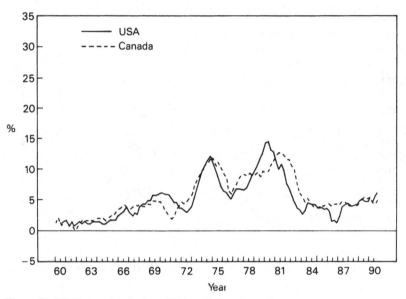

Figure D.4.3 Rates of inflation: USA and Canada, 1960–90
Source: International Financial Statistics, International Monetary Fund, Washington D.C.

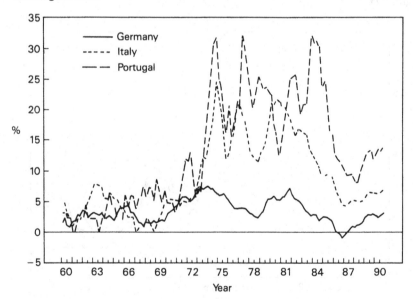

Figure D.4.4 Rates of inflation: Germany, Italy and Portugal, 1960–90
Source: International Financial Statistics, International Monetary Fund, Washington D.C.

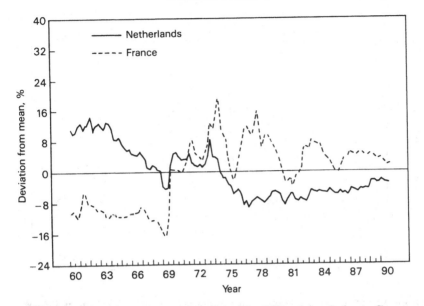

Figure D.4.5 Real exchange rates: Netherlands and France in relation to Germany, 1960–90
Source: International Financial Statistics, International Monetary Fund, Washington D.C.

tendency towards convergence recently but inflation differentials with Germany are still substantial and highly persistent. (And we can say the same for Ireland, Spain, and the United Kingdom.) The issue is then, can or should the EC try to get more uniformity in its monetary policy and price behaviour?

Similarly, real exchange rates might be expected to converge as policy differentials are eliminated. The convergence in real exchange rates (in relation to the Deutschmark) for the Netherlands and France and for Italy and Portugal over the period 1960–90, is shown in Figures D.4.5 and D.4.6. Figure D.4.7 shows the movement of the real exchange rate for Canada (in relation to the USA) over the same period. It should be noted that the fluctuations in the real exchange rate for Portugal (in relation to Germany) are not much larger than those for Canada (in relation to the USA). It may be, therefore, that it is not critical that exchange rates be damped further. The most problematic example is Italy, where the real exchange rate has fallen by nearly 40% over the last 12 years.

To summarize, I would emphasize two points. First, both inflation differentials and deviations from purchasing power parities (PPP) across countries in the EMS are persistent. But second, if current trends continue

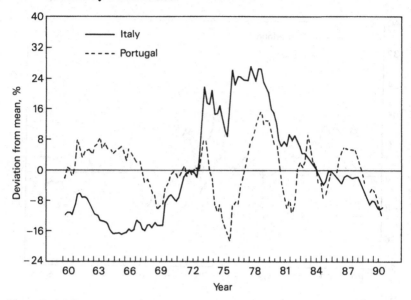

Figure D.4.6 Real exchange rates: Italy and Portugal in relation to Germany 1960–90
Source: International Financial Statistics, International Monetary Fund, Washington D.C.

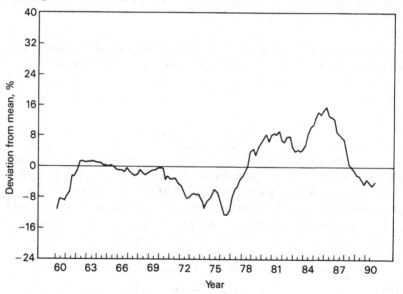

Figure D.4.7 Real exchange rate: Canada in relation to the USA, 1960–90
Source: International Financial Statistics, International Monetary Fund, Washington D.C.

(note the qualification), these differentials will not be much larger than those which existed in the Bretton Woods period within the US, or between the US and Canada. For this reason I would not expect them to be a large impediment to trade. It might be possible to do better, but this is probably good enough. The chapter by Frankel and Phillips in this volume comes, I think, to the same conclusion by other means. (I would be curious to see how their method works during the Bretton Woods period, especially the 1950s, when there was presumably little worry about the collapse of the system.)

D.4.2 Convergence in theory

This chapter has been concerned with modelling inflation differentials, which are substantial and persistent for (say) Italy and Portugal. One interpretation of the chapter is that monetary policy does not lead, in the authors' theoretical framework, to sustained divergences of inflation rates, unless policies are themselves divergent. The theory is based on Taylor's staggered wage contracts. In the basic model there is very little persistence of inflation differentials once policies are harmonized: $n - 1$ period's worth, where n is the length of the longest contract. Given what we know about explicit labour contracts, inflation rates could be expected to converge quite rapidly. The authors seem to find this unappealing, and suggest two extensions designed to generate more persistence: imperfect credibility and lack of common knowledge. (I am not sure what they have in mind for the latter.)

By and large I think they find much the same thing that Stanley Fischer, John Taylor, and John Driffill and I found several years ago: that with or without credibility, disinflationary policies in these kinds of models act quickly and have very small costs. Given what the data have revealed, however, we must conclude either that policies have yet to converge or that there is more persistence in prices than this class of models allows.

The same issue arose a couple of years ago at the Federal Reserve, where the costs and benefits of moving to zero inflation were evaluated. A number of studies found that with Fischer/Taylor contracts the costs of disinflation were very small, much less than the sacrifice ratios computed for actual disinflations, even with modest amounts of credibility. I had the misfortune (with Rao Aiyagari) of presenting these results to the president of the Minneapolis Federal Reserve Bank, who decided that theory was not very informative on this matter. I cannot say that I disagree with him.

This is not a criticism of this chapter, just a different interpretation of their results. Before we turn to extensions of the theory, I think we have to consider whether the kinds of inertia present in Taylor and Fischer contracts are a good enough approximation of real economies to be used in serious policy evaluation. These contracts are a great improvement over their predecessors, I think, and about as good as anything since then. But I think we still have some work to do in this area if we want to make precise statements about the likely effects of changes in the nature of monetary policy. Whether imperfect credibility or lack of common knowledge will do the trick remains to be seen.

D.4.3 Credibility in practice

This chapter talks a lot about 'credibility' without saying exactly how it might be achieved. But as I follow the deliberations on the EMS, it strikes me that a more interesting question is what kinds of institutional arrangements are effective in establishing this mysterious and useful state. I should not single out this chapter, since most academic work, including my own, does the same thing. But I think the really tough practical question is how to design a good central bank for a community with decentralized political institutions.

In conclusion, I would like to pose the question: are existing inflation differentials a problem for the European Community? Probably not; quite large differentials existed among countries during the Bretton Woods period, among US cities, and between the US and Canada, all of which have experienced healthy trading relations.

From a theoretical perspective, the degree of persistence of inflation differentials and deviations from PPP are puzzling. This is a general problem, not unique to the findings of this chapter, but one worth exploring. In this chapter, the authors make some interesting efforts to go beyond earlier contributions.

From a practical perspective, I think the interesting issue is the design of good monetary institutions. Central bankers will not take much comfort from this, but as an academic economist I find this is a fascinating experiment. I feel reassured by this conference that the central bankers are more advanced in this regard than I am.

REFERENCES

Backus, D. and J. Driffill (1987) 'Credible Disinflation in Closed and Open Economies', *Ricerche Economiche*, **41**, 326–40.
Fischer, S. (1986) 'Contracts, credibility, and disinflation', in S. Fischer, *Indexing, nflation and Economic Policy*, Cambridge, Mass.: MIT Press.
Taylor, J. (1983) 'Union wage settlements during a disinflation', *American Economic Review*, **73**, 981–93.

Discussion

MICHAEL DOOLEY

Miller and Sutherland focus on the case where a new exchange rate arrangement implies a significant reduction in the rate of currency depreciation and inflation. The more familiar models developed in their chapter suggest that the costs of such a reform depend upon the credibility of the new exchange rate regime, the inertia in wage setting behaviour, and the level chosen for the nominal exchange rate at the time of the reform. A novel aspect of the chapter is that uncertainty about the beliefs of other private wage setters can make individuals who believe the regime change to be credible behave as if the new regime is not fully credible.

The chapter makes several contributions to our understanding of the issues. First, overlapping wage contracts and inertia are not a potent source of inflationary pressure following the reform. To see this it is useful to modify slightly the figure used in their chapter. Figure D.4.8 shows the price level and the level of the nominal exchange rate. Prior to the reform, the level of these two variables had moved together for a long time so that the real exchange rate was constant. At the origin, the exchange rate is fixed but the price level for one or more of the reasons listed above continues along its former trajectory for a time. Clearly the real exchange rate remains above its long run equilibrium until the price level falls back to the $P = 0$ axis.

In the models developed in this chapter wage setters receive a clear signal that the price level (and the real exchange rate) are too high since this causes a recession. The interesting aspect of the argument is that inflation only lasts until the price level starts to return towards equilibrium ($t_0 - t_1$ in Figure D.4.8) but the recession lasts until the deflation wipes out the over-valuation of the real exchange rate ($t_0 - t_2$ in Figure D.4.8). Moreover, the magnitude of the over-valuation is likely to be quite limited during the first year of the reform since it starts at zero and grows, at most, at the rate of desired fall in the inflation implied by the new trajectory for the nominal exchange rate. In most cases in the context of countries joining the exchange rate mechanism (ERM) this is in the neighbourhood of 3% so the average real appreciation in the first year is, at most, only 1.5%.

This suggests that the costs of reform will be very sensitive to the level at which the nominal exchange rate is initially set. The first model developed

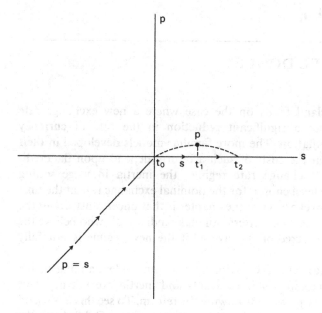

Figure D.4.8 Prices and nominal exchange rates

by Miller and Sutherland suggests that the key to avoiding an unnecessary loss in output is simply to set the initial level of new parity for the exchange rate at a level that anticipates the fact that wages set partly by habit will become too high relative to the market exchange rate prevailing before the announcement of the new regime. In particular, the first simple model offered suggests that setting the exchange rate at a 'strong' level will increase the fall in output but will curb inflation only slightly more rapidly compared with setting the level of the exchange rate in a way that accommodates existing contracts.

With forward-looking wage setting, overlapping contracts do not generate inflation after the exchange rate is fixed. These relationships can be seen clearly using Figure 4.1 in the chapter. With two overlapping contracts and constant price inflation, each wage contract is set so that for the first half of the contract period the wage is too high and for the second half the wage is too low. At t_0 the contract set at t_1 is exactly right in that the level of the wage is consistent with the level of prices. If the price level is credibly pegged at this level, there is no inflation implied by the lagged wage contract. Moreover, if wage-setting behaviour is forward looking, it is also clear that the new contract (last set at t_2) will also be set at a level consistent with the price level at t_0. If there was a distribution of old contracts set on expectations of continued inflation the price level would fall until all such contracts were re-negotiated. If the government chooses to set the price level, or what is the same thing in this model, the exchange rate, at a level that increases the gap between lagged wages and the equilibrium nominal wage, this will result in a deeper recession and a more rapid deflation. The lesson again seems to be that if there is credibility there is no reason to try, initially, to set an over-valued exchange rate peg in order to curb inflation. It is comforting that very similar results are reported by Bayoumi and Chada (1991) in work that uses the International Monetary Fund's multi-country model.

The third model reminds me of the well-known beauty contest example used by Keynes to explain behaviour in speculative markets. Wage setters consider themselves well informed about the 'beauty' of the government's commitment to the new exchange rate but are not sure that others are as well informed. The implications of this model seem to me the same as a model in which the government's policy is in fact not credible. In seeking to protect their real wage, workers will continue for a time to set inflationary wage settlements and suffer the resulting loss in output. This is an interesting idea to work through since it might apply to a case in which interest groups that are protected from a fall in output would misrepresent their expectations. Such models should remind us that credibility must be augmented by a list of assumptions about information, behaviour, and institutional arrangements before the happy news from rational expectations and credibility shines through.

In general, the good news from these models seems to be at odds with the experience of countries undertaking reform programmes. Inflation seems to be more stubborn and nominal interest rates remain relatively high as compared with partner countries. Moreover, there is no clear impact on activity following a reform. One possibility, of course, is that the reform is not fully credible in that the market expects at least one more exchange rate adjustment. But it is also possible that factors outside those considered in the models are important.

Another empirical regularity that follows reform programmes is large private capital inflows into the reforming country. This would not be predicted by the type of model developed in the chapter. Clearly, if nominal interest rates remain high relative to the world interest rate in such models it is because the reform is not credible. In this case, the expected devaluation of the exchange rate would just offset the interest rate differential and no capital inflow is predicted. Moreover, the recession predicted in most versions of the model would reduce the demand for money perhaps inducing a capital outflow. Different expectations would have to be posited for wage setters and financial markets to generate an inflow, a set-up not likely to convince the sceptical.

An alternative explanation for the capital inflow is that, given interest rates, there is a portfolio shift toward domestic bonds in the reforming country. In most cases, reform programmes have included some deregulation of capital markets in the reforming country in addition to the exchange rate reform. The period of high inflation that preceded the reform was often associated with administrative controls designed to protect the tax base of domestic financial instruments on which the inflation tax was levied. The reduction of such controls, and in the case of potential ERM members, the unification of capital market rules and institutions, could account for a large capital inflow associated with financial market reform but not caused by the new exchange rate policy.

Such a coincidence presents the central bank in the reforming country with a difficult problem, particularly in the case where the exchange rate target is not fully credible. In the short run, capital inflows might seem to be responding to the relatively high domestic interest rate. But if the central bank maintains its target for a monetary aggregate all the inflow must be sterilized. This means that the central bank must sell to the market instruments denominated in the domestic currency and the proceeds must be invested in reserve assets. Since domestic nominal interest rates will remain above the rate earned on reserve assets until the private sector is convinced the exchange rate target is credible, the central bank will show losses that could be quite large and could persist for some time. Even if the capital inflow is temporary, the losses for the central bank will continue until the credibility of the new exchange rate regime is established. In these circumstances, the losses can become a fiscal problem for the government.

In the meantime, some observers are sure to ask why the central bank is intervening in the domestic market to keep nominal interest rates above those in partner countries and why the central bank has become a fiscal liability. The answer is that a failure to sterilize capital inflows of this type will generate growth in the monetary base unless capital is perfectly mobile. A rapid expansion of the monetary base is not consistent with price stability. In fact, the growth of the monetary base might contribute to the lack of credibility of the exchange rate target.

Unlike the simple models we like to work with, capital inflows may not reflect an increase in the demand for money, and certainly do not reflect an increase in the demand for the monetary base. It seems important that the central bank should give a commitment to sterilizing these inflows, or what is the same thing, announce an aggregate monetary target that it believes is consistent with price stability. During the initial months of a transition to a new exchange rate regime it will be difficult to know if nominal interest rates should be equalized or whether some credibility risk premiums on the domestic asset is necessary. A clear commitment to a monetary or credit aggregate could be useful in these circumstances.

REFERENCES

Bayoumi, Tamim and Bankim Chada (1991) 'The Transition Effects of Entry into the ERM', Mimeo, International Monetary Fund, Washington, DC.
Miller, Marcus and Alan Sutherland, Ch. 4 this volume.

5 Inflation in fixed exchange rate regimes: the recent Portuguese experience

SÉRGIO REBELO

1 Introduction

One of the classical problems in macroeconomics is that of how to achieve and maintain a low level of inflation. This problem is thought to have at least one easy solution: a high inflation country can peg its currency to that of a low inflation economy, thereby 'importing' a low inflation rate. This textbook advice has been used with success in several countries and in different time epochs. Most recently, France has achieved one of the lowest rates of inflation in the world by pegging the French franc to the Deutschmark.

In an attempt to lower its rate of inflation in order to join the European monetary system (EMS) Portugal has, since October 1990, followed an exchange rate policy that essentially pegs the Portuguese escudo to the ECU. The results of this policy in terms of inflation convergence have so far been disappointing: the rate of inflation has failed to decline by more than 3% since 1990. And instead of simplifying the task of the central bank, the adoption of a fixed exchange rate regime has generated new policy dilemmas. The slow decline of inflation has kept nominal interest rates at high levels that have forced the central bank to impose capital controls. The difficulties involved in enforcing these controls have led the monetary authorities to allow some short term volatility in the exchange rate in the hope that this element of risk will reduce the temptation to circumvent capital controls and arbitrage out the difference between domestic and foreign nominal rates.[1]

The reason why the slow convergence of inflation is surprising is that it is strikingly at odds with the simple one-good paradigm often used in international finance. This model predicts that when country A pegs its currency to that of country B the rate of inflation in A converges instantaneously to that of country B. Adding more tradable goods to the model does not eliminate this prediction of instantaneous inflation convergence, so it is clear that non-tradables must be considered.

128

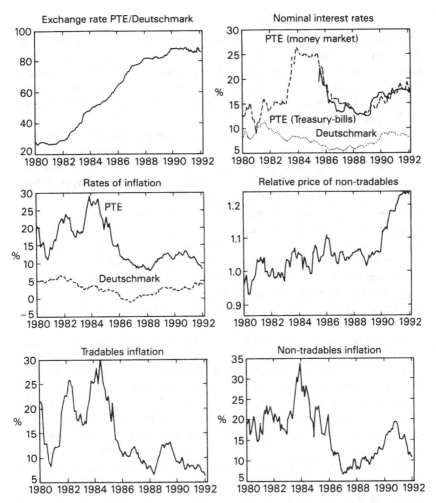

Figure 5.1 Exchange rate, interest rates and inflation in Portugal, 1980–92

Suppose that the prices of tradable goods have been equalized in the two countries; when can the rate of inflation in country A remain above that of country B? The price level is a weighted average of the price of tradables (P_t^T) and the price of non-tradables (P_t^{NT}):

$$P_t = \omega P_t^T + (1 - \omega)P_t^{NT}$$

The price of tradables will expand at the rate of inflation in country B. Deflating both sides of this expression by the price of tradables,

$$P_t/P_t^T = \omega + (1 - \omega)(P_t^{NT}/P_t^T)$$

it becomes obvious that for the rate of inflation in country A to be higher than that of country B (so that P_t/P_t^T increases over time), the relative price of non-tradables, P_t^{NT}/P_t^T, must increase in a persistent manner. Figure 5.1 shows that this increase in the relative price of non-tradables has, in fact, been the main force that has worked against a rapid decline in the Portuguese rate of inflation.[2]

In this chapter I try to go beyond the simple inflation arithmetic described above to construct a fully articulated model that is consistent with the facts suggested by the panels of Figure 5.1 which give the movement in a number of key variables from 1980–92: (i) tradables inflation has, essentially, converged; (ii) the relative price of non-tradables has increased over time;[3] (iii) nominal rates of return for assets denominated in Portuguese escudos are higher than those of assets with similar risk denominated in Deutschmarks.[4] Table 5.1 provides information on the evolution of other important macroeconomic variables. I will focus on two more relevant facts about the Portuguese economy suggested by this table; (iv) the last few years have been periods of fast economic growth; and (v) there has been an appreciation of the real wage rate.

Section 2 sets up an open economy model with capital controls to study three candidate explanations for the protracted increase in the relative price of non-tradables: (i) the process of convergence to the steady state from a low stock of capital; (ii) an increase in the government demand for non-tradables; and (iii) an increase in the prdouctivity of the tradable sector. Section 3 re-examines these three potential sources of slow inflation convergence in a model with free international capital mobility. While the focus of Sections 2 and 3 is on the behaviour of real variables, in Section 4 I discuss briefly how money can be introduced in the models so that the nominal interest rate can be determined. The main findings are summarized in Section 5.

2   An economy with capital controls

To explain the empirical regularities described in the introduction, it is easiest to focus first on the facts that pertain to real quantities. These facts can be explored in an economy without money which will be the basic building block for the rest of our analysis. The model used is related to three lines of research in international macroeconomics: the Scandinavian model of inflation (e.g. Aukrust (1977) and Lindbeck (1979)), the international models of the 1980s, with their emphasis on inter-temporal

Table 5.1. *Rates of growth[a] of selected economic variables and GDP ratios, Portugal 1980–91*

	GDP	Investment	Government consumption	Public employment	Wage rates	Exports	Imports	Machinery imports
1980	6.99	14.19	11.81	2.83	0.06	8.22	17.38	—
1981	2.84	11.99	4.96	-1.88	-1.84	-2.39	11.32	—
1982	3.71	4.32	0.82	21.27	-5.29	-0.45	0.90	—
1983	-0.20	-6.72	1.24	3.58	-8.15	18.53	-4.30	—
1984	-1.33	-23.78	1.30	-1.12	1.24	17.30	2.45	-17.13
1985	2.59	-5.25	5.82	6.16	4.41	5.64	-5.62	7.26
1986	4.60	6.00	3.54	1.40	4.15	-7.84	-9.41	23.93
1987	4.33	13.28	3.47	4.50	1.48	8.37	18.38	35.32
1988	3.92	14.39	10.93	2.47	1.94	5.87	15.18	26.53
1989	5.36	2.96	6.33	2.47	3.39	10.53	3.57	10.82
1990	4.30	4.48	7.59	2.47	3.88	3.02	4.51	12.07
1991[b]	2.47	2.76	3.44	2.47	—	1.78	5.92	—

Year	Government deficit[c]	Total public debt[c]	Balance of trade[c]	Current account balance[c]	Net private transfers from abroad[c]	Net EC transfers[c]	Unemployment rate
1980	10.37	50.46	-20.82	-5.36	12.82	—	8.0
1981	12.61	60.82	-22.27	-12.07	12.54	—	7.7
1982	10.95	64.67	-21.20	-14.00	12.07	—	7.5
1983	9.62	71.08	-14.29	-7.14	10.60	—	7.9
1984	9.55	74.98	-10.80	-3.00	11.23	—	8.6
1985	15.20	75.69	-7.46	-1.75	10.43	—	8.7
1986	12.87	82.58	-5.94	-4.07	9.37	—	8.6

Table 5.1. (*cont.*)

1987	11.28	83.75	− 10.17	1.28	9.68	–	7.1
1988	8.29	85.87	− 13.75	− 2.52	9.02	1.69	5.8
1989	5.07	82.42	− 11.30	0.38	8.65	1.71	5.3
1990	6.37	76.85	− 11.84	− 0.34	7.81	1.48	5.3
1991	4.02	75.83	− 11.87	− 1.05	7.00	1.81	5.3

Notes:

[a] Logarithmic growth rates; all variables in real terms.

[b] All data for 1991, except Public employment, are estimates from Banco de Portugal *Annual Report.*

[c] As per cent of gross domestic product.

Sources: International Financial Statistics for GDP at market prices, Gross fixed capital formation, Government consumption, Exports, Imports; *OECD Main Economic Indicators* for Public employment; Unemployment rate; *Banco de Portugal Annual and Quarterly Reports* for Government deficit, Government debt, Balance of trade, Current account balance, Net private transfers from abroad, Net EC transfers; *Instituto Nacional de Estatística* for Real wage rate; *Direcção Geral do Comércio Externo* for Machinery imports.

optimization (e.g. Obstfeld (1981), Svensson and Razin (1983), Greenwood (1984), Persson and Svensson (1985), and Frenkel and Razin (1987)), and the recent international real business cycle literature (e.g. Mendoza (1991), Baxter and Crucini (1992) and Backus, Kehoe and Kydland (1992)).

To simplify the notation I will assume that the population is constant and express all variables in per capita terms. The economy is inhabited by a large number of infinitely lived individuals who seek to maximize their utility defined as:

$$U = \sum_{t=0}^{\infty} \beta^t \frac{1}{1-\sigma} \{[(C_t^T)^\gamma (C_t^{NT})^{1-\gamma}]^{1-\sigma} - 1\} \quad \sigma > 0, \gamma > 0, 0 < \beta < 1 \quad (1)$$

where C_t^T denotes the per capital consumption of tradable goods and C_t^{NT} the per capita consumption of non-tradables.

There are two factors of production, capital (K_t) and labour. In each period every household supplies inelastically N units of labour which are allocated to the tradables (N_t^T) and non-tradables industry (N_t^{NT}):

$$N_t^T + N_t^{NT} = N \quad (2)$$

Capital is accumulated in the two industries according to:

$$K_{t+1}^T = \phi(I_t^T/K_t^T)K_t^T + (1-\delta)K_t^T \quad (3a)$$

$$K_{t+1}^{NT} = \phi(I_t^{NT}/K_t^{NT})K_t^{NT} + (1-\delta)K_t^{NT} \quad (3b)$$

where δ denotes the rate of depreciation, while I_t^T, K_t^T, I_t^{NT} and K_t^{NT} represent, respectively, the investment flow and the stock of capital in the tradables and non-tradables industries. The concave function $\phi(\cdot)$ reflects the presence of adjustment costs to investment, as in Lucas and Prescott (1971), Abel and Blanchard (1983), and Hayashi (1982). This function is assumed to be twice continuously differentiable and to have two properties that guarantee the absence of adjustment costs in the steady state: $\phi(\delta) = \delta$ and $\phi'(\delta) = 1$. These adjustment costs serve two purposes. In this section they prevent the model from predicting implausible short-term reallocation of capital between the two sectors. In Section 3, in which the possibility of borrowing and lending in the international capital market is introduced, adjustment costs are necessary so that the model does not predict implausibly large capital inflows and an instantaneous adjustment toward the steady state. Equations (3a) and (3b) implicitly assume that adjustment costs are identical in the two sectors. This symmetry assumption is adopted given the absence of direct information that can be used to parameterize the adjustment cost functions.

The production of tradables (Y_t^T) and the production of non-tradables (Y_t^{NT}) are carried out according to Cobb-Douglas production functions:

$$Y_t^T = A_t^T (K_t^T)^{1-a} (N_t^T)^a, \quad 0 < a < 1 \tag{4}$$

$$Y_t^{NT} = A_t^{NT} (K_t^{NT})^{1-v} (N_t^T)^v, \quad 0 < v < 1, v > a. \tag{5}$$

The assumption that $v > a$ implies that the non-tradable good is more labour intensive than the tradable good. This standard assumption is motivated by the fact that non-tradables tend to be produced mostly in the service sector which is labour intensive.

For convenience, it is assumed that the output of the tradable sector can be used for consumption or for investment but that the production of non-tradables is suitable only for consumption:

$$Y_t^T = C_t^T + I_t^T + I_t^{NT} + G_t^T + TB_t \tag{6}$$

$$Y_t^{NT} = C_t^{NT} + G_t^{NT} \tag{7}$$

The variables G_t^T and G_t^{NT} denote, respectively, the amount of public consumption of tradables and non-tradables. To keep government policy as simple as possible I will assume that public consumption is financed through lump sum taxes. The trade balance, denoted by TB_t, is one of the determinants of the evolution of the country's net asset position vis-à-vis the rest of the world, which will be denoted by B_t:

$$B_{t+1} = (1 - r_t^*)B_t + TB_t + TRF_t \tag{8}$$

In this equation r_t^* denotes the world real interest rate and TRF_t represents net transfers from abroad. I assume in this section that B_t, TB_t and TRF_t are all constant, so that $B = -(TB + TRF)/r^*$. This corresponds to a situation in which the economy can run a constant trade deficit which is financed with income from assets held abroad or with transfers. The private sector cannot borrow or lend in the international capital markets so, except for the presence of a trade deficit, this economy functions as a closed economy model.

Although I did not introduce exogenous technological progress to economize on notation, I will interpret all the variables as being detrended by their steady state growth rate.

For exposition purposes I will describe the competitive equilibrium under rational expectations for this economy by assuming the simplest possible market structure. This structure involves spot labour markets and one period credit markets. Firms hire factors of production seeking to maximize profits. Households choose the mix of goods they consume and make savings decisions in order to maximize utility. There are, as usual, many other market structures that would support the equilibrium that I describe.

Table 5.2. *Parameters used in baseline scenario*

Parameters	Benchmark indicators
$A^T = 1$	
$A^{NT} = 2.57$	$p = 1.5$
$a = 0.40$	Aggregate labour share = 53%
$v = 0.73$	
$N = 1$	
$\xi = -1$	
$\beta = 0.96$	$r = 0.04$
$\sigma = 5$	
$\gamma = 0.58$	Share of tradables in consumption = 58%
$\delta = 0.05$	Investment share = 26%
$TB/Y = -0.09$	
$TRF/Y = 0.089$	
$G^T/Y^T = 0.06$	Share of government consumption in GDP = 12%
$G^{NT}/Y^{NT} = 0.20$	Fraction of non-tradables in government consumption = 1/3
$N^T = 0.46$	
$N^{NT} = 0.54$	

2.1 Calibrating the model

Although there are a few properties that can be studied analytically, to explore fully the dynamics of this model it is necessary to assign values to its parameters and compute approximate numerical solutions. The results described in this chapter were obtained with the linear approximation methods of King, Plosser and Rebelo (1988).

It is very difficult to find empirical studies for the Portuguese economy which can be used to help calibrate the parameters of the model. Estimating these parameters as in Christiano and Eichenbaum (1990) is not feasible since the number of available observations is extremely small. I am left with the option of choosing a baseline scenario and resorting to sensitivity analysis. Table 5.2 summarizes the parameters used in this basic scenario. These parameters were chosen so that each time period represents one year.

The value of N (which represents the number of hours worked) was normalized to one. Since the labour supply is exogenous, N is an irrelevant scale parameter. A^T is also a scale parameter that is normalized to one. A^{NT} was chosen so that the steady state relative price of non-tradables is 1.5.

The value of β was chosen so as to be consistent with the steady state real interest rate (r) of 4%.[5] I assumed, as in Lundvik (1991) and in Correia, Neves and Rebelo (1992), that the international real interest rate coincides with the autarchic steady state real interest rate of our economy. In the model with free capital mobility considered in Section 3, this rules out scenarios in which the country is always a net borrower or a net lender in the steady state (see Becker (1980)). A consequence of this assumption is that, in the economy of Section 3, most macroeconomic variables display a random-walk type behaviour.

The parameter σ was set to be 5 instead of 2, which is the most commonly used parameter value. A higher value of σ was used so that the model can produce realistic values for the rate of growth of gross domestic product (GDP).[6] The elasticity of substitution between tradables and non-tradables is assumed to be one (momentary utility is Cobb-Douglas in equation (1)).

The value of γ was chosen so that the steady state fraction of non-tradables consumption coincides with the weight of non-tradable consumption that underlies the price index in Figure 5.1 (42%). The value of a, the share of labour in the tradables sector, was set at 40%.

The share of government consumption in GDP was set equal to 12% (the average value for the post-war period). I assumed that two-thirds of government expenditure was devoted to non-tradables. Given the value of γ, this implied that in the steady state, 46% of labour is used in the tradables sector and 54% in the non-tradables sector.

The parameter ζ, which represents the elasticity of $\phi'(\cdot)$ (the first derivative of the adjustment cost function) is set equal to -1. This produces realistic speeds of adjustment for the various experiments that I will consider.

The remaining parameters were chosen so that the model reproduces some features displayed by the Portuguese economy in the post-war period, documented in Correia, Neves and Rebelo (1992). The value of v was chosen so that the steady state aggregate labour share coincides with the mean of the labour share (53%). The depreciation rate δ was set equal to 5% so that the steady state investment share coincides with the mean investment share (26%). The share of the trade balance in GDP in the steady state was set equal to -9%. Since Portugal has had a chronic trade deficit that has been financed with net private transfers from abroad (mainly composed of emigrants remittances) I assumed that the ratio of net private transfers to GDP is -8.9%. The values of the trade balance and of the flow of net transfers imply the steady state value of B, the stock of net foreign assets: $B = - (TB + TRF)/r^*$.

2.2 Transitional dynamics

Since the model just described has a structure that is similar to that of the two-sector neo-classical growth model it can potentially exhibit complicated dynamics (deterministic cycles or chaos) of the type studied by Benhabib and Nishimura (1985) and Boldrin (1986). But for all the parameters used in the simulations the model displayed a turnpike property. As in the standard Solow-Cass-Loopmans neo-classical model the economies studied have a stable steady state to which they converge regardless of their initial stock of capital.

One important feature of this convergence process – the evolution of the relative price of non-tradables – can be analysed with pencil and paper if we abstract for a moment from the presence of adjustment costs. Profit maximization by firms ensures that the following two conditions, involving the relative price of non-tradables, p_t, will be satisfied:

$$aA_t^T(K_t^T)^{1-a}(N_t^T)^{a-1} = p_t v A_t^{NT}(K_t^{NT})^{1-v}(N_t^{NT})^{v-1} \tag{9}$$

$$(1-a)A_t^T(K_t^T)^{-a}(N_t^T)^a = p_t(1-v)A_t^{NT}(K_t^{NT})^{-v}(N_t^{NT})^v \tag{10}$$

These conditions require that, at the margin, labour and capital be equally valuable in both sectors. This implies that the capital-labour ratio in the two sectors will be proportional:

$$\frac{a}{1-a}(K_t^T/N_t^T) = \frac{v}{1-v}(K_t^{NT}/N_t^{NT}) \tag{11}$$

and that p_t can be expressed as:

$$p_t = \eta(A^T/A^{NT})(K_t^T/N_t^T)^{v-a} \tag{12}$$

where η is a positive function of the two share parameters, v and a.

Consider an economy with a level of capital stock that is below the steady state. As the economy converges towards its steady state level it increases its capital stock, as well as the capital-labour ratio used in the production of tradables and non-tradables. If v is greater than a, that is, if non-tradables are more labour intensive than tradables, the relative price of non-tradables will rise as the economy marches towards its steady state. In other words, as the capital-labour ratio of the economy rises, the price of the good that is capital intensive – the tradable good – falls.

Countries that peg their currency to that of a low inflation country often do it as part of a policy reform package that might include measures such as tax reform, strengthening property rights, dismantling of trade barriers, and reductions in government consumption.[7] It is reasonable to expect that these reforms will raise the steady state capital stock and set in motion transitional dynamics.

The transitional dynamics of this model are broadly similar to those of the neo-classical growth model described in King and Rebelo (1992). Even though these dynamics deserve to be explored more fully, to con-

Table 5.3. *Alternative shock paths*

	Number of time periods							
	1	2	3	4	5	10	20	∞
Temporary shock	3.00	1.80	1.08	0.65	0.39	0.03	0.00	0.00
Permanent shock Type I	3.00	3.00	3.00	3.00	3.00	3.00	3.00	3.00
Permanent shock Type II	3.00	4.80	5.88	6.53	6.92	7.46	7.50	7.50

serve space I will focus my attention on the behaviour of the rate of inflation.[8]

I searched for initial values for the two capital stocks, K^T and K^{NT} which would be consistent with a maximum output growth rate of 2%. This corresponds to a 4% rate of growth if we think of the steady state growth rate of the economy as 2% per annum.[9] I also required that there be no re-allocation effect associated with the initial capital stocks. When we choose arbitrarily the stocks of capital in the two industries there is generally a tendency to concentrate the investment in one of the industries. This re-allocation effect can have an important impact on the behaviour of the relative price p. This effect was eliminated by simulating the economy with small initial levels of the two capital stocks so that the re-allocation effect occurred before the levels of the capital stock associated with a 2% growth rate were reached. The initial conditions for the capital stocks turned out to be such that K^T and K^{NT} are, respectively, 341% and 282% below their steady state levels.[10] This implies that real GDP is 6.5 times smaller than its steady state values. In this rather extreme scenario the real rate of return measured in terms of installed capital goods is of the order of 8%.

Table 5.4 shows that even with these very low stocks of capital as an initial condition, it is difficult to generate high rates of inflation. The differential between the rates of inflation of tradables and non-tradables associated with the transition dynamics of the model is only 0.38%. The initial rate of growth was (by construction) 2% in the first period and this declined slowly in the following periods. The real wage rate (measured in terms of tradables) increased over time but at a slow rate – about 1% per year.

Before I re-examine these adjustment dynamics with free capital mobility I would like to use this model to study two potential sources of slow inflation convergence considered by Froot and Rogoff (1992): shocks to

Table 5.4. *Economy with capital controls: differences between inflation rates of tradables and non-tradables*

	Number of time periods				
	1	2	3	4	5
Transitional dynamics	0.38	0.38	0.38	0.38	0.38
Temporary shock to A^T	1.11	− 0.42	− 0.25	− 0.15	− 0.09
Permanent shock to A^T (Type I)	1.41	0.01	0.01	0.01	0.01
Permanent shock to A^T (Type II)	1.88	0.66	0.40	0.25	0.16
Temporary shock to G^{NT}	0.17	− 0.07	0.04	− 0.03	− 0.02
Permanent shock to G^{NT} (Type I)	0.12	− 0.00	− 0.00	− 0.00	− 0.00
Permanent shock to G^{NT} (Type II)	0.05	0.19	0.05	0.03	0.01

the productivity of the tradables sector and to the government demand for non-tradables. I will consider three possible paths for each of these shocks which are depicted in Figure 5.2. The first path corresponds to a temporary shock and coincides with the impulse-response function of an AR(1) process with a first-order serial correlation equal to 0.6. The second path corresponds to a permanent 3% increase. The third path corresponds to a permanent increase that is smoothly distributed over time. This path coincides with the impulse response function of an AR(2) process with first and second order partial auto-correlations equal to 1.6 and − 0.6, respectively. These three different paths are also described in Table 5.3.

2.3   Increases in the productivity of the tradables sector

Equation (12) shows that increases in the productivity of the non-tradable sector can generate an increase in p_t provided that the response of N^T to this shock is not too strong. Differences in the evolution of the productivity of the tradables sector have, in fact, been one of the explanations for the failure of purchasing power parity (Balassa (1964) and Samuelson (1964)).

Table 5.4 shows the impact on inflation of the three different shock trajectories described in Table 5.3 and depicted in Figure 5.2. All these

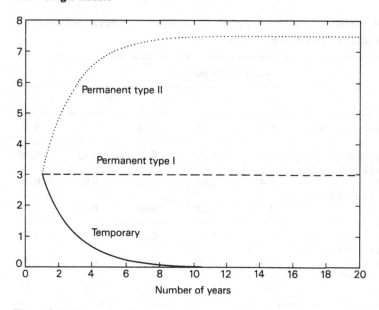

Figure 5.2 Alternative shock paths

shocks raise the real wage and the rate of growth, although only the type II permanent shock does so in a persistent manner. The response of the real variables to the two first types of shocks is qualitatively similar. In both cases Y^T, C^T, N^T rise, while Y^{NT}, C^{NT}, N^{NT} fall. Investment increases in the two sectors in order to spread the effect of the shock over future consumption. In the case of the permanent, type II shock the responses are more complex. I^T and N^T decline in the first few periods while N^{NT} increases initially and then drops below its previous steady state value.

These shock patterns produce inflation effects between 1% and 2% in the initial period and significantly smaller effects in the following periods.

2.4   Increases in the government demand for non-tradables

Froot and Rogoff (1992) considered that the increase in government demand for non-tradables was an important factor underlying the slow convergence of Italian inflation. In contrast, I found that the effects of government expenditure increases on the rate of inflation were extremely small. Table 5.4 shows that the largest effect (for a type II permanent shock) was of the order of 0.19%. In all cases, the initial increase in the government demand for non-tradables was 3%. Since non-tradables expenditures represent two-thirds of overall government expenditure, the initial increase in total government expenditures is two-thirds (3% + $\hat{p}_t$), where $\hat{p}_t$ represents the percentage increase in the relative price of non-tradables. The value of $\hat{p}_t$ is negligible (which is why the inflation effects are small) so the initial increase in government expenditure is 2%.

In all three cases there was an increase in the real wage, a short-lived impact on economic growth, a rise in Y^{NT} and in N^{NT} and a fall in Y^T and C^{NT}. Investment falls in the two sectors. When the shock is permanent the overall capital stock of the economy declines in a permanent manner as the result of a Rybczynski-type effect. As Baxter (1990) emphasized, the steady state capital-labour ratios in the two sectors of a neoclassical model are constant and independent of the pattern of government expenditure. A permanent shock to government expenditure shifts demand toward the non-tradable sector. Since this sector is labour intensive this means that the overall capital stock has to be smaller in the new steady state.

3   Introducing free movement of capital

In this section, I re-examine the three potential sources of appreciation in the relative price of non-tradables in a setting in which private agents can borrow and lend freely in the international capital market at rate r^*.[11] I assumed that $1/\beta$ equals $(1 + r^*)$ so that there exists a steady state in which the value of net foreign assets (B) is constant. Any value of B is compatible with the steady state; economies with larger net foreign assets will simply enjoy higher levels of consumption. All the variables in this economy display a random-walk type of behaviour. Any shock to the system, even temporary, generally produces a permanent effect.

The first line of Table 5.5 shows the impact of an instantaneous liberalization of capital flows. The small inflation effect associated with transitional dynamics in Section 2 is now concentrated in a single period generating an 8.8% inflation differential between tradables and non-tradables. If the liberalization of international capital flows is gradual, as in the second line of Table 5.5 the jump in p_t associated with the inflow of foreign capital can be spread over two or three periods. In the example reported in the table the inflation differential takes on values between 2% and 3% during the first three years.[12]

The effects of shocks to productivity in the tradables sector and to the government demand for non-tradables are, with few exceptions, similar to those of Section 2. The inflation effects are of the same order of magnitude and the qualitative impact of the shocks is similar for most variables. The main new aspect that is introduced in the analysis is the behaviour of the trade balance. The balance of trade deteriorates with permanent

Table 5.5. *Economy with free capital mobility: differences between inflation rates of tradables and non-tradables*

	Number of time periods				
	1	2	3	4	5
Transitional dynamics instantaneous liberalization	8.8	0.05	0.09	0.13	0.16
Transitional dynamics gradual liberalization	2.26	3.41	1.77	0.94	0.54
Temporary shock to A^T	0.88	-0.32	-0.19	-0.11	-0.07
Permanent shock to A^T (Type I)	1.61	-0.00	-0.00	-0.00	-0.00
Permanent shock to A^T (Type II)	2.77	0.49	0.30	0.18	0.11
Temporary shock to G^{NT}	0.06	-0.01	-0.01	-0.01	-0.01
Permanent shock to G^{NT} (Type I)	0.04	-0.00	-0.00	-0.00	-0.00
Permanent shock to G^{NT} (Type II)	-0.15	0.05	0.05	0.04	0.04

shocks to tradables productivity and with temporary shocks to government expenditure. An improvement in the balance of trade is associated with temporary productivity shocks and with permanent shocks to government expenditure.

4   Explaining the nominal facts

So far all the attention has been focused on the behaviour of real quantities but some of the most prominent facts discussed in the introduction have to do with variables such as the nominal interest rate. The introduction of money via a cash-in-advance constraint, as in Lucas (1981), allows us to derive explicitly an expression for the nominal interest rates. Since in the simulations that I studied the rates of inflation generated by the cash-in-advance model were virtually identical to those shown in Tables 5.3 and 5.4, I will only briefly discuss the novel aspects associated with the introduction of money.

Given that the economy has adopted a fixed exchange rate regime the nominal price of tradables, P_t^T is given by the product of the exchange rate (e) and the international price of tradables (P_t^{T*}): $P_t^T = P_t^{T*}$. Monetary policy is assumed to be passive: the stock of money is made endogenous by the choice of the exchange rate e.

Anticipated inflation has, in this economy, effects that are similar to those of output taxation. This is particularly clear in the equation that determines the steady state capital stock:

$$[\beta/(1 + \pi)](1 - a)A_t^T(K_t^T)^{-a}(N_t^T)^a + 1 - \delta = 1/\beta \tag{13}$$

The left-hand side of this expression represents one plus the real interest rate which, as usual, has to equal $1/\beta$, to be consistent with zero consumption growth. Since $1/\beta$ is assumed to be equal to $1 + r^*$, so equation (13) can also be interpreted as equating the domestic real rate of return to the international real rate of return.

As in the standard neo-classical model (see Stockman (1981)) higher rates of inflation (π) act like a tax on investment depressing the steady state capital stock. When the rate of inflation is equal to $1/\beta - 1$ (the Friedman rule) the steady state of this economy coincides with that of the models of Sections 2 and 3. The distortionary effects of inflation are quantitatively small in this model, as in Cooley and Hansen (1988).

The nominal interest rate is related to the real rates by familiar Fisher-type formulas:

$$(1 + r_t^n) = (1 + r_t^T)(P_{t+1}^T/P_t^T) \tag{14}$$

$$(1 + r_t^n) = (1 + r_t^{NT})(P_{t+1}^{NT}/P_t^{NT}) \tag{15}$$

P_{t+1}^T/P_t^T is the expected tradables inflation (which is exogenous to our small open economy) while P_{t+1}^{NT}/P_t^{NT} is the expected inflation in terms of non-tradables.

As was emphasized by Dornbusch (1983) and Bruno (1976) in a similar context, there are two real interest rates in this model; one for loans denominated in tradable goods (r_t^T) and the other for loans denomninated in terms of non-tradables (r_t^{NT}). These two rates, which are related by a simple condition:

$$(1 + r_t^T) = (p_{t+1}/p_t)(1 + r_t^{NT}) \tag{16}$$

coincide only in the steady state (where the relative price of non-tradables is constant).

To verify whether the model with capital controls described in Section 3 is consistent with the 'nominal facts' described in the introduction (the rate of inflation and the nominal interest rate are higher than in other countries) we need to supply more information about the foreign country to which the currency is pegged. A natural assumption is that that country is in the steady state, so that its relative price of non-tradables is constant and the international real interest rate (r^*) is equal to $(1/\beta - 1)$. Under these assumptions the rate of inflation and the nominal interest rate in the foreign country councide with the values of these variables in the steady state of our economy. This means that the model is successful in reproducing the two 'nominal facts' since both the rate of inflation and the nominal interest rate are higher than their steady state values. In a monetary version of the Section 2 economy, the nominal interest rate depends on the equilibrium choices of the consumption of the two goods. In contrast, the rate of inflation under free capital mobility is independent of these choices.

The main new insight obtained by introducing money into the model is related to the Walters (1990) critique. Walters has argued that, since free capital mobility and fixed exchange rates will ensure that all the countries in the exchange rate mechanism (ERM) have the same nominal interest rates, economies with high inflation will have low (perhaps negative) real interest rates. This will create inflationary pressures that will undermine the credibility of the fixed exchange rate. This critique does not apply to the monetary version of the model in this section. In this model free capital mobility and a fixed exchange rate ensure the convergence of nominal interest rates but they also ensure that the tradables real interest rate converges. It is the non-tradables real interest rate that will take on low values but this is not inconsistent with capital mobility nor is it the source of inflationary pressures.

5   Summary and conclusions

In this chapter, I have examined the extent to which the slow convergence of inflation in Portugal could be the result of real forces that produce an appreciation in the relative price of non-tradables. In the experiments that I considered, the effects of shocks to the productivity of the tradable sector and to the government demand for non-tradables produce an inflation differential between tradables and non-tradables of between 1% and 3%. These effects were generally concentrated in a single period. This largely reflects the fact that I considered shocks that were not anticipated from the standpoint of the first period but that were perfectly foreseen after that. A more sophisticated modelling of the evolution of the shocks and of the expectations of the private sector could probably generate more persistence in the effects that I isolated.

The process of transition toward the steady state of an economy with low capital stock can also be responsible for an appreciation of the relative price of non-tradables. While this appreciation occurs slowly in an economy with free capital mobility, it can produce large inflation differentials between tradables and non-tradables in a period in which international capital flows are liberalized.

Although I experimented with different parameter values and avoided reporting results that were too sensitive to parameter configuration, more sensitivity analysis is warranted given the low degree of confidence that can be attached to some of the parameter values and to the paths followed by the shocks. One avenue that seems promising is to consider non-unitary elasticities of substitution between tradables and non-tradables.

I view the experiments considered here as first steps in evaluating whether real forces play an important role in the inflation convergence process. The reason why this is an important question is that if this is the case, the Walters critique does not apply. Two economies linked by a fixed exchange rate and free capital mobility can have different rates of inflation. The economy with a high inflation rate will have a low (perhaps negative) non-tradables real rate of interest but the tradables real interest rate will be the same in both countries. This real interest rate configuration does not in itself fuel the inflation process and undermine the fixed exchange rate regime.

To put it differently, the models in this chapter suggest that it is not necessary for the rate of inflation to be identical in two countries linked by fixed exchange rate regimes. To join a fixed exchange regime such as the European monetary system, the convergence of inflation for tradable goods should be enough. Higher rates of inflation associated with movements in the relative price of non-tradables caused by real factors are compatible with a fixed exchange rate regime.

There are some obvious shortcomings and extensions of the analysis considered in this chapter. The behaviour of other macroeconomic variables, such as the balance of trade and the current account provide important additional information that should be considered when evaluating the outcome of the different experiments. The description of government policy in the economy is another area in which there is plenty of room for refinement. Incorporating distortionary taxation and public debt may increase the role of government shocks in the inflationary process.

The commitment of the Portuguese monetary authorities to a fixed exchange rate regime is extremely recent. It started in October of 1990 and was strengthened on 6 April, 1992 when Portugal joined the exchange rate mechanism of the EMS. As more data becomes available on the recent periods it will be useful to compare the Portuguese experience with those of Spain and Italy.

Two theoretical developments provide a natural follow up to the analysis in this chapter. The first is the study of a dynamic version of the Scandinavian model that incorporates capital mobility. The second is the study of the credibility issues, emphasized by Miller and Sutherland in

Chapter 3 of this volume, against the backdrop of the theoretical models considered here.

NOTES

I benefited from conversations with José Ramalho, José Scheinkman and Nathan Sheets, from the comments of David Backus, Antonio Pinto Barbosa, Isabel H. Correia, Francesco Giavazzi, Tryphon Kolllintzas, Michael Moore, João C. Neves, Guido Tabellini and seminar participants at Athens University, and from the research assistance of José M. Tavares. The essay was completed during my visit to the Institute for International Economic Studies in Stockholm. I am grateful to the Institute for its support and to Graziela Kaminsky, Assar Lindbeck, Torsten Persson, and Lars Svensson for many helpful suggestions. Any errors or shortcomings are my own.

1 Recent empirical analyses of the link between inflation and exchange rate policy in Portugal include Cunha and Machado (1992) and Barbosa (1992). Theoretical analyses of the effects of financial integration include Gaspar and Macedo (1991), Antão and Brito (1992), and Gaspar and Pereira (1992).

2 The data that underlies the figures, with the exception of the German rate of inflation and nominal interest rate, were compiled from several issues of the Banco de Portugal *Quarterly Bulletin*. The German rate of inflation is based on the consumer price index, while the nominal interest rate corresponds to the Public Authority bond yield. Both of these series were extracted from *International Financial Statistics* published by the International Monetary Fund, Washington. The method employed in the construction of separate price indices for tradables and non-tradables is described in Nascimento (1990). Goods were classified as tradables or non-tradables depending on their characteristics but goods whose price is controlled directly by the government (e.g. gas and motor oil) were included in the non-tradables category. The 'jumps' observed in the relative price of non-tradables (e.g. in January 1990) are generally due to the liberalization of these government-controlled prices.

3 The weights used by the Instituto Nacional de Estatística to construct the consumer price index changed in 1988. The rates of inflation for 1988 have to be interpreted with caution because they are artificially influenced by this change.

4 Figure 5.1 depicts two series for securities denominated in Portuguese escudos: the long series corresponds to money market loans with maturities from 30–60 days; the short series corresponds to the yield on Treasury bills with 30 days maturity.

5 This is the average real rate of return to capital in the USA during the post-war period (see Prescott (1986)).

6 Giovannini (1985) discusses evidence that is consistent with the view that the elasticity of inter-temporal substitution $(1/\sigma)$ is lower in less-developed countries.

7 Argentina's Convertibility Act, enacted in April 1991, is a recent example of implementation of a reform package that includes pegging to a low inflation currency (the US dollar).

8 Inflation is measured as the growth rate of the consumption deflator. To study the rate of inflation associated with the transition to the steady state, I

constructed a deflator using the values of C^T and C^{NT} in period zero. To study the inflation effects of shocks to productivity and to government expenditures, I constructed the consumption deflator using the steady state values of C^T and C^{NT}.

9 This economy does not grow once it reaches the steady state, but it would be trivial to introduce steady state growth while preserving all the properties discussed next.

10 The linear approximation techniques used here may produce poor results for levels of the capital stock that are far from the steady state (see King and Rebelo 1992). Ideally, the results presented here should be complemented by those obtained with an approximation technique that does not rely on local approximations, e.g. the method proposed by Mulligan (1992).

11 See Razin (1984) for a similar analysis in a two-period setting.

12 This example was constructed by finding the international real interest rate such that the country would not change its foreign asset position in the first period. It was assumed that 50% of the difference between this rate and 4% was eliminated each period and that this was foreseen by private agents. This is not exactly equivalent to a liberalization of the capital markets partly because changes in the international real interest rate affect the return on foreign asset holdings. Since the value of B is very small, however, this effect is negligible.

REFERENCES

Abel, A. and O. Blanchard (1983) 'An Intertemporal Equilibrium Model of Savings and Investment,' *Econometrica*, **51**, 675–92.

Antão, M. and P. Brito (1992) 'Financial Liberalization and Adhesion to EMS – The Dynamics of Adjustment in Portugal', in J. Amaral, D. Lucena and A. Mello, *The Portuguese Economy Towards 1992*, Dordrecht and London: Kluwer Academic Publishers.

Aukrust, O. (1977) 'Inflation in an Open Economy: A Norwegian Model', in L. Krause and W. Salant, eds *Worldwide Inflation*, The Brookings Institution, Washington, DC.

Backus, D., P. Kehoe and F. Kydland (1992) 'International Real Business Cycles', *Journal of Political Economy*.

Balassa, B. (1964) 'The Purchasing Power Parity Doctrine: A Reappraisal', *Journal of Political Economy*, 584–96.

Barbosa, A. (1992) 'Inflation in Portugal, 1979–1992: An Empirical Investigation', in progress, New University of Lisbon.

Baxter, M. (1990) 'Fiscal Policy, Specialization, and Trade in the Two Sector Model: The Return of Ricardo?', Working Paper 250, Rochester Center for Economic Research.

Baxter, M. and M. Crucini (1992) 'Explaining Saving/Investment Correlations', *American Economic Review*.

Becker, R. (1980) 'On the Long-Run Steady State in a Simple Dynamic Model of Equilibrium with Heterogeneous Households', *Quarterly Journal of Economics*, **95**, 375–82.

Benhabib, J. and K. Nishimura (1985) 'Competitive Equilibrium Cycles', *Journal of Economic Theory*, **35**, 284–306.

Boldrin, M. (1986) 'Paths of Optimal Accumulation in Two-Sector Models', in

W. Barnett, J. Geweke, and K. Shell, eds, *Economic Complexity: Chaos, Sunspots, Bubbles and Non-linearity*, Cambridge: Cambridge University Press.

Bruno, M. (1976) 'The Two-Sector Open Economy and the Real Exchange Rate', *American Economic Review*, 66, 566–77.

Christiano, L. and M. Eichenbaum (1990) 'Current Real Business Cycle Models and Aggregate Labor Markets', mimeo, Northwestern University.

Cooley, T. and G. Hansen (1988), 'The Inflation Tax in a Real Business Cycle Model', *American Economic Review*, 79, 733–48.

Correia, I., J. Neves, and S. Rebelo (1992) 'Business Cycles in Portugal: Theory and Evidence', in J. Amaral, D. Lucena and A. Mello (eds), *The Portuguese Economy Towards 1992*, Dordrecht and London: Kluwer Academic Publishers.

Cunha, L. and J. Machado (1992) 'Inflação em Contexto de Integração de Mercados: O Caso Português', mimeo, New University of Lisbon.

Dornbusch, R. (1983) 'Real Interest Rates, Home Goods, and Optimal External Borrowing', *Journal of Political Economy*, 91, 141–53.

Frenkel, J. and A. Razin (1987) *Fiscal Policies and the World Economy*, Cambridge, Mass.: MIT Press.

Froot, K. and K. Rogoff (1992) 'The EMS, the EMU and the Transition to a Common Currency', *NBER Macroeconomics Annual 1991*.

Gaspar, V. and B. Macedo (1991) 'Financial Integration and Macroeconomic Stabilization, mimeo, New University of Lisbon.

Gaspar, V. and A. Pereira (1992) 'The Impact of Financial Integration and Unilateral Public Transfers on Investment and Economic Growth', mimeo, New University of Lisbon.

Giovannini, A. (1985) 'Savings and the Real Interest Rate in LDCs', *The Journal of Development Economics*, 17, 197–217.

Greenwood, J. (1984) 'Non-Traded Goods, the Trade Balance, and the Balance of Payments', *Canadian Journal of Economics*, 17, 806–23.

Hayashi, F. (1982) 'Tobin's Marginal q and Average q: A Neoclassical Interpretation', *Econometrica*, 50.

King, R. and S. Rebelo (1992) 'Transitional Dynamics and Economic Growth in the Neoclassical Model', *American Economic Review*.

King, R., C. Plosser and S. Rebelo (1988) 'Production, Growth and Business Cycles: I – The Basic Neoclassical Model', *Journal of Monetary Economis*, 21, 195–232.

Lindbeck, A. (1979) 'Imported and Structural Inflation and Aggregate Demand: the Scandinavian Model Reconstructed', in A. Lindbeck (ed.), *Inflation and Employment in Open Economies*, Amsterdam, New York and Oxford: North-Holland.

Lucas, R. (1981), 'Equilibrium in a Pure Currency Economy', *Economic Inquiry*, 18, 203–20.

Lucas, R. and E. Prescott (1971) 'Investment under Uncertainty', *Econometrica*, 39.

Lundvik, P. (1991) 'Business Cycles in a Small Open Economy: Sweden 1871–1987', mimeo, Institute for International Economic Studies, Stockholm.

Mendoza, E. (1991) 'Real Business Cycles in a Small Open Economy', *American Economic Review*, 81, 797–818.

Mulligan, C. (1992) 'Computing Transitional Dynamics in Recursive Growth Models: the Method of Progressive Paths', mimeo, University of Chicago.

Nascimento, T. (1990) 'Indicadores de Inflação', *Quarterly Bulletin*, Banco de Portugal, Vol. 12, n. 4.

Obstfeld, M. (1981) 'Macroeconomic Policy, Exchange Rate Dynamics and Optimal Asset Accumulation', *Journal of Political Economy*, **89**, 1142–61.

Persson, T. and L. Svensson (1985) 'Current Account Dynamics and the Terms of Trade: Harberger-Laursen-Metzler Two Generations Later', *Journal of Political Economy*, **93**, 43–65.

Prescott, E. (1986) 'Theory Ahead of Business Cycle Measurement', *Federal Reserve Bank of Minneapolis Quarterly Review*, 9–22.

Razin, A. (1984) 'Capital Movements, Intersectoral Resource Shifts and the Trade Balance', *European Economic Review*, **26**, 135–52.

Samuelson, P. (1964) 'Theoretical Notes on Trade Problems', *Review of Economics and Statistics*, 145–54.

Stockman, A. (1981) 'Anticipated Inflation and the Capital Stock in a Cash-in-Advance Economy', *Journal of Monetary Economics*, **8**, 387–93.

Svensson, L. and A. Razin (1983) 'The Terms of Trade and the Current Account: The Harberger-Laursen-Metzler Effect', *Journal of Political Economy*, **91**, 97–125.

Walters, A. (1990) 'Sterling in Danger: The Economic Consequences of Pegged Exchange Rates', mimeo.

Discussion

MICHAEL MOORE

According to some versions of purchasing power parity (and interest rate parity), a credible fixed or quasi-fixed exchange rate ensures that the inflation rate (and nominal interest rate) will converge to those of the reserve currency country. In the experience of many countries in the European monetary system (EMS), this convergence has been very slow. Rebelo's chapter is motivated by the fact that Portugal has experienced this lack of convergence since the Escudo began to track the ECU in October 1990.

His approach to analysing the problem is to simulate a model taken from the real business cycle literature modified by the Scandinavian model. In essence he argues that (a) if the capital stock is below the steady state and (b) if non-tradables are more labour intensive than tradables, then the relative price of non-tradables rises as the economy moves towards the steady state. This determines the adjustment of inflation and interest rates.

This discussion is critical of Rebelo's strategy for the following reasons. First, it is argued that whatever its pedagogic merits, the weaknesses of dividing goods into traded and non-traded categories present substantive difficulties for empirical applications. Second, even the most uncritical exponents of the real business cycle approach should be concerned about a model that purports to explain *nominal* magnitudes like inflation and interest rates by *real* variables. The third point is that Rebelo's arguments are essentially presented in a closed economy framework.

D.5.1 Traded versus non-traded goods

The utility function of the representative individual takes the following form:

$$U = \sum_{t=0}^{\infty} \beta^t \frac{1}{1-\sigma} [(C_t^T)^\gamma (C_t^{NT})^{1-\gamma})^{1-\sigma} - 1] \quad \sigma > 0, \gamma > 0, 0 < \beta < 1 \quad (D.1)$$

where C_t^T and C_t^{NT} are consumption of tradables and non-tradables respectively. In Rebelo's simulations, γ, the 'share' parameter is set to 0.43; σ, the inverse of the inter-temporal elasticity of substitution, is 5 and the subjective discount rate is assumed to be 0.96. The aggregate consumption price index corresponding to this utility function is the unit utility expenditure function:[1]

$$P_t = E(P_t^T, P_t^{NT}, 1) = \bar{k}(P_t^T)^\gamma, (P_t^{NT})^{1-\gamma} \qquad (D.2)$$

where $\bar{k}$ is a constant, and P_t, P_t^T, and P_t^{NT} are the aggregate price level, the price of traded goods and the price of non-traded goods respectively. Equation (D.2) implies that the inflation differential i.e. the gap between the home and foreign inflation rates is proportional to the rate of change of the real exchange rate:

$$\dot{P}_t - \dot{P}_t^T = (1 - \gamma)\dot{p}_t \qquad (D.3)$$

where $\dot{p}_t = \dot{P}_t^{NT} - \dot{P}_t^T$. There are a number of technical points which arise from equation (D.3). First, Rebelo uses an aggregate price index which is a weighted arithmetic mean of the prices of tradables and non-tradables i.e.

$$P_t = \omega P_t^T + (1 - \omega)P_t^{NT} \qquad (D.4)$$

Equation (D.4) is inconsistent with the utility function which is being used and it is not clear how to interpret ω.

Second, there is no discussion about what is meant by 'traded' goods. Presumably, it means those goods for which instantaneous purchasing power parity (PPP) holds. It is perfectly possible, however, that no such goods exist (Fraser, Taylor and Webster (1991)).[2] Third, it is not obvious why consumer preferences should be separable across a purely production characteristic of goods such as transportability. Furthermore, whether or not a good is transportable is not fixed. On the contrary, it is endogenous and depends on the internal terms of trade. Examples of this include some health and education services which have changed from being local goods to internationally traded services. This is undoubtedly because their relative prices have risen.

D.5.2 Nominal versus real magnitudes

Rebelo presents three variations on the model in the text. The first is a closed economy with no money from which most of the simulations are drawn; the second is a closed 'monetary' economy and the final economy has an external financial asset. Money is introduced through a binding cash-in-advance constraint:

$$\phi^T P_t^T (C_t^T + I_t^T + G_t^T) + \phi^{NT} P_t^{NT}(C_t^{NT} + G_t^{NT}) \le M_t^d \tag{D.5}$$

I_t^T, G_t^T, G_t^{NT} are investment in traded goods and government purchases of traded goods and non-traded goods respectively. Φ^T and Φ^{NT} are the fractions of traded and non-traded expenditures which require advance funding. In the simulations, Φ^T is set to unity and Φ^{NT} is $\frac{1}{2}$.

It is not at all clear why traded and non-traded goods should have different cash-in-advance requirements. No justification is offered by Rebelo and in the absence of a currency substitution framework, it is difficult to think of one which is convincing.

If Φ^T and Φ^{NT} are both set to unity, equation (D.5) amounts to the standard one sector cash-in-advance constraint. As is well known, this asserts rather than explains the quantity equation and primarily provides a nominal anchor for an otherwise real model. The model does exhibit, however, the classical non-neutrality whereby higher rates of anticipated inflation act like a tax on investment, depressing the stock of capital in the steady state. Cooley and Hansen (1989) examined this non-neutrality in the context of a simulated real business cycle model of the USA and they found that its real effects are small for moderate rates of inflation such as Portugal's. A surprising feature of Rebelo's 'monetary' model is that there is no domestic financial asset other than cash. Consequently, there is no explicit nominal rate of interest even though this is one of the two principal variables which the author wishes to explain for Portugal. The nominal interest rate is defined implicitly through the Fisher effect:

$$r_t^n = r_t^T + \dot{P}_t^T = r_t^{NT} + \dot{P}_t^{NT} \tag{D.6}$$

r_t^n, r_t^T and r_t^{NT} are the nominal rate of interest and the return on capital in the traded and non-traded sectors respectively. There does not appear to be anything fundamentally monetary about the analysis.

D.5.3 Open versus closed economies

The last of the three models is also the first model to have open economy characteristics. In an attempt to examine the impact of capital controls, Rebelo introduces an external financial asset. The absence of such an asset implies that in the earlier models, the current account surplus was identically zero at all times. Since most of the intuitions and simulations are derived from these earlier models, it is hard to avoid the conclusion that the 'openness' of the economy is not an essential feature of the results. In fact the openness seems to be an after-thought which is required to define the nominal price of traded goods:

$$P_t^T = eP_t^{T'} \tag{D.7}$$

e is the domestic price of foreign currency and $P_t^{T'}$ is the price of traded goods in foreign currency. Equation (D.7) is also required to justify the internal terms of trade $p_t = P_t^{NT}/P_t^T$. In the simulations, however, this open-economy relationship is never actually used. A purely domestic nominal price index is decomposed into two categories. The aggregate price index is then related to one of its nominal components (labelled 'traded goods') and a relative price (labelled 'traded' to 'non-traded' goods) along the lines of equation (D.3). This equation, however, is tautologically true for any binary division of goods.

D.5.4 Conclusion

In this discussion, it has been argued that Rebelo's attempt to simulate recent Portuguese inflation and interest rate experience is not convincing. In order to explain nominal magnitudes in a small open economy, it is not a good strategy to base the essential results on a closed barter economy.

NOTES

1. The constant $\bar{k}$ is a non-linear function of σ and γ.
2. Indeed, there is a lot of empirical evidence against long-run PPP. For a summary of this and a theoretical discussion see Moore (1991).

REFERENCES

Cooley, Thomas F. and Gary D. Hansen (1989) 'The Inflation Tax in a Real Business Cycle', *American Economic Review*, Vol. 79, **4**, 733–48.
Fraser, Patricia, M.P. Taylor and A. Webster (1991) 'An Empirical Examination of Long-Run PPP as Theory of International Commodity Arbitrage', *Applied Economics*, Vol. 23, **11**, 1749–60.
Moore, Michael J. (1991) 'Covered Purchasing Power Parity, Ex-Ante PPP and Risk Aversion', Working Paper AF/91–7, Queen's University of Belfast, November.

Discussion

GUIDO TABELLINI

The problem addressed in this chapter is a fundamental problem for several countries, not just for Portugal. It is almost a 'stylized fact': when a high inflation country attempts to bring down inflation by fixing the exchange rate, it experiences a large and lasting appreciation of the price of non-tradable relative to traded goods. In Spain and Italy, for instance, lack of inflation convergence is attributable to a prolonged increase in the relative price of non-tradable relative to traded goods. The same was true of the Southern Cone countries during their stabilization attempts in the late 1970s and early 1980s (see *World Development*, 1985). Understanding why this relative price change occurs, and why it lasts for so long, is thus central to our understanding of inflation convergence in a fixed exchange rate system.

In the literature two explanations can be found for the appreciation of the relative price of non-tradables. The first and most popular one argues that the appreciation is due to some distortion: lack of credibility of the exchange rate peg (*World Development*, 1985), public sector wages growing too fast for non-economic reasons (CEPR, 1991), or some microeconomic rigidities in the labour market or in specific markets for non-tradables (for instance, backward-looking wage indexation in the non-tradable sectors – *World Development* 1985). Central to these explanations is some non-neutrality of the nominal exchange rate regime.

The second kind of explanation, on the other hand, tells a real equilibrium story. The appreciation is a real phenomenon that does not reflect any distortion. Perhaps the oldest example is the Balassa (1964) hypothesis that productivity growth is higher in the traded goods sector. More recently, Froot and Rogoff (1992) have suggested that the relative price change in some countries in the European monetary system (EMS) has been caused by a surge of public expenditures in non-tradable goods. Rebelo in this chapter combines these two examples in a standard two-sector neo-classical growth model. He adds a third possible explanation for the relative price change. During the adjustment to the steady state, the capital-labour ratio rises. If the non-tradable sector is labour intensive, this results in a prolonged increase in its relative price.

These two kinds of explanation have strikingly different implications. If, indeed, the relative price change reflects a distortion then eventually it needs to be corrected either through fiscal policy or by a future nominal devaluation. According to the real equilibrium approach, however, the relative price change is the correct response of the economy to some real phenomenon unrelated to the exchange rate regime. The worries about lack of inflation convergence are wrong, and a mistake was made at Maastricht when inflation was included as one of the convergence critieria.

Hence, it is extremely important to make a distinction between these two alternative explanations. Rebelo is to be commended for setting up a coherent framework where the evaluation of at least one of the two candidate explanations is possible.

The conclusion suggested by this evaluation, though, is not favourable to the real equilibrium story. As remarked in the chapter, this neo-classical model is very successful at providing qualitative predictions consistent with the stylized facts. But the model fails miserably in the quantitative aspect. The order of magnitude of the change in the relative price predicted by the model is far too small compared with the actual change. Since 1990 (the year when the exchange rate was pegged), the relative price of non-tradables in Portugal has risen by over 10%. In the most favourable case, and summing all three possible reasons for the change (transitional dynamics, shock to public consumption and productivity shock), the theoretical model only predicts a relative price change of less than 2.5% in the immediately subsequent year. Moreover, the predicted price change does not continue over the next period. We know, however, from the experience of the other high-inflation European countries that the price of non-tradables continued to appreciate for several years. On this ground alone, the real equilibrium explanation does not come out well.

But there are other problems with this explanation, not evident from the data described in the chapter. A prediction of the model, implied by the

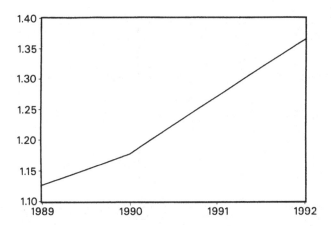

Figure D.5.1 Labour share of income, manufacturing sector, Portugal relative to other OECD countries
Note: Labour share of income is computed as relative unit labour cost divided by the relative export prices of manufactures, both in a common currency
Source: Economic Outlook, Organisation for Economic Cooperation and Development, Paris

Cobb-Douglas production function, is that the income shares of labour and capital remain constant in both sectors over time. This prediction is not borne out by the facts; on the contrary a systematic pattern emerges. Figure D.5.1 displays the labour share of income in the manufacturing sector in Portugal relative to other OECD countries. This measure is both higher than unity and rising very rapidly, indicating that the share of capital – and hence profitability in general – in the Portuguese manufacturing sector is lower and diminishing relative to the other countries. Figures D.5.2–D.5.4 indicate that the same phenomenon is occurring in the other high inflation countries within the EMS, Italy, Spain and the UK, although on a smaller scale. The relative labour share in the manufacturing sector in the low-inflation countries in the EMS (France, Germany, Belgium, Denmark and the Netherlands) is, on the other hand, lower than unity and slowly declining – Figure D.5.5. Thus, these figures suggest an important 'stylized fact'. Labour costs are squeezing profit margins in the high inflation countries relative to their low inflation partners in the EMS.

I conjecture that it would be difficult to account for this stylized fact within the neo-classical growth model, even allowing for a more general production function. On the other hand, this stylized fact is consistent with the distortion-explanations of the lack of inflation convergence, and

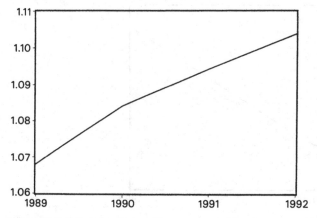

Figure D.5.2 Labour share of income manufacturing sector, Italy relative to other OECD countries
Source: Economic Outlook, Organisation for Economic Cooperation and Development, Paris

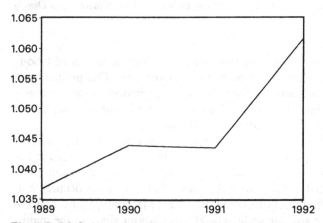

Figure D.5.3 Labour share of income manufacturing sector, Spain relative to other OECD countries
Source: Economic Outlook, Organisation for Economic Cooperation and Development, Paris

more generally with the idea that the appreciation of non-tradables relative to traded goods is not sustainable. Rapidly rising public sector wages, or backward-looking wage indexation, or lack of credibility of the exchange rate peg, put upward pressure on nominal wages. The non-traded goods sector can pass on the wage increases through higher prices, because this sector is shielded from foreign competition. In the traded

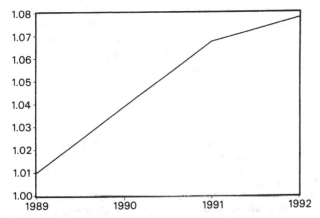

**Figure D.5.4 Labour share of income manufacturing sector, United Kingdom rela-
tive to other OECD countries**
Source: Economic Outlook, Organisation for Economic Cooperation and Development, Paris

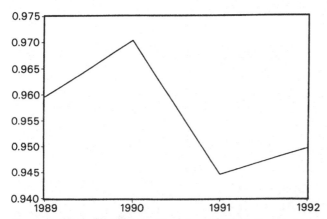

**Figure D.5.5 Labour share of income manufacturing sector, average of Denmark,
France, Belgium and the Netherlands relative to other OECD countries**
Source: Economic Outlook, Organisation for Economic Cooperation and Devel-
opment, Paris

goods sector this is not possible. Hence both a higher price of non-
tradables relative to traded goods can be seen as well as a profit squeeze in
the traded goods sector.

Summarizing then, a very important question has been addressed in this
chapter, and I certainly learnt a lot from the analysis. But what I think I
learnt is that the answer to the question posed in the chapter is probably

not in the real equilibrium model studied by Rebelo. The next step in this line of research is to formulate the alternative class of explanations, based on some underlying distortion, in a coherent model, and to enquire into its empirical validity with the same rigour and with the same demanding standards imposed by Rebelo in this chapter.

REFERENCES

Balassa, B. (1964) 'The Purchasing Power Parity Doctrine: A Reappraisal', *Journal of Political Economy*, 584–96.
Centre for Economic Policy Research (1991) 'Monitoring European Integration – The Making of Monetary Union', Annual Report, London.
Froot, K. and K. Rogoff (1992) 'The EMS, the EMU and the Transition to a Common Currency', *NBER Macroeconomics Annual 1991*, Cambridge Mass.: MIT Press.
World Development (1985) 'Symposium on Stabilization in the Southern Cone', special issue of *World Development*, vol. 13, n. 8.

6   Models of economic integration and localized growth

GIUSEPPE BERTOLA

1   Introduction and overview

European economies are fast approaching complete integration, with elimination of legal restrictions to trade and factor mobility, increasing credibility of fixed exchange rates, and better coordination of economic policies. The legal and institutional process of economic integration among the 'core' countries of the European Community (EC) will be essentially complete by the end of 1992. As linguistic and cultural barriers to economic interaction weaken as well, Europe should soon become as much of a single economic entity as the United States of America. The question naturally arises of what difference this will make to overall economic performance on the one hand, and to regional developments on the other.

If economic borders represented artificial restrictions in an otherwise undistorted economic system, their elimination would necessarily yield welfare improvements at the aggregate level. An integrated Europe should then enjoy increased production efficiency and faster capital accumulation. Baldwin (1989) and Rivera-Batiz and Romer (1991) studied the effects of economic integration in models of investment-driven economic growth. Increasing returns to scale are crucial to the mechanics of growth in models which account for use in production of non-accumulated factors (such as land and labour). Since constant returns to accumulation of knowledge and/or physical capital are necessary for investment to sustain steady growth, aggregate production must have increasing returns to scale as a function of accumulated and non-accumulated factors together.[1] Economic integration increases the extent to which such economies of scale may be exploited, and affords a step increase in the level and the rate of growth of aggregate production.

The less developed (or 'catching-up') European regions and countries, however, look with some trepidation at the dissolution of economic borders. Countries like Spain, Portugal, and Greece have only recently begun the process of integration. Given the large differences between status-quo income and productivity levels in these and the core countries it is legitimate to wonder whether integration will lead to convergent or divergent developments. At the theoretical level, if increasing returns to scale are as important as recent models of endogenous growth suggest, and if they may be exploited along geographical dimensions as well as over time, then removal of obstacles to factor reallocation may well lead to concentration of production and growth in privileged regions. Within a given country or region, in fact, production is concentrated (in cities) and specialized. If sectoral and geographical developments are considered from the point of view of endogenous-growth theories, as in Rauch (1991), it will be found that divergent economic development is not inconsistent with the increased efficiency and faster aggregate growth emphasized by Baldwin (1989). Geographic concentration of production and growth might indeed be necessary to exploit the scale economies made possible by economic integration.

Inasmuch as removal of economic barriers and the resulting concentration of production and growth do yield welfare improvements at the aggregate level, the implications of endogenous-growth models are no different from those of standard distortion-free models of international economic policy, as surveyed by Baldwin (1984). At the normative level, the owners of those factors of production which are hurt (rather than helped) by economic integration should receive compensation financed by taxing those factors of production which gain disproportionately. In so far as such policies may be difficult to design and implement under the constraints of real-life policy-making, institutional resistance to potentially beneficial reforms may explain persistent implementation of inferior policies, as well as an economy's growth behaviour in endogenous-growth models such as those of Persson and Tabellini (1991), Perotti (1990), Bertola (1991a), and Alesina and Rodrik (1991).

With endogenous growth, however, the welfare effects of economic integration are amplified by changes in growth rates, and need not represent a welfare improvement: with increasing returns to scale at the aggregate level, the economy cannot feature the perfect, complete markets that would ensure optimization of the integrated economy's production possibilities. Accordingly, it is important to consider which corrective policies might be desirable following the elimination of the status-quo mobility restrictions. Even in the presence of the dynamic or static scale economies that make unceasing endogenous growth possible, *geographic* concentration of production need not be socially optimal, and the models of geographic location with externalities or increasing returns studied by

Krugman (1991), Burda and Wyplosz (1991), and others are relevant to the analysis of post-1992 economic developments in Europe. To clarify the point, in this chapter a stylized model of integration and growth is outlined which distinguishes the aggregate scale economies that are dynamically necessary to sustain endogenous growth on the one hand, and localized scale economies on the other. The latter may lead to privately optimal, but socially harmful concentration of production: when external linkages exist between social returns in different localities, private investment decisions are statically as well as dynamically distorted away from the first-best accumulation path. Free factor mobility may compound the two distortions and lead to a deterioration of social productivity and of growth.

In Section 2 a brief outline is given of the aggregate structure of endogenous-growth models, and in Section 3 economic integration among endogenously-growing economic entities is discussed. Modelling economic integration by simply juxtaposing closed-economy models of endogenous growth yields quite dramatic implications. If one of two formerly independently growing economic entities being integrated is even slightly less conducive to production and innovation, then it will shrivel down as in Rauch (1991). Frightening as this may be for agents with equity in this disappearing region, the outcome is likely to be socially preferable to the status quo.

In Section 4 a stylized model of linkages across endogenously-growing localities is proposed, and the implications for the static and dynamic effects of economic integration discussed. The results may not be as dramatic, but are potentially much more worrying. In Section 5 it will be found that the same asymmetries that would make one country disappear in simpler, linkage-free models can now lead to *slower* rather than faster growth in an integrated economy where factor mobility is completely unrestrained. In this setting, a case can be made for distortionary policy interventions along with redistributive ones. The concluding Section 6 sketches the positive and normative implications of the model for post-1992 Europe, and outlines directions for further research.

2   Investment and macroeconomic growth

Omitting time indexes, let output Y be produced according to

$$Y = AK^{\alpha}L^{\beta}, \tag{1}$$

where A indexes the level of disembodied productivity as well as the productivity of factors other than capital K and labour L, such as land. While the supply of L is exogenously given, capital is endogenously accumulated by decisions to invest rather than consume current output. Measuring aggregate consumption C in the same units as output and letting P denote the consumption price of a newly installed capital unit, the stock of capital evolves over time according to

$$\dot{K} = (Y - C)/P - \delta K, \tag{2}$$

where the dot denotes a time derivative and δ is the rate of depreciation of the aggregate capital stock. Depreciation may be taken to reflect continuous 'melting' of each existing unit of capital or (equivalently, if the relevant risk can be diversified away by individual investors) disappearance of a randomly chosen portion of existing capital units, which become obsolete and cease to yield income to their owners.

It would be realistic, and essential to the study of transitional issues, to assume that the decision to invest rather than consume is *irreversible*, i.e. that the installed stock of capital cannot be converted back into consumption goods at any price. For simplicity, however, privately optimal investment decisions can be analysed from a long-run perspective under the assumption that the $\dot{K} > \delta K$ constraint never binds.

Let $\tilde{a}$ denote the after-tax share of aggregate output accruing to the owners of the capital stock K, or the profit share for short. The size of this parameter depends not only on technology, but also on the structure of output and factor markets on the one hand, and on the fiscal treatment of different types of income on the other. If output and product markets are competitive, then $\tilde{a} = a$ and the income flow accruing to every unit of capital equals $aAK^{a-1}L^{\beta}$, or the marginal productivity of capital. For a general $\tilde{a}$, but maintaining the assumption that profit rates are uniform across units of capital, optimality of private investment decisions requires that

$$rP = \tilde{a}AK^{a-1}L^{\beta} - \delta P + \dot{P}, \tag{3}$$

where r denotes the interest rate on consumption loans. In words, investment decisions must satisfy an intuitive economic criterion. On the left-hand side of (3) is the instantaneous return from investing P units of consumption goods in the financial market at rate r. On the right-hand side, operating profits are added to capital gains or losses caused by physical depreciation or obsolescence at rate δ on the one hand, and to changes at rate $\dot{P}$ in the resale price of the undepreciated portion. If physical and financial investment are both unconstrained, then their returns must be equalized, as in (3).

A specification of savings behaviour closes the model. Let $1/\sigma$ denote the inter-temporal elasticity of substitution in consumption, and let ρ denote the consumer's discount rate. If consumable resources can be transferred to the future at the instantaneously riskless rate r, then optimal consumption paths satisfy the Euler condition

$$\frac{\dot{C}}{C} = \frac{r - \rho}{\sigma} \tag{4}$$

at the individual consumer's level and, if σ and ρ are the same across individuals, at the aggregate level as well.

Rearranging (3), we obtain

$$r = \tilde{a}\,\frac{A}{P}\,K^{a-1}L^{\beta} - \delta + \frac{\dot{P}}{P}.$$

With $a < 1$ in (1), higher K levels decrease the return r to investment for given parameters. Hence, the rate of consumption growth (4) converges to zero along a path of capital accumulation if the parameters are constant.

Per-capita production and consumption do grow over time in reality. In the neo-classical literature following Solow (1956), long-run growth is driven by exogenous dynamics in disembodied productivity A (or, equivalently, in the consumption price of capital P). More recent contributions let the dynamics of A and/or P be *endogenous* to the economy's savings behaviour instead. To offset the tendency of capital accumulation to depress returns to further investment, the parameters of microeconomic investment problems are taken to depend on aggregate capital accumulation. To capture this idea, it might be simply assumed that

$$A = \eta K^{\mu}, \quad P = K^{-\nu}: \tag{5}$$

if $\mu + \nu = 1 - a$, then the rate of return on investment can be written

$$r = \tilde{a}\eta L^{\beta} - \delta - \nu\,\frac{\dot{K}}{K} \tag{6}$$

There is now no tendency for ongoing capital accumulation to depress private incentives to further investment. Combining (6) with (1) and (4), we, in fact, obtain steady growth rates:

$$\frac{\dot{Y}}{Y} = \frac{\dot{C}}{C} = (1 - \nu)\frac{\tilde{a}\eta L^{\beta} - (\delta + \rho)}{\sigma + (1 - \sigma)\nu} \equiv \vartheta \quad \text{with} \quad \frac{\dot{K}}{K} = \vartheta/(1 - \nu). \tag{7}$$

Growth is endogenous to the economy's technological and institutional structure, in that a different income share of capital $\tilde{a}$, a different depreciation rate δ, or a different level of the productivity indicator η would all affect balanced growth rates.

Since the relationships in (5) are taken to be external to individual agents' investment decisions, the growth rate resulting from decentralized market inter-actions need not be socially optimal. One way or another, social returns to investment must be constant rather than decreasing for unceasing endogenous growth to be possible. As at least another factor of production with positive productivity is present (labour, or L), the economy's dynamic equilibrium cannot be supported by complete, competitive markets where the income of each factor reflects its true social productivity. More than one distortion may be present, of course, and the rate of economic growth can be slower as well as faster than the socially optimal one.

Changes in the level of L also have growth-rate effects in this framework. Of course, the functional relationship is not meant to imply that large countries (like China) should grow faster than small countries (like Luxembourg): the productivity indicator η is certainly not constant across economies which differ so drastically across technological and institutional dimensions. Rather, the productivity effect of L is a metaphor for efficiency gains afforded by larger markets. From this perspective, it is quite meaningful to explore the role of increasing returns to scale in economic integration, and it is especially interesting to model labour mobility along with investment decisions and endogenous growth.

Before turning to the macroeconomics of integration and growth in the next sections, however, the microeconomic rationale for the assumptions made in (5) need to be briefly discussed. Relationships similar to (1), (2), and (5) hold true at the aggregate level in all endogenous-growth models which imply a constant rate of balanced growth. The original Romer (1986) model assumes that only part of capital's contribution to aggregate production is privately appropriable, and the consumption price of capital is constant. When the production function has constant elasticity a to the privately-owned capital stock, growth can be endogenously sustained in the long run if $A = K^\mu$ with $\mu \geq 1 - a$, and the rate of growth is constant if this holds with equality. In the Romer (1987) model of innovation and monopolistic competition, an imperfect market structure similarly prevents investors from appropriating all of the contribution of cumulated investment to aggregate production flows. More generally, disembodied productivity might be taken to depend on the level of aggregate output rather than on the stock of capital (as in Bertola, 1991a): along a balanced growth path, the two grow at the same rate, and the assumption might be rationalized on the basis of static production externalities as in Hall (1988).

To obtain constant returns to investment, Grossman and Helpman (1991, Ch. 3), Romer (1990), and other models of innovation assume that new knowledge (product designs and patents) becomes progressively cheaper as more and more production is invested rather than consumed. In the reduced form relationships above, this is modeled by $P = K^{-\nu}$ if K

denotes a measure of the economy's accumulated stock of knowledge. This is perhaps more appealing than the contemporaneous-externality assumption, since innovative activity can to some extent free ride on previous efforts, because knowledge property rights are only imperfectly protected by patent and copyright laws. The Grossman and Helpman (1991, Ch. 4) model of increasing product quality similarly features knowledge spillovers, albeit at the individual product rather than at the economy-wide level. Successful development of (patented) improvements bestows monopoly profits on the innovating firm, but also opens the way to further improvements – which will undermine the previous inventor's monopoly power. Hence, investment decisions jointly and endogenously determine the growth rate and the rate δ at which private returns to investment vanish. Market-determined rates of innovation and product obsolescence need not coincide with the socially optimal ones and, depending on parameter values, the economy may grow too fast or too slow in *laissez-faire* equilibrium.

3   Economic integration and endogenous growth

The reduced-form relationship in (7) has the same qualitative properties regardless of whether contemporaneous externalities or learning spillovers are present. For simplicity, in the remainder of this chapter interactions of factor mobility and endogenous growth are studied on the basis of the aggregate relationships above, with implicit rather than explicit reference to the microeconomics of innovation and growth. By implication, it will not be possible to obtain precise normative results, which would require an understanding of the microeconomic process of innovation.[2]

Consider two economic entities, each characterized by the technology in (1):

$$Y_1 = A_1 K_1^\alpha L_1^\beta, \quad Y_2 = A_2 K_2^\alpha L_2^\beta. \tag{8}$$

Entities 1 and 2 will be referred to as *localities*. In the context of this chapter, they might be viewed as two of the European economies being integrated in '1992', or as regions within them. To keep things simple, the two localities are taken to use symmetric technologies, but potentially different amounts of the three factors K, L, and A. Also, Y_1 and Y_2 are measured in common units: the localities produce homogeneous goods, and it is technologically possible to convert production into the capital stock of either locality. Again for simplicity, let the price at which investment can take place be common across countries, normalize it to unity, and set the depreciation rate δ to zero.[3]

To complete the symmetry assumptions, localities 1 and 2 are inhabited by consumers with common inter-temporal preference parameters ρ and σ. Relationships similar to (3) and (4) then need to hold true in each location if savings and investment decisions are unconstrained. Returns to investment and growth rates would in general differ across localities if no market spanned location boundaries. If the two localities do exchange output, conversely, they necessarily engage in *inter-temporal* trade in this single-good model, and capital accumulation must satisfy the aggregate constraint

$$\dot{K}_1 + \dot{K}_2 = Y_1 + Y_2 - (C_1 + C_2)$$

rather than a constraint similar to (2) for each of the two localities. In the absence of taxes or financial market imperfections, returns to investment must be equalized: with $P = 1$, $\delta = 0$, the common interest rate must equal

$$\tilde{a}_1 A_1 K_1^{\alpha-1} L_1^{\beta} = \tilde{a}_2 A_2 K_2^{\alpha-1} L_2^{\beta} \tag{9}$$

if gross investment is positive in both localities, and consumption grows at the same rate in the absence of parameter changes.

To model unceasing endogenous growth, we might want to suppose that $A_1 = \eta_1 K_1^{\mu}$, $A_2 = \eta_2 K_2^{\mu}$, each locality's disembodied productivity (or price of capital goods) depending only on the same locality's stock of capital. Endogenous growth is the equilibrium outcome if $\mu = 1 - \alpha$, and this technology would support unceasing growth even if the two localities were completely isolated from each other.

Autarkic growth rates differ from each other unless $\tilde{a}_1 \eta_1 L_1^{\beta} = a_2 \eta_2 L_2^{\beta}$. When equality obtains (the case studied by Rivera-Batiz and Romer, 1991), the two localities are symmetric for the purpose of growth-rate determination and it is unnecessary to study re-location of factors and of production. If this condition does not hold with equality, conversely, only *one* of the localities will grow (or indeed produce anything in the long run) if output and capital markets are integrated. Suppose for concreteness that

$$\tilde{a}_1 \eta_1 L_1^{\beta} > \tilde{a}_2 \eta_2 L_2^{\beta}, \tag{10}$$

then returns to investment in locality 1 will dominate returns to investment in locality 2 in the integrated economy. Unless $\tilde{a}_2$ changes endogenously (or by policy action), all of the less productive locality's capital stock is predicted to flow out to the more productive location, or to disappear asymptotically if capital cannot instantaneously flow out of 1 and into 2 because of convex adjustment costs (as in Rauch, 1991) or irreversibility constraints. The simplicity of the model is, of course, responsible for the unrealistic sharpness of this result. The counterpart in a model with many goods would be complete specialization of locality 2 in (say) tourism or agriculture, while growth-promoting activities and spillovers would be concentrated in locality 1.

If labour is immobile in the integrated economy, every agent's consumption would grow forever at locality 1's relatively fast autarkic rate of growth. Such fast growth, however, need not be much of a consolation for owners of the factors of production which remain stuck in (now unproductive) locality 2. While economic integration would benefit owners of K_2 by increasing the rate of return on their asset, owners of L_2 and of land would see their income sources become worthless as all capital flows out. If appropriate compensation is not easy to provide, then the non-capitalist agents in 2 should resist economic integration and restrain capital outflows (see Bertola, 1991a, for a discussion of factor-income distribution in an endogenous-growth model).

Labour mobility will be considered next. If L_2 is allowed to move, *all* of it will migrate immediately (in the absence of adjustment costs) or in the medium/long run (in their presence). When locality 1's stock of labour rises from L_1 to $L_1 + L_2$, its (and the aggregate) rate of economic growth accelerates as the return to investment increases from $a_1 \eta_1 L_1^\beta$ to $a_1 \eta_1 (L_1 + L_2)^\beta$. In most models of endogenous growth, faster growth is good from the social planner's or representative individual's point of view – so nothing is really wrong with all capital or even all workers flowing to the privileged locality. If the assumptions under consideration are the appropriate ones for modeling localized endogenous growth, then redistributive policies should be implemented to let all agents benefit from the increase in the size of the social welfare pie (and policies intended to correct the inter-temporal distortions on the saving/consumption margin might be needed as well). Using a model where the incentives to factor mobility reflect social as well as private returns to concentration of production and growth, we would be led to predict that '1992' will result in massive re-location of production from (say) Portugal to (say) Germany, and to evaluate such an outcome as socially desirable. Capital and labour mobility should therefore not be restricted, and policy-makers should passively accept this outcome.

4   Geographic linkages

Under the assumptions of the previous section, economic integration would leave locality 2 with no domestic production and, if the model is taken literally, no population either. Only truly immobile factors such as land, whose contribution to production is captured by the parameter η in the expression above, would remain in localities where $\tilde{a}$ and/or η are relatively low for (respectively) institutional and technological reasons. On the eve of the 1992 liberalization of factor movements, this is an unpleasant scenario for peripheral countries – and especially so for their governments, which would be deprived of a constituency by the flight, not only of physical factors of production, but of voters as well.

The progressive liberalization of capital and goods movements, however, appears to have induced capital flows *into* countries and regions where institutional and technological factors might be thought of as less conducive to high private returns to investment. If returns to capital were constant in each location, then human capital, infrastructures, and the very nature of land should make it preferable to invest in central Europe rather than (say) Portugal or Spain. But the latter, not the former regions have been experiencing capital inflows in the recent past.

In contrast to the simple-minded endogenous growth model above, standard static international trade theory and neo-classical growth models *à la* Solow (1956) assume decreasing returns to a given locality's capital stock. This can readily explain the tendency of capital to flow from capital-rich to capital-poor regions, and in fact constant returns to capital accumulation or concentration *within* each locality do not appear very realistic. The idea of congestion externalities caused by the concentration of production, and a tendency of capital to flow towards capital-poor countries at a given time, are not difficult to reconcile with endogenous, investment-driven growth. To ensure unceasing endogenous growth, returns to investment should be constant over time, but not necessarily within each locality; constant returns to accumulation are implied by, but do not require, constant returns to accumulation in each individual locality.

To see this, consider the following simple-minded extension of the model introduced above. Again taking the two localities to be symmetric for simplicity, suppose that disembodied productivity (or investment-good prices) in each locality may depend on the other locality's stock of capital and, for the sake of argument, let this dependence take a constant-elasticity Cobb-Douglas form:

$$A_1 = \eta_1 K_1^\mu K_2^{\mu*}, \quad A_2 = \eta_2 K_2^\mu K_1^{\mu*}, \tag{11}$$

It is not difficult to verify that if $\mu + \mu^* = 1 - a$ then both localities have positive, endogenously-growing production in steady state, regardless of whether or not their output and capital markets are integrated. The simple functional forms in (11) capture the idea that production and investment need not take place independently in the two locations under study.[4] The resulting model makes it possible to study economic integration among localities which maintain a distinct identity even when perfect, costless mobility of goods and factors is allowed for. In fact, location issues could not be addressed if we simply wrote aggregate output as a function of aggregate factor inputs in the integrated economy, as implicitly done by Baldwin (1989) when studying Europe-wide growth developments.

The linkage-free case above, with $\mu^* = 0$, would imply that one or the other of the localities shrinks into non-existence if $\eta_1 \neq \eta_2$, or that the location of production is a matter of indifference if $\eta_1 = \eta_2$. In the general $\mu^* \neq 0$ case, the model can be used to paint a broad picture of factor mobility and growth interactions, and the specification captures the aggregate aspects of microeconomically detailed models of locational and/or sectoral linkages which could be written along the lines of Krugman (1991) or Grossman and Helpman (1991).

In the absence of capital or labour mobility, returns to investment would generally differ across localities. If $a + \mu < 1$, returns to investment and the growth rate of consumption will decrease as the local capital stock grows. Endogenous growth, however, is sustained by the growth of the other location's capital stock which, with $\mu^* > 0$, has a positive effect on productivity across location boundaries. Under conditions of autarky, these geographical spillovers have the same role as disembodied productivity in Solow-style growth models.[5] Returns to investment and growth rates would tend to converge over time as the ratio of capital stocks approaches the level that ensures steady, balanced growth. Combining (11) and the appropriate versions of (1), we find from (9) that

$$\frac{K_1}{K_2} = \left(\frac{L_1^\beta \tilde{a}_1 \eta_1}{L_2^\beta \tilde{a} \eta_2} \right)^{\frac{1}{2\mu^*}} \tag{12}$$

equalizes private returns to investment in the two localities. If capital mobility becomes possible at some point along the transition path to the balanced-growth point (12), then a stock-shift of capital (or prolonged capital flows if adjustment costs are present) will occur to ensure that (12) holds with equality. Such flows of capital from capital-rich to capital-poor locations are once again similar to those that would take place in a neo-classical model of growth with decreasing returns to capital accumulation and exogenous productivity increases.

When (12) holds, private returns to investment in either locality are a geometric average of the expressions in (10), and output and consumption all grow at the common rate

$$\vartheta = \frac{\sqrt{\tilde{a}_1 \eta_1 L_1^\beta} \sqrt{\tilde{a}_2 L_2^\beta \eta_2} - \rho}{\sigma} \tag{13}$$

for a given allocation of labour L_1, L_2. Remarkably, the symmetry assumptions above yield (13) *regardless* of the absolute size of μ^*, or of the intensity of productivity (or innovation) spillover across localities. Even very small spillover will ensure that growth is balanced in the long run. By the symmetry assumptions above, the growth rate is maximized when $L_1 = L_2$ for a given $L_1 + L_2$. The next section studies the consequences of allowing L mobility across localities.

5   Labour mobility

Since neither locality disappears upon economic integration, the analysis of labour mobility is not as trivial in the presence of linkages as in their absence. Let localities 1 and 2 grow steadily at the rate in (13), and let the L_i units of labour located in i ($i = 1, 2$) collectively earn a portion $\tilde{\beta}_i$ of total production i. If individual units of labour share equally in the wage bill, then wages in the two countries are given by $\omega_i = \tilde{\beta}_i Y_i / L_i$. Taking (11) to hold with equality,

$$w_1 = \tilde{\beta}_1 \sqrt{\eta_1 L_1^\beta} \sqrt{\eta_2 L_2^\beta} \frac{K_1}{L_1}, \quad w_2 = \tilde{\beta}_2 \sqrt{\eta_2 L_2^\beta} \sqrt{\eta_1 L_1^\beta} \frac{K_2}{L_2}. \tag{14}$$

With $\tilde{\beta} = \beta$, these wage rates would equal labour's marginal contribution to aggregate (local) production, as would be implied by a competitive labour market. In general, however, $\tilde{\beta}$s might take on different values, subject to the obvious constraint $\tilde{\beta}_i + \tilde{a}_i \leq 1$. The remainder share $1 - \tilde{\beta}_i - \tilde{a}_i$, if non-zero, is paid to those immobile factors of production (such as land, or government) whose productivity is summarized by η_i.

If labour can move freely across the two localities, then wage rates should be equalized, at least in the long run. Combining (14) and (12) yields the non-trivial solution

$$\frac{L_1}{L_2} = \left(\frac{\tilde{\beta}_2 \eta_2}{\tilde{\beta}_1 \eta_1} \right)^{\frac{1}{\beta - 2\mu^*}} \tag{15}$$

to the condition $\omega_1 = \omega_2$, and two trivial solutions as well: if either $L_1 = K_1 = 0$ or $L_2 = K_2 = 0$, then $\omega_1 = \omega_2 = 0$. Further, $r = Y_1 = Y_2 = 0$ as well in this case, because full concentration of factors so reduces the externality assumed in (11) as to make no production viable in either locality.

Figures 6.1a and 6.1b plot the return to capital, the (logarithm of) the relative wage rate in the two localities, the (logarithm of) relative capital stocks, and total output $Y_1 + Y_2$ as a function of $L_1 = 1 - L_2$. The total supply of capital (also normalized to one) flows freely across the two locations to equalize private investment returns at the level displayed in the top panel.

In both figures, $\eta_1 = 0.12$ and $\eta_2 = 0.10$, so that locality 1 is a priori more productive than locality 2. Both figures take $a = 0.3$, $\beta = 0.5$, and (for simplicity) $\tilde{a}_i = a$, $\tilde{\beta}_1 = \tilde{\beta}_2$. The cases depicted in the figures differ in how growth-promoting externalities are distributed across localities: in Figure 6.1a, $\mu = 0.5$ and $\mu^* = 0.2$, so that production displays strongly localized increasing returns to scale. In Figure 6.1b, $\mu = \mu^* = 0.35$, to imply that much of each locality's growth-promoting external effects stem from economic activity in the other locality.

A square marks the point in investment return – labour allocation space, corresponding to (15), where wage rates as well as investment returns are equalized at non-zero levels. Free labour mobility does *not* maximize the return to investment, and of course there is no reason why it should in the presence of externalities. More worryingly, the factor-income equalization point (15) is *unstable* in Figure 6.1a, at least if labour mobility is taken to be driven by point-by-point wage differentials (a more precise specification of transitional dynamics is beyond the scope of this chapter). As L_1 diverges from L_2, the wage differential increases without bounds, and myopic labour moblility decisions tend to concentrate production so much as to bring the integrated economy towards one of the stable (and quite bleak) points where $Y_1 = Y_2 = 0$.

The picture would be qualitatively similar for all parameter choices such that $\mu^* < \beta/2$. Thus, the closer the present model is to the naive, localized-externality model studied in Section 3 above under the assumption that $\mu^* = 0$, the more likely it is that attempts to exploit the factor rewards indexed by β will cause the external source of productivity indexed by μ^* to dry up. The Cobb-Douglas assumption is too strong in this context, but of course qualitatively similar results would obtain if output were assumed to be very low rather than zero upon full concentration of production. In fact, the steady-state allocation in (15) is not only globally unstable, but it also reflects a distorted productivity signal. If the two localities differ in their a priori productivity and $\eta_1 > \eta_2$, then (15) would imply $L_1 < L_2$ for $\mu^* < \beta/2$.

In Figure 6.1b, where $\mu^* > \beta/2$, the outcome of privately optimal market inter-actions is less dramatic, but also sub-optimal. Factor mobility decisions converge to the stable point marked by a square, where $L_1 > L_2$ appropriately reflects the higher productivity of locality 1. Private optimal mobility decisions, hwoever, still imply excessive concentration of factors and production. In fact, disembodied productivity (or, more generally, non-privately appropriable factor returns) as shown in (11) introduces allocative distortions across geographical locations as well as the more familar inter-temporal distortions. A social planner interested in maximizing total (discounted) output should first of all choose an allocation that is statistically optimal. When capital is mobile across

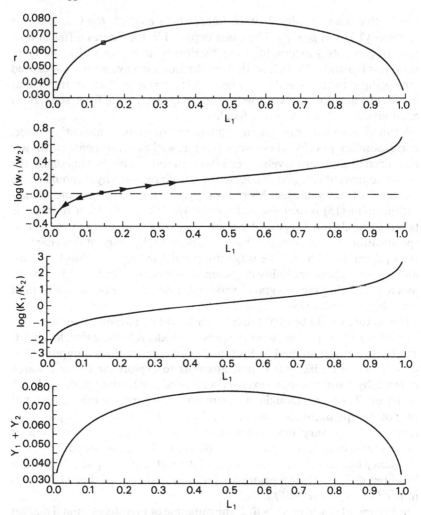

Figure 6.1 (a) Private equilibrium

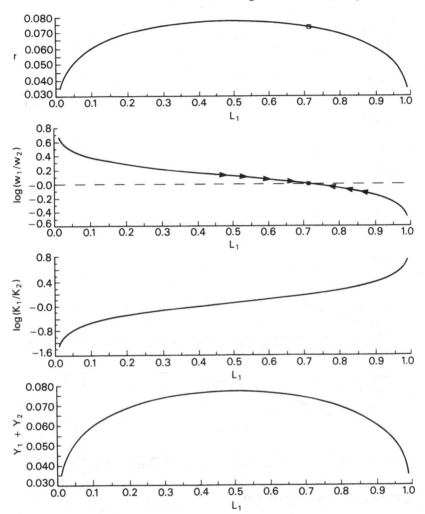

Figure 6.1 (b) Private equilibrium

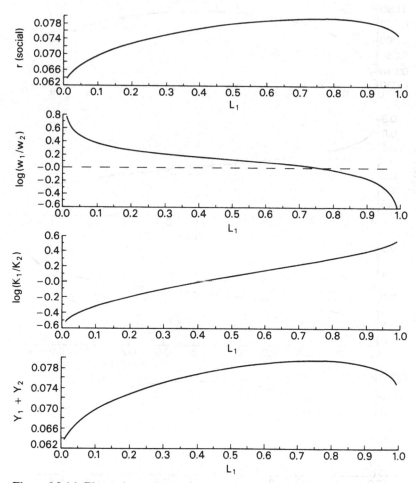

Figure 6.2 (a) Planner's equilibrium

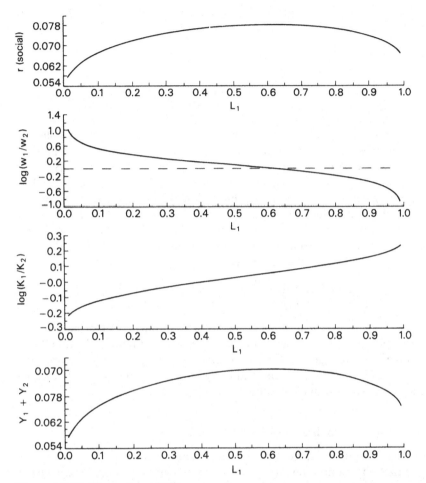

Figure 6.2 (b) Planner's equilibrium

locations, the social planner should choose K_1 so as to set to zero the derivative

$$\frac{\partial Y_1 + Y_2}{\partial K_1}$$

$$= \frac{\partial(K_1^{1-\mu^*}(1 - K_1)^{\mu^*} L_1^\beta \eta_1 + (1 - K_1)^{1-\mu^*} K_1^{\mu^*} L_2^\beta \eta_2)}{\partial K_1} \quad (16)$$

From the social point of view, a unit of capital located in locality 1 should be rewarded with a portion of locality 2's output, and vice versa. Condition (16) has no closed-form solution and needs to be solved numerically, but it is intuitive and easy to show that when $\mu^* > 0$ the socially optimal allocation of capital distributes a given (unitary) capital stock more equally across locations than would be the case in market equilibrium.

When the social planner can choose labour allocations as well, the marginal returns to labour as well as to capital should be equalized across locations, and this is the case when

$$\left(\frac{L_1}{L_2}\right)^{\beta - 1} \frac{\eta_1}{\eta_2} \left(\frac{K_1}{K_2}\right)^{1 - 2\mu^*} = 1.$$

Figures 6.2a and 6.2b display the socially optimal counterparts to the corresponding market-determined quantities in Figure 6.1a and 6.1b. Unlike private agents, the social planner recognizes the asymmetry implied by different η levels, and chooses a factor allocation that maximizes output as well as investment returns.

5   Europe, and directions for further research

In this chapter inter-actions between factor mobility decisions, social productivity, and long-run growth have been discussed. The stylized models emphasize the role of externalities in shaping aggregate outcomes. Not surprisingly, the results suggest that market inter-actions are unlikely to yield socially optimal outcomes. When a geographic dimension is added to the productivity spillovers or innovation externalities of recent growth models, it can be seen that free factor mobility need not optimize the overall performance of an integrated economy. More specifically, private mobility decisions lead to excessive concentration of production.

To prevent the undesirable side effects of economic integration, the geographical linkages among productive activity in different localities should be internalized to individual agents' optimization problems by appropriate tax instruments. In the context of the model discussed in Sections 4 and 5 above, what is needed is *distortionary* taxation as well as lump-sum redistribution. Choosing $\tilde{\beta}_1$ and $\tilde{\beta}_2$, for example, the fiscal authorities of a united Europe could prevent the excessive concentration of production resulting from the market's failure to take cross-location spillovers into account, and bring the private incentives displayed in Figure 7.1 closer to the socially-optimal ones of Figure 6.2.

To formulate precise policy implications it would of course be necessary to specify more precisely what microeconomic features of real-life economies correspond to the aggregate external spillovers assumed in equation (11). To this end, the analysis of economic integration in an endogenous-growth context should probably be framed in terms of more than two localities or sectors, and the simple model above can be straightforwardly adapted to the purpose. Disembodied productivity of factors located in i might be taken to depend on the capital stock located in n locations, for example expressing it in the form $A_i = \Pi_{j=1}^{n}(v_j K_j)^{\epsilon_j}$. While constant-elasticity assumptions should probably be taken to approximate reality only in narrow neighbourhoods, the relative strength of cross-locality productivity spillovers would depend on how easily goods and information can cross the boundaries of the localities being considered. In turn, transportation and communication should be easier when the economic units under consideration are geographically close to each other, or share a common language. It would also be possible to allow for idiosyncratic fluctuations in productivity or demand conditions across localities, and to analyse the role of factor mobility in allowing efficient re-allocation in response to such shocks (as in Bertola, 1991b).

As it stands, the analysis of this chapter suggests caution in welcoming the concentration of production that might result from full integration of European economies. The geographic as well as inter-temporal dimensions of realistic distortions will need to be taken into account when planning a tax structure for a united Europe. The models considered in this chapter suggest that a tendency towards production concentration can indeed be expected in post-1992 Europe if economic growth is driven by private investment decisions, and that it might be wise to limit such concentration not only for the questionable purpose of preventing a disappearance of peripheral economies and cultures, but to promote aggregate European economic development as well.

NOTES

I would like to thank the editors, discussants, and conference participants at Banco de Portugal for very valuable comments.
1 Increasing returns to scale are not necessary to sustain growth if there are no factors of production in fixed supply, as in models proposed by Lucas (1988), Tamura (1991), and others, or if they become asymptotically unnecessary to production, as in Jones and Manuelli (1990).

2 A detailed specification of the econmy's structure would also be necessary to take the theory to the data in quantitative rather than qualitative fashion. Available statistics need not correctly account for the heterogeneity of production flows and investment vintages of firms and sectors that is essential to the more sophisticated endogenous-growth theories. In particular, the economic depreciation rate δ appearing in (3) is a notoriously elusive concept, and plays a crucial role in the Grossman-Helpman model of increasing product quality.

3 More generally, we could denote with P_i the price of K_i and allow for investment-price dynamics and/or for capital depreciation. This would have no essential consequences for the exercises which follow.

4 It will be recalled from Section 2 that disembodied productivity might equivalently be written in terms of output instead of capital stock, and that models of knowledge spillovers would have very similar implications. The geographical spillovers considered here are qualitatively similar to those modelled by Grossman and Helpman (1990) and by Tamura (1991).

5 Implicitly, the specification in (11) allows the two localities to interact even in the absence of trade opportunities. This may be taken to reflect disembodied flows of knowledge across the boundaries of the locations. Communication difficulties because of language differences or geographical distance and other obstacles to such external flows may be modelled by a weight applied to the other locality's capital stock. A small weight, like lower overall productivity η, would reduce returns to investment and slow down growth.

REFERENCES

Alesina, Alberto, and Dani Rodrik (1991) 'Distributive Policies and Economic Growth,' National Bureau of Economic Research Working Paper No. 3668, March.

Baldwin, Richard (1989) 'The Growth Effects of 1992', *Economic Policy, 9*, 248–81.

Baldwin, Robert (1984) 'Trade Policies in Developed Countries', in R.W. Jones and P.B. Kenen (eds), *Handbook of International Economics*, Vol. I, Amsterdam, New York and Oxford: North-Holland.

Bertola, Giuseppe (1991a) 'Factor Shares and Savings in Endogenous Growth', National Bureau of Economic Research Working Paper No. 3851, September.

(1991b) 'Flexibility, Investment, and Growth', National Bureau of Economic Research Working Paper No. 3864.

Burda, Michael, and Charles Wyplosz (1991) 'Human Capital, Investment and Migration in an Integrated Europe', Centre for Economic Policy Research Discussion Paper No. 614, December.

Grossman, Gene M. and Elhanan Helpman (1990) 'Comparative Advantage and Long Run Growth', *American Economic Review*, **80:4**, 796–815.

(1991) *Innovation and Growth in the Global Economy*, Cambridge, Mass.: MIT Press.

Hall, Robert E. (1988) 'The Relation between Price and Marginal Cost in US Industry', *Journal of Political Economy*, **96**, 921–47.

Jones, Larry E. and Rodolfo Manuelli (1990) 'A Model of Optimal Equilibrium Growth', *Journal of Political Economy*, **98**, 1008–38.

Krugman, Paul (1991) *Geography and Trade*, Leuven, Belgium: Leuven University Press and Cambridge, Mass.: MIT Press.

Lucas, Robert E. Jr. (1988) 'On the Mechanics of Economic Development', *Journal of Monetary Economics*, **22**, 3–42.

Perotti, Roberto (1990) 'Political Equilibrium, Income Distribution and Growth', working paper, MIT.

Persson, Torsten, and Guido Tabellini (1991) 'Politico-Economic Equilibrium Growth: Theory and Evidence', Centre for Economic Policy Research Discussion Paper No. 581, October.

Rauch, James E. (1991) 'Balanced and Unbalanced Growth', working paper, University of California, San Diego.

Rebelo, Sergio (1992) 'Growth in Open Economies', in K. Brunner and A. Metzler (eds), *Carnegie-Rochester Series on Public Policy* (forthcoming).

Rivera-Batiz, Luis A. and Paul M. Romer (1991) 'Economic Integration and Economic Growth', *Quarterly Journal of Economics*, **CVI**, 531–555.

Romer, Paul M. (1986) 'Increasing Returns and Long-Run Growth', *Journal of Political Economy*, **94**, 1002–37.

   (1987) 'Growth Based on Increasing Returns Due to Specialization', *American Economic Review, Papers and Proceedings*, **77**, 56–72.

   (1988) 'Capital Accumulation in the Theory of Long-Run Growth', in Robert J. Barro (ed.), *Modern Business Cycle Theory*, Cambridge, Mass: Harvard University Press.

Solow, Robert M. (1956) 'A Contribution to the Theory of Economic Growth', *Quarterly Journal of Economics*, **70**, 65–94.

Tamura, Robert (1991) 'Income Convergence in an Endogenous Growth Model', *Journal of Political Economy*, **99(3)**, 522–40.

Discussion

JOÃO CÉSAR DAS NEVES

In this chapter, Giuseppe Bertola discusses the issues of economic integration in the framework of an endogenous growth model in the Romer-Lucas tradition. The main question addressed is whether the dissolution of economic borders leads to an 'eventual concentration of production and growth in privileged regions'.

This research, triggered by the single European market which was due to be implemented by the end of 1992, can be related to a very old development problem, formulated by Albert Hirschman as the acceptance of the 'mutual-benefit claim'. This was defined as:

the assertion that economic relations between these two groups of countries [underdeveloped countries and advanced industrial countries] could be shaped in such a way as to yield gains for both (Hirschman, 1981)

According to Hirschman, this hypothesis was rejected by both the Marxians and the Marxists, the latter adopting the 'imperialism' model. The rest of the economics profession upheld a dynamic version of the 'invisible hand', where economic inter-action promoted development.

More recently, this debate has been transformed by the 'endogenous growth school' in the discussion of the 'convergence' issue: whether there is a tendency for poor countries to approach the level of the rich. The general conclusion of this debate can be summarized in the words of a popular handbook:

the lower-income countries do not tend systematically to converge toward the higher-income countries. For countries that began in a position of relative prosperity, there is some tendency for the lower-income countries to grow at a faster rate. Therefore, the data indicate some tendency for convergence among the group of relatively prosperous countries. (Barro, 1990. See also the related discussion of the 'equilibrium of poverty', Neves 1990)

Bertola approaches this problem using a two-country neo-classical one-sector model, analysing the cases of autarky, capital mobility and labour mobility. Endogenous growth is obtained through a special formulation for disembodied productivity (A).[1]

This parameter A – the 'measure of our ignorance' according to Denison – is assumed to depend positively on the level of capital stock (K). Two alternative formulations are considered: one in which A depends only on domestic capital, and another where there are 'geographic linkages' through spillovers of the external capital into domestic technology.

My main comment has to do with the general structure of the model. Although its simplicity is very commendable, I wonder if the main philosophy of the 'endogenous growth school' can be captured in a model with only one productive sector and one type of capital stock. A few problems arise from this.

The main driving force of growth in the model is the level of the capital stock; this gives the model an undesirable dependence on size that generates a few paradoxes. For instance, as the growth rate depends positively on the size of the labour force this would qualify India and China as rich and dynamic countries and Switzerland and Sweden as under-developed.

On the other hand, the main results of this very stylized model are somewhat trivial. As a matter of fact, the role played by the spillovers hypothesis is to eliminate the strange case in which one of the two countries disappears.

Table D.6.1. *Evolution of real gross domestic product ratio, 1960–85 and 1960–91*

	Belgium/ France	Ireland/ United Kingdom	Portugal/ European Community	Greece/ European Community	Canada/USA	Mexico/USA	Haiti/USA	European Community/ USA
G	0.9249	1.5945	1.4482	1.4066	1.1834	1.0880	0.6142	1.0825

Table D.6.2. *Real gross domestic product ratio*

Europe	Belgium/ France	Ireland/ United Kingdom	Portugal/ European Community	Greece/ European Community	European Community/ USA
1960–75	0.9508	1.3106	1.2554	1.4459	1.1329
1976–91	0.9726	1.2166	1.1535	0.9728	1.0466

America	Canada/USA	Mexico/USA	Haiti/USA
1960–70	1.0921	1.1079	0.7093
1971–85	1.0836	0.9820	0.8659

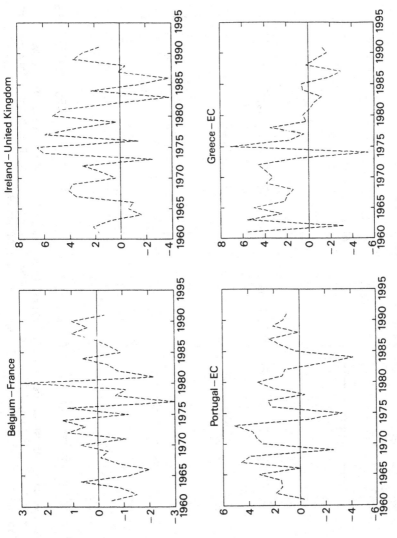

Figure D.6.1 Relative growth rate differentials, 1960–91, selected EC countries

Source: Commission des Communauté's Européenes, 'Rapport Economique Annuel 1990–91', *Economie Européene*, no. 46, December 1990.

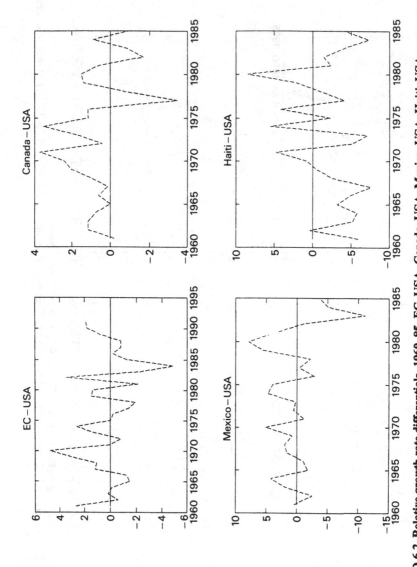

Figure D.6.2 Relative growth rate differentials, 1960–85, EC–USA, Canada–USA, Mexico–USA, Haiti–USA
Source: Summers R. and A. Heston, 'A New Set of International Comparisons of Real Product and Price levels: Estimates for 130 Countries 1950–1985', *Review of Income and Wealth*, vol. 34, No. 1, March 1988.

Table D.6.3. *Correlation coefficients of real GDP growth rates*

Europe	Belgium/ France	Ireland/ United Kingdom	Portugal/ European Community	Greece/ European Community	European Community/ USA
1960–91	0.8329	0.0874	0.7682	0.6558	0.5445
1960–75	0.8591	0.1485	0.7822	0.4464	0.6515
1976–91	0.5818	0.0027	0.5886	0.7126	0.4933
Non-EC membership	—	0.3841	0.7751	0.5205	
Member of EC	—	0.0036	0.3799	0.6238	

America	Canada/USA	Mexico/USA	Haiti/USA
1960–85	0.8148	0.1127	0.1277
1960–70	0.8973	0.4199	0.2039
1971–85	0.7939	0.0602	0.0807

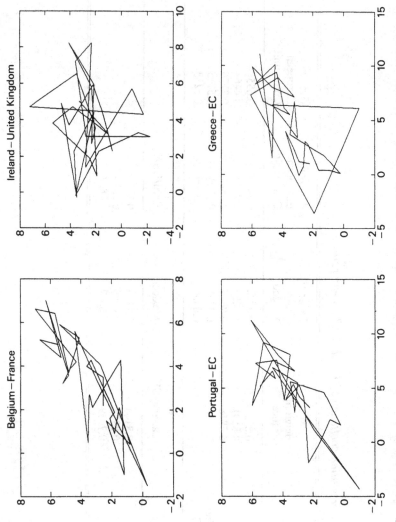

Figure D.6.3 Correlation between annual growth rates, Belgium-France, Ireland-United Kingdom, Portugal-EC, Greece-EC
Source: As for Figure D.6.1

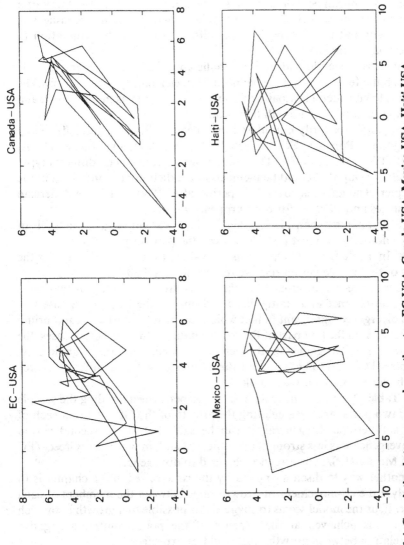

Figure D.6.4 Correlation between annual growth rates, EC-USA, Canada-USA, Mexico-USA, Haiti-USA
Source: As for Figure D.6.1

If the dynamic of the framework was elaborated somewhat more, in the Romer-Lucas tradition, this would not be needed.

The main conclusion of the chapter is to suggest 'caution in welcoming the concentration of production that is likely to result from full integration of European economies'. This conclusion raises the possibility of a reduction of growth at the periphery following integration. The issue is so important and fascinating that it is difficult to resist the temptation to investigate it further.

Only a very simple and even symbolic empirical analysis can be made here, but a few things can be deduced from elementary data analysis. The idea is to consider a few pairs of poor/rich countries as in the model, and look at their relative growth behaviour.

The pairs arbitrarily considered are: Belgium/France, Ireland/United Kingdom, Portugal/EC, Greece/EC, Canada/USA, Mexico/USA, Haiti/USA and EC/USA. These situations capture several different types of relationship that could be included in the dichotomy considered in the chapter. The analysis covers the period after 1960–85 for the American countries and 1960–91 for the European countries.

The first point to consider is whether there was convergence in levels of gross domestic product (GDP) between the pairs of poor and rich countries. In Table D.6.1, G represents the value of the poor/rich ratio at the end of the sample period relative to 1960 level, (1960 = 1).

It can be seen that after 1960 there was divergence only in two cases (Belgium/France and Haiti/USA) and only in the Haiti/USA case was this divergence significant (a fact which can be related to the 'equilibrium of poverty' in the first part of Barro's quotation). In all the other cases, the poor country has gained on the rich one, in some cases very significantly. Figures D.6.1 and D.6.2 present the annual growth rate differentials for each pair throughout the sample.

In Table D.6.2 the same calculation was performed dividing the sample into two parts, and recalculating the growth of the GDP ratio in each of the sub-periods. In general, it can be said that in the second period convergence was less strong than in the first and, in two cases (Greece/EC and Mexico/USA) convergence changed to divergence.

Another way to discuss empirically the issue raised in the chapter is to analyse the co-movement of growth rates between the members of each pair. If, as the model seems to suggest, it is possible that growth in the rich country is achieved at the expense of the poor country, a negative correlation between growth rates could be expected.

Table D.6.3 and Figures D.6.3 and D.6.4 present the correlation between annual growth rates of the two members of each pair. Division in sub-periods is also made in Table D.6.3 and, for three of the pairs for which it was significant, the sample was also divided in relation to the date of EC membership.

This analysis clearly points towards positive correlations and, in most cases, very high ones with three exceptions: the pairs of low income countries, Mexico and Haiti, with the USA (again the 'equilibrium of poverty'), and the Ireland/United Kingdom pair.

Nevertheless, the correlations are almost always lower in the later period. This finding is reinforced if it is connected with the lower convergence speed in that period which was noted before. If the later period is considered to indicate the effects of greater integration, because of advances in institutional reform, then the conclusion of the model is somewhat upheld.

Nevertheless the very different world economic climate that existed in each of the periods should be noted. The general instability in the world economy since the mid-1970s has much more to do with this lack of convergence than the effects of integration.

For all these reasons, the data seems to indicate a happier picture than the cumulative process of the model. All this can only point towards the continuation of research, to which Bertola has made a valuable contribution.

NOTE

1 The consumption price of a newly installed capital unit (P) is also considered endogenous in the first part of the chapter, but this relationship is not implemented when the integration issue is considered in the model.

REFERENCES

Barro, R. (1990) *Macroeconomics*, 3rd edition, John Wiley & Sons, Inc.
Hirschman, A.O. (1981) 'The Rise and Decline of Development Economics', in *Essays in Trespassing. Economics to Politics and Beyond*, Cambridge: Cambridge University Press.
Neves, J. (1990) *Da validade Científica do Conceito de Equilibrio de Pobreza*, Centro de Estudos Fiscais, Ministério das Finanças, Lisbon.

Discussion

CHARLES WYPLOSZ

This is a very interesting chapter. In just a few equations Giuseppe Bertola manages to summarize much of the literature on endogenous growth and extend it to a two-country framework. This by itself is enough to make the chapter rewarding to study carefully.

The purpose of the chapter is to consider how the move from autarky to capital and labour mobility affects the location of activities. The motivation is '1992' which Giuseppe Bertola takes seriously. Many observers believe that, in fact, '1992' is just the last relatively limited step in the completion of the Treaty of Rome. There has in essence been a free market in goods, capital and labour for some time although some barriers to capital mobility remained until the dismantling of capital controls on 1 July 1990 and there is still room for greater mobility among the most skilled jobs, such as lawyers, medical doctors and university professors. It might have been more fruitful if Bertola had applied his ideas to the southern European countries which joined the European Community in the mid-1980s. This observation might take a bit of glamour off the dramatic conclusions that he reaches, for we know that nothing so dramatic as he envisages has occurred among the older core of EC countries. The true drama is the European Monetary Union, a logical implication of capital mobility-cum-fixed exchange rates (Wyplosz (1986)).

The central message of the chapter is obviously right. Removing barriers to the mobility of factors of production is expected to be a Pareto improvement. Under some conditions – spelled out for example in Eichengreen (1990) – it may substitute for, or complement the benefits from, trade in goods. While the gut reaction of economists is to think that mobility is good, the man in the street, or his favourite politician, seem to believe that there is something wrong with labour mobility. As the man in the street is more often right than economists, Bertola proposes an answer: because of market distortions, increased labour mobility may deliver Pareto-inferior outcomes. The argument is not only correct and very general, it is one that needs to be emphasized at a time when migration (from the south, and now the east) is capturing the political agenda in several countries. The next step is to identify the empirically important market distortions.

The distortions that we usually worry about when thinking of the location of economic activities are externalities, chiefly congestion and network externalities. Bertola focuses on a particular network externality, the increasing returns which lead to endogenous growth. It looks like a highly promising lead. Indeed, increasing returns require some form of market distortion to allocate the rent and these distortions have growth effects, which are quantitatively much more important than any level effect. In some cases they are hair raising. One particularly spectacular case is the 'national park' effect, when whole regions or countries – depending on what one means by locality – become empty. The principle at work is clear. If private capital has external effects so that the social returns from investment are constant, moving factors of production has permanent growth effects. Then if a region is more productive, all capital and labour should move there, leaving a valueless national park in the other region. I have a problem, though, with the required condition (10):

$$\tilde{a}_1 \eta_1 L_1^\beta > \tilde{a} \eta_2 L_2^\beta$$

To fulfil this equation, we need one of three conditions – or a combination thereof – to be satisfied. First, there is the case where $\tilde{a}_1 > \tilde{a}_2$, the share of labour is higher in region 2. I find it hard to believe that it is exogenous and would remain unchanged while desertification is under way. Second, there is the case where $\eta_1 > \eta_2$. I believe that η, which could be land productivity, more realistically stands for a sort of disembodied technology productivity. With greater mobility of factors of production, it is unlikely that technologies do not travel. If Ghana has a smaller η than Korea, it is because of other factors but more of that later. Finally, there is the case where $L_1^\beta > L_2^\beta$, region 1 has a larger labour force. This is where this class of endogenous models is at its weakest since it predicts that larger countries grow faster, a result so contradicted by casual evidence that even Paul Romer has not tried to defend it. In the end, it should not be surprising that countries do not melt away, at least in the way predicted by the model.

Bertola is clearly aware of this. That is why he proposes another model with less dramatic, but equally perplexing, conclusions. He introduces capital spillover effects so that the capital of region 1 increases productivity in region 2. The results are quite interesting. With capital mobility only, the outcome is Pareto optimal. The reason is clear: the externality is internalized by capital flows. Add labour mobility and the outcome is inefficient, with too much concentration in one region. Again the reason is clear: as labour moves it does not internalize its effect on capital productivity. Hence Bertola's conclusion that growth could be permanently sub-optimal and that policy action is well-advised. Unfortunately, this result also hinges on the unpleasant role of population size in Romer-type endogenous growth models, and is therefore unconvincing.

Much of the literature on endogenous growth, I feel, is dealing with concepts which need to be clarified. What are the capital spillovers modelled here? Bertola notes that they are more likely to be at work in a small area, like a metropolitan area. These externalities, indeed, might explain that big cities grow out of their hinterland because infrastructure services (for example, roads, administration, cinemas, and so on) benefit more than their immediate neighbourhood. Yet these effects are not likely to be extended far enough to cover a whole country in the spirit of '1992'.

In the end, Bertola pays a high price for his methodological choice. These days endogenous growth is too tempting to be easily resisted. I believe that he could get many of the same results without endogenous growth, or with some other form of endogenous growth. This is the issue that I wish to explore informally.

Solow-type models are actually quite illuminating. With one good, we find again the national park result. If disembodied technology differs among regions, it is impossible simultaneously to equalize across two regions, except by pure luck, the marginal productivities of labour and capital. The less productive factor will migrate elsewhere. With two goods, though, this result disappears, the relative price of goods does the balancing job and we are back in trade theory. So we need to think about other externalities. One idea is that there are costs of migration which are larger at the social level than at the individual level: for example, receiving and integrating large numbers of economic refugees. This would also imply inefficiently high labour mobility, and seems to conform to what the man in the street worries about. Bertola dismisses such costs, because he sees them as transitory, barely slowing down the process. Unless, in the spirit of Barro, we see individuals as perpetuating themselves forever through their descendants, if each migrant incurs a fixed cost and faces a finite stream of income there is an important externality to consider.

One lesson that I have learnt from the endogenous growth literature is the importance of human capital, with or without externalities. Some results (Barro (1991), Mankiw et al. (1991)) show that when human capital is accounted for, Solow-type growth does very well. If we want to raise the level of interest by having growth effect, I would rather use the Lucas-type of endogenous growth mechanism. This explains why Ghana's apparently disembodied productivity does not match that of Korea. We could even allow for heterogeneous human capital and begin to understand why often those who migrate are the most skilled people. In doing so, we would have plenty of externalities to cope with (knowledge, for example), with or without permanent growth effects.

In the end, Bertola has put forward a very important research agenda. While his particular modelling strategy here may fail to capture the quantitatively most important factors, his central theme is undoubtedly right. I look forward to further variations on this theme.

REFERENCES

Barro, Robert (1991) 'Economic Growth in a Cross Section of Countries', *Quarterly Journal of Economics*, **106**, May, pp. 407–44.

Eichengreen, Barry (1990) 'One Money for Europe? Lessons from the US Currency Union', *Economic Policy*, **10**, April, pp. 117–88.

Mankiw, N. Gregory, David Romer and David N. Weil (1990) 'A Contribution to the Empirics of Economic Growth', unpublished paper, Harvard University, December.

Wyplosz (1986) 'Capital Controls and Balance of Payments Crises', *Journal of International Money and Finance*, **5**, June, pp. 167–80.

7   Shocking aspects of European monetary integration

TAMIM BAYOUMI and
BARRY EICHENGREEN

1   Introduction

From all appearances the process of European monetary unification continues to gather momentum. Nearly four years have passed since the last significant realignment of exchange rates of members within the European monetary system (EMS). All significant controls on capital movements among member countries have been removed. Discussions of the establishment of a European central bank and a single currency are proceeding apace. If the current timetable is observed the transition will have been completed by the end of the decade.

At the same time there remain serious questions about the advisability of a European Monetary Union (EMU) voiced, in the most recent round of discussions, by the governments of the United Kingdom and Spain. By definition, EMU involves a sacrifice of monetary autonomy. In response to country-specific shocks, governments will no longer have the option of adopting a monetary policy which differs from that of the union as a whole. Insofar as monetary policy is useful for facilitating adjustment to disturbances, adjustment problems may grow more persistent and difficult to resolve.

These concerns are reinforced to the extent that it is believed that completion of the internal market will place new limits on the use of fiscal policy. Not only will individual governments have lost autonomy over the use of seigniorage to finance budget deficits but, insofar as the 1992 process renders factors of production increasingly mobile, constraints will be placed on their ability to impose tax rates significantly different from those of their neighbours. Limits on their ability to tax in the future will limit their ability to run budget deficits in the present; hence all important fiscal instruments may be constrained.[1] The sacrifice of monetary autonomy is potentially all the more serious.

The weight that should be attached to these arguments depends on the incidence of shocks. If disturbances are distributed symmetrically across countries, symmetrical policy responses will suffice. In response to a negative aggregate demand shock that is common to all EMU countries, for example, a common policy response in the form of a common monetary and fiscal expansion should be adequate. Only if disturbances are distributed asymmetrically across countries will there be occasion for an asymmetric policy response and the constraints of monetary union may then be felt. This has been widely understood, of course, since the seminal work on the theory of optimum currency areas by Mundell (1961).

In light of the attention attracted by EMU, we possess remarkably little evidence on the incidence of shocks to the European economy. In this chapter, therefore, we analyse data on output and prices for 11 European Community (EC) member countries in order to extract information on aggregate supply and aggregate demand disturbances. We use the structural vector auto-regression approach for isolating disturbances developed by Blanchard and Quah (1989) and extended by Bayoumi (1992). We examine the time-series behaviour of real gross domestic product (GDP) and the price level. To recover aggregate supply and demand disturbances, we impose the identifying restrictions that aggregate demand disturbances have only a temporary impact on output but a permanent impact on prices, while aggregate supply disturbances permanently affect both prices and output.

To assess the magnitude of disturbances to the European economy, a standard of comparison is required. The United States of America is the obvious possibility. It is a smoothly functioning monetary union. Its local authorities possess fiscal autonomy. It can be divided into regions that are approximately the economic size of Community countries, and supply and demand disturbances to each region can be calculated. If it turns out, for example, that supply shocks are less correlated across US regions than across the member countries of the Community, then there can be no presumption that asymmetric shocks will necessarily threaten the success of EMU. If, on the other hand, shocks to EC countries are significantly more asymmetric than shocks to US regions, then adoption of a single currency could give rise to serious problems.

The empirical framework allows us not just to identify aggregate supply and demand disturbances but to examine the economy's speed of adjustment. Comparing the responses of US regions and EC countries provides suggestive evidence on the structural implications of the single market. If the responses of US regions are more rapid than those of European countries, this would suggest that the creation of a unified internal market in Europe will encourage factor mobility and create other mechanisms which will facilitate the Community's adjustment to shocks. Evidence from the USA is useful, therefore, for gauging the extent to which monetary unification and the rest of the 1992 programme is likely to accelerate the response to shocks, as argued by the Commission of the European Communities (1990).[2]

The remainder of this chapter is organized as follows. In Section 2 we review the theoretical literature on optimum currency areas and what it says about asymmetric shocks. Previous empirical work on the issue is also surveyed. In Section 3 the framework used to identify supply and demand disturbances is set out. A description of our data and its properties is given in Section 4, while Section 5 contains the results of the statistical analysis. Our conclusions are given in Section 6.

2   Optimum currency areas: theory and evidence

The point of departure for the literature on optimum currency areas was Mundell (1961).[3] Mundell observed that an exchange rate adjustment which permitted the pursuit of different monetary policies in two countries (say, the USA and Canada) was of little use if the disturbance in response to which the policies were adopted depressed one region within both countries (say, western Canada and the western United States) while simultaneously stimulating other regions within both (say, eastern Canada and the eastern United States). In this case, there is an efficiency argument for forming one currency area comprised of the two western parts and a second currency area made up of the eastern parts. In response to this disturbance, the western regions can then adopt one policy, the eastern regions another, and the exchange rate between them can adjust accordingly, while preserving the advantages of a common currency in the form of reduced exchange rate risk and lower transaction costs within the eastern and western regions. In Mundell's framework, then, the incidence of disturbances across regions is a critical determinant of the design of currency areas.[4]

One strand of subsequent literature explored the determinants of the incidence of shocks. Kenen (1969) highlighted the degree of industry or product diversification as a determinant of the symmetry of disturbances. When two regions are highly specialized in the production of distinct goods the prices of which are affected very differently by disturbances, he argued, asymmetric shocks are more likely than when the two regions have the same industrial structure and produce the same goods.[5]

A second direction taken by the subsequent literature analysed mechanisms other than exchange-rate-cum-monetary policy that might facilitate adjustment. Following Meade (1957), Mundell emphasized labour mobility. The greater the propensity for labour to flow from depressed to prosperous regions, he argued, the less the need for different policy responses in the two regions to prevent the emergence of pockets of high unemployment. Ingram (1973) noted that even where labour remains imperfectly mobile, capital mobility has typically reached high levels.[6] Hence capital flows can substitute for labour migration as a mechanism for reallocating resources across regions. But physical capital mobility eliminates the need for labour mobility only under restrictive assumptions.[7]

Given that the markets for labour and physical capital do not respond instantaneously to region-specific shocks, a number of authors have analysed market mechanisms and the policy measures that can insure against region-specific risk. Atkeson and Bayoumi (1991) explore the extent to which financial capital mobility can substitute for physical capital mobility. In their model, agents can diversify away the risk of region-specific shocks by holding financial assets the returns on which are uncorrelated with region-specific sources of labour and capital income. Sachs and Sala-i-Martin (1991) have suggested that regional problems can be alleviated through transfers of purchasing power from booming to depressed regions accomplished by federal fiscal systems. This creates a presumption that currency areas should coincide with fiscal jurisdictions.

This predominantly theoretical literature suggests an agenda for empirical research: (i) identifying the incidence of shocks, (ii) isolating their determinants, and (iii) analysing the market and policy responses. A remarkable feature of the scholarly literature – and of the debate over EMU – is how little empirical analysis has been devoted to these questions.

One approach to gauging the extent of asymmetric shocks has been to compute the variability of real exchange rates, since changes in relative prices reflect shifts in demand or supply affecting one region relative to another. Poloz (1990) compared regional real exchange rates within Canada with national real exchange rates between France, the UK, Italy and Germany. He found that real exchange rates between Canadian provinces were more variable than those between the four EC countries. Since Canada runs a successful monetary union, the implication is that the Community should be able to do likewise. Eichengreen (1990a) extended Poloz's analysis, using consumer price indices, to four US regions (North East, North Central, South and West) and ten Community countries. He found that real exchange rates within the EC have been more variable than real exchange rates within the US, typically by a factor of three to four. De Grauwe and Vanhaverbeke (1991) similarly considered real exchange rates of regions within individual European countries. Using data on unit labour costs for different regions within

Germany, France, Spain, the UK and the Netherlands in the period 1977–85, they found that real exchange rates were significantly less variable within European countries than between them. One interpretation is that the European Community as a whole is significantly further from being an optimum currency area than are the individual countries making up the Community.

In a related analysis, Eichengreen (1990a) analysed the covariance of real share prices in Toronto and Montreal and in Paris and Dusseldorf. In theory, the prices of equities should reflect the present value of current and expected future profits. If shocks are asymmetric, profits will rise in one market relative to the other. Real share prices in Toronto and Montreal were found to move more closely together than real share prices in Dusseldorf and Paris. There was evidence of convergence between Paris and Dusseldorf over time, but even in the 1980s the ratio of real share prices between Paris and Dusseldorf was five times as variable as the ratio for Toronto and Montreal.

A limitation of the approaches which focus on relative prices, as pointed out by Eichengreen (1990a), is that they conflate information on the symmetry of shocks and on the speed of adjustment. If real share prices in two regions move together, this may indicate either that the two regions experience the same shocks or that capital is quick to flow from the region where the rate of return has fallen to the one where it has risen. Similarly, if the relative prices of the products of two regions show little variability, this may reflect either that their product markets experience the same supply and demand disturbances or that factors of production are quick to flow out of the region where prices have begun to fall and into the region where they have begun to rise, thereby minimizing relative price variability.

This has led other authors to focus on the behaviour of output rather than prices. Cohen and Wyplosz (1989) were first to use the time series of output to investigate the asymmetry of shocks.[8] They transform data on real GDP for France and Germany into sums and differences, interpreting movements in the sum as symmetric disturbances, movements in the difference as asymmetric disturbances. They remove a trend component from the sum and the difference using a variety of time-series techniques, and interpret the standard deviation of the de-trended series relative to the standard deviation of the original as a measure of the contribution of temporary disturbances to overall variability. They find that symmetric shocks are much larger than asymmetric shocks. (In other words, the variability of the sum is larger than the variability of the difference.) By their interpretation, symmetric shocks are predominantly permanent, while asymmetric shocks are predominantly temporary. (De-trending the sum eliminates much of its variability, while de-trending the difference has a smaller effect.)

The limitation of this approach is much the same as the one that focuses on prices. Observed movements in real GDP reflect the combined effects of shocks and responses. Using this methodology it is impossible to distinguish their separate effects.[9]

Independent evidence on the response to disturbances may permit information about the symmetry and magnitude of shocks to be extracted. Recent investigations have focused on the responsiveness of labour markets. The Organisation for Economic Cooperation and Development (OECD 1985) assembled data comparing inter-regional labour mobility within the USA and within EC countries. The tabulations suggest that mobility within the US has been two or three times as high as mobility within European countries. De Grauwe and Vanhaverbeke (1991) found a much higher degree of inter-regional labour mobility in northern European countries such as Germany, the UK and France than in southern countries like Spain and Italy. While they do not provide comparisons with the US, their numbers are consistent with those of the OECD study.

The problem with such evidence, again, is that a high degree of observed labour mobility may reflect either an exceptionally responsive labour market or exceptionally asymmetric regional labour market shocks. Eichengreen (1990b) therefore estimated time-series models of regional unemployment differentials for both Europe and the United States. He examined the speed with which rates of unemployment in individual EC countries converged to their long-run relationship to the EC average and compared his findings with data showing the speed at which regional unemployment rates in the US converged to the average for the USA as a whole. The results suggest that regional unemployment rates adjust to one another about 20% more rapidly in the United States than national unemployment rates adjust to one another within the EC.

Given the costs of migration, the movement of labour is a plausible mechanism mainly for adjusting to permanent shocks. Work on responses to temporary disturbances has focused on portfolio diversification and fiscal redistribution. Using data for US regions, Atkeson and Bayoumi (1991) estimate that recipients of capital income succeed in using portfolio diversificaton to insure against a significant proportion of region-specific income fluctuations, but that recipients of labour income do so only to a very limited extent.

On the effects of fiscal federalism, Sachs and Sala-i-Martin (1991) conclude that the US fiscal system offsets about one-third of a decline in regional personal incomes relative to the national average. In other words, when incomes in one US region fall by $1 relative to incomes in the

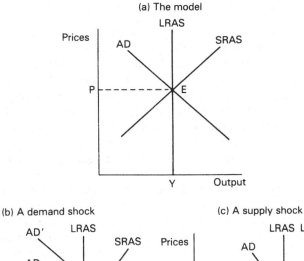

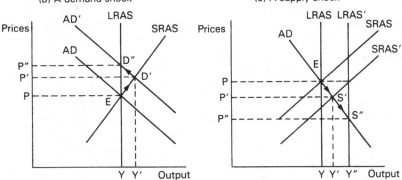

Figure 7.1 The aggregate demand and supply model

nation as a whole, the fall in tax payments by that region to Washington, DC plus inward transfers from other regions via the expenditure side of the government budget is about 33 cents. Disposable income therefore falls by only 67 cents.[10]

These studies uniformly point to the conclusion that adjustment to region-specific shocks, whether by markets or by policy, is faster in the USA than in Europe. Hence, the smaller variability of output and prices across regions in the US than across countries in Europe may reflect the fact that the US exhibits either a faster response to larger, more asymmetric shocks or a faster response to smaller, less asymmetric shocks. The approaches utilized in previous studies thus fail to provide enough information to distinguish disturbances from responses.

3   Methodology

It is for this reason that we take an alternative approach to identifying disturbances. Our point of departure is the familiar aggregate demand and aggregate supply diagram, reproduced as the top panel in Figure 7.1. The aggregate demand curve (labelled AD) is downward sloping in the price output plane, reflecting the fact that lower prices, by raising money balances, boost demand. The short run aggregate supply curve ($SRAS$) is upward sloping, reflecting the assumption that wages are sticky and hence that higher prices imply lower real wages. The long run supply curve ($LRAS$) is vertical, since real wages adjust to changes in prices in the long run.[11]

The effect of a shock to aggregate demand is shown in the left half of the lower panel. The aggregate demand curve shifts from AD to AD', resulting in a move in the equilibrium from initial point E to the new intersection with the short run curve, D'. This raises both output and prices. As the aggregate supply curve becomes more vertical over time, the economy moves gradually from the short run equilibrium D' to its new long run equilibrium, D''. This movement along the aggregate demand curve involves the return of output to its initial level, while the price level rises to a level which is permanently higher. (Depending on the price mechanism, there could be cycling around the new long run equilibrium.) Hence the response to a permanent (positive) demand shock is a short term rise in output followed by a gradual return to its initial level, and a permanent rise in prices.

The effect of a supply shock is shown in the right-hand bottom panel of Figure 7.1. Assume that the long run level of potential output rises, say because of a favourable technology shock. The short and long-run supply curves move rightwards by the same amount, as shown by $SRAS'$ and $LRAS'$. The short run effect raises output and reduces prices, shifting the equilibrium from E to S. As the supply curve becomes increasingly vertical over time, the economy moves from S' to S'', implying further increases in output and reductions in prices. Unlike demand shocks, supply shocks result in permanent changes in output. In addition, demand and supply have different effects on prices; positive demand shocks raise prices while positive supply shocks reduce them.

This framework is estimated using a procedure proposed by Blanchard and Quah (1989) for decomposing permanent and temporary shocks to a variable using a vector auto-regression (VAR) and extended by Bayoumi (1992).[12] Consider a system where the true model can be represented by an infinite moving average representation of a (vector) of variables, X_t, and an equal number of shocks, ϵ_t. Formally, using the lag operator L, this can be written as:

$$X_t = A_0\epsilon_t + A_1\epsilon_{t-1} + A_2\epsilon t_{2-2} + A_3\epsilon_{t-3} \ldots$$

$$= \sum_{i=0}^{\infty} L^i A_i \epsilon_t \tag{1}$$

where the matrices A_i represent the impulse response functions of the shocks to the elements of X.

Specifically, let X_t be made up of the change in output and the change in prices, and let ϵ_t be demand and supply shocks. Then the model becomes

$$\begin{bmatrix} \Delta y_t \\ \Delta p_t \end{bmatrix} = \sum_{i=0}^{\infty} L^i \begin{bmatrix} a_{11i} & a_{12i} \\ a_{21i} & a_{22i} \end{bmatrix} \begin{bmatrix} \epsilon_{dt} \\ \epsilon_{st} \end{bmatrix} \tag{2}$$

where y_t and p_t represent the logarithm of output and prices, ϵ_{dt} and ϵ_{st} are independent supply and demand shocks, and a_{11i} represents element a_{11} in matrix A_i.

The framework implies that while supply shocks have permanent effects on the level of output, demand shocks only have temporary effects. (Both have permanent effects upon the level of prices.) Since output is written in first difference form, this implies that the cumulative effect of demand shocks on the change in output (Δy_t) must be zero. The model implies the restriction,

$$\sum_{i=0}^{\infty} a_{11i} = 0. \tag{3}$$

The model defined by equations (2) and (3) can be estimated using a VAR. Each element of X_t can be regressed on lagged values of all the elements of X. Using B to represent these estimated coefficients, the estimating equation becomes,

$$\begin{aligned} X_t &= B_1 X_{t-1} + B_2 X_{t-2} + \ldots + B_n X_{t-n} + e_t \\ &= (I - B(L))^{-1} e_t \\ &= (I + B(L) + B(L)^2 + \ldots)e_t \\ &= e_t + D_1 e_{t-1} + D_2 e_{t-2} + D_3 e_{t-3} + \ldots \end{aligned} \tag{4}$$

where e_t represents the residuals from the equations in the VAR. In the case being considered, e_t is comprised of the residuals of a regression of lagged values of Δy_t and Δp_t on current values of each in turn; these residuals are labelled e_{yt} and e_{pt}, respectively.

To convert equation (4) into the model defined by equations (2) and (3), the residuals from the VAR, e_t, must be transformed into demand and supply shocks, ϵ_t. Writing $e_t = C\epsilon_t$, it is clear that, in the two-by-two case considered, four restrictions are required to define the four elements of the matrix C. Two of these restrictions are simple normalizations, which define the variance of the shocks ϵ_{dt} and ϵ_{st}. A third restriction comes from assuming that demand and supply shocks are orthogonal.[13]

The final restriction, which allows the matrix C to be uniquely defined, is that demand shocks have only temporary effects on output.[14] As noted above, this implies equation (3). In terms of the VAR it implies,

$$\sum_{i=0}^{\infty} \begin{bmatrix} d_{11i} & d_{12i} \\ d_{21i} & d_{22i} \end{bmatrix} \begin{bmatrix} c_{11} & c_{12} \\ c_{21} & c_{22} \end{bmatrix} = \begin{bmatrix} 0 & . \\ . & . \end{bmatrix} \tag{5}$$

This restriction allows the matrix C to be uniquely defined and the demand and supply shocks to be identified.[15]

Clearly, interpreting shocks with a permanent impact on output as supply disturbances and shocks with only a temporary impact on output as demand disturbances is controversial. Doing so requires adopting the battery of restrictions incorporated into the aggregate-supply-aggregate-demand model of Figure 7.1. It is possible to think of frameworks other than the standard aggregate-supply-aggregate-demand model in which that association might break down. Moreover, it is conceivable that temporary supply shocks (for example, an oil price increase that is reversed subsequently) or permanent demand shocks (for example, a permanent increase in government spending which affects real interest rates and related variables) dominate our data. But here a critical feature of our methodology comes into play. While restriction (5) affects the response of output to the two shocks, it says nothing about their impact on prices. The aggregate-supply-aggregate-demand model implies that demand shocks should raise prices while supply shocks should lower them. Since these responses are not imposed, they can be thought of as 'over-identifying restrictions' useful for testing our interpretation of permanent output disturbances in terms of supply and temporary ones in terms of demand. Only if this over-identifying restriction is satisfied can we be confident of our interpretation of disturbances with permanent and temporary effects on output as supply and demand disturbances, respectively.

4 Data

Annual data on real and nominal GDP spanning the period 1960–88 were obtained from the OECD annual *National Accounts* for the 11 principal members of the European Community. This same source provided an aggregate measure of output and price performance for the EC as a whole.[16] These same data were collected for 11 additional OECD countries: six members of the European Free Trade Area (EFTA) – Sweden, Switzerland, Austria, Finland, Norway and Iceland – plus the United

States, Japan, Canada, Australia and New Zealand. For each country growth and inflation were calculated as the first difference of the logarithm of real GDP and the implicit GDP deflator. The GDP deflator was used to measure prices since it reflects the price of output rather than the price of consumption. This distinction is particularly important for regional US data since the integration of the domestic goods markets minimizes differences in regional consumer price indices.[17]

For US regions, annual data on real and nominal gross product for the separate states were collected for 1963–86. The gross product series for the states, produced by the US Department of Commerce, is described in the *Survey of Current Business* (May 1988). It measures gross output produced by each state and hence represents the regional equivalent of the gross domestic product series in the OECD data. The data were aggregated into the eight standard regions of the United States used by the Bureau of Economic Analysis, namely New England, the Mid-East, the Great Lakes, the Plains, the South East, the South West, the Rocky Mountain states and the Far West. As is the case for EC countries, these regions differ considerably in size; the Rocky Mountain region is the smallest, with under 3% of US population, while the Mid-East, South East and Great Lakes each contain around 20% of the US population. Growth and inflation for each region were calculated in the same way as for the OECD series, namely as the first difference in the logarithm of real gross product for the state and of the state's gross product deflator.

Before analysing these data, we consider them in their unprocessed form. Table 7.1 shows standard deviations and correlation coefficients for the logarithm of the growth in output and of inflation across eleven countries of the Community and the eight regions of the United States for the full data period.[18] The correlations are measured with respect to Germany in the case of the European Community and the Mid-East for the US.[19] The standard deviations indicate that output fluctuations have generally been somewhat smaller across EC countries than across US regions, while inflation variability has been higher in Europe. The correlation coefficients indicate that output growth is generally more highly correlated across US regions than EC regions, although two regions (the South West and the Rocky Mountains) show relatively idiosyncratic behaviour. For inflation, the correlation coefficients are much more highly correlated across US regions than EC countries, presumably reflecting the existence of a common currency.

In Tables 7.2 and 7.3 the analysis of correlations is extended. The share of the variance of output growth and inflation explained by the first principal component (the orthogonal component most correlated with the underlying series) is shown for different groups of countries or regions

Table 7.1. *Standard deviations and correlation coefficients with anchor areas. (Logarithms of raw data)*

	Growth of real GDP		Inflation	
	Standard deviation	Correlation	Standard deviation	Correlation
EC countries				
Germany	0.022	1.00	0.017	1.00
France	0.018	0.74	0.031	0.47
Belgium	0.022	0.73	0.024	0.57
Netherlands	0.022	0.79	0.028	0.68
Denmark	0.025	0.67	0.023	0.69
United Kingdom	0.021	0.54	0.052	0.48
Italy	0.023	0.52	0.054	0.33
Spain	0.027	0.56	0.044	0.26
Ireland	0.022	0.09	0.050	0.49
Portugal	0.034	0.57	0.074	− 0.07
Greece	0.035	0.66	0.067	0.00
US regions				
Mid-East	0.025	1.00	0.020	1.00
New England	0.031	0.94	0.020	0.98
Great Lakes	0.040	0.88	0.022	0.98
Plains	0.027	0.85	0.023	0.94
South East	0.027	0.76	0.022	0.72
South West	0.022	0.40	0.035	0.89
Rocky Mountains	0.024	0.27	0.024	0.84
Far West	0.033	0.66	0.018	0.96

Notes: All variables are measured in logarithms, so that 0.027 indicates at standard deviation of approximately 2.7 percent.
Source: See text.

over several time periods. The results confirm the greater coherence of price and output movements among US regions than among EC countries. For the full period, the first principal component explained 74% of the variance in output movements for US regions but only 57% for EC countries. For inflation the comparable figures are 92% and 59% respectively.

For both the USA and the European Community the first principal component explained the largest share of the variance in output in the 1970s and the smallest share in the 1960s. This presumably reflects the fact that all countries and regions experienced an unusually severe recession following the first oil shock. For both the US and the EC the first

Table 7.2. *Percentage of variance explained by the first principal component across different groups of countries: raw data*

	European Community (11 countries)	Other 11 OECD countries	EC core	EC periphery	EFTA	Control group
Growth of real GDP						
Full period	57	42	73	49	43	49
1963–71	40	39	73	35	51	49
1972–79	62	39	82	49	43	53
1980–88	44	46	54	42	42	57
Inflation						
Full period	59	54	64	70	53	57
1963–71	44	37	46	38	42	36
1972–79	39	46	58	52	44	59
1980–88	73	61	82	69	68	58

Notes: (a) Since the percentage of variance explained varies with the number of countries in the group, it is not useful to compare the results from the first two columns with those in the subsequent columns. The control group comprises USA, Japan, Canada, Australia, New Zealand and Iceland.
(b) The European Community excludes Luxembourg.

principal component explained the largest share of the variance in inflation in the 1980s, presumably reflecting the extent to which price-level trends in both the US and Europe were dominated by disinflation after 1980.

In Table 7.2, contrasts in the behaviour of output and prices in the EC and in the 11 other industrial economies in our sample are shown. Although the first principal component explained a larger share of the variance of output in the EC than in the other industrial countries, this appears to be because of the similar reaction of EC members to the oil shock and to other events in the 1970s, rather than to the EMS and the first steps toward completion of the internal market in the 1980s. In contrast, there is weak evidence of the effects of the EMS in the larger share of the variance of inflation explained for the EC than for the other economies in the 1980s.

The failure to discern a large difference in the coherence of output movements between the Community countries and the other industrial economies reflects divergent movements not among what might be regarded as the 'core' members of the EC (Germany, France, Belgium,

Table 7.3. *Percentage of variance explained by the first principal component across different groups of US regions*

	Eight US regions	Six 'core' regions	Six 'peripheral' regions
Growth of real GDP			
Full period	74	85	73
1966–72	79	88	78
1973–79	92	94	92
1980–86	78	92	74
Inflation			
Full period	92	93	92
1966–72	84	90	83
1973–79	70	77	67
1980–86	98	99	98

Notes: The core regions comprise the Mid-East, New England, Great Lakes, Plains, South East and Far West while the peripheral regions are the Mid-East, Plains, South East, South West, Rocky Mountains and Far West.

Luxembourg, the Netherlands and Denmark)[20] but between the core and the EC 'periphery' (the UK, Italy, Ireland, Greece, Portugal and Spain). In each sub-period, the first principal component explained much less of the variance in output growth among peripheral countries, and generally less for inflation. The coherence of price and output trends among the EFTA countries was similar to that among the members of the EC periphery. The final column of Table 7.2 shows the results for a control group, made up of the five countries in our sample which are not members of the EC or of EFTA plus Iceland. Iceland, an EFTA member, is included in the control group in order to make the number of countries in each group equal.[21] Again, the behaviour of this control group was not dissimilar to that of the EC periphery.

Table 7.3 shows an analogous breakdown for the United States. The second column, which excludes the South West and Rocky Mountains, can be thought of as the US 'core'.[22] The third column, which excludes the Great Lakes and New England, is intended to simulate a US 'periphery'. The second column confirms that output movements were more closely synchronized, most notably in the 1980s, when the South West and Rocky Mountains were removed. This presumably reflects the very different composition of production in these two regions (dominated by oil in the

South West and by other minerals and raw materials in the Rocky Mountain states). There is less difference in the behaviour of inflation, as if the integration of production markets encompasses even those regions where the composition of local output is different.

The third column confirms that the picture is reversed when the Great Lakes and New England are removed. Compared with Table 7.2, however, the contrast between columns is quite small, substantiating the view of greater coherence of price and output trends among US regions than within the EC and among other countries.

5   Results

To recover disturbances, we estimated bivariate VARs for each country and region in the sample. In all cases, the number of lags was set to 2, since the Schwartz Bayesian information criterion indicated that all of the models had an optimal lag length of either one or two.[23] A uniform lag of two was chosen in order to preserve the symmetry of the specification across countries. For the EC and other countries, the estimation period was 1963–88, while for US regions it was 1966–86. For the OECD countries, the estimation period includes a potential change in regime, namely the break-up of the Bretton Woods fixed exchange rate system in the early 1970s. Chow tests of the structural stability, however, produced no evidence of a shift in the early 1970s. Limited analysis using data sets which excluded the Bretton Woods period showed similar results to those reported.

In nearly every case, the estimation and simulation results accord with the aggregate-demand-aggregate-supply framework discussed in Section 3. The 'over-identifying restriction' that temporary shocks, in order to be interpreted as demand disturbances, should be associated with increases in prices while permanent shocks, in order to be interpreted as supply disturbances, should be associated with falls in prices was generally observed. In only three of the 30 cases, namely Norway, Ireland and the Rocky Mountain region of the United States, was it impossible to interpret the results using the aggregate-demand-aggregate-supply framework. Henceforth, we therefore refer to the permanent and temporary shocks as supply and demand disturbances.

In Figure 7.2 some illustrative results are displayed. Output and price impulse-response functions are shown for the EC and for the US as a whole.[24] The impulse-response functions for output shown in panels (A) and (B) illustrate the restriction that aggregate demand shocks have only temporary effects on the level of output while supply shocks have permanent output effects. Positive demand shocks produce a rise in output

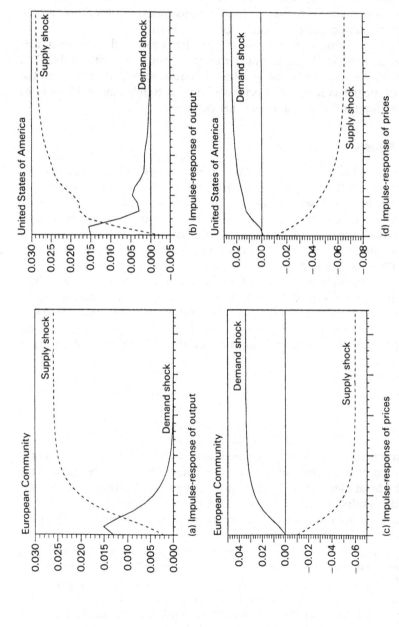

Figure 7.2 Impulse-response functions for the European Community and the USA

initially, which then reverts to its baseline level; the return to zero is imposed by the methodology, but the smooth adjustment path is not. By comparison, positive supply shocks produce a steady rise in output to a new higher equilibrium level. The impulse-response functions for prices in panels (C) and (D) show that the 'over-identifying restriction' is satisfied. While both permanent and temporary shocks have long-run effects on the price level, temporary ('demand') shocks produce a gradual rise in prices over time, while permanent ('supply') shocks produce a steady decline in prices, as predicted by the aggregate-demand-aggregate-supply framework.

Three additional features of the impulse-response functions stand out.

(i) Demand shocks are more important than supply shocks for output in the short run. (By construction, they become progressively less important over time.) No such regularity holds for prices.

(ii) The impulse-response function for the US appears to show a faster response to shocks than that for the EC.

(iii) In contrast to the results for speed of response, the magnitude of response is remarkably similar for the US and for the EC, implying that the underlying shocks may be of a similar magnitude. (These are all issues to which we return later.)

In Figure 7.3 the underlying demand and supply shocks for the EC and US aggregates are shown. In the case of the EC, large negative disturbances to supply are evident in 1973–75 and 1979–80, corresponding to the two oil shocks, along with a large negative supply shock in 1968 which is more difficult to interpret. The demand disturbances illustrate the different response of the EC to the first and second oil crises; there was a large positive demand shock in 1976, while from 1980 onwards demand shocks were negative. In the case of the US the effects of the oil crises are also clearly evident, while the rapid recovery of the 1980s seems to be associated with a series of positive supply shocks (perhaps reflecting tax cuts which were supply-side friendly). There was a major negative demand shock in 1982, corresponding to the policy of disinflation pursued by the Federal Reserve System.

We now turn to the results for individual EC countries and US regions. We first examine the correlation of aggregate demand and supply shocks across EC members and standard US regions in order to identify similarities and differences between the two groups. We next consider comparisons over time in order to study whether the shocks to the EC have become more correlated as a result of the convergence of macroeconomic policy. Finally, we compare the magnitude of underlying demand and supply disturbances in Europe and the US and contrast their speed of adjustment.

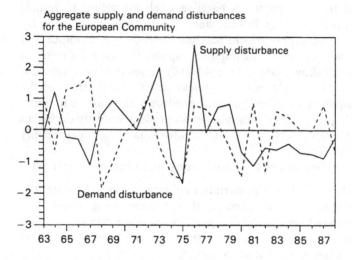

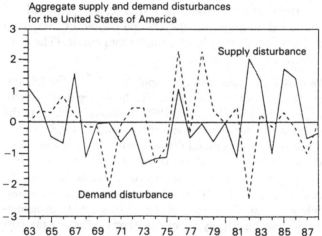

Figure 7.3 Aggregate demand and supply shocks for the European Community and the USA

5.1 Correlations

The first column of data in Table 7.4 shows correlation coefficients measuring the association of supply shocks in Germany with those in other EC countries. German supply shocks were highly correlated with those experienced by four of its close neighbours: France, the Netherlands, Denmark and Belgium. All four had correlation coefficients of 0.5

Table 7.4. *Correlation coefficients between anchor areas and other regions: underlying shocks*

	Supply shocks	Demand shocks
EC countries		
Germany	1.00	1.00
France	0.54	0.35
Belgium	0.61	0.33
Netherlands	0.59	0.17
Denmark	0.59	0.39
United Kingdom	0.11	0.16
Italy	0.23	0.17
Spain	0.31	− 0.07
Ireland	− 0.06	− 0.08
Portugal	0.21	0.21
Greece	0.14	0.19
US regions		
Mid-East	1.00	1.00
New England	0.86	0.79
Great Lakes	0.81	0.60
South East	0.67	0.50
Plains	0.30	0.51
South West	− 0.12	0.13
Rocky Mountains	0.18	− 0.28
Far West	0.52	0.33

Notes: The correlation coefficients refer to the entire data period: 1962–88 for the European Community and 1965–86 for the regions of the United States.

and 0.65, while the other six EC countries had lower correlations, in the order of − 0.1 to + 0.3.[25]

The bottom half of the table shows the same results for US regions (with the Mid-East being taken as the US centre analogous to Germany in the EC). The data display a similar pattern but with higher correlations than those of EC countries. The three US regions neighbouring the Mid-East (New England, the Great Lakes and the South East) had correlations of over 0.65, while the other four regions had lower correlations. The correlation between the Far West and the Mid-East was still relatively high (over 0.5), but that between the South West and the Mid-East was negative (presumably reflecting the importance of the oil industry in states like Texas and Oklahoma).

In effect, then, both the EC and the US appear to divide themselves into a 'core' of regions characterized by relatively symmetric behaviour and a 'periphery' in which disturbances are more loosely correlated with those experienced by centre. As in Europe, the US 'core' is made up of areas that are neighbours of the centre region (the only exception being the Far West).

The results for demand disturbances, reported in column 2, are more difficult to characterize. All of the correlations for EC countries were in the range − 0.1 to + 0.4. As with supply disturbances, there is some evidence that demand disturbances are more highly correlated across core countries than among the members of the EC periphery. The simple arithmetic means of the respective sets of correlation coefficients are 0.31 and 0.10. The 'core-periphery' distinction is less strong, however, for the demand shocks than for the supply shocks.

The correlation of regional demand disturbances for the US was higher than the analogous correlation for Europe. This is what could be expected in that US regions are members of a monetary union and should therefore experience similar monetary and (perhaps) fiscal shocks. The other three members of the US core regions all had correlation coefficients with the Mid-East in excess of 0.5. The Far West and the Plains had correlation coefficients of more than 0.33, while the two remaining regions had more idiosyncratic demand shocks.

In Figure 7.4 the correlation coefficients of demand shocks (on the vertical axis) and the correlation coefficients supply shocks (on the horizontal axis) are juxtaposed. (The top panel is for Germany and the other EC countries, while the lower panel is for the Mid-East and other US regions). While the distinction between 'core' (with highly correlated supply shocks) and a 'periphery' is evident in both panels, it is also clear that the US regional data are characterized by higher correlations.

In Table 7.5 the correlations between demand and supply shocks are summarized using principal components analysis. Results are reported for three successive sub-periods as a way of exploring the extent to which supply and demand shocks in EC member countries have grown more similar over time. The first two columns compare the 11 member countries of the EC with the 11 other industrial economies. For the full sample period, aggregate supply and aggregate demand shocks for the EC countries were more correlated. The first principal component explained 31–33% of the variance for the 11 EC countries; for the others it explained only 26%. This pattern of higher correlations among EC countries generally held for sub-periods. There is, however, little or no evidence of convergence over time. There is no apparent tendency for the difference in the percentage of the variance explained for the EC and for the other 11 industrial countries to increase over time.

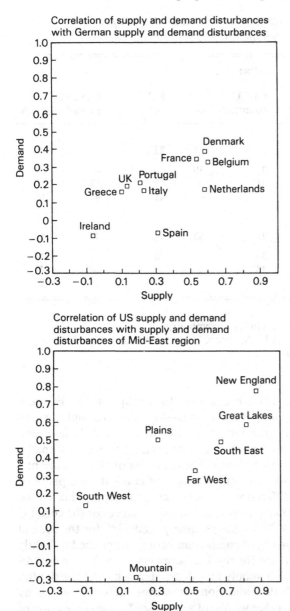

Figure 7.4 Correlation of demand and supply shocks with anchor areas

Table 7.5. *Percentage of variance explained by the first principal component for geographic groupings*

Regions	European Community[a]	Other 11 OECD countries	EC core	EC periphery	Control group[b]	USA
Supply shocks						
Full period	33	26	54	32	33	49
1963–71	34	33	39	40	42	53
1972–79	44	41	63	41	51	65
1980–88	35	37	62	41	47	68
Demand shocks						
Full period	31	26	53	36	41	51
1963–71	30	34	58	30	37	44
1972–79	40	38	50	49	48	49
1980–88	40	34	54	43	56	75

Notes:
[a] The European Community excludes Luxembourg.
[b] The control group comprises USA, Japan, Canada, Australia, New Zealand and Iceland. The sample period is 1962–88.

In columns 3–5 the results are extended to distinguish the EC core (Germany, France, Belgium, the Netherlands, Denmark and Luxembourg), the EC periphery (the UK, Italy, Spain, Portugal, Ireland and Greece), and a control group of other countries (the US, Japan, Canada, Australia, New Zealand and Iceland). The countries of the EC core had more correlated supply and demand shocks than either the periphery or the control group. The difference is most striking for supply shocks: the first principal component explained 54% of the variance for the core EC countries, compared to 32% for the periphery, and 33% for the control group. In fact, the first principal component actually explained a slightly lower percentage of variance for the EC periphery than for the control group. This is true for both supply and demand shocks and for the full data period. There is little indication, moreover, of convergence by newcomers to the EC – in other words, of a tendency for the correlation of disturbances among members of the EC periphery to rise over time compared to the correlation of disturbances among members of the control group.

The sixth column shows the results for the eight US regions. Their correlations are similar to those for the EC core but noticeably higher than those for the EC periphery and the control group. The correlations were considerably higher when the South West and Rocky Mountains were excluded than when all eight US regions were included. When the Great Lakes and New England were excluded, the correlations fell. Thus, the correlation of supply and demand disturbances across US regions is highly sensitive to the regions included. The core EC countries were consistently near the bottom of the range defined by the correlations for these sub-sets of US regions.

To summarize, the results for both the US and EC suggest that it is possible to distinguish core regions for which supply and demand shocks are highly correlated, and a periphery in which the correlation of shocks is less pronounced. Whether the eight US regions are compared with the 11 EC members or whether the comparison is limited to the EC and US core countries/regions, disturbances tended to be more highly correlated in the US.[26] Only if the core EC countries are compared with all eight US regions are the correlations of similar magnitude, although it should be recalled that in the case of demand shocks the higher US correlations may reflect the impact of uniform economic policies.

5.2   Size of shocks

In addition to looking at the symmetry or correlation of shocks across regions, our methodology can also be used to estimate their relative size. The larger the size of the underlying shocks, the more difficult it may be to maintain a fixed exchange rate, and the more compelling may be the case for an independent economic policy response. This is particularly true of supply shocks, which may require more painful adjustment.

In Table 7.6 the standard deviations of the aggregate demand and aggregate supply disturbances are given for the EC countries and the US regions. For the EC, the magnitude of supply shocks, like the correlation of supply shocks, suggests the existence of two distinct groups of countries. The core countries all have standard deviations in the range of 0.01 to 0.02 (1–2% per annum). The standard deviations for the periphery all range from 0.02 to 0.04 (2–4% per annum). Broadly speaking, then, the peripheral countries experience supply shocks twice as large as the core countries.

The supply shocks to US regions are similar to those experienced by the EC core and uniformly lower than those of the EC periphery. The standard deviation for the US South West, which at 0.019 is the largest for any US region, is still lower than that for any of the members of the EC periphery. There is also some indication that the US regions, particularly

Table 7.6. *Standard deviations of aggregate supply and aggregate demand shocks*

	Supply shocks	Demand shocks
EC countries		
Germany	0.017	0.014
France	0.012	0.012
Belgium	0.015	0.016
Netherlands	0.017	0.015
Denmark	0.017	0.021
United Kingdom	0.026	0.017
Italy	0.022	0.020
Spain	0.022	0.015
Ireland	0.021	0.034
Portugal	0.029	0.028
Greece	0.030	0.016
US regions		
Mid-East	0.012	0.019
New England	0.014	0.025
Great Lakes	0.013	0.033
Plains	0.016	0.022
South East	0.011	0.018
South West	0.019	0.018
Rocky Mountains	0.018	0.015
Far West	0.013	0.017

Notes: All variables are measured in logarithms, so that 0.027 indicates a standard deviation of approximately 2.7 percent.

those in the core, experience smaller supply shocks than member countries of the EC core; five of the eight US standard deviations are below 0.15, compared to only one of five for the EC core countries.

The results for demands shocks, shown in the right hand column, are quite different. Demand shocks in the EC core countries are slightly smaller than those of the EC periphery. Germany and France, for example, have the lowest standard deviations. More striking, however, is the comparison betwee the US and the EC. In contrast to the results for supply shocks, the US regions actually have somewhat larger standard deviations than the EC countries.

This finding is not a reflection of larger aggregate disturbances to the US as a whole; the standard error for the US aggregate, using OECD data, is 0.153 – lower than that for most EC countries. The high variability of

demand affecting US regions may therefore reflect the greater specialization of industrial production in the US (for data on the concentration
of industry within the US, see Krugman (1991), Appendix D). The large
region-specific demand disturbances would then reflect shifts in demand
from the products of one region to those of another region. This suppo-
sition is supported by the ranking of the size of demand disturbances
across US regions. The largest demand disturbances are those for the
Great Lakes, Mid-East, Plains and New England regions, all of which are
relatively specialized while the South East and Far West, which are more
sectorially diversified, have lower variability. If this interpretation is
correct, the evidence suggests that completion of the internal market in
Europe may well magnify aggregate demand disturbances by leading to
increased specialization.[27]

In Figure 7.5 (A)–(D) the size of disturbances against their correlation
with that of the centre country or region are juxtaposed. The vertical axis
measures the standard deviation of the disturbance, while the horizontal
axis shows the correlation. Panel A shows the results for supply shocks in
EC countries, B the results for supply shocks in US regions. Panels (C)
and (D) show the results for the demand disturbances. The panels are
plotted using the same scales to aid comparison. The supply disturbance
panels vividly illustrate the different behaviour of the core and periphery
for both the EC and the US. It is also clear, however, that the shocks
affecting the US periphery were much smaller than those affecting the EC
periphery, making the lack of correlation with the anchor region somewhat less of an issue. The data for the demand disturbances, on the other
hand, show relatively little pattern, although the relatively large shocks
experienced by US regions is evident.

5.3 Speed of adjustment to shocks

In addition to isolating underlying disturbances, our procedure permits
the responses of economies to shocks to be analysed. This can be done by
looking at the impulse response functions associated with the structural
VARs. Two issues of interest can then be addressed. How does speed of
adjustment by EC countries characterized by relatively low factor mobility but adjustable exchange rates compare with speed of adjustment by
US regions characterized by high factor mobility but fixed exchange
rates? Is there evidence of consistent differences among EC countries
associated with openness or other structural characteristics?

In Figures 7.6 and 7.7 the impulse-response functions for output are
displayed for the EC countries and for US regions. In Figure 7.6 the
responses to supply shocks are shown; the top panel displays the impulse-

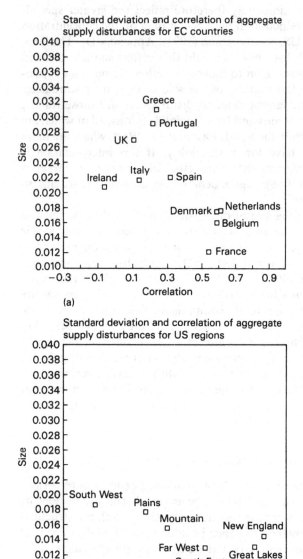

Figure 7.5 (a and b) The size and correlation of the demand and supply disturbances

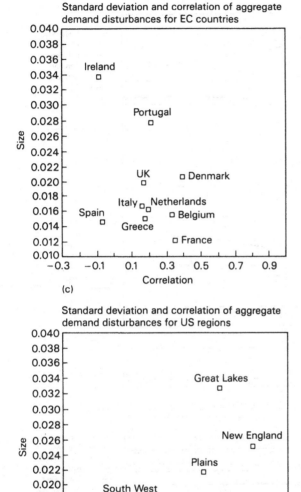

Figure 7.5 (c and d) The size and correlation of the demand and supply disturbances

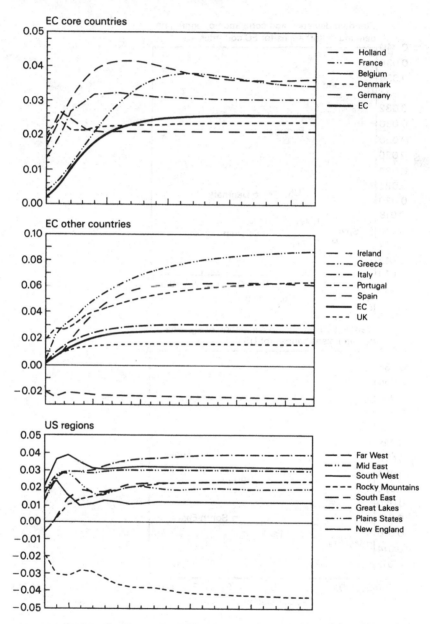

Figure 7.6 Impulse-response functions – supply shocks

responses for the core EC countries, the middle panel the responses for the remaining EC economies, and the bottom panel the responses for US regions.[28] A noticeable feature is the faster speed of adjustment for the US regions despite the lack of an exchange rate instrument within the US currency area. The bulk of the adjustment by the US regions to supply shocks occurred within three years; for EC countries it typically took substantially longer. A simple measure of the speed of adjustment is the ratio of the impulse-response function in the third year to its long run level, a high value indicates a fast adjustment, a low value a relatively slow adjustment. The average value of this statistic across US regions was 0.94, as opposed to 0.72 across EC countries. Interestingly, the average value for the EC core was also somewhat higher than that for the periphery.

The impulse-response functions to demand shocks shown in Figure 7.7, show a similar pattern. Again, the US regions appear to exhibit significantly faster responses than EC countries. One measure of the speed of this adjustment is to take the value of the impulse-response function after five years; a low value will now represent speedy adjustment. The values of the statistic were generally lower across US regions than EC countries, confirming the visual impression.

These VAR decompositions have allowed the analysis to proceed considerably further than simple comparisons of growth and inflation rates permit. The distinction between EC core and periphery is much less clear when the raw data are analysed. For example, the standard deviations of untransformed GDP growth rates for Italy and the UK were quite similar to those for Germany and France, while US regions tended to show relatively large variability in output growth. Our decomposition, by differentiating supply and demand disturbances from responses, allows the sources of this variability to be identified more precisely. Differences among countries and regions in the extent to which output variability and its sources are correlated with analogous variables in the centre country or region are less striking in the raw data than in the transformed series, rendering the former more difficult to interpret. Moreover, the calculations of the impulse-response functions allowed us to analyse the different set of issues revolving around speed of adjustment to shocks which cannot be addressed using the raw data.

6   Summary and implications

In this chapter we have used structural vector auto-regression to identify the incidence of aggregate supply and demand disturbances in Europe and to analyse the response of the economies of the European Community. A strong distinction emerges between the supply shocks affecting the

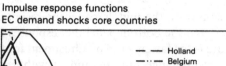

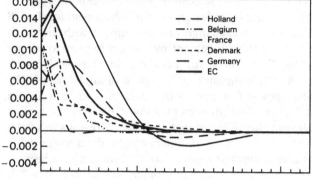

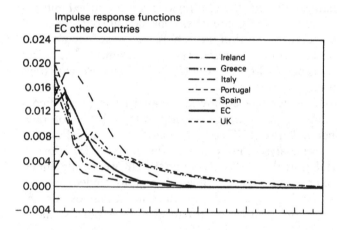

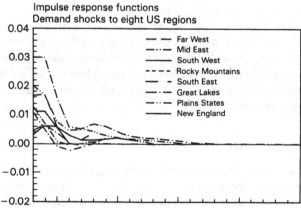

Figure 7.7 Impulse-response functions to a demand shock

countries at the centre of the European Community – Germany, France, Belgium, the Netherlands and Denmark – and the very different supply shocks affecting other EC members – the United Kingdom, Italy, Spain, Portugal, Ireland and Greece. Supply shocks to the core countries were both smaller and more correlated across neighbouring countries. The demand shocks experienced by the core countries were also smaller and more inter-correlated, although the difference on the demand side was less dramatic. There was also little evidence of convergence in the sense of the core-periphery distinction becoming less pronounced over time.

Our analysis of the American monetary union similarly suggests the existence of an economic core comprised of the Eastern Seaboard, the Mid-West and the Far West, along with a periphery comprised of the Rocky Mountain states and the South West. Shocks to the US core and periphery showed considerably more coherence than shocks to the analogous European regions. Only if the EC core is compared with the entire US (core and periphery together) were the magnitude and coherence of aggregate supply and demand disturbances comparable. The US does, however, contain two (relatively small) regions, the South West and the Rocky Mountains, where the underlying disturbances were relatively idiosyncratic.

Our impulse response functions indicate that the US regions adjust to shocks more quickly than do EC countries, in spite of the lack of the exchange rate instrument. This finding, which holds for both aggregate demand and aggregate supply shocks, plausibly reflects greater factor mobility in the United States than in Europe.

What are the implications of this analysis for the debate over EMU? Our finding that supply shocks are larger in magnitude and less correlated across regions in Europe than in the United States underscores the possibility that the European Community may find it more difficult, initially, to operate a monetary union than the United States. Large idiosyncratic shocks strengthen the case for policy autonomy and suggest that significant costs may be associated with its sacrifice. Our finding that the adjustment to shocks is faster in the US than in Europe emphasizes this point.

The strong distinction that emerges in our analysis between on the one hand, a core of EC member countries that experienced relatively small, highly-correlated aggregate supply disturbances, and on the other, a second group of countries, in which supply disturbances were larger and more idiosyncratic, is consonant with arguments that have been advanced for a two-speed monetary union (e.g. Dornbusch 1990). Information on other dimensions of the performance of these economies will be required, however, before we are in a position to pass judgement on the case for and against a two-speed EMU. Nevertheless, our analysis of disturbances suggest that for the time being, Germany and its immediate EC neighbours (the EC core) come much closer than the Community as a whole to representing a workable monetary union along American lines.

The conclusions reached in the preceding two paragraphs on the outlook for monetary unification in the EC reflect the fact that the results are based on historical data. The incidence of supply and demand shocks could well change with the completion of the 1992 programme and the transition to EMU. As market structures grow more similar across European countries, the incidence and correlation of supply disturbances should also become more similar. As factor mobility increases, the speed of adjustment to shocks should rise approaching, if not necessarily matching, US levels. On the other hand, demand disturbances may grow less correlated across European countries as market integration leads to increased regional specialization.[29] Changes on the supply side will make monetary union easier to operate, while those on the demand side will introduce further difficulties,; but both set of changes will work to make the incidence of supply and demand shocks across European nations resemble more closely those experienced in the United States. Thus, the comparative evidence for the US reported in this chapter remains a logical benchmark for those seeking to forecast the performance of the European economy once the transition to monetary and economic union is complete.

NOTES

We wish to thank Peter Kenen, Jeff Frankel and our conference discussants, Giorgio Basevi and Patrick Minford for helpful comments on earlier drafts. The text does not necessarily reflect the views of the Bank of England.

 1 The argument that deficit spending will be constrained follows from the observation that investors will hesitate to purchase the additional bonds issued by a jurisdiction running a budget deficit if the implied debt service exceeds its capacity to raise revenues. The force of this argument is disputed. For reviews of the debate see Eichengreen (1990a), Bayoumi and Russo (1992) and Goldstein and Woglom (1991).
 2 This change in response could take place through a number of different mechanisms. Horn and Persson (1988) suggest that EMU, by increasing the credibility of policy-makers' commitment to price stability, might enhance wage flexibility. The Commission of the European Communities (1990) argues similarly that EMU, by increasing the credibility of fiscal authorities' commitment not to bail out depressed regions, will encourage workers in such areas to moderate wage demands. Marsden (1989) suggests that increased product market integration, by reducing product market power at the national level, will make the derived demand for labour more price elastic, rendering wage setting more responsive to market conditions. Bertola (1988) presents argu-

ments suggesting that once exchange rates are immutably fixed, workers will respond by adjusting on other margins, notably inter-regional migration. We discuss some potential limitations of the US-European comparisons below.

3 Here we review only selected aspects of the optimum currency area literature as they bear on the issues. A more comprehensive survey is given in Ishiyama (1975).

4 Symmetry of shocks is not the only criterion for the choice of an optimal currency area. Other factors such as the cost of operating an independent currency, size of trade with other regions, and (possibly) similarity of public preferences are also important. When comparing the current EC with the US, however, many of these differences are relatively small. In particular, both regions represent continent-wide industrial areas with a high degree of internal trade and similarly sized populations. Accordingly, this chapter will focus on the issue of the symmetry and size of the underlying shocks in EC countries as compared with those across US regions.

5 The Commission of the European Communities (1991) presents evidence on the similarity of industrial structure across EC countries and argues that product market integration will increase the scope of intra-industry trade, rendering national industrial structures increasingly similar over time. Krugman (1991, 1992) suggests in contrast that completion of the internal market may lead to greater regional specialization and thereby magnify geographical differences in industrial structure. We return to this issue later.

6 The essence of this argument appears also in Scitovsky (1967).

7 If technology exhibits increasing returns, a shock which requires the expansion of one sector at the expense of another may require the inter-sectoral re-allocation of both factors of production for full efficiency to be achieved. See Eichengreen (1991). A taxonomy of cases is provided by Helpman and Krugman (1985).

8 Weber (1990) has extended their analysis of other EC countries.

9 De Grauwe and Vanhaverbeke (1991) study the variability of output across regions *within* European nations, arguing that this holds economic policies constant. But since it fails to hold the responsiveness of market adjustment mechanisms constant (such as, for example, internal migration and wage flexibility), which may themselves vary across regions, it remains difficult to distinguish disturbances from market responses. Eichengreen (1991) estimated models of internal migration for the United Kingdom, Italy and the United States and similarly found support for the hypothesis of greater labour mobility in the US.

10 Using different econometric methods, von Hagen (1991) has suggested that regional co-insurance in the US is closer to one-tenth than one-third. More recently, Bayoumi and Masson (1991) have arrived at estimates which are close to those of Sachs and Sala-i-Martin. In any case, fiscal redistribution across US regions is much more extensive than across EC member countries. In terms of the automatic stabilizer response to cyclical movements within regions, Atkeson and Baymoui (1991) present evidence that the behaviour of US regions and EC countries is similar.

11 Although this is usually thought of as a closed economy model, it is readily extended to include trade and the exchange rate. Textbook descriptions of the model include Dornbusch and Fischer (1986) Ch. 11, and Hall and Taylor (1988) Ch. 4–5.

12 Quah (1991) discusses the issue of identifying restrictions for *VARs*. An important assumption which is required to ensure uniqueness of the decomposition is that the underlying series (growth and inflation in this case) are fundamental in a World sense, as pointed out by Lippi and Reichlin (1990).

13 The conventional normalization is that the two variances are set equal to unity, which together with the assumption of orthogonality implies $C'C = \Sigma$, where Σ is the variance covariance matrix of e_y and e_p. When we wish to calculate the variance of the shocks themselves, however, we report results using the normalization $C'C = \Gamma$, where Γ is the correlation matrix of e_y and e_p. (See Bayoumi, 1991, for a discussion of this decomposition.) These two normalizations gave almost identical paths for the shocks, except for a scaling factor, and hence are used inter-changeably.

14 This is where our analysis, based on the work of Blanchard and Quah (1989), differs from other *VAR* models. The usual decomposition assumes that the variables in the *VAR* can be ordered such that all the effects which could be attributed to (say) either a_t or b_t are attributed to whichever comes first in the ordering. This is achieved by a Choleski decomposition (Sims, 1980).

15 Note from equation (4) that the long run impact of the shocks on output and prices is equal to $(I - B(1))^{-1}$. The restriction that the long run effect of demand shocks on output is zero implies a simple linear restriction on the coefficients of this matrix.

16 Two different measures of the EC aggregate are available from the OECD, one based on conversions of local currency data using 1985 dollars, and a second based on a weighting of the EC real GDP and GDP deflator indices. Since the two data sets gave very similar results, only those based on 1985 dollar exchange rates are reported.

17 For evidence and comparisons with Europe, see Eichengreen (1990a).

18 Since the data are in logarithms, a standard deviation of 0.012 implies an average deviation of 1.2%.

19 Germany is the largest economy in Europe, and has played the anchor role in the exchange rate mechanism, making it the obvious standard for comparison. The Mid-East, which is the most important region in the US financially and, arguably, economically, is taken as the analogous 'anchor' region of the US. These choices are retained in all subsequent analysis. Patrick Minford, in his comments, raised the question of whether our results for Europe are sensitive to the choice of Germany as the anchor area. In fact, this turns out not to be the case, as we elaborate below.

20 Luxembourg (which is otherwise excluded from the analysis because of its small size) was included in this part of the analysis in order to make the number of countries equal in each group. It should be stressed that the results from principal components analysis depend upon the number of series involved in the comparison. Hence it is not useful to compare the results for the EC 11 with (say) those for the six members of the EC periphery. Note that we have arbitrarily divided the EC countries and US regions into a core and periphery on the basis of our priors and by eyeballing correlation coefficients. In future work we plan to use cluster and discriminant analysis to sort these countries more systematically into groups, thereby getting at the issue known in Europe as 'variable geometry'.

21 We include six regions in each column and therefore render our principal-

components analysis as consistent as possible. Since growth and inflation rates are relatively variable in Iceland, and since its supply and demand shocks are fairly loosely correlated with those of other countries, its inclusion will tend to make shocks to other countries appear coherent compared to the control group. For details, see Bayoumi and Eichengreen (1991).

22 We show later that the two excluded regions respond differently to shocks from the rest of the US.

23 We also estimated VARs with three lags because, in contrast to the Schwartz Bayesian statistic, the Akaike information criterion showed the optimal lag to be above 2 in some of the models; this specification produced very similar results.

24 These results were obtained by estimating VARs on aggregate data for the US and EC, not by aggregating results obtained using regional US and national European data.

25 The same result holds when another member of the 'core', say France, is substituted for Germany as the anchor area. The result for the 'periphery' also continues to hold: on average, the peripheral countries do not exhibit a higher correlation with the other members of the core than they do with Germany. Nor do the peripheral countries exhibit as high a correlation with one another (or with a hypothetical anchor area like the UK or Italy) as do the countries of the core.

26 This is particularly true if account is taken of the fact that several of the peripheral US regions are quite small. Together the Rocky Mountains and South West contain less than 12% of the US population.

27 Our results concerning the magnitude of disturbances are broadly consistent with the more impressionistic evidence presented by Krugman (this volume). Both studies suggest that market integration of the type that characterizes the US leads to regional specialization and large region-specific shocks. The main difference is that Krugman, basing his interpretation on Blanchard and Katz (1992), argues that these region-specific disturbances are permanent, whereas our evidence suggests that the component of disturbances associated with US-style market integration is largely temporary. One explanation for this difference in interpretation is the following. Blanchard and Katz identify a single regional disturbance the long-run effect of which on activity (measured by employment) is slightly larger than its initial impact, hence the view that disturbances have permanent effects. We identify two disturbances, with permanent and temporary effects on activity. The permanent disturbance typically has a long-run effect which is much larger than its impact effect, while the temporary disturbance has no long-run effect (see Figures 7.6 and 7.7). A weighted average of these two paths can give an aggregate response of the type identified by Blanchard and Katz, while still implying a large role for temporary disturbances in regional activity. Hence we believe our results are not inconsistent with those in the work of Blanchard and Katz, rather they result from a more detailed disaggregation of the underlying data.

28 The larger scale required for the EC periphery is another illustration of the relative large shocks they experience.

29 Note that our estimates for successive sub-periods (in Table 7.5), including pre- and post-EMS decades, suggesting that market integration works only slowly to alter the incidence of supply and demand disturbances.

REFERENCES

Atkeson, A. and T. Bayoumi (1991) 'Do Private Markets Insure Against Regional Shocks in a Common Currency Area – Evidence from the US', unpublished manuscript, University of Chicago.

Bayoumi, Tamim (1991) 'A Note on the Decomposition of Vector Autoregressions', unpublished manuscript, Bank of England, London.

(1992) 'The Effects of the ERM on participating Economies', *IMF Staff Papers*, 39, Washington, DC.

Bayoumi, Tamim and Massimo Russo (1992) 'Fiscal Policy and EMU', paper included in a conference volume, *EMU and ESCB after Maastricht*, Financial Markets Group, London School of Economics.

Bayoumi, Tamim and Barry Eichengreen (1991) 'Is There a Conflict Between EC Enlargement and European Monetary Unification?', unpublished manuscript, Bank of England and University of California at Berkeley.

Bayoumi, Tamim and Paul Masson (1991) 'Fiscal Flows in the United States and Canada: "Lessons for Monetary Union in Europe",' unpublished manuscript, International Monetary Fund, Washington, DC.

Bertola, G. (1988) 'Factor Flexibility, Uncertainty and Exchange Rate Regimes', in Marcello de Cecco and Alberto Giovannini (eds), *A European Central Bank?*, Cambridge: Cambridge University Press, pp. 99–119.

Blanchard, Olivier and Lawrence Katz (1992) 'Regional Evolutions', unpublished manuscript, Cambridge, Mass.: MIT and Harvard University.

Blanchard, Olivier and Danny Quah (1989) 'The Dynamics Effects of Aggregate Demand and Supply Disturbances', *American Economic Review*, 79, pp. 655–73.

Cohen, Daniel and Charles Wyplosz (1989) 'The European Monetary Union: An Agnostic Evaluation', Centre for Economic Policy Research Discussion Paper No. 306, London.

Commission of the European Communities (1990) 'One Market, One Money: an Evaluation of the Potential Benefits and Costs of Forming an Economic and Monetary Union', *European Economy*, 44 (October).

De Grauwe, Paul and Wim Vanhaverbeke (1991) 'Is Europe an Optimum Currency Area? Evidence from Regional Data', Centre for Economic Policy Research Discussion Paper No. 555, London.

Dornbusch, Rudiger (1990) 'Two-Track EMU, Now!', in Karl Otto Pohl et al., *Britain and EMU*, London: Centre for Economic Performance, pp. 103–12.

Dornbusch, R. and S. Fischer (1986) *Macroeconomics*: 3rd Edition, New York: McGraw Hill.

Eichengreen, Barry (1990) 'Is Europe an Optimum Currency Area?', Centre for Economic Policy Research Discussion Paper No. 478, forthcoming in Herbert Grubel (ed.), *European Economic Integration: The View from Outside*, London: Macmillan.

(1990b) 'One Money for Europe? Lessons from the US Currency and Customs Union', *Economic Policy*, 10, pp. 118–87.

(1991) 'Labor Markets and European Monetary Unification', unpublished manuscript, University of California at Berkeley.

Goldstein, Morris and G. Woglom (1991) 'Market-Based Fiscal Discipline in Monetary Unions: Evidence from the US Municipal Bond Market', unpublished manuscript, International Monetary Fund, Washington.

Hall, R. and J. Taylor (1988) *Macroeconomics: Theory, Practice and Policy*, New York: Norton.

Helpman, Elhanan and Paul Krugman (1985) *Market Structure and Foreign Trade*, Cambridge, Mass.: MIT Press.

Horn, H. and Torsten Persson (1988) 'Exchange Rate Policy, Wage Formation and Credibility', *European Economic Review*, 32, pp. 1621–36.

Ingram, James (1973) 'The Case for European Monetary Integration', *Princeton Essays in International Finance* No. 98 (April), Princeton, New Jersey.

Ishiyama, Yoshihide (1975) 'The Theory of Optimum Currency Areas: A Survey', *IMF Staff Papers*, 22, Washington, DC, pp. 344–83.

Lippi, M. and L. Reichlin (1990) 'A Note on Measuring the Dynamic Effects of Aggregate Demand and Supply Disturbances', unpublished manuscript.

Kenen, Peter B. (1969) 'The Theory of Optimum Currency Areas: An Eclectic View', in Robert A. Mundell and Alexander K. Swoboda (eds), *Monetary Problems of the International Economy*, Chicago: University of Chicago Press.

Krugman, Paul (1991) *Economic Geography and International Trade*, Cambridge, Mass.: MIT Press.

(1993) 'Lessons of Massachusetts for EMU', Ch. 8, this volume.

Marsden, D. (1989) 'Occupations: The Influence of the Unemployment Situation', in W.T.M. Molle and A. van Mourik (eds), *Wage Differentials in the European Community*, Avebury: Gower, pp. 105–39.

Meade, James (1957) 'The Balance of Payments Problems of a Free Trade Area', *Economic Journal*, 67, pp. 379–96.

Mundell, Robert (1961) 'A Theory of Optimum Currency Areas', *American Economic Review*, pp. 657–65.

Organisation for Economic Cooperation and Development (1985) *Flexibility in the Labour Market*, Paris.

Poloz, Stephen S. (1990) 'Real Exchange Rate Adjustment Between Regions in a Common Currency Area', unpublished manuscript, Bank of Canada.

Quah, Danny (1991) 'Identifying Vector Autoregressions. A Discussion of P. Englund, A. Vredin and A. Warne: Macroeconomic Shocks in Sweden 1925–86', unpublished manuscript, London School of Economics, September.

Sachs, J. and X. Sala i Martin (1991) 'Fiscal Policies and Optimum Currency Areas: Evidence from Europe and the United States', paper given at a conference Establishing a Central Bank, Georgetown University, 1–2 May 1991.

Scitovsky, Tibor (1967) 'The Theory of Balance-of-Payments Adjustment', *Journal of Political Economy*, 75, pp. 523–31.

Sims, Christopher (1980) 'Macroeconomics and reality', *Econometrica*, 48, pp. 1–49.

von Hagen, Jurgen (1991) 'Fiscal Arrangements in a Monetary Union: Evidence from the US', unpublished manuscript, Indiana University.

Weber, A. (1990) 'EMU and Asymmetries and Adjustment Problems in the EMS: Some Empirical Evidence', Centre for Economic Policy Research Discussion Paper No. 448, London.

Discussion

GIORGIO BASEVI

I shall start my discussion by briefly recalling the authors' main findings, and the policy implications that they suggest should be drawn from them.

After having devised a model that allows empirical identification of supply and demand shocks, and the speed of the economy's reaction to them, the authors obtain a number of results, some of which are relevant to the question of the overall feasibility of a European Monetary Union (EMU), while others are relevant to the question of which countries will find it easier to move into such a union.

On the question of the overall feasibility of EMU, the authors first find that supply shocks have been larger in magnitude and less correlated across regions in Europe than in the United States. This would imply that the European Community as a whole may find it more difficult to operate a monetary union than the United States.

The same inference is drawn from the finding that adjustment to shocks is faster in the US than in Europe, as this suggests that factor mobility is greater in the former country.

Moreover, it would seem that a smooth working of monetary union in Europe will not be fostered by further economic integration: the finding that US regions experience relatively large demand shocks compared to their European counterparts suggests, according to the authors, that the completion of the single European market will push the member countries into a more specialized economic structure, thereby magnifying the asymmetric nature of demand shocks.

On the question of which countries will more easily form an economic and monetary union, the authors identify a strong distinction between a core of EC members that experience relatively small and highly correlated aggregate supply disturbances, and a group of peripheral EC members whose supply disturbances are larger and less correlated with those of the centre. From this evidence, the authors infer that a two-speed monetary union is a more viable avenue towards EMU, with the core EC countries moving ahead to form it.

Although I think it is difficult not to agree with the empirical analysis of the chapter, and with the implication that the road to EMU is a difficult one, particularly for the peripheral members, I also think that the authors should agree that, on purely logical ground, their suggested implications do not follow from the evidence. More specifically, comparison between the EC and the US in terms of regions and their different structures, shocks, and reactions to them, would have to include, in the set of situations to be compared, one that refers to a counter-factual history and one that refers to two alternative futures.

The counter-factual history would have to tell us what would have been the difference between the peripheral and the core regions of the US – in terms of structure, shocks, and speed of adjustment – had they not been members of the US monetary union. The alternative future histories from which we would like to draw our conclusions should include both a consideration of what may happen to the peripheral regions should they join EMU at one and the same speed as the core regions, and a consideration of what may happen if they were to join the union at a later date, or stay out of it altogether. Unfortunately we cannot observe what did not happen in the US, even though it might have happened, nor compare two future alternative events, only one of which, necessarily, will happen. Although this is obvious enough, yet I think it must be stated. In fact, if we do not consider what might happen to the peripheral European regions should they stay out of EMU or not proceed at the same speed as the core regions, and unless we do so in the light of what we might guess could have happened to the US peripheral regions had they been left out of the union (say with Mexico and the rest of Central America), we would be tempted to reach conclusions too rapidly and possibly incorrectly.

It seems to me that the real question raised in this chapter is not one of social optimality, but rather one of economic efficiency. In other words, the question is not really whether it is beneficial for the members of the EC to form an economic and monetary union, but whether the path to it is viable, i.e., whether the 'traverse' that leads to it is such as to make all members better off during the process. The suggestion of the chapter is that some members, the peripheral countries, may find the path too costly if they have to proceed at the same speed as the others.

To argue this, we must consider the alternative paths of a common and a two-speed participation, and also the possibility that no path at all is taken towards EMU, i.e. that a country (or a set of countries) on the periphery may finally have to stay out of EMU.

I think it is better to say from the beginning, that in considering these options, I have in mind a country like mine, i.e. Italy. I submit that such a peripheral country, if it were to renege on its engagement to EMU and stay out of it altogether, would have to revert to a sort of crawling peg for its exchange rate, much as in the old European monetary system

(Giavazzi and Spaventa, 1990). At worst, such a country would be in danger of losing its status as a full member of the European Community. On the other hand, if it were to aim at full EMU participation but to proceed towards it at a lower speed, it would have to keep its exchange rate fixed, but adjust it once or twice before entering fully the economic and monetary union.

For reasons on which I have no time to elaborate, but which are in my view obvious and mainly political, I think it is inconceivable that Italy would opt out of EMU. Thus the question is simply whether it should proceed towards EMU at the same speed as the others or at a lower speed.

I proceed from the assumption that with a fixed exchange rate, Italy will be unable, even through the convergence process that should be implemented until 1996, to recover the competitive position it has lost through higher inflation. Thus, to make sense of the final entry into EMU, the lira would have to be depreciated, possibly at the time of the revision of other parities, when the last phase of the unification programme is entered into. To wait for that date, however, and in the meantime try to converge to the monetary and fiscal requirements laid down at Maastricht would, in my opinion, be disastrous for Italy, even assuming it to be possible. Its impaired competitive position would make the necessary fiscal and monetary restraint required from now until the end of 1996, more costly. A realignment of the lira is thus required now, or at least within the current year, together with a serious launching of the stabilization programme requested by the European Community. The realignment must be substantial, i.e. enough to make it clear that it will not be followed by further realignments in the future, not even at the end of the convergence programme (except for what may be required within the overall and last revision of parities necessary for the final conversion of national currencies into the ECU).

Now, if the realignment is to be substantial, then Italy need not move at a lower speed towards EMU. On the contrary, a lower speed will only make for renewed loss of competitiveness during the convergence process. In fact, Italy could not credibly return to the crawling peg system that characterized the EMS before 1987, while at the same time committing herself to a stricter system at a later stage. Thus the exchange rate would have to be kept fixed also in the two-speed option and, worse than in the one-speed option, it would continue to bind the economy, exacerbating Italy's current problems.

But what are these problems and how are they related to the regional differences that the authors identify, both within countries and among the core and the peripheral countries of Europe?

One problem related to the subject of the chapter under discussion is that, instead of gaining for Italy a faster and less painful convergence to a lower degree of inflation, the exchange rate constraint seems to have taken the strength out of the economy's productive structure. What has happened is not just the textbook re-allocation away from tradable towards non-tradable goods sectors because of an over-valued exchange rate for the currency. The strait-jacket of monetary and exchange rate policies, together with the pressure to reduce government expenditure and increase fiscal revenues in relatively quick and politically less costly ways, appear to have bitten deeply in the sectors of the economy that are exposed to these policy instruments; the development of the sectors that hide from competitive constraints or legal regulations have been comparatively favoured.

I am not just referring to the traditional recourse to a hidden economy that wrongly appeared to be, some years ago, a sign of strength of the Italian society. I refer rather to the illegal and criminal activities which, in Italy, are experiencing a boom in the middle of a recession. This 'sector' thrives both in tradable and non-tradable industries and services.

When there is a situation where exchange rate and fiscal pressures are affecting the ability of the legal economy to remain competitive, while the government is retrenching and diminishing the quantity and quality of its essential services, the stage is set whereby illegal production and criminal activities can act at a comparative advantage. These activities can easily employ the labour force that cannot find better employment in the legally productive sectors. They hire labour on less regulated terms and they are less sensitive to the exchange rate constraint. When they produce exportable products that are illegal (such as drugs) they face a rather inelastic demand curve for them; they can even provide efficiently some non-tradable services that should be traditionally reserved to the Government – such as security of a sort (for those who accept protection), faster bureaucratic tracks, and other social privileges.

Thus the country as a whole, and not just the traditionally less developed regions in it, drifts into a very efficient, but not very enviable, economic specialization. As has been argued in recent contributions at the border of international and regional economics (Abraham and Von Rompuy, 1991), such a process of acquired comparative advantage may be self-reinforcing. In fact, in so far as capital and skilled labour are more complementary in production with efficient and legal government services, than is unskilled labour, there will be pressure for capital and skilled labour to migrate to the legally more reassuring regions and countries, leaving the unskilled labour to be hired for labour-intensive illegal and criminal activities. These may even attract more of the unskilled labour coming from outside the Community, particularly from the African continent, while the relatively more trained immigrants from Eastern Europe will be attracted by the more advanced regions and countries in the core of the EC.

Clearly, this dark picture is one in which the forces involved in the process towards EMU are just part of the complex field of forces that have historically generated such a perverse development. I am convinced, however, that today the political and economic situation in which Italy finds herself is extremely critical, and that a wrong choice, even on matters that seem far from these problems, such as the timing and the speed of adoption of the monetary and fiscal policies required by EMU, could unchain a perverse involution of the country into economic, social and political decline.

In a recent CEPR report on EMU (1991), the authors stress that the fabric of EMU must be acceptable to all members in order to be viable: it must be incentive-compatible.

We may thus wonder, if the picture of the situation in Italy that I have just drawn is correct, what incentives would countries in the core of the EC have to offer and why should they accept an attempt at a faster, rather than a two-speed, movement towards EMU. My answer would be that these countries have much to lose by letting any peripheral country of the EC specialize in the industries and services that are now flourishing in Italy. These produce exportable products and services of a kind that other countries should not wish to import, and yet are bound to import unless something is done about redressing the perverse specialization of their drifting partners. We certainly do not want some of the peripheral countries of Europe to become, for the core countries, what some of the Central and South American countries are for the United States, in terms of the illegal products and financial activities that they export.

There is no time to argue now what should be done about all this. But at least, to come back to EMU and the Maastricht programme, it seems to me that there are at least three implications.

(1) The peripheral countries, and in particular Italy, should not be encouraged to move at a lower speed towards EMU. The lira should be devalued soon and credibly, and then the stage should be set for a serious programme to join EMU at the same time as the other main partners in the project.

(2) Programmes of financial transfers by the EC to the less developed

regions and countries should be limited, in so far as they have mainly contributed to the corruption of government administration in the recipient countries (and again, I have mainly Italy in mind), in which the illegal sectors of the economy have been able to flourish.

(3)   The social and labour market side of European integration should not be designed so as to make it even more difficult for the less advanced regions to specialize within the legally productive and labour intensive sectors, while giving further incentive to the illegal sectors. The entrepreneurs in these latter sectors certainly do not care about labour legislation when hiring their manpower. The position taken by the United Kingdom at Maastricht appears to me, in this respect, economically much sounder than the one taken by the other main EC countries.

REFERENCES

Abraham, F. and Paul van Rompuy (1991) 'Convergence-divergence and the implications for Community Structural Problems', International Economics Research Paper No. 18, Centrum voor Economiche Studien, KUL.

Centre for Economic Policy Research (1991) *Monitoring European Integration: the Making of Monetary Union*, Annual Report, Centre for Economic Policy Research, London.

Giavazzi, F. and L. Spaventa (1990) 'The New EMS' in P. de Grauwe and L. Papademos (eds), *The European Monetary System in the 1990s*, London: Longman.

Discussion

PATRICK MINFORD

To travel hopefully is often better than to arrive. In Stage II we are travelling hopefully; this chapter is about what may happen if we arrive. Some of us hope that we will not make it – the authors seem to agree with those concerns. My fellow discussant, Giorgio Basevi, has added his concerns from one of the countries which in this chapter is classified as on the 'periphery'; I might add that if a peripheral country in the authors' optimal currency area sense, such as Italy or Britain, were to be forced into the 'core', then these countries would risk becoming peripheral in the more usual sense of being retarded in growth.

There are two main arguments advanced for EMU. The first promotes the gain in monetary policy credibility and so in price stability that could come from a single independent European central bank, able to avoid and prevent the time-inconsistency of national policy-making. The second states that the gains from reduced transactions costs and exchange rate uncertainty outweigh the losses from the lack of national exchange rate (and interest rate) adjustment to differential (or 'asymmetric') regional shocks.

This last argument centres around the 'optimal currency area' debate and is the focus of this chapter. This investigates the extent to which the EC regions (countries) have differential shocks and adjust more slowly than US regions, which are taken to be the benchmark for a successful monetary union. The authors find that a 'core' of EC countries are similar to the US but that a 'periphery' group exhibits high shock asymmetry and slow response speeds. They conclude that this is further evidence for a variable-speed EMU.

The chapter is clear and well-executed and I am in agreement with at least one part of the authors' conclusion – that a large number of countries are not ripe for EMU. The chapter is a good contribution to the burgeoning literature attempting to find evidence about EMU – much of it reviewed at the start of this chapter. As the authors note, however, there are vast problems in the sort of work they are doing: namely 'to distinguish the separate effects' of shocks and responses.

D.7.1 Structure and reduced forms

What we ideally want is (a) the shocks to structural equations and (b) the effects of these with and without EMU, given optimal policy responses (this is, after all, about optimal currency areas!). Instead, what we have here is a decomposition of reduced form shocks to output and prices, in the EC countries and in US regions. Bayoumi and Eichengreen emphasize their decomposition into 'demand' and 'supply' – but these are not structural shocks, merely those effects on output that are temporary versus those that are permanent. The temporary effects reflect transitory supply shocks, fiscal and monetary responses, temporary fiscal transfers (or their absence), and the effects of floating or the exchange rate mechanism in the EC and of a common exchange rate in the US regions. The permanent effects include all supply variables integrated of order one (that is, whose first differences are stationary) – such as oil prices, tax rates, public spending, factor prices – and the permanent responses to them – whether fiscal, monetary or institutional.

Therefore I cannot see that the authors have done much more, qualitatively, than other recent work comparing European output and relative price variability inside countries with that between countries – for example, De Grauwe and Vanhaverbeke (1991), whom they cite, or von Hagen and Neumann (1991). This can be seen by comparing the Table 7.1, correlations of raw output data, with Table 7.4 which gives decomposed data: the rankings of core and periphery countries is much the same. (I presume the same holds for raw versus decomposed response speeds and impulse patterns, though the raw data are not given.)

It is interesting to have decompositions, of course, but this leads me to ask exactly how useful these decompositions are. The distinction between permanent shocks to output and temporary ones is not really between 'supply' and 'demand' shocks, though the authors adduce evidence of price responses to argue that it closely corresponds to it. But in any case why is this relevant to optimal currency areas? When the role of the exchange rate and interest rates is to dampen shocks because wages and prices do not move sufficiently rapidly, then both types of shock are candidates for dampening (a permanent shock because the adjustment path to it may be inefficiently slow, and specifically may involve excessive unemployment). If one uses as a guide Poole's (1970) analysis extended to the open economy, then only domestic monetary shocks would be dampened better by fixed rates, but with all others there is a *prima facie* case for floating. There would be some interest, therefore, in a decomposition into domestic monetary shocks and the rest.

Even then, shocks would need to be distinguished from responses, something that in principle – in spite of all the work they have done – the authors do not succeed in doing, any more than their predecessors did. To do it, however, requires a different methodology altogether. A structural model must be estimated and then simulated under the alternative regimes, assuming optimal policy responses. From this can be estimated the relative macroeconomic variability (welfare cost) of EMU (and for that matter of US monetary union). There have been attempts – including work by Hughes Hallett and Vines (1992), the EC Commission (1990), using Multimod, and Hughes Hallett, Rastogi and myself (1992) using the Liverpool models.

For all the difficulties with such an approach, it is at least complementary to the work in this chapter and would be worth bringing into the picture. As it happens, generally the results obtained support the authors' conclusions. For example, in the Liverpool work we found that for the EC as a whole the weighted variances of macro variables of interest would rise by two-thirds in EMU compared with floating (much more for the UK); it was found that EC differential shocks were approximately 50% greater. (The correlation of EC countries with Germany is around 0.5 against around 0.75 for US regions with the Mid-East).

D.7.2 *Some detailed points*

Is the US really a good benchmark? This is an illustration of the confusion between shocks and responses. For suppose that fixing (abolishing) exchange rates produces more violent regional fluctuations so reducing their correlations with the centre and slowing their speed of adjustment. Then the US correlations would be biased downwards, for purposes of comparison with an EC where exchange rates have mostly been flexible.

Is the *VAR* method appropriate? It assumes that prices and output are both integrated of order one (i.e. that growth and inflation are both stationary). This is implausible for inflation at any rate (and for growth in some regions will not there also be supply shocks that affect the growth rate?). The authors claim to have tested for this assumption and found it appropriate for most countries, yet I am suspicious given the generally low power of tests for unit versus high roots. If it really is important to distinguish permanent shocks to output levels and growth rates, then the Kalman filter may provide a better approach. Also by specifying prices in relative price terms (real exchange rates) I would have more faith in price stationarity.

The use of correlations with a main 'central' region is obviously arbitrary. The authors could add to the chapter by displaying the correlation matrix between regions and then using clustering techniques to group the countries into possible currency areas. It seems quite plausible that there are sub-groups with a claim to be an optimal area – for example, Germany/Benelux, and UK/Ireland.

D.7.3 *Some wider points of general relevance*

In another chapter in this volume, Paul Krugman argues that integration leads to more regional differentiation through industrial specialization. This, it seems to me, does not necessarily conflict with the findings of this chapter. Integration also will lead to some diversification of industries within regions (if only because state politicians have a strong interest in diversification), and to the dominance of common economy shocks (because of tighter links on the demand side). The net effect should be to increase the correlations looked for and found by these authors.

Last, what is the policy implication of all this for Europe? Surely it is that EMU will remain premature even in 1999. Integration in the EC, as this chapter shows, falls far short of that of the US. Cross-border labour mobility in the EC is trivial compared with cross-regional migration in the US; this suggests a much greater need for relative price flexibility between countries of the EC, implying a crucial role for exchange rate flexibility. True, the lack of labour mobility will mean that national fiscal authorities have a more stable tax-base from which to carry out some fiscal stabilization, albeit limited by the new EC fiscal guidelines. Nevertheless, severe differential national shocks are likely to overwhelm this modest capacity, as witnessed by the incapacity of other countries in the exchange rate mechanism to offset German monetary tightness in the current recession.

If, in spite of all this, EMU were to go ahead, the conclusion must be that the infrastructure of political union would need to be put rapidly in place. An independent European central bank would need strong political backing, to give it legitimacy and to take the flak from unpopular actions. A central budget would be needed to boost national fiscal stabilizers. The necessary political union would have to come from willing cooperation by soverign states, since these have the most legitimacy with which to endow the new framework and the greatest power to frustrate it. Ultimately, the only logical participants at Maastricht were the Germans: they stressed that political union was the price of monetary union. They were right but they allowed themselves to be ignored and the Maastricht result was an inconclusive mishmash. We have a cart blocking the road with no horse in sight.

REFERENCES

De Grauwe, P. and W. Vanhaverbeke (1991) 'Is Europe an Optimum Currency Area? Evidence from Regional Data', Centre for Economic Policy Research Discussion Paper No. 555, London.

Hughes Hallett, A. and D. Vines (1991) 'Adjustment difficulties within a European Monetary Union: Can they be Reduced, Centre for Economic Policy Research Discussion Paper No. 517, London.

Minford, P., Hughes Hallett, A. and A. Rastogi (1992) 'The Price of EMU Revisited', Centre for Economic Policy Research Discussion Paper No. 656, London.

Poole, W. (1970) 'The optimal choice of monetary instrument in a single stochastic macro model', *Quarterly Journal of Economics*, **84**, 197–221.

Commission of the European Communities (1990) 'One Money, One Market: an Evaluation of the Potential Benefits and Costs of Forming an Economic and Monetary Union, *European Economy*, 44 (October).
von Hagen, Jurgen and Manfred Neumann (1991) 'Real exchange rates within and between currency areas: How far away is EMU', Centre for Global Business, Indiana University, Graduate School of Business, Discussion Paper 62.

8   Lessons of Massachusetts for EMU

PAUL KRUGMAN

1   Introduction

Over the past decade the European Community has made great strides towards becoming a fully unified economic entity. Border obstacles and regulatory barriers to an integrated market for goods and services have been removed in the drive towards 1992; now, as the economic and monetary union (EMU) moves forward, an integrated capital market and eventually a common currency seem all but assured. By the end of the twentieth century Europe should, in many respects, constitute as unified and integrated an economy as the United States of America.

Most economists (myself included) view this as a generally good thing. Yet at any given time not everyone in the USA is entirely happy to be part of such a unified, integrated economy. In particular, over the past decade several regional economies within the United States have been subject to large adverse shocks – shocks which have arguably been so large precisely because the US economy is so integrated – for which they have had essentially no policy recourse simply because the US already has the common currency that EMU is supposed to produce for Europe.

The most intellectually influential of the regional crises in the US has been the recent slump in New England – the events are dramatic enough to be worth noting in any case, but proximity to certain univerisities has not hurt their academic visibility! The New England story is by now familiar in the US, but may be worth reviewing for Europeans.

New England is a region of about 10 million people. Like other regions in the US, it is highly specialized. Its 'export' base – those industries that sell primarily to customers outside the region – is concentrated in several narrow high technology sectors: mini-computers, advanced medicine, precision military hardware. During most of the 1980s, these sectors thrived. As computing power grew, many businesses shifted from the large mainframe computers made by IBM to the mini-computers manufactured by Massachusetts firms such as Digital Equipment; the large Reagan-era defence budgets concentrated on high-technology hardware, for example, the Patriot missile manufactured by Massachusetts-based Raytheon, and so on. This export boom had both a multiplier and an accelerator effect on the local economy: employment grew in non-traded sectors such as retailing, and a commercial real estate boom led to a surge in construction employment. In late 1987 Massachusetts had an unemployment rate of only 2.5%, less than half the national average.

But then the bottom fell out. Demand shifted away from New England products: personal micro-computers began to displace office mini-computers, defence spending fell. The building boom collapsed as an excess supply of new construction in the region became apparent. Within the space of three years the unemployment rate nearly quadrupled.

If New England had been a sovereign country, it might have devalued its currency and/or pursued an expansionary monetary policy. In fact, not only were these options not available, but a budget crisis forced fiscal policy to move in a pro-cyclical direction, exacerbating the slump.

When will the New England economy turn around? Based on previous regional experience in the US (which will be discussed later), the maximum likelihood answer is never. To be more specific: there is no reason to expect the New England region ever to regain its pre-slump share of US employment. The unemployment rate should gradually decline, and move towards the national average, but this will happen primarily through emigration of labour rather than through a return of jobs.

The argument of this chapter is that the New England experience is a particularly grim illustration of some of the difficulties that EMU will face at a regional level. The combined effects of 1992 and EMU will reinforce many of the conditions that allow a regional crisis of this kind. These include:

> *Regional specialization*: US regions are much more specialized than areas of corresponding size in Europe. This greater degree of specialization has been fostered by the greater integration of the US market, an integration that Europe now seeks to emulate. Increased specialization in turn leads to:
> *Instability of regional exports*: Because US regions are highly specia-lized, shifts in tastes and especially in technology lead to large and erratic shifts in exports. European regions can look forward to similar shocks,[1] with the effect of these export shifts assigned by:
> *Pro-cyclical capital movements*: Regional export booms are reinforced by investment booms. Although balance of payments

data are not available, there is little question that New England experienced capital inflows during its boom years, magnifying the boom, and that these changed to capital outflows during the slump, helping to deepen that slump. Economic and monetary union will, of course, help to make capital more mobile within Europe, actually reinforcing instability at this level, while also contributing to:

Divergent long-run growth: US regions show marked differences in growth rates, with no tendency to return toward historical levels of relative output or employment (indeed, there is high serial correlation of growth). This divergence has a great deal to do with high factor mobility, which will of course be reinforced in Europe both by 1992 and by EMU. When the export basket of a US region falls on hard times, that region normally simply sheds capital and labour rather than experiencing a real depreciation sufficient to acquire new export sectors.

The argument of this chapter, then, is that 1992/EMU will combine to make American-style regional crises more common and more severe within the European Community. And it is immediately apparent that Europe will have a problem if it starts to experience American-style regional slumps without American-style fiscal federalism. The argument suggests, in other words, that some kind of policy reform will be necessary if the increasingly unified European economy is not to pay an even higher price for that unification than the US does.

The rest of the chapter is in four parts. Section 2 offers some theoretical analysis of the reasons why 1992/EMU will lead to greater regional instability and greater divergence in regional growth rates. Section 3 offers a rough survey of empirical evidence bearing on this analysis. In Section 4 the implications for stabilization policy are analysed. Finally, Section 5 offers a speculative look at the longer-term issues of regional growth policy.

2   Integration, regional specialization and regional stability

Most economists believe that international trade and factor mobility promote equalization of factor prices; this is probably correct although I will put forward a few doubts in Section 5. It might be imagined, on first thoughts, that eliminating explicit obstacles to trade, harmonizing regulations that would otherwise segment markets, and increasing the mobility of labour and capital, would lead not only to convergence in factor prices but to convergence in economic structure and in growth rates. In fact, however, both theory and evidence suggest that the contrary is the case: a more integrated market leads to divergence in both the economic structure and the growth rates of regions.

We may consider each of these issues in turn.

2.1 Integration and specialization

It is, of course, the essential point of most trade theory that economic integration allows regions to specialize. At one time, most agricultural land was devoted to producing foodstuffs for local consumption; today, most agricultural regions in the US are highly specialized, devoted to producing a few crops for which the soil and climate are highly suited, but correspondingly vulnerable to market fluctuations in those crops.

For regional issues both in the US and in the EC, however, the key aspect of regional specialization is the dependence of regional economies on export clusters held together by Marshallian external economies. Thus the New England boom and slump were tied to the fortunes of Route 128; the fortunes of northern California to those of Silicon Valley; and so on. Are such regional clusters more likely to form in a more integrated economy?

The answer is definitely yes. A reduction in the transactions costs between two regions, whether these costs take the form of transportation expenses, tariffs, or disparities in regulation, will make it more likely that any given degree of external economies will be sufficient to lead to geographical concentration of an industry.

This point can be made crudely in a diagram such as Figure 8.1. In the diagram we imagine an industry which can operate in either of two locations, each of which also has a local demand for the industry's products. We also assume that demand is completely price-inelastic, so that we may take the total industry output OO as fixed, with sales of OQ in one region, QO^* in the other. The industry is assumed to be perfectly competitive but subject to location-specific external economies; thus the downward-sloping schedule CC (measured from the left) represents the supply curve in the first region, the schedule C^*C^* (measured from the right) the supply curve in the second.

Now we ask: is it possible for both regions to produce in this industry, or will external economies lead the industry to concentrate in one location? Consider a situation in which each region is self-sufficient, with OQ produced in the first region, QO^* in the second. As drawn here, this would give the first region a cost c that is lower than the other region's cost c^* – a cost advantage that may be the result either of a larger local market, or because of some factor cost advantage. But this will not necessarily lead to concentration of the industry. If the transaction cost

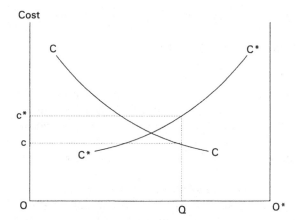

Figure 8.1 Geographical concentration

between the regions exceeds $c^* - c$, a geographically dispersed industry is
a stable equilibrium. If the transaction cost should then be reduced,
however, say by harmonization of regulations and elimination of border
posts, the result would be a snowballing of advantage: the cost advantage
in Region 1 would lead to an expansion of its industry and a contraction
of the industry in Region 2; this would reinforce the cost disparity, and so
on until the process produced a geographically concentrated industry.
Other industries might, of course, end up concentrated in Region 2 in the
same way. So a reduction of transaction cost would ordinarily lead to a
divergence between regions in terms of their industrial structure, and
increased specialization of any particular region.

It might be objected, with considerable justification, that this is too
'black-boxy' an approach. In particular, what we call external economies
are often market-size effects; will not greater integration of markets make
it less necessary to be in the same country as other firms in order to have
access to the forward and backward linkages they generate? (For
example, will we need a Silicon Valley when hackers can do everything
they want from cabins in the woods?)

The answer is yes – but the presumption is still that increased integration
will lead to greater geographical concentration of industries. A highly
stylized example (suggested in Krugman (1991) but sketched out at
slightly greater length here) may make the point. Imagine an industry
consisting of a number of symmetric firms, all of whom in addition to
selling to a market of final consumers find their output used as intermediate inputs by each other. We suppose that each firm sells a total of x units,
with a fraction μ sold as intermediate goods within the industry and the

rest to consumers outside the industry. Consumers are in two locations, 1 and 2, with equal final demand.

Some special cost and pricing assumptions will make this a tractable model. First, assume that firms charge customers a price p that is independent of the actual cost of delivering the product.[2] This implies that they must absorb any transportation costs. Second, assume that production costs take the form $F + cx$, where F is a fixed cost that must be incurred for every production facility. Third, assume that there is a transportation cost t for every unit shipped between locations. We may now ask the following: when is a concentration of the industry in only one region an equilibrium?

Suppose that all production were concentrated in one location. Then each firm would sell $(1 - \mu)x/2$ units to final consumers in each location, plus an additional μx units to other firms in the cluster. Clearly, if a firm were to choose to produce in only one place it would choose the location of the existing cluster, in order to minimize transportation costs. (Note that this is a kind of external economy which holds the cluster together, but it is an external economy which is derived from market size – in Hirschmann's terminology, it is a backward linkage effect). But the firm might choose to open another plant. This would mean incurring an extra fixed cost F, but would save transport costs $t(1 - \mu)x/2$. Thus geographic concentration of the industry will be an equilibrium only if $F > t(1 - \mu)x/2$.

This criterion is more likely to be satisfied the higher is F (loosely, the more important are economies of scale; the higher is μ); in other words, the stronger are intra-industry linkages and, crucially for the argument in this chapter, the lower are transportation/transaction costs t. This may at first seem surprising. The lower are transportation costs, the less necessary is it to be close to an industry cluster in order to benefit from its linkages, and thus we might expect to find that the incentive to concentrate would be less. In this example, however, lower transport costs make geographical concentration more attractive for each individual firm, and as long as this concentration occurs, it will take place at the cluster.

The important point is that even when we attempt to formalize the emergence of external economies in a way that does not simply assume that they are localized, the idea that lower transport costs fosters geographical concentration still seems to hold.

Now imagine two continents. On one continent national governments have traditionally thrown up barriers to trade that have limited the formation of geographically concentrated industries. The other has long been run by a single government the constitution of which prohibits obstacles to inter-regional trade. We would then expect to find that regional economies on the first continent would be more diversified and hence more similar in structure than those on the second.

As we will see in the next section, a comparison between Europe and the United States does in general fit this description.

Presumably the United States gains from the efficiencies of specialization, from the greater ability to exploit external economies and linkages that concentration of industries provides. The penalty is that regional economies, being less diversified, are more subject to technology and demand shocks. This leads to a greater risk of severe region-specific recessions. It also leads, in the presence of high factor mobility, to large divergences in long-term growth rates.

2.2 Factor mobility and long-run growth

It is possible to imagine an economy in which free movement of goods and services allows extensive regional specialization, with any individual industry highly concentrated geographically, but with immobile factors of production. Economies of this kind are, in fact, a staple of theoretical models of international trade in the presence of external economies. The US economy, however, is characterized by high mobility of capital and labour as well as of goods and services. Economic and monetary union will ensure high mobility of capital within Europe; it remains to be seen whether the Single European Act will eventually result in mobile labour or whether language and cultural barriers will continue to make European labour relatively immobile.

What is the effect of increased factor mobility? I will argue first, that high mobility of capital in particular tends to magnify regional economic fluctuations; and second, that high mobility of both capital and labour tends to produce divergent economic growth over time.

The first point is fairly obvious. Consider a region that is highly specialized, relying on a few industrial clusters for its exports to other regions. A positive shock to the demand for the products of these clusters will ordinarily raise the expected return on investment in the region. If capital were immobile, this increase in investment demand would primarily be reflected in a rise in the regional cost of capital. With mobile capital, however, the result will be an inflow. (It is, in fact, more usual than not for export booms driven by external demand to produce current account deficits rather than surpluses; see the comparison of Puerto Rico and Portugal by Eichengreen (1990), which is discussed further in Section 3.) As long as some of the capital expenditure falls on non-traded goods, this will have an accelerator effect that increases the impact of export fluctuations on regional employment, both in booms and in slumps.

The point about long run growth is a little more subtle, or at least unfamiliar. Again consider a situation in which industries are geographically concentrated but factors of production are immobile. Suppose that in such a situation a region received an adverse shock to the demand for its export industries. The effect would be to drive down the relative wages and other factor costs in the region; but this would attract additional employment, and perhaps allow the region to snatch some industrial clusters away from other, higher-cost regions. There would therefore be some mean reversion in terms of gross regional product: regions that have been unlucky in their heritage of industries from the past will have lower costs than lucky regions, and will therefore be more likely to break into industries in the future. We would expect this process to put limits on the extent of regional divergence in growth.[3]

Suppose, on the other hand, that factors of production are highly mobile. Then an unfortunate region will not have lower factor prices for very long: capital and labour will move to other regions until factor payments are equalized. This means, however, that there is no particular reason to expect a region whose traditional industries are faring badly to attract new industries. It can simply shed people instead. The implication is that relative output and employment of regions should look more like a random walk than like a process that returns to some norm.

Note that this argument is rather different from the standard idea of uneven development or core-periphery formation, in which divergent growth emerges as a deterministic process because initially successful regions enjoy a cumulative advantage over initially less successful regions. While many authors, myself included, have emphasized the possibility of such even development, the growth of the sunbelt in the USA and in the Iberian countries suggests that such systematic unequalizing forces are not strong in today's industrial world. The story is instead one in which the point is not the existence of a strong force for divergence but the absence of a force for convergence of output and employment (factor prices and per capita income *do* converge). As a result, random shocks just cumulate over time. This corresponds to Henry Ford's characterization of history as 'one damn thing after another'.

I have argued, then, that the combination of 1992 and EMU will produce a European economy that is (a) more subject to region-specific shocks, because in an integrated market regions will become more specialized and (b) likely to exhibit greater disparity in regional growth rates, because with increased factor mobility regions will tend to adjust to shocks by adding or shedding resources rather than by adding or shedding industries.

So far, however, this is just a theoretical argument. Next I turn to a survey of some relevant evidence.

3   Evidence on integrated markets and monetary unions

Analysts of potential developments in Europe are fortunate in having a reasonably good model: the United States. The US shows how a continent-sized single market and currency union works in practice, and both examining that example and contrasting it with the EC offers considerable insight. Admittedly, there are some differences – the language and cultural uniformity of the US will not be matched by Europe in the forseeable future. Nonetheless, I will focus on the US-EC comparison to buttress my case on three issues. First is the proposition that an integatrated market leads to greater specialization at the regional level. Second is the proposition that this specialization leads to greater short-run regional instability, an instability reinforced by capital mobility. Finally, we need to document the proposition that long-run growth tends to be more divergent in an integrated market with high factor mobility.

3.1   Regional specialization

In some earlier work (Krugman 1991) I made a crude comparison of regional specialization in the US and in Europe. Regions were defined at a very aggregate level, exploiting the fact that the 'Great Regions' of the US – the North-east (New England plus Middle Atlantic), the Mid-west (East North Central and West North Central), the South, and the West – are comparable in population and economic size to the four major European countries. So if policy regimes had been comparable we might have expected a roughly similar degree of economic differentiation among major US regions and among major European countries. Indeed, we might have expected localization to have proceeded further in Europe, if only because the distances involved in the US are so much larger. The analysis above suggests, however, that because of the history of trade barriers we should find European nations less specialized than US regions.

The comparisons reported below use employment statistics for (more or less) two-digit industries for European countries, which can be compared with regional employment statistics for (more or less) the same industries for US regions.

Using this data, indices of regional/national divergence are constructed as follows. Let s_i be the share of industry i in total manufacturing employment in some region/country; and let an asterisk indicate that we

Table 8.1. *Indices of industrial specialization*

US regions, 1977

	North-east	Mid-west	South	West
North-east	–	0.224	0.247	0.242
Mid-west	–	–	0.336	0.182
South	–	–	–	0.271

EC countries, 1985

	France	Federal Republic of Germany	Italy	United Kingdom
France	–	0.200	0.197	0.083
Federal Republic of Germany	–	–	0.175	0.184
Italy	–	–	–	0.184

Sources: US Census of Manufactures, 1977.

are referring to some other region/country. Then the index is

$$\Sigma_i |s_i - s_i^*|$$

Suppose that two regions had identical industrial structures, i.e., that shares of employment were the same for all i, then the index would be zero. A little less obviously, if two regions had completely non-overlapping industry structures, the index would be 2 (because each share in each region would be counted in full). So the index is a rough way of quantifying differences in structures, and hence regional specialization.

This index was calculated for twelve pairs of regions/countries: for US regions compared with one another, and for Europe's big four compared with one another. The results are shown in Table 8.1.

In spite of greatly excessive aggregation both of industries and of geographical units, the basic result is clear: European nations are less specialized than US regions.

The result can be emphasized by focusing on two particularly revealing cases: the specializations of the Mid-west and the South, on the one hand, and of Germany and Italy, on the other. In both cases we are, in effect, comparing a traditional heavy industrial producer with a traditional light, labour-intensive producer. And as we see in Table 8.2, which compares employment shares in selected sectors, the patterns of revealed comparative advantage in key industries are similar.

Table 8.2. *Industrial specialization, 1985. (Percent share of manufacturing employment)*

	Germany	Italy	Mid-west	South
Textiles	3.7	9.1	0.3	11.7
Apparel	2.6	5.6	2.4	10.6
Machinery	15.8	12.9	15.0	7.1
Transport equipment	13.2	10.4	12.8	5.9
Sum of share differences $(\Sigma_i |s_i - s_i^*|)$	35.2		62.6	

But the degree of specialization in accord with this revealed comparative advantage is very different. At one extreme, the Mid-west has essentially no textile industry, compared with Germany's still substantial one. At the other, the South produces far less machinery than Italy.

A final illustrative comparison involves the automotive industry. Table 8.3 compares the regional distribution of the US auto industry with the national distribution of the European industry. What it shows is that the US industry is far more localized. (In essence, the US industry is a Mid-western phenomenon, with only a scattering of assembly plants in other parts of the country.)

These are at best illustrative comparisons. Other work on US data, and recent US experience, shows that such aggregative numbers fail to do justice to the subtleties and yet crucial significance of regional specialization. To take the most obvious example, aggregate industry statistics lump together a variety of electronics-related sectors in such a way that tests for geographic concentration fail to reveal the existence of either Silicon Valley or Route 128. Yet not only are these agglomerations very

Table 8.3. *Distribution of automobile production, 1985. (Percent share of total production)*

United States of America		European Community	
Mid-west	66.3	Germany	38.5
South	25.4	France	31.1
West	5.1	Italy	17.6
North-east	3.2	United Kingdom	12.9

Source: Motor Vehicle Facts and Figures, Detroit: Motor Vehicle Manufacturers' Association, 1988.

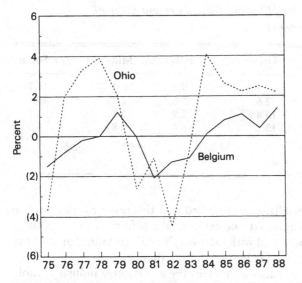

Figure 8.2 Annual rates of employment growth, Ohio and Belgium
Sources: US Department of Labor, *Handbook of Labor Statistics*, 1989; OECD,
Main Economic Indicators, Historical Statistics, 1990

real, they are sharply distinct, to such an extent that the severe slump that
hit the Massachusetts industry was hardly felt in the West. While I cannot
document this, it is hard to escape the impression that regional specialization at a very fine-grained level has gone considerably further in the US
than in Europe.[4]

3.2   Short-run growth

A full analysis of the prevalence of short-term region-specific shocks
would require a fairly elaborate analysis. In particular, I would like to see
a study along the lines of the recent paper by Blanchard and Katz (1992)
carried out in tandem for comparably-sized geographical units in the US
and in Europe. In this chapter I will restrict myself to an illustrative
comparison, in order to provide some suggestive support for the proposition that regional shocks are larger in the highly specialized regions of
the US, than they are in Europe.

The comparison is between the state of Ohio and the nation of Belgium.
Both are old industrial areas, located in their continent's 'rust belt'; both
are essentially manufacturing areas. (Illinois would have been in some
ways a more obvious candidate, but the presence of the large service-

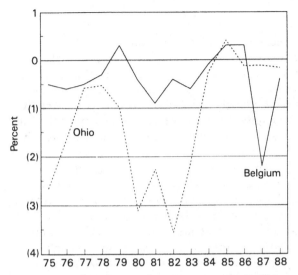

Figure 8.3 Adjusted rates of employment growth, Ohio and Belgium

exporting metropolis of Chicago makes it less than comparable with any small European nation.)

It is immediately apparent that employment growth is much more unstable in Ohio than in Belgium. Figure 8.2 compares annual rates of growth of employment in the two areas from 1975–88; evidently Ohio has experienced much more variation. The standard deviation of the Ohio growth rate is 2.75 compared with 1.05 for Belgium.

To some extent the greater instability in Ohio can be attributed to the instability of the US economy as a whole: over the period, the standard deviation of employment growth in the US was 1.69 compared with 1.02 for the European Community. To correct for this, Figure 8.3 compares two differences: the difference between the growth in Ohio employment and US employment on the one hand, and the difference between Belgian and EC employment growth, on the other. Although the contrast between the two is now somewhat less, this normalized Ohio employment growth is still substantially more variable, with a standard deviation of 1.23 compared with 0.61 for Belgium.

This is hardly a conclusive demonstration. We need to do a global comparison rather than focus on a single pair of regions, and we need to do a more elaborate time series analysis rather than assume that first differences are a sufficient statistic. Nonetheless, Figures 8.2 and 8.3 help confirm the point that the specialization of US regions leads to greater instability in regional economies.

3.3   Long run growth

In their illuminating recent paper, Blanchard and Katz (1992) have produced a striking set of stylized facts about growth at the state level within the United States. The picture that emerges is one of large differences in growth rates that are, however, almost entirely due to differences in the rate of employment growth rather than to changes in relative income per worker or per capita. We may, for example, compare the two largest states: from 1960–88 employment in California rose 86% relative to employment in New York, but the relative per capita income of the two states was unchanged. As Blanchard and Katz point out, this is consistent with the view that US states are subject to large, persistent shocks, to which they adjust through migration rather than changes in wage rates.

The Blanchard-Katz time series analysis suggests, in fact, that the conventional international adjustment mechanism, in which countries that suffer adverse shocks restore full employment through real depreciation, is virtually absent within the United States. While wages do decline somewhat in states that suffer adverse shocks, there is no discernible tendency for states to recover lost jobs. Instead, workers simply move out until the unemployment rate falls to its normal level.

The historical European adjustment process has been completely different. Table 8.4 makes the point, comparing the rates of employment growth in major US states and in the major EC countries. In spite of images of 'Bread and Chocolate' and political tensions over immigrants, migration has played very little role in European countries. Instead, real wages have adjusted so as to allow employment in each country to grow at roughly the rate of natural increase of the employable population. The slowest-growing major EC country, the UK, has maintained almost exactly the same rate of employment growth as the EC average.

The result has been that even though rates of growth in per capita income and productivity are more nearly equal among US states than among European countries, the spread of overall growth rates is much larger: over the 1960–88 period real gross domestic product (GDP) in the slowest-growing major EC country, the UK, grew at 2.5% compared with 4% for Italy, a difference of 1.5%. Over the same period, US sunbelt states on average grew more than 3% faster than old industrial states in the North-east.

The obvious implication, then, is that if Europe moves toward US levels of regional specialization and factor mobility, disparities in economic growth rates among countries and regions can be expected to increase substantially.

Table 8.4. *Annual rates of employment growth, EC and USA, 1960–88*

European Community	0.3
France	0.5
Italy	0.1
United Kingdom	0.3
United States of America	2.2
California	3.2
New York	1.0

The next question is how likely the increases in regional instability and in growth disparities will affect the need for policy intervention.

4   Integration, monetary union and stabilization policy

If regional shocks are likely to be larger in a more integrated and unified Europe, we might be tempted to look to the possibilities of regional stabilization policies. There are then three points that need to be made. First, within a monetary union stabilization policy must take the form of fiscal intervention. Both logic and US experience suggest, however, that regional governments in an integrated market with high factor mobility will be unable to pursue counter-cyclical fiscal policies, and will indeed tend to act pro-cyclically. This then puts the weight of stabilization at the regional level on fiscal actions, both automatic and deliberate, at a higher level; essentially fiscal federalism is the major regional stabilizer within the US, and the minor size of the EC budget poses questions about how an integrated EC economy will actually function.

4.1   The primacy of fiscal policy

It is a familiar point, but one perhaps worth re-emphasizing, that in a monetary union old-fashioned Keynesianism with its emphasis on fiscal policy comes back into its own. Aggregate monetary policy can stabilize aggregate demand shocks, but region-specific demand shocks resulting from changes in tastes and technology cannot be smoothed out in this way. By definition, countries and regions have no monetary policy. At the same time, with the high capital mobility that goes with EMU there should be little crowding out from fiscal expansion because the regional money supply will automatically accommodate the expansion.

The only reason to suspect that regional fiscal policy might be ineffective would be the argument that in highly integrated markets any increase in regional spending would fall primarily on goods produced elsewhere – in effect, that the multiplier would be very small. At first sight, such figures as are available would seem to confirm this; for example, Eichengreen (1990) found that the ratio of imports (goods and services) to GDP in Puerto Rico was more than 0.6. In a way, however, this high ratio is misleading, because it consists to a large extent of imports of intermediate goods. A more relevant number is the share of value-added or employment generated by sectors that are essentially oriented to the local market rather than national or international markets. While it is difficult to make such estimates rigorously, most studies have found that even within the US more than half of a state's output and work force is oriented toward the internal market. (As a recent example, see Porter's (1991) study of Massachusetts.)

So the natural tool of regional stabilization is fiscal policy. Unfortunately, in an integrated market this tool tends to become largely unavailable.

4.2   The immobility of local fiscal policy

It is an initially surprising fact that state governments in the US make no effort to use their budgets as a stabilization tool. In fact, almost without exception they disconnect even the automatic stabilizers: every state but Vermont has the requirement that the budget should be balanced.[5] Thus state level fiscal policy moves in a strongly pro-cyclical direction, magnifying regional booms and slumps.

It could be the case that the insistence on budget balance at the state and local level is the result of conservative prejudice, and that within an EMU the more sophisticated European governments would follow more stabilizing policies. We may, however, offer another hypothesis: that the insistence on budget balance reflects a more or less appropriate response at the state level to the realities of the regional business cycle.

Why should state governments follow a policy of continuous budget balance? We may note, first, that to the extent that state business cycles are associated with national fluctuations in employment, states can rely on national monetary policy to do the stabilizing role. This job will not be done perfectly, but state governments are unlikely to be able to second-guess the Federal Reserve productively.

When we turn to state-specific shocks, we can argue that it would be appropriate for a state to use borrowing to offset any decline in revenue that results from a temporary downturn in the state economy. But as noted above, it appears that at the state or regional level there is essentially no such thing as a temporary downturn! That is, the Blanchard and

Katz evidence (1992) suggests that states work their way out of high relative unemployment not by increasing employment but by reducing their labour force. If a state does badly relative to the national average in one period, there is no reason to expect it to compensate with an exceptionally good performance later.

Putting these arguments together, we see that there may be little case for attempting to make a stabilizing state or regional fiscal policy possible. Responding to aggregate shocks is not part of the state's appropriate role; responding to state-specific shocks could easily become fiscally irresponsible, since such shocks tend to be permanent. Thus the costs of pro-cyclical fiscal policy that result from a constitutional prohibition on deficits may be outweighed by the advantages of enforced responsibility.

The problem with all of this is that while factor mobility is high, it is not instantaneous. If workers could instantly move from distressed regions to successful ones, then there would be no case for regional stabilization policy. Given the transition periods – Eichengreen (1990) estimated that only 40% of a region-specific unemployment shock is eliminated each year; Blanchard and Katz found that after a state-specific shock, unemployment actually grew for a time and then took six years to fade away – there is still a case for some counter-cyclical policy at the regional level.

In the US, this role is largely played by automatic stabilizers resulting from the importance of the Federal budget.

4.3   Federalism as an automatic stabilizer

It is straightforward to see how the role of a large Federal budget acts as a stabilizer of regional economies. Consider a regional economy that may be described in the short run by an old-fashioned multiplier model:

$$Y = C + I + G + X - M$$

$$C = (1 - s)(1 - t)Y$$

$$M = mY$$

But suppose that taxation and government spending may be split into two parts. Some taxes are Federal, others state:

$$t = t_F + t_s$$

And while Federal spending in the region can be taken as given, state spending must be adjusted to equal state tax revenue:[6]

$$G = G_F + t_s Y$$

It then follows that the multiplier on changes in regional exports is

$$\frac{dY}{dX} = \frac{1}{1 - t_s - (1 - s)(1 - t)}$$

It is immediately apparent that for any given overall level of taxation, the multiplier is larger the greater the share of taxes that is collected at the state or regional (or, in the European context, national) level. That is, a system with little fiscal federalism will have a harder time coping with the instability of exports from highly specialized regions than a system like that of the US, with its largely Federal systems of social insurance, defence, and so on.

We have argued, then, that greater integration of markets and greater factor mobility, together with the loss of national monetary policy, will create new problems of stabilization at the European regional level. The United States has long had these problems. While the US does not cope with the problems perfectly (as the current travails not only of New England but of the North-east, in general, and increasingly also of California, demonstrate) a highly federalized fiscal system helps a good deal. The lack of such a system in Europe therefore is a real problem.

This may seem to be an unusual focus for a discussion of regional issues. Most regional analysis focuses not on problems of stabilization but on longer run issues of development, and on equalizing versus unequalizing forces. While I have not made these issues central, I conclude the chapter with a brief discussion of these more traditional concerns.

5 Development and regional inequality

This chapter has followed Blanchard and Katz (1992) in supposing that large differences in growth rates among US regions are generated by a largely random process. Integrated markets lead to regional specialization along essentially arbitrary lines, but with the pattern of specialization then locked in by external economies. When random shocks to demand or technology benefit some regions at the expense of others, factors of production migrate to the successful regions, short-circuiting the mechanisms that might otherwise have led these regions to acquire new specialties.

This mechanism is somewhat in contrast to models of uneven development in which a systematic process leads to growth differences. In the familiar view, which can be formalized in terms of both endogenous growth models like those of Grossman and Helpman (1991) and in terms of models of economic geography, success and failure are self-reinforcing through external economies that apply at a level that extends beyond that of individual industries. For example, successful regions will generate

backward linkages, not simply within industries for their specific intermediate products, but across all industries because of the geographic
concentration of population and purchasing power. Similarly, they may
generate forward linkages through the availability of general purpose
inputs such as power and transportation. I have argued (Krugman 1991)
that such large-scale linkages explain the nineteenth century emergence of
a concentration of US manufacturing in a narrow stretch of the North-
east and inner Mid-west.

Why, then, does the argument in this chapter focus on the milder
random mechanism? The basic answer is that at least since World War II
the experience of regional growth, both in the US and in Europe, has
suggested that the forces tending to generate a core-periphery pattern
have reached their limit or may even be weakening. In the US the
traditional manufacturing belt is both spreading to the south and facing
growing competition from other areas; in Europe there has been a process
of convergence between north and south.

Why this should be the case is less clear. It may be that new technologies
of transportation and communication make it easier for industries to flee
high land costs and take advantage of immobile labour in peripheral
regions that prefers to receive low wages at home rather than migrate to
take advantage of high wages at the centre. This is, however, speculative
at this point. What is clear is that in the US the employment shares of the
traditional manufacturing states have been steadily declining since World
War II. Thus we need to postulate a mechanism for uneven growth that
does not predict that past success is always self-reinforcing.

This does not mean that all of the issues associated with core-periphery
stories become irrelevant. The main policy concern in regional economics
is with the fate of those workers who, for whatever reason, are immobile,
and who can end up stranded in a declining region – the Mezzogiorno
problem. Essentially the same social and distributional problems arise,
however, when the decline of a region simply reflects specialization in
what turns out to be the wrong product – Detroit does not present any
prettier a picture than Appalachia.

In this chapter, however, I will simply avoid the question of what the
policy response to this kind of regional issue should be, for three reasons.
First, it is much less related to the EMU than the stabilization problem.
Second, it would need an entirely separate paper. Finally, I do not at
present have any useful ideas to offer!

6   Summary and conclusions

Since official documents on EMU tend to focus only on the potential
benefits, academics have an obligation to point out various clouds that

may go with the silver lining. This chapter falls in that category. It does not argue that EMU will be a bad thing, but it points out that the combination of 1992 and EMU will tend to produce some new stabilization problems at the regional level.

Theory and the experience of the US suggest that EC regions will become increasingly specialized, and that as they become more specialized they will become more vulnerable to region-specific shocks. Regions will, of course, be unable to respond with counter-cyclical monetary or exchange rate policy. Furthermore, in an environment of high factor mobility such shocks will tend to have permanent effects on output, which will tend to immobilize fiscal policy as well.

In the US the heavily federalized fiscal system offers a partial solution to the problem of regional stabilization. Unless there is a massive change in European institutions, this automatic cushion will be absent.

None of this is an argument against EMU. Some advocates of EMU seem to suggest, however, that *every* aspect of policy management will become easier. But as virtually any US state governor can attest, an integrated continental market does not solve all local problems, and can even make some of them worse.

NOTES

1 The recent EC document 'One Market, One Money' (European Commission, 1990) addresses this issue, but in a one-sided way. Section 6.2 is entitled 'Will asymmetric shocks diminish in EMU?'; the possibility, and indeed the likelihood, that such asymmetric shocks will actually increase is not even contemplated.

2 This can be justified by a limit-pricing argument in the face of an alternative source of supply. It has the unfortunate effect of eliminating any possibility of forward linkages via supply of intermediates, which can only be brought back in a model with a more elaborate market structure (see Krugman 1991).

3 A highly stylized formulation of international competition with external economies but immobile factors is given in Krugman (1987). In that formulation, historical accident can have persistent effects on the relative income of two countries/regions, but only over a limited range. The reason for the limit is that with sufficiently low relative wages a region can, as suggested in the text, start to snatch other regions' industrial clusters.

4 One problem with asserting that an integrated Europe will become more specialized, however, is that US statistics show that regional specialization has been declining since World War II (see Krugman 1991, ch. 3). I suspect, however, that this is largely statistical illusion; specialization may have become more difficult to measure, but not necessarily less in fact.

5 Actually, matters are a bit more complicated. What is required is usually not a balanced budget, but the maintenance of a state balance. That is, states maintain what amounts to a bank account; they can use surpluses to increase this account, and draw it down in times of need, but are forbidden to go into

debt. In principle, they could practice counter-cyclical policies by building up the accounts in good years, then drawing them down in bad; but few do this. Adding to the confusion is the proliferation of quasi-autonomous agencies, which are allowed to borrow and which in effect allow states to go into debt after all. For example, toll highways are typically financed by bond issues; other capital spending may be financed by borrowing backed by a special allocation of revenue. Last year the government of New York offered a classic example of how to evade its budget restrictions by creating a dummy agency which borrowed money to buy Attica prison from the state, which then leased the facility back for a fee sufficient to cover the debt service. In spite of abuses, however, it is not too misleading to think of states as running balanced budgets.
6 State budgets could be balanced either by adjusting spending or by raising taxes. I choose the 'read my lips' assumption for convenience.

REFERENCES

Blanchard, O. and L. Katz (1992) 'Regional Evolutions', in *Brookings Papers in Economic Activity*, 1.

Eichengreen, B. (1990) 'One Money for Europe? Lessons from the US Currency and Customs Union', *Economic Policy*, 10, pp. 118–87.

Commission of the European Communities (1990) One Market, One Money: an Evaluation of the Potential Benefits and Costs of Forming an Economic and Monetary Union, *European Economy*, 44 (October).

Grossman, G. and E. Helpman (1991) *Innovation and Growth in the Global Economy*, Cambridge, Mass.: MIT Press.

Krugman, P. (1987) 'The narrow moving band, the Dutch disease, and the competitive consequences of Mrs. Thatcher', *Journal of Development Economics*, 27: 41–55.

Krugman, P. (1991) *Geography and Trade*, Cambridge, Mass.: MIT Press.

Porter, M. (1991) *A competitive strategy for Massachusetts*, mimeo, Harvard Business School.

Discussion

ALESSANDRA CASELLA

This paper exhibits features we have come to expect from Paul Krugman's work: it is rich in ideas, seductive in taking us through simple logical arguments to surprising conclusions, and so self-confident in the discussion of its assumptions and its premises that reading it is at the same time great fun and a continuous challenge. Krugman's ideas point to several directions for future work; I am certain that these suggestions will be followed, and will prove productive and important.

The central thesis of the chapter is that increased economic integration makes regions more sensitive to idiosyncratic shocks, while at the same time increasing labour mobility. Evidence from the USA suggests that the result is a permanent divergence of growth rates, even while income levels per capita are equalized. Applying this reasoning to Europe, Krugman concludes that the benefits of economic integration should be evaluated with more scepticism, and regions should become aware that a common market may mean exactly the opposite of a common destiny.

The logical argument proceeds through four main points, which I will discuss in turn: (1) trade leads to regional specialization; (2) specialization leads to regional instability; (3) specialization combined with labour mobility leads to divergent growth rates; and (4) permanent idiosyncratic shocks require temporary fiscal measures to ease the pain of the transition; because of the permanence of the shocks these measures are best administered at the federal level.

D.8.1 Trade leads to regional specialization

It is possible to think of situations where this statement would not be true, and Paul Krugman has been responsible for pointing out most of them in his research on trade and imperfect competition. Indeed, Krugman has convinced us all that these exceptions are of more than academic interest, and the example of regions which are highly integrated (think, for example, of the Deutschmark area in Europe) confirms that specialization is not the inevitable outcome of integration. Still, the fundamental economic proposition remains – specialization in response to trade is the main source of gains from free exchange, at any level of economic activity.

What is called into question, in my opinion, is the identification of the relevant economic unit. What is a 'region' and to what extent can we identify an economic region with a given political border? We do not expect economic regions to coincide with political jurisdictions; they may be much smaller, and a country will in general contain many different economic regions. Political borders may also overlap, and therefore be common to two or more countries, implying that specialization of the region would not coincide with 'national' specialization. I remember old economic maps of Europe, where similar industries were represented with similar colours and political borders were ignored. Studying contemporary maps of this type would be a first step in furthering our understanding of the question. It is an important point, well-known to all but easily forgotten in policy discussions.

D.8.2 Specialization leads to regional instability

If regions specialize, they become subject to idiosyncratic shocks. What are the possible mechanisms of defence? First of all, diversification. In economic models with rational – if possibly not too pleasant – individuals, workers specializing in particular skills may reduce the riskiness of their investment in human capital by getting married and pooling family income. Similarly, economic regions may share common resources with other regions with different specializations. If the relevant unit of analysis here is the country, then a country composed of several regions, with different activities the shocks to which are not likely to be correlated, may be able to protect its citizens from the vagaries of sectoral shocks.

As an alternative, it would theoretically be possible to hedge against idiosyncratic shocks through the creation of optimal portfolios. Exactly because the shocks are not common to the entire economy, in a world rich with financial markets it would be conceivable to spread the risk through private portfolios. The practical likelihood of this scheme may not be too high at present, but it should not be entirely ruled out.

Finally, it would be possible to buy insurance. This is very similar to the creation of an optimal portfolio, with the explicit recognition of an extra step of intermediation. In this context, if individual countries are not sufficiently diversified, and if they cannot borrow in the face of temporary shocks, we can think of fiscal federalism as a sort of insurance. (This is not, however, the argument made by Krugman.)

D.8.3 Specialization combined with labour mobility leads to divergent growth rates

The main empirical support of Krugman's theoretical arguments is a recent paper by Blanchard and Katz presenting evidence of divergent growth rates among US states. According to these authors, while employment growth rates differ consistently across states, unemployment rates and wages do not, suggesting that states in the US tend to be hit by permanent idiosyncratic shocks to which workers react by re-locating (Blanchard and Katz, 1992). In this discussion, these factors will be taken as established.

We are used to thinking that labour mobility is an efficient response to idiosyncratic shocks. It allows the incomes of workers remaining in the declining sector to approximate to incomes in the expanding industries.

While the 'region' may lose, from an economic point of view, the individuals will not (ignoring inevitable short-run adjustment costs). In contrast, Krugman claims that low labour mobility would be a better response to a regional shock. Wages would then be pushed down, and low labour costs may make the region attractive to an expanding industry, possibly causing its re-location, and giving new impetus to local growth.

Two assumptions are present in this argument. First, it is assumed that wages would indeed be pushed down. In Europe this prediction seems doubtful. If different economic regions belong to the same country, it is likely that strong pressures will be exerted towards wage equalization. In Italy, for example, consistently higher unemployment rates in the south have not given rise to differences in wages. Such differences are resisted by trade unions, and probably viewed as politically unacceptable. In addition, the movement to a common currency may create forces towards more similar rewards to labour. The example of German unification, with equal compensation for workers of different productivity, is a natural example. To what extent this is a result of money illusion, and to what extent this was a politically inevitable move is unclear, but the difficulties experienced by the former German Democratic Republic are beyond doubt.

The second assumption in Krugman's analysis is that a decline in the price of factors other than labour may not be sufficient to trigger a re-location of expanding industries. While labour can move, land cannot, and a natural effect of declining economic health in a region should be a fall in the price of land. I do not see any a priori reason to discount the importance of land prices on the decisions of industries to re-locate. The problem is that such decline in land prices is not observed by Blanchard and Katz. Indeed, they find that house prices in the US tend to decline sharply after a negative shock to employment, but return to their previous level over time. The result is puzzling, and does not accord easily with the migration-led story presented by Blanchard and Katz, and subscribed to by Krugman. More empirical evidence on this point would be interesting.

My main concern is that labour markets in a unified Europe may work in ways that are fundamentally different from those discussed in this chapter. In this respect I do not believe that the American experience is a mirror of things to come, at least in the medium term. I believe that labour mobility in a single market will increase, but will remain lower than in the United States. At the same time, as mentioned above, I do not see wages acquiring the flexibility they have in the American market. My feared scenario then is the opposite of the one discussed by Krugman: it is a world where sectoral shocks trigger large unemployment without the equilibrating force of labour mobility, and where wages do not respond.

Barry Eichengreen has presented evidence on the low mobility of labour across regions in Europe (Eichengreen, 1991). Again, more work on this question is needed.

D.8.4 Fiscal federalism

Krugman's argument in favour of fiscal federalism is unusual. In his opinion, different states taking part in the economic and monetary union retain their ability to use fiscal policy effectively. Since the negative shocks which affect them are permanent, however, stabilization policies are not appropriate. What is needed is some temporary measure to make the transition less painful while workers re-locate or, in the best scenario, re-train. Local governments are ill-equipped to provide temporary assistance in response to permanent shocks because they may become the prey of local interests, and be unable to stop supporting the local economy. Thus the argument relies on two elements: first, the permanence of the shocks; second, the larger freedom of action of the federal government. While the first point derives from the Blanchard and Katz analysis, and is here taken as given, the second is problematic.

National governments have not been particularly successful in providing assistance to regions with long-term development problems. They have not been successful in solving those problems, and migration has not eliminated the disparity. Governments have not, therefore, been able to phase out the aid slowly as in Krugman's model. An obvious example is government intervention in southern Italy. There the common view sees government intervention, in the form of transfers from the north to the south, as the force preventing migration. Indeed, according to a popular argument the transfers may have been due in part to the desire to limit migration to the north in an effort to avoid social tensions. Whatever the political forces behind the problem, it is generally agreed that the national government is hardly unconstrained in its actions towards the south.

D.8.5 Is all this true?

Having reviewed the logical structure of the chapter, and enjoyed its many ideas and suggestions, I must conclude by asking whether or not we believe its main argument. It is impossible not to notice the contrast between Krugman's thesis, and the chapter by Bayoumi and Eichengreen in this volume.

To summarize briefly, Krugman states the following: the dispersion of regional shocks is higher in the United States than in Europe. Such dispersion is a natural result of economic integration, and we can predict that it will become high in Europe. Labour mobility will also increase and Europe will replicate the pattern of divergent regional growth rates experienced by the United States. The reasoning suggests that economic integration may be painful, and will require the support provided by fiscal federalism.

For their part, Bayoumi and Eichengreen argue: the dispersion of regional shocks is higher in Europe than in the United States. This disparity reflects structural differences that will not be altered by economic integration. Labour mobility will also remain low. The result is that Europe is not an optimum currency area, unlike the United States. Economic integration, and monetary unification in particular, will be difficult.

Thus the authors of the two chapters claim opposite facts and apply different theories but reach the same conclusion. While I am confident that the different empirical results can be explained, I do not think we know enough to subscribe wholeheartedly to either interpretation. At this stage, the main message of these two chapters is that three people whose economic intuition we have learnt to respect are uneasy about economic integration in Europe. Exactly why they are uneasy, however, is not yet clear.

REFERENCES

Bayoumi, Tamim and Barry Eichengreen 'Shocking Aspects of European Monetary Integration' Chapter 7, this volume.
Blanchard, Olivier and Lawrence Katz (1992) 'Regional Evolutions', *Brookings Papers in Economic Activity*, No. 1.
Eichengreen, Barry (1991) 'Is Europe an Optimum Currency Area?', National Bureau of Economic Research Working Paper 3579, Cambridge, Mass.

Discussion

PAUL DE GRAUWE

Most European citizens (outside Germany) take it for granted that monetary union can only be beneficial. This rosy picture of benefits of economic and monetary union (EMU) has been given a strong boost by the publication of a report by the Commission of the European Community entitled 'One Market, One Money'. In this intellectual environment it is refreshing to read a paper like Paul Krugman's that contains a strong warning that EMU could also lead to great economic problems in the Community.

The essence of Krugman's argument can be summarized as follows. Increased market integration leads to more specialization of industrial activities. In a world of increasing returns, this is likely to lead to regional concentration of industrial activities. As a result, shocks in demand are more likely to have asymmetric effects, with some regions (and countries) being affected more severely than others. In addition, with free factor mobility, factors of production move quickly from the region (country) which is adversely affected towards regions (countries) that experience a positive demand shock. Thus, asymmetric shocks tend to have permanent effects on the growth rates of regions and countries. The implications for EMU are that the macroeconomic adjustment problem in a future monetary union will be intense, because countries will no longer be able to use the exchange rate as a policy instrument while they will be subject to more rather than fewer asymmetric shocks. The only way this adjustment problem can be made less severe is by centralizing a significant part of the national budgets so that the automatic inter-regional redistributive mechanism can play a role in the future EMU.

My comments about this thesis are twofold. First, I want to produce some additional evidence that tends to corroborate Krugman's analysis of the concentration effect of market integration. Second, I want to take issue with some of the policy conclusions.

D.8.6 Market integration and regional disparities

Krugman compares the disparities in long-term growth rates between the individual states in the USA with the disparities between European countries and finds evidence that these disparities are larger in the United States than in Europe. This suggests that market integration leads to more unequal growth. A similar kind of evidence is found when the disparities in regional growth rates *within* European countries are compared with the disparities of growth rates *between* European countries. This is shown in Table D.8.1.

From Table D.8.1 it can be seen that the regional disparities of growth rates within European countries tend to be larger than the national disparities in Europe. Since it is reasonable to assume that the degree of market integration between regions of the same countries is greater than the degree of integration between countries, this evidence suggests that

Table D.8.1. *Divergencies in regional and national growth rates of output*

Countries	Period	Annual percentage change
OECD	1976–90	0.48
European monetary system	1976–90	0.48
Regions in		
France	1976–86	0.78
W. Germany	1976–86	0.51
Netherlands	1976–86	0.71
Spain	1981–86	1.45
United Kingdom	1976–88	0.72

Note: Divergence is defined as the standard deviation of the average growth rates over the relevant periods.
Source: The national data are from Organisation for Economic Cooperation and Development, *Economic Outlook*, various issues. The regional data are from *Eurostat, Banque de données régionales.*

integration may increase the dispersion of growth rates. Although this evidence cannot be considered to be complete, it tends to strength the hypothesis formulated by Krugman.

D.8.7 The policy implications

The main policy implications of Krugman's analysis are that policy reform will be needed in Europe. More specifically, Europe will need more centralization of national budgets, so that the Federal European budget can play a stabilizing role when asymmetric shocks occur. The European monetary union will then resemble more closely the monetary union of the United States, where the Federal budget tends automatically to redistribute resources towards regions affected by a negative economic shock. This policy conclusion can be criticized on two grounds.

First, even if Europe moves towards a more integrated market, it is very unlikely that the degree of labour mobility will come near to that achieved within the US or within the same countries in Europe. Cultural and language barriers will continue to present barriers to labour mobility. This has important implications for the logic of Krugman's article. It means that when one country experiences a negative shock, there will not be a major outward migration from the country (as in the US when a region experiences such a shock). Thus future negative disturbances are unlikely to lead to a permanent decline in the growth rate of the countries in the EC. As a result, a much greater pressure will be exerted on relative real wages to accommodate such negative shocks. Put differently, a European country facing a negative disturbance will not be confronted with a large exodus of its working population. By the same token, it will have to adjust through a relatively large decline in its *relative* real wage.

It is often stated that real wage rigidity will prevent this from happening. There is a lot of evidence, however, which points out that large changes in *relative* real wages have, in fact, occurred during the 1980s in countries experiencing large negative shocks. The Netherlands, which was affected very badly by the recession of the early 1980s, saw its relative unit labour costs decline by more than 20%. This happened without any significant devaluation of the guilder. Something similar occurred in Belgium; the real exchange rate of the Belgian franc (measured by unit labour costs) declined by 25% during the 1980s. Of this decline about 10% can be attributed to nominal devaluations.

These adjustments in relative labour costs allowed these countries to catch up with the growth rates observed in other European countries. The negative disturbance had no permanent effect. In addition, the adjustment took place without any transfer from the Community budget.

A second criticism I have with Krugman's policy conclusion is the following. National governments in a future monetary union will not lose all their instruments of economic policy. In particular, national budgetary policies will continue to play the role of automatic stabilizers. Thus, a country experiencing a large negative shock will be able to let its budget deficit increase so as to accommodate the shock, at least if governments are sensible enough not to take the Maastricht requirement of no more than a 3% budget deficit too seriously. My prediction is that they will be sensible enough, and they will not let their economic policies be guided exclusively by the dictates of central bankers' view of the world.

Apart from fiscal policies, national governments will continue to use other instruments of policy, in particular incomes policies. In fact, incomes policies were the main instrument used by the Netherlands and Belgium to bring about macroeconomic equilibrium after the shocks of the early 1980s. In this respect, European countries are quite different from states in the USA which do not have such instruments at their disposal.

In conclusion, monetary union in Europe will not leave nation states without instruments to stabilize their economies. Whereas in the US the only regionally stabilizing institution is the Federal budget, this is not so in Europe where nation states will continue to maintain a panoply of instruments. The urgency of centralizing the national budgets into the hands of a Federal European authority therefore is weak.

9   Financial and currency integration in the European monetary system: the statistical record

JEFFREY FRANKEL, STEVEN PHILLIPS
and MENZIE CHINN

1   Introduction

The Maastricht Treaty set out convergence of interest rates as one of the key criteria for deciding whether a country in the European Community (EC) can joint the European monetary union (EMU) when it is established in the late 1990s. Specifically, long-term interest rates should be within two percentage points of the average of the three member countries with the lowest rates. There is wisdom in such a test criterion. Politicians occasionally declare their support for regional integration without fully realizing the degree of loss of economic independence that is implied. If a country's interest rate is tied closely to that of its neighbours, it cannot independently use monetary policy to stimulate domestic demand. The criterion of interest rate convergence is a clear test of whether a country is in fact prepared to make the sacrifice of monetary sovereignty that joining EMU will require.

Interest rate convergence comprises two distinct kinds of integration. First, it implies the elimination of capital controls and other barriers to the movement of capital across national boundaries, which we call financial integration or 'country integration'. Second, it implies the elimination of investor perceptions that the exchange rate is likely to change in the future, which we call 'currency integration'. In this chapter, the recent statistical record on both kinds of integration up to 1991 is tested.

Another of the criteria set out at Maastricht was exchange rate stability: the currency must not have been devalued within the preceding two years, and must have remained within the normal ± 2.25% margins of the exchange-rate mechanism. Of central concern to investors is the credibility of future exchange rate stability. Though related to historical exchange rate stability, credibility among investors is less immediately observable.

The absolute magnitude of 3-month interest rate differentials (*vis-à-vis*

Table 9.1. *Average absolute interest rate differentials*

	September 1982–December 1986	January 1987–May 1990
Austria	0.730	0.410
	(0.204)	(0.150)
Belgium	4.528	2.405
	(0.492)	(0.357)
Denmark	1.059	1.797
	(0.390)	(0.423)
France	5.087	3.200
	(0.588)	(0.501)
Ireland	7.516	4.586
	(0.687)	(1.221)
Italy	10.144	6.280
	(0.804)	(0.606)
Netherlands	0.673	0.663
	(1.186)	(0.219)
Norway	6.962	not avail.
	(0.348)	
Portugal[a]	14.912	10.884
	(1.581)	(1.179)
Sweden	6.512	5.619
	(0.657)	(0.405)
Spain	9.302	8.751
	(1.395)	(1.170)
Switzerland	1.069	0.643
	(0.414)	(0.261)
United Kingdom	5.229	6.341
	(0.666)	(0.420)

Notes:
Standard errors in parentheses; $N/3$ independent observations assumed.
[a] Regression includes a dummy for data revision after December 1987 when Portuguese interest rate switched from 30–90 day maturity to 1–7 days.

those in Germany) is reported for 13 European countries in Table 9.1.[1] The sample period from September 1982 to May 1990 is broken at January 1987, the date of the last major currency realignment. In every case, the mean absolute interest differential is statistically significant, even when conservative standard errors are used to allow for the likelihood of serial correlation.[2] Every country, except Denmark and the United Kingdom, however, showed a smaller interest differential during the later period 1987–90, than during the earlier period 1982–86.[3] When we fit ordinary least squares (OLS) regressions against a time trend, we confirm that most countries' interest rate differentials on average narrowed after the formation of the European monetary system (EMS) in 1979. (Norway showed a widening trend during the period 1982–86, whereafter our data source gives out.) Seven of the time trends have the appearance of being statistically significant. In descending order of the estimated rate of narrowing they are: Italy, Ireland, France, Spain, Belgium, Switzerland, and Sweden.[4] Only in Austria, the Netherlands and Switzerland were interest rate differentials smaller than 100 basis points during the 1987–90 sub-period. Of these, only the Netherlands is a member of the European Community.

Why have interest rates gradually narrowed? And why do substantial gaps still remain? International interest rate differentials are created by two categories of barriers. First, country barriers, defined as obstacles to the free movement of capital across national boundaries; these include capital controls, different tax treatment of domestic and foreign income, information barriers, default risk, and risk of future capital controls. Second, currency barriers, defined as those factors that apply to the possibility of changes in the exchange rate in question regardless of the political jurisdiction in which assets are issued or held; they include the exchange risk premium and expectations of depreciation.

The two kinds of barriers need not move together. It was argued in the early phase of the EMS that the success in stabilizing European exchange rates had been accomplished entirely by means of country barriers (e.g., Rogoff, 1985). France, for example, strengthened its capital controls in 1981. In other words, exchange rate stability can increase even while financial (or country) integration decreases.

The central aim of this chapter is to separate out the effects of country barriers and currency barriers, and to see the extent to which country integration and currency integration have contributed to the recent gradual narrowing of overall interest differentials. We begin by using forward rate data to decompose the total interest rate differential of Table 9.1 into a covered interest differential term, which measures country barriers, and other terms, which represent currency factors. We will then proceed to a detailed analysis of the currency factors.

2   How rapidly have country barriers diminished?

The differential for interest rates of common maturities can be decomposed as follows:

$$i - i^{GY} = (i - i^{GY} - fd) + (fd - \Delta s^e) + \text{depreciation})$$

| (interest differential) | (covered interest differential) | (exchange risk premium) | (expected depreciation) |

where GY superscript denotes the German variable, fd is the forward discount for a consistent maturity, and Δs^e is the expected depreciation over a consistent horizon.

This equation merely breaks the nominal interest rate differential into its constituent parts: a covered interest differential, which reflects the country premium, and the exchange risk premium plus expected rate of depreciation, which together constitute the currency premium.[5]

Covered interest parity has in the past proved a useful test of whether or not a country has become integrated into international financial markets. The positive covered interest differential that existed for Germany in the early 1970s disappeared when controls on capital inflow were removed in 1974.[6] The negative differential that had existed for the United Kingdom in the 1970s disappeared when controls on capital outflow were removed in 1979.[7] Negative differentials persisted for France and Italy into the 1980s, reflecting effective capital controls.[8]

Frankel (1989, 1991) reported statistics for absolute covered interest rate differentials *vis-à-vis* London Eurodollars, for the period September 1982–April 1988.[9] All countries showed an average trend of narrowing differentials, except for three that already had small differentials at the beginning of the period (Austria, Belgium, and the United Kingdom). Eight had downward trends that appeared to be statistically significant. In descending order they were: Portugal, Spain, France, Denmark, Italy, Germany, Switzerland, and the Netherlands.[10]

Estimates of time trends in the magnitude of covered interest rate differentials for European countries *vis-à-vis* German interest rates are given in Table 9.2. All show a downward trend except for Belgium and Ireland. The trends for five of the countries appear statistically significant even if conservative standard errors are used. (In many cases there is so little evidence of serial correlation that conventional standard errors could as well be used.) In order of estimated speed of integration, they are: Portugal, France, Spain, Denmark, and the Netherlands.

Evidently the 'country' component of European interest rate differentials has generally diminished, indicating enhanced financial integration. We now turn to the 'currency' component.

3   Has the exchange risk premium diminished?

The risk premium, defined as $(fd - \Delta s^e)$, is the second of the three components of the interest differential in equation (1). It is the difference in the expected rate of return on otherwise identical assets denominated in different currencies. Such a difference in expected returns would in theory be compensation to risk-averse investors for holding assets in currencies

Table 9.2. Time trends in absolute covered interest rate differentials from September 1982

Country	Constant	Trend	$\bar{R}^2$	Durbin–Watson statistic	n	End of sample period
Austria	0.297 (0.217)	−0.010 (0.032)	−0.01	1.82	78	April 1989
Belgium	0.163 (0.123)	0.011 (0.016)	0.00	2.02	90	February 1990
Denmark	4.859[b] (0.918)	−0.330[a] (0.134)	0.17	0.31	82	August 1989
France	3.300[b] (1.186)	−0.869[b] (0.143)	0.27	0.79	100	December 1990
Ireland	−0.636 (2.157)	0.248 (0.306)	0.01	0.85	83	September 1989
Italy	1.680 (0.947)	−0.142 (0.114)	0.04	1.43	100	December 1990
Netherlands	0.236[b] (0.063)	−0.039[b] (0.008)	0.21	1.78	100	December 1990
Norway	1.252[a] (0.576)	−0.164 (0.140)	0.06	0.47	50	October 1986
Portugal[c]	16.378[b] (4.823)	−3.290[b] (0.879)	0.37	0.33	98	December 1990
Sweden	0.381 (0.202)	−0.012 (0.029)	−0.01	1.68	84	September 1989
Spain	3.821[b] (1.523)	−0.448[a] (0.184)	0.14	1.24	100	December 1990

Switzerland	0.218[a]	− 0.011	0.01	1.97	85	September 1989
	(0.098)	(0.014)			
United Kingdom	0.135	− 0.018	0.06	1.20	100	December 1990
	(0.099)	(0.012)			

Notes:
Trend coefficients are annualized. Standard errors are in parentheses; $N/3$ independent observations assumed.
[a] Significant at 5% level.
[b] Significant at 1% level.
[c] See Note a on preceding table.

that they view as risky. Much has been written both for and against the existence of a large and variable risk premium.

We cannot directly observe s^e, but we can observe the average response from a survey of market participants (Δs^e). Survey data that include the minor European currencies are collected by the *Currency Forecasters' Digest* of White Plains, New York. The data consist of 'combined consensus' values (harmonic means) from surveys of approximately 45 exchange rate forecasters from major banks, multinational companies and forecasting firms.[11]

These survey data were first used in Chinn and Frankel (1991), to test for the presence of a time-varying risk premium of the sort studied in many tests of bias in the forward market. In that paper the exchange rates *vis-à-vis* the dollar of 17 countries were studied. We regressed expected depreciation, as measured by the survey data, against the forward discount, to see if it was possible to reject the hypothesis of a unit coefficient. When the countries were tested individually, only a few showed statistically significant evidence of a time-varying risk premium. These included two out of the nine EMS currencies tested (Ireland and Belgium). Two more out of four non-EMS-European currencies tested showed evidence of such a time-varying risk premium (Norway and Austria). When all 17 currencies were pooled, there was significant evidence overall of a time-varying risk premium at the three-month horizon.

We now test for the existence of a time trend in the risk premiums of European currencies. We measure the absolute risk premium against the Deutschmark as:

$$ARP = |fd^{(\text{loc}/\text{DM})} - \Delta s^{e\,(\text{loc}/\text{DM})}| \tag{2}$$

The results are reported in Table 9.3 for the period February 1988 to December 1991. Unfortunately, we do not have expectations data going as far back as the covered interest rate differentials analysed in the preceding section.[12]

It appears that over this recent four-year period, the risk premium fell for the Danish krone, French franc, Irish punt, Norwegian krone, Swedish krone, and the pound sterling at statistically significant rates for at least one of the forecast horizons (either 3 or 12 months). The Norwegian krone and the pound sterling showed statistically significant declines in the risk premium at both forecast horizons. On the other hand, the risk premium showed no clear trend for the Belgian franc, the Italian lira, or the Dutch guilder.[13]

It is interesting to note that the most pronounced decline in the risk premium was among countries that joined the EMS during the sample period, either officially (Spain and the United Kingdom) or *de facto* and

Table 9.3. Time trends in absolute risk premium February 1988–December 1991

Country	k	Constant	Trend	$\bar{R}^2$	Durbin–Watson statistic	n	Assumed MA[a]
Belgium	3	2.480[c] (1.010)	0.259 (0.440)	−0.02	1.686	45	
	12	0.960[c] (0.158)	−0.062 (0.070)	−0.00	1.629	45	
Denmark	3	2.145[c] (0.429)	−0.180 (0.187)	−0.00	1.768	47	
	12	1.643[c] (0.249)	−0.318[c] (0.108)	0.14	1.531	47	
France	3	3.283[c] (1.864)	−0.284 (0.781)	−0.01	0.927	47	MA(1)
	12	1.041[c] (0.080)	−0.139[c] (0.021)	0.01	2.254	47	MA(6)
Ireland	3	3.543[c] (0.602)	−0.460[b] (0.222)	0.09	1.265	47	MA(1)
	12	2.377[c] (0.411)	−0.326 (0.179)	0.04	1.994	47	
Italy	3	4.131[c] (1.578)	−0.727 (0.618)	0.06	1.424	47	MA(1)
	12	1.776[c] (0.339)	−0.010 (0.148)	−0.01	1.659	47	
Netherlands	3	0.985[c] (0.335)	0.138 (0.155)	−0.00	1.774	47	
	12	0.635[c] (0.196)	−0.032 (0.085)	−0.02	1.602	47	

Table 9.3. (*cont.*)

							MA
Norway	3	6.087ᶜ (0.817)	−0.883ᶜ (0.335)	0.10	1.862	47	
	12	6.940ᶜ (0.587)	−1.656ᶜ (0.256)	0.47	1.920	47	
Sweden	3	6.456ᶜ (1.794)	−1.136 (0.619)	0.17	1.276	47	MA(3)
	12	6.911ᶜ (0.816)	−1.374ᶜ (0.136)	0.23	1.824	47	
Spain	3	8.549ᶜ (0.835)	−0.883ᶜ (0.036)	0.10	2.032	47	
	12	7.470ᶜ (1.026)	−0.898ᶜ (0.434)	0.20	1.317	47	MA(3)
Switzerland	3	0.843 (0.564)	0.593 (0.377)	0.07	1.809	47	MA(1)
	12	0.591ᶜ (0.279)	−0.476ᶜ (0.136)	0.22	1.598	47	MA(7)
United Kingdom	3	6.985ᶜ (0.905)	−1.363ᶜ (0.396)	0.19	2.126	47	
	12	5.433ᶜ (0.724)	−1.248ᶜ (0.242)	0.43	1.401	47	MA(4)

Notes:
Trend coefficients are on an annual basis. Standard errors are in parentheses.
[a] Assumed MA indicates order of moving average process assumed in calculating Hansen-Hodrick robust standard errors.
[b] Significant at 5% level.
[c] Significant at 1% level.

unilaterally (Norway and Sweden). It is further interesting to note that the risk premium appeared to increase for the one European currency in the sample unrelated to the EMS, the Swiss franc. This correlation with the exchange rate regime bolsters confidence that the movements in the measured risk premium are genuine.

4   The EMS target zone

The European monetary system has been in operation since 1979. Realignments, 11 altogether, were recurrent during the first eight years. The history is illustrated in Figure 9.1, which presents central rates around the Deutschmark, in normalized log form so that they can be read as percentage deviations. Only the Dutch guilder was able to maintain a nearly fixed rate against the Deutschmark, undergoing just two small devaluations.

There has been a period of exchange rate stability since January 1987, the month of the twelfth (and possibly final) realignment. Giavazzi and Spaventa (1990) argue that 1987 marked the beginning of a 'New EMS'. A series of policy steps and institutional reforms were taken during the subsequent five years with the aim of enhancing exchange rate stability. (A chronology is given in Appendix 9B.) It is not possible to say, however, whether there will be a future realignment. More relevantly to the determination of interest differentials, it is not possible to tell whether investors *think* there might be a future realignment. In the remainder of the chapter we test the recent credibility of the EMS with participants in the foreign exchange market.

Recent research on the EMS starts from the theory of the target zone introduced by Krugman (1991). He examined the case where the commitment of the authorities to intervene to defend the target zone was completely credible, and showed the effect of investor awareness that the foreign exchange market would become a one-way bet as the exchange rate neared the target zone boundary.

Empirical studies, such as the one by Flood, Rose and Mathieson (1990), showed that the European data of the 1980s did not fit the standard target zone model. The simplest test of target zone credibility is that proposed by Svensson (1991a): expected future exchange rates were found to lie nearly always outside contemporaneous EMS target zones for the period 1979 to early 1990. This result suggested that the market during this period usually perceived a strong probability of realignment. Expectations were inferred from interest rates using the assumption of uncovered interest parity (requiring that no risk premium should exist).

Our goal here is to update the tests of exchange rate expectations, to see

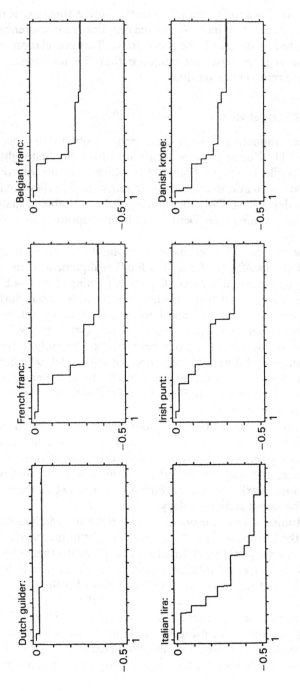

Figure 9.1 EMS currencies, March 1979 – December 1991 (log of Deutschmark central rates)

in particular if the credibility of the EMS has been enhanced over the period 1988–91.Our main methodological innovation is the use of the *Currency Forecasters' Digest* survey data, supplementing interest rate differentials as a measure of market expectations.[14] The potentially important advantage of using survey data is immunity to errors introduced by exchange risk premiums. If the existence of a large exchange risk premium meant that the apparent finding of expected rates outside the band were spurious, this would still be evidence that investors had little faith in exchange rate stability. After all, they would not demand a risk premium if they were confident that the exchange rate would not change. Nevertheless, we wish to distinguish empirically between the exchange risk premium, considered in the preceding section, and expectations of exchange rate changes.

As noted above, it is a controversial question whether the exchange risk premium is large enough and variable enough to render the forward discount or interest rate differential deficient measures of the expected future spot rate. Recent tests using the survey data for a number of minor currencies, such as the tests of the European currencies reported in the preceding section, turned up more evidence of a time-varying risk premium than did earlier studies of the major currencies.

In addition to the question of EMS credibility per se, we are also interested in the question whether the empirical failure of the standard target zone model noted above might reflect simply an erroneous assumption of uncovered interest rate parity. The alternative explanation of the empirical results, advanced by Bertola and Svensson (1990), is based on time-varying credibility. Our analysis suggests a particularly good reason to believe that EMS credibility changed over this period. We use the Bertola–Svensson framework to estimate an expected realignment term, and observe how it changes over time.

We begin by reviewing the standard evidence on EMS credibility based on interest rate differentials. If there is no risk premium and uncovered interest parity holds, we can use interest rates and contemporaneous spot rates to construct expected future exchange rates and see whether they lie within the target bands.[15] In Figure 9.2 expected future exchange rates at the one-year horizon are plotted, as deviations from then-current central rates. Vertical lines indicate dates of realignment against the Deutschmark, while the horizontal lines indicate the target zone boundaries. The period is March 1979 to the January 1987 realignment.

Figure 9.2 provides striking evidence on the historical credibility of the EMS. Only the Dutch guilder was, on the whole, expected to remain inside its contemporaneous band. The other five currencies were, for the most part, expected to violate the limits against the Deutschmark. The

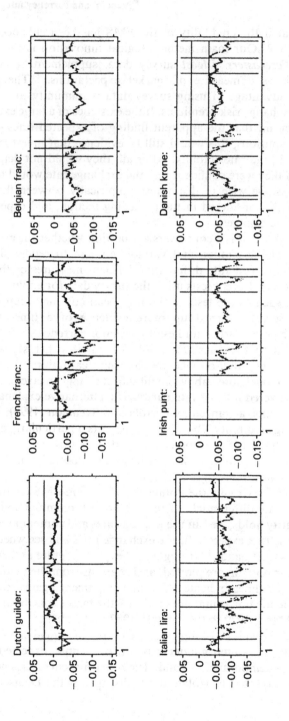

Figure 9.2 One-year expectations based on interest rate differentials, March 1979–January 1987 (Deviations from current central rate of the Deutschmark)

evidence supports the view that the EMS had low credibility during its first eight years; the many devaluations during this period apparently did not come as a surprise.

5 Have expected future exchange rates fallen inside the bands since 1988?

We now proceed to the period February 1988 to December 1991. The Spanish peseta and British pound are added to the original set of six currencies. Actual spot rates of the Deutschmark price of each currency are presented in Figure 9.3, in normalized log form. While the Dutch guilder remained close to its central rate,[16] the other currencies showed more variability, and several came close to their lower limits in this period. The strength of the Spanish peseta within its Deutschmark target zone in 1990–91 was atypical.

To assess the credibility of the current EMS target zones, we first updated the interest rate test; Figure 9.4 shows the 12-month expectations that would be implied by uncovered interest parity. Figure 9.4 may be compared to Figure 9.2 for the earlier period. All eight currencies showed smaller expected deviations from current central rates than in the pre-1987 period. Sample means from the two periods are compared in Table 9.4; t-statistics indicate a statistically significant increase in credibility for all five currencies tested.

We note an upward trend in the 12-month expectations within the 1988–91 period. During the second half of this period, most values were within the target zones, a remarkable finding compared with earlier results. These results, however, are only valid under the assumption of uncovered interest parity. We therefore turn to our alternative measure of expectations – the survey data.

In Figure 9.5 the forecasts at the one-month horizon for the period February 1988 to December 1991 are shown.[17] The forecasts typically were within the official limits. Figure 9.6 shows the forecasts at a 3-month horizon; they also were within the bands by the second quarter of 1988. At both horizons, forecasts (with the exception of the guilder) were often close to the lower limits of the band, a possible symptom of imperfect credibility.

A more stringent test can be made by using longer time horizons. Figure 9.7 shows 12-month expectations, which were often outside the target zone. Prior to 1990, the forecasts for the currencies of France, Denmark, Belgium, and Italy were typically 1–3 percentage points below their lower Deutschmark limits. In January 1990, however, forecasts for these four currencies began to strengthen, crossing inside the band limits by the

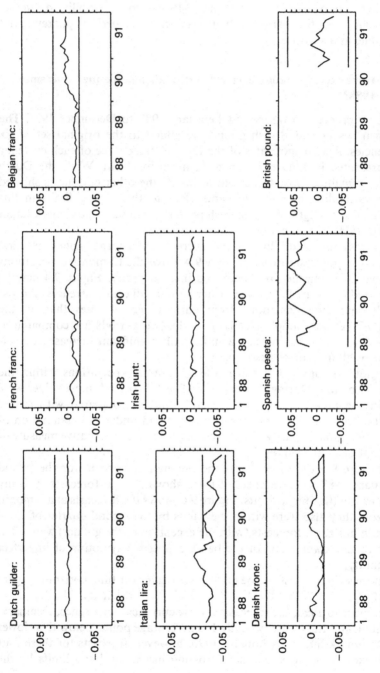

Figure 9.3 EMS spot exchange rates, February 1988–December 1991 (Log deviation from central rate of the Deutschmark)

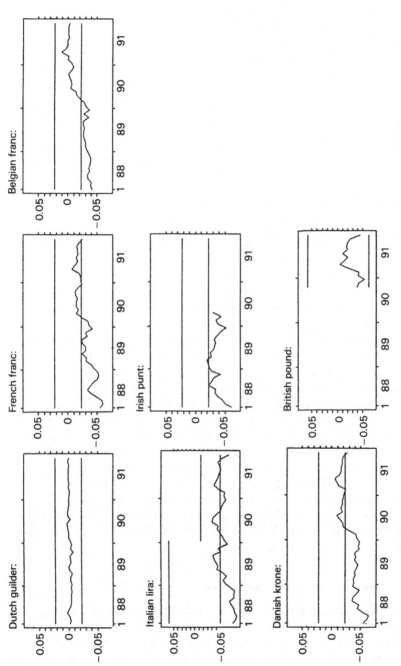

Figure 9.4 Twelve-month expectations, using interest rate differentials, February 1988–December 1991 (Log deviation from central rate of the Deutschmark)

Table 9.4. *Mean 12-month expectations (from interest rates) as deviations from Deutschmark central rates*

Currency	Mar. 1979– Dec. 1986 %	Feb. 1988– Dec. 1991 %	Difference of means	T-test of inequality
France	− 5.57	− 2.87	+ 2.70	+ 5.98
Belgium	− 4.95	− 1.94	+ 3.01	+ 11.60
Denmark	− 5.17	− 3.14	+ 2.03	+ 6.27
Netherlands	− 0.531	− 0.162	+ 0.369	+ 2.24
Italy	− 8.40	− 7.42	+ 0.98	+ 1.49
		− 2.13[b]	+ 6.27	+ 14.46
Ireland	− 6.50[a]	NA	NA	NA

Notes: Percentages approximated as log deviations × 100.
[a] Irish interest rate data available for 1982–1986 only.
[b] The central rate of the lira shifted with the narrowing of the target zone in January 1990. The February 1988–December 1989 mean was − 7.42%; the January 1990–December 1991 mean was − 2.13%.

second quarter of that year. In 1991, the 12-month forecasts were typically inside the target zone.

It should be noticed that the survey-based forecasts shown in Figure 9.7 are similar to the forecasts based on interest rates shown in Figure 9.4 for the same period and time horizon. The exception is the Irish pound, where the survey data showed greater credibility: since mid-1988, most of the 12-month forecasts have been inside the Deutschmark target zone.

Quarterly forecasts over a time horizon of five years are presented in Figure 9.8. Although forecasts for most of the currencies were several percentage points below the lower limits, some showed an upward trend. Several drew near to the target zone during 1990–91, or crossed into it (most clearly the Belgian franc).

With credibility apparently greater than before, currencies within the EMS might seem more likely to conform at present to the basic target zone model developed by Krugman and others. We now re-examine this question using the recent data.

6   Reassessing the performance of target zone models

The standard target zone model is built on an equation that determines the exchange rate as a function of economic fundamentals, such as the money supply and real income, and rationally expected depreciation. The fundamentals are assumed to evolve exogenously, in accordance with a

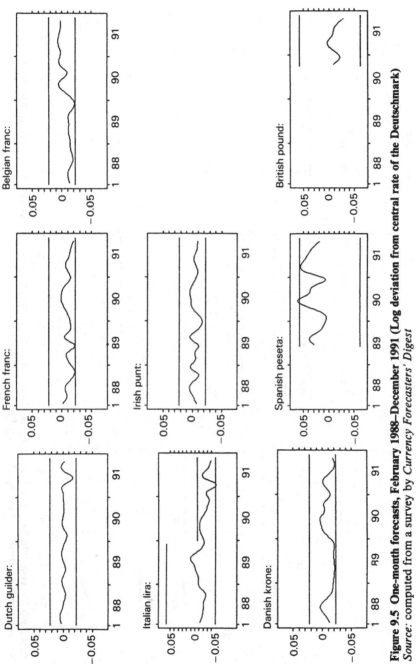

Figure 9.5 One-month forecasts, February 1988–December 1991 (Log deviation from central rate of the Deutschmark)
Source: computed from a survey by *Currency Forecasters' Digest*

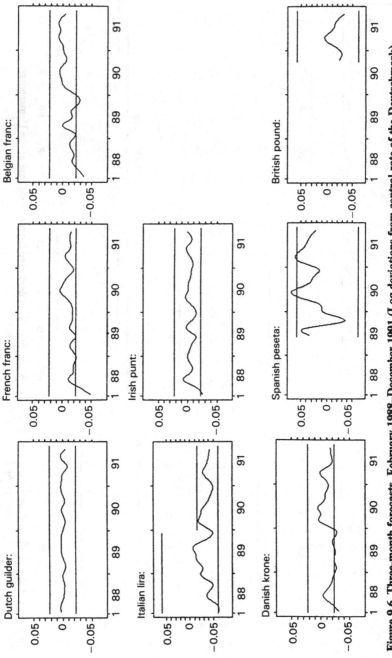

Figure 9.6 Three-month forecasts, February 1988–December 1991 (Log deviations from central rate of the Deutschmark)
Source: computed from a survey by *Currency Forecasters' Digest*

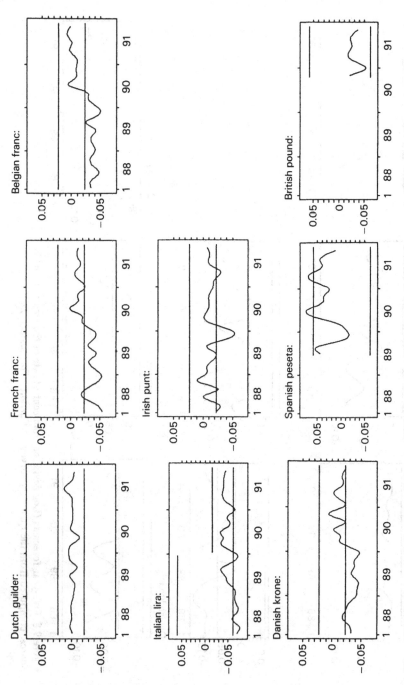

Figure 9.7 Twelve-month forecasts, February 1988–December 1991 (Log deviations from central rate of the Deutschmark)
Source: computed from a survey by *Currency Forecasters' Digest*

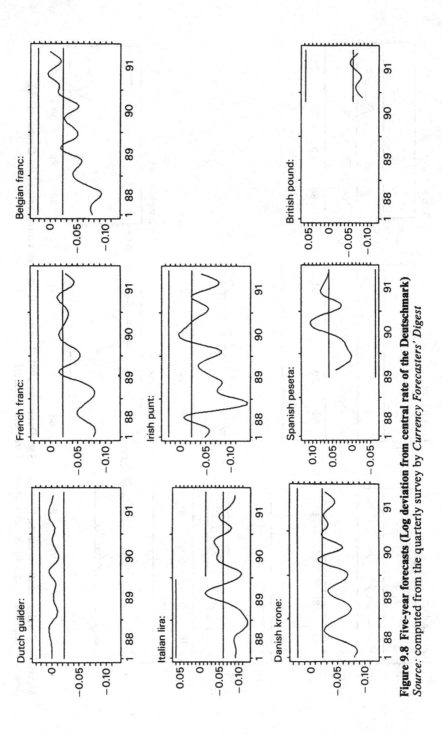

Figure 9.8 Five-year forecasts (Log deviation from central rate of the Deutschmark)
Source: computed from the quarterly survey by *Currency Forecasters' Digest*

Table 9.5. *Correlation coefficients: spot position in band and expected change over 12-month horizon*

	Survey data	Interest rate differential	Survey data	Interest rate differential
	(Feb. 1988–Dec. 1991)		(Jan. 1990–Dec. 1991)	
Belgium	+ 0.716	+ 0.823	+ 0.476	+ 0.760
	(0.000)	(0.000)	(0.025)	(0.000)
Denmark	+ 0.106	− 0.196	− 0.014	− 0.392
	(0.493)	(0.186)	(0.954)	(0.058)
France	+ 0.067	+ 0.006	− 0.308	− 0.519
	(0.665)	(0.965)	(0.163)	(0.009)
Ireland	+ 0.105	NA	+ 0.077	NA
	(0.498)		(0.732)	
Netherlands	− 0.232	− 0.262	− 0.346	− 0.316
	(0.129)	(0.075)	(0.115)	(0.133)
Italy	− 0.059[a]	+ 0.491[a]	− 0.414	− 0.360
	(0.794)	(0.017)	(0.056)	(0.084)

Notes:
Marginal significance levels in parentheses.
[a] To end-December 1989.

continuous-time stochastic process (analogous to a random walk), except that discrete changes in the money supply occur when the authorities intervene to defend the band. The solution for the exchange rate has the important property that, near the bands, speculation will help to stabilize the exchange rate, lessening the need for actual intervention. This phenomenon has been called the 'honeymoon effect'. The model is predicated on the assumption that the commitment to defend the band is entirely credible.

The first rigorous empirical evaluation of the target zone model was the study of the EMS in May 1990 by Flood, Rose and Mathieson (1990). They found negligible evidence in favour of the specification. Phillips (1990) obtained similar results for the 'mini-snake' of the 1970s.

These tests required a number of auxiliary assumptions in addition to the basic assumption of target zone credibility including the absence of a risk premium, flexibility of goods prices, and a reliable estimate of the elasticity of the demand for money with respect to the interest rate. We focus here on a key prediction of the theory that does not depend on these assumptions: a negative relationship between the *level* of the exchange rate (within the band) and its *expected rate of change*. This relationship is the basis for the stabilizing honeymoon effect.

In Table 9.5 correlations between the exchange rate and its own expected rate of change are presented, using both measures of expectations (one based on survey data and the other on interest differentials). For the entire four-year period, there were more positive than negative coefficients, and none of the latter were statistically significant. Indeed, the Belgian franc was significantly positive. We also report results for the second half of the period. Signs were negative during 1990–91 for Denmark, Netherlands, Italy and France (and significantly so on the interest rate test for France). These results suggest that credibility increased between the first and second sample periods.

7   Estimation of the realignment term

The Krugman model was not designed to deal with time-varying credibility, but the Bertola–Svensson (1990) version was. Bertola and Svensson allowed for a probability of realignment. The model can thus explain why investors who observe the exchange rate move close to the boundary might expect a further movement in the same direction rather than a reversal. Rose and Svensson (1991) were the first to implement the Bertola–Svensson model (on the franc/Deutschmark rate for the period March 1979 to May 1990). Svensson (1991c) extended the procedure to five other currencies in the EMS. Weber (1992) pursued the implications of time-varying realignment fears for the relationship between the level of the exchange rate and its expected rate of change. All of these studies measured expectations by interest rate differentials.

In this section we use the Bertola–Svensson framework to estimate a term showing investor perception of the importance of possible realignments. This measure is based on the overall expected rate of change of the exchange rate, but differs in that expectations of mean-reversion within the target zone have been filtered out, leaving a more pure measure of realignment perceptions.

The expected change in the exchange rate is a weighted average of (i) the expected magnitude of the realignment conditional on one taking place, and (ii) the expected reversion to the centre of the band conditional on there being no realignment. How can we measure expected reversion conditional on no realignment? Since no realignments in fact took place during the period January 1987 to December 1991, we estimated the *ex post* relationship between the level of the exchange rate and its next-period change during this period, and invoke rational expectations to argue that this was the process conditionally perceived by investors.

Results are given in Table 9.6 for the OLS regressions of the change in the exchange rate against its past level for time horizons of 1, 3, 6 and 12

Table 9.6. *Expected mean reversion within the band: estimates of β_1*

Currency of:	$k = 1$ mth (59 obs.)	$k = 3$ mths (57 obs.)	$k = 6$ mths (54 obs.)	$k = 12$ mths (48 obs.)
Belgium	− 0.653	− 0.167	− 0.356	− 0.629
	(0.0555)	(0.112)	(0.207)	(0.238)
Denmark	− 0.123	− 0.393	− 0.853	− 1.06
	(0.0631)	(0.186)	(0.173)	(0.219)
France	− 0.140	− 0.424	− 0.769	− 0.977
	(0.0723)	(0.174)	(0.200)	(0.033)
Ireland	− 0.427	− 0.931	− 1.31	− 0.768
	(0.114)	(0.131)	(0.805)	(0.125)
Netherlands	− 0.382	− 0.746	− 1.11	− 1.17
	(0.138)	(0.205)	(0.111)	(0.204)
Italy	− 0.154	− 0.523	− 0.727	− 1.37
	(0.0775)	(0.146)	(0.187)	(0.122)

Notes:
Based on monthly observations from January 1987 to end-December 1991 (December 1989 for Italy). Standard errors, in parentheses, based on Newey-West covariance estimators.

months.[18] The estimates of the auto-regressive coefficient β_1 are satisfactory in a number of respects. As would be expected, the absolute magnitude of the coefficient is larger the longer the horizon considered (with the single exception of the 12-month Irish forecast). The simple linear form appears to be adequate. We tested for quadratic and cubic terms β_2 and β_3 in Table 9.7, and found relatively little evidence to support such non-linearity.

Section VI of Frankel and Phillips (1991) showed how it is possible to subtract this measure of expected reversion conditional on no realignment from overall expected depreciation, to derive a measure q of the perceived importance of possible future realignment. The realignment term q reflects both the perceived probability of realignment and its expected magnitude. We focus on the 12-month horizon, the longest for which survey data are available on a monthly basis. We believe this will give the most accurate result.

Results from applying this procedure to the survey measure of expected depreciation for the period 1988–91, are presented in Figure 9.9. Reversion within the band was 'filtered out' to arrive at the estimated realignment term q. The estimates tended to be close to zero for the guilder, suggesting a low probability of realignment (or a very small expected magnitude of realignment). For the other currencies, the q

Table 9.7. *Test of $B_2 = B_3 = 0$: marginal significance*

Currency of:	$k = 1$ mth	$k = 3$ mths	$k = 6$ mths	$k = 12$ mths
Belgium	0.000[a]	0.000[a]	0.000[a]	0.091
Denmark	0.432	0.498	0.478	0.000[a]
France	0.413	0.067	NA	0.298
Ireland	0.447	0.182	0.435	NA
Netherlands	0.000[a]	0.001[a]	0.319	0.575
Italy	0.954	0.919	NA	NA

Notes:
Chi-square (2) test of $B_2 = B_3 = 0$, based on Newey-West covariance estimators.
[a] Denotes significance at the 5% level.
NA denotes computational problems.

estimates were usually negative, indicating some perception of possible devaluation of the central rate against the Deutschmark. But there is quite bit of fluctuation, and the perceived importance of realignments was substantially diminished for all examined currencies during the 1990–91 period.

Figure 9.10 is analogous to Figure 9.9, but interest rate differentials were used to measure expectations instead of the survey data. We were thus able to estimate q beginning just after the last EMS realignment in January 1987. Again, we note an improvement in credibility after early 1990.

In Table 9.8 summary statistics are reported for the expected rates of mean-reversion. Mean absolute values during the 1987–91 period for those currencies using $\pm 2.25\%$ bands range from 0.2 to 0.9% per year. Compared to historic levels of interest rate differentials within the EMS, such values seem relatively small. The implications would be that observed interest rate differentials reflect mostly imperfect credibility and expectations of realignment. But the more recent evidence suggests that realignment concerns are becoming smaller. If so, expected mean-reversion within the band may now represent the larger portion of overall expected exchange rate changes in a newly credible EMS.

8   Conclusions

On the specific question of the standard target zone model, we found that tests based on survey data were no more supportive than those based on uncovered interest parity, suggesting that the risk premium is not the explanation for the empirical failure of the model. A more likely expla-

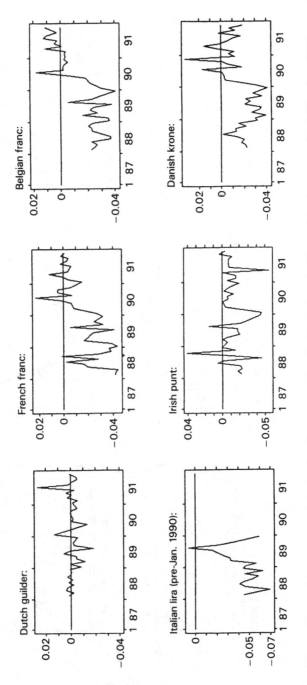

Figure 9.9 q estimates – expected rate of realignment against the Deutschmark, 12-month horizon, annualized (Based on CFD survey)

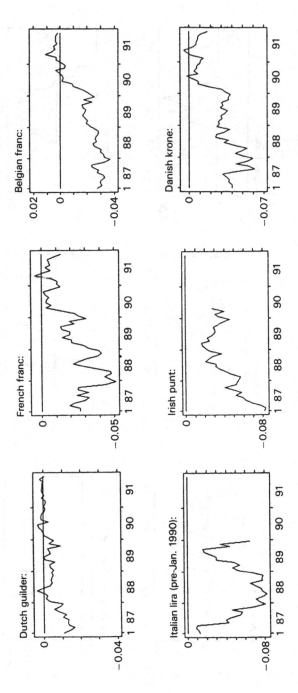

Figure 9.10 q estimates – expected rate of realignment against the Deutchmark, 12-month horizon, annualized (Based on uncovered interest parity)

Table 9.8. *Magnitude of expected rates of mean-reversion (Annualized percentages)*

Currency of:	Mean	Mean absolute	Minimum	Maximum
Belgium	− 0.07	0.44	− 1.06	0.99
Denmark	− 0.26	0.86	− 2.75	1.31
France	− 0.27	0.64	− 1.88	1.01
Ireland	0.01	0.23	− 0.48	0.93
Netherlands	0.01	0.17	− 0.70	0.81
Italy	0.67	1.69	− 4.46	2.25

Notes:
Approximate percentages based on log differences. Based on OLS estimation for the period January 1987 to end-December 1991 (December 1989 for Italy).

nation is time-varying credibility, as put forward by Bertola and Svensson. Our estimates show that the term representing the perceived importance of realignment was high during much of the sample period, but that it was smaller during 1990–91.

More generally, our results suggest that currency factors are a more important component of interest rate differentials than are capital controls and other barriers to the movement of capital across country boundaries. Tests of covered interest parity showed that 'country barriers' have been relatively small in Germany, the Netherlands, and Belgium, since the beginning of the 1980s (as well as for some countries that were not official members of the EMS: Switzerland, Austria, and the United Kingdom). For the other members, (Portugal, Spain, France, Italy, and Denmark) the covered interest rate differential diminished in the late 1980s. Thus currency factors are the most important remaining components of the interest differentials. But both currency factors – the exchange risk premium and expected depreciation – now show signs of diminishing as well. Investor faith in the exchange rate stability provided by the EMS seems to have improved particularly in 1990–91 relative to 1988–89.

NOTES

We would like to thank Barry Eichengreen for presenting this paper at the conference in Estoril on 16–18 January, 1992. We also thank Rudiger Dornbusch, Barry Eichengreen, Robert Flood, Alberto Giovannini, David Romer, Andrew Rose and Lars Svensson for helpful comments. We would also like to thank the

Center for German and European Studies and the Institute for Business and Economic Research, both at the University of California at Berkeley and the Group for International and Comparative Economic Studies of University of California, Santa Cruz, for research support. The views reflected in the chapter are those of the authors only and not of any institution.

1. The interest rate data used in the table, and throughout the chapter, are end-of-period inter-bank rates, if available. If inter-bank rates are not available, 3-month time deposit rates or other substitutes are used. Most of the data are as described in NBER Working Paper 2309. A data appendix, available on request, describes the changes, including updating. Data for the updating was obtained from *World Financial Markets* for April 1988–September 1989, and the 3-month money market rates from *The Economist* from October 1989 for the absolute interest rate regressions.

2. The standard errors are calculated assuming only one-third the number of observations, to allow for the fact that the observations may not be independent.

3. The interest rate for Denmark is a highly regulated 3-month time deposit rate, which may account for the result.

4. It must be noted that high levels of serial correlation mean that the appearance of statistical significance may be illusory, despite the use of conservative standard errors. For this reason the regression results are reported only in the Appendix [Table A1]. Correcting for high serial correlation by taking first differences does not yield trends that are truly significant statistically.

5. Frankel (1991) performs a similar decomposition of the *real* interest differential for a sample of 25 countries.

6. See Dooley and Isard (1980); and Giavazzi and Pagano (1985, p. 27).

7. The United Kingdom liberalization is explained and analysed in Artis and Taylor (1989).

8. Giavazzi and Pagano (1985, pp. 27–8), and Wyplosz (1986), among others.

9. The forward rate data were mostly from Barclays Bank, as reported by Data Resources, Inc. The interest rate data for this period were primarily from *World Financial Markets*, which discontinued this series subsequently. The Data Resources information was used to extend the series for France, Germany, Italy, the Netherlands and the United Kingdom.

10. It is clear from Braga de Macedo and Torres (1989) that the magnitude of Portugal's covered interest differential fell sharply in the first half of 1986, and remained relatively small in 1987–89.

11. These data are proprietary, and were obtained by subscription at the Institute for International Economics, where one author is a Visiting Fellow. We formed an estimate of the implied forecast of intra-EMS exchange rates using the ratio of the relevant forecasts against the dollar. Contemporaneously dated forward rates are available from the same source, as described in Frankel and Phillips (1991).

12. The forward rate observations are chosen to match the survey dates, and thus differ from the end-of-period forward rate data used in the test of covered interest parity.

13. There does not appear to be much evidence of serial correlation which might bias downwards the standard errors. GMM standard errors were calculated for those regressions where there appeared to be some evidence of serial correlation (see Table 9.3).

14. This section in large part replicates the results in Frankel and Phillips (1991). The sample there, however, ended in July 1991, whereas in this instance the sample period has been updated to December 1991, the month of the Maastricht meeting. (The reader is referred to the 1991 article for the technical details of the theory and tests.)

15. This basic test of target zone credibility was first performed by Svensson (1991a) for the Swedish krone. Here we replicate the findings of Flood, Rose and Mathieson (1990) for the EMS. We thank these authors for access to their data. Giovannini (1990) conducts an equivalent test for the French franc and Italian lira.

16. The Dutch have apparently followed a Deutschmark target zone of about ± 0.5% since 1983, i.e. much narrower than the standard EMS bands of ± 2.25%.

17. For an extra degree of protection to the confidentiality of the original *Currency Forecasters Digest* data, we have applied a data-smoothing technique to the series plotted in these figures. We do not believe that the qualitative conclusions are materially affected by this procedure.

18. For the lira, we limited the test to the period before the narrowing of Italy's target zone in January 1990. Because estimation of mean-reversion is sensitive to the length of period, we did not attempt to estimate the relationship for the EMS newcomers – Spain and the United Kingdom.

Appendix 9A: Interest rate differentials

Table A1. *Trends in absolute interest rate differentials from September 1982*

Country	Constant	Trend	$\bar{R}^2$	Durbin–Watson statistic	End of sample period
Austria	0.695[b] (0.288)	− 0.026 (0.042)	0.00	0.47	September 1989
Belgium	5.745[c] (0.465)	− 0.562[c] (0.061)	0.74	0.48	May 1990
Denmark	0.897 (0.597)	0.127 (0.087)	0.06	0.23	August 1989
France	6.614[c] (0.468)	− 0.615[c] (0.061)	0.77	0.30	May 1990
Ireland	9.053[c] (1.185)	− 0.764[c] (0.168)	0.42	0.3	September 1989
Italy	12.440[c] (0.615)	− 1.043[c] (0.080)	0.85	0.56	May 1990
Netherlands	0.665[b] (0.282)	0.000 (0.036)	− 0.01	0.35	May 1990
Norway	6.049[c] (0.516)	0.448[c] (0.126)	0.43	0.70	October 1986
Portugal[a]	15.349[c] (2.301)	− 0.442 (0.436)	0.49	0.08	May 1990
Sweden	6.741[c] (0.828)	− 0.162 (0.107)	0.06	0.30	May 1990
Spain	11.194[c] (1.692)	− 0.557[b] (0.220)	0.17	0.13	May 1990

Switzerland	1.551^c		0.20	0.31	May 1990
	(0.471)	−0.175^c			
		(0.061)			
United Kingdom	4.162^c	0.407^c	0.39	0.41	May 1990
	(0.693)	(0.090)			

Notes:

Trend coefficients are annualized. Standard errors in parentheses; $N/3$ independent observations assumed.

[a] See Note *a* on preceding table.

[b] Significant at 5% level.

[c] Significant at 1% level.

Appendix 9B. EMS developments, 1986–91

1986

February   Single European Act set 31 December, 1992 as date for completion of internal market with free movement of goods, services, labour and capital within the European Community.

1987

12 January   EMS realignment (the eleventh, and possibly final)

January   France and Italy announced changes in their exchange rate management.

September   Basle–Nyborg Agreement. Committee of central bank governors agreed to strengthen the ERM by providing for intramarginal intervention and more liberal short-term finance of intervention.

1988

13 June   Agreement to free capital movements in the EC. Germany softened previous opposition to EC central bank; France and Italy persuaded to remove major capital controls over next two years.

28 June   Hanover summit. Britain rejected proposal for European central bank and single currency. Committee on economic and monetary union set up with Jacques Delors, President of the European Commission, as Chairman.

14 July   Bundesbank's President denied he was opposed to the concept of a European currency.

1989

17 April   Report of the committee on economic and monetary union (the Delors committee). A three-stage transition to economic and monetary union (EMU) proposed, but no timetable specified:

                Stage 1: Liberalization of capital movements; enlargement of ERM membership; more powers given to EC Committee of central bank governors.
                          Exchange rate realignments still permitted.

                Stage 2: Exchange rate bands to be narrowed from ± 2.25%, realignments permitted only in exceptional circumstances. Economic policy guidelines, not binding, to be set at the Community level. European system of central banks (ESCB) to be set up, absorbing existing monetary arrangements.

                Stage 3: Exchange rates to be irrevocably locked.
                          ESCB to replace the national central banks.
                          Adoption of single currency will complete this stage.

19 June   Spain joined the ERM.

June 27   European Council decided to begin Stage 1 of the transition to EMU on 1 July 1990. (According to the Delors Report, 'a decision to enter upon the first stage should be a decision to embark on the entire process'.)

November	Dismantling of the Berlin Wall.
December	Strasbourg summit. Agreement that by December 1990 an inter-governmental conference would convene to prepare the changes in the Treaty of Rome to allow EMU to go ahead. West Germany after initially favouring a slower pace, agreed to this schedule as its EC partners gave their stamp of approval to German monetary unification.

1990

8 January	Lira bands narrowed from ± 6% to the standard ± 2.25%. Lower limit unchanged.
6 February	Germany: apparently sudden decision of Chancellor Kohl in favour of rapid movement towards a German currency union.
March	France: minister announced that French franc will never again be devalued in the EMS.
March	European Commission released its plan for EMU; similar to Delors' Report, but centrally-set rules for members' budget deficits dropped. Plan to be discussed by EC finance ministers on 31 March.
31 March	Ashford Castle meeting of EC finance ministers. Eleven of 12 ministers agreed on main features of a new European central bank.
April	East and west German governments agreed on terms of monetary conversion and union, to be enacted 2 July, 1990.
28 April	Dublin summit. Declaration that changes in Treaty of Rome relating to EMU must be ratified by end of 1992 (thus **possible** for Stage 2 to begin in January 1993). 14 December, 1990 chosen as date for conference on EMU.
18 May	Treaty to unify east and west Germany signed. West Germany agreed to set up a DM 115 billion fund to support East Germany to the end of 1994.
June	Belgian central bank declared Deutschmark exchange rate as its main policy target.
1 July	Stage 1 of EMU began. Complete removal of capital controls, as previously scheduled. Exceptions: Ireland, Spain, Portugal, and Greece (deadline 1992). German monetary unification.
August	European Commission finalized its contribution to the forthcoming Rome conference on EMU. (See March 1990.) Recommended that the ECU should replace existing currencies (rather should than fixing permanent exchange rates among them). Proposed that Stage 2 should start in January 1993 leading, after 'a short duration', to full monetary union.
September	Meeting of finance ministers in Rome revealed large differences over timing of EMU. Belgium, France and Italy called for Stage 2 to start January 1993 and Stage 3 soon afterwards. Germany and the Netherlands were against setting any deadlines, arguing that economic convergence must come first.

8 October	Britain joined the ERM, using bands of ± 6%.
22 October	Norway unilaterally linked its currency to EMS.
27 October	Rome summit. Breakthrough in favour of EMU deadlines. Eleven of 12 agreed that Stage 2 of EMU should begin in January 1994 (subject only to mild conditions).
	European central bank to be set up at start of Stage 2, to begin conducting monetary policy in Stage 3.
	Timing of Stage 3 was vague, but apparently before 2000.
	Countries would be permitted to stay outside Stages 2 and 3 if they chose to do so.
13 November	EC central bankers unveiled their draft statutes for a future European central bank: first objective to be maintenance of price stability.
22 November	UK Prime Minister, Mrs Margaret Thatcher, resigned.
14 December	Rome summit. Inter-governmental conference on EMU began work on a treaty to be signed by October 1991. Draft treaty, published by European Commission, to be used as working base.

1991

April	Spain removed virtually all capital controls.
April	Speculation that Britain and Spain would narrow their exchange rate bands to ± 2.25%.
13 May	*Financial Times* reported that many EMU negotiators had now accepted that a 'two-speed' transition to EMU was inevitable.
	Reported that Bundesbank's President would resign; resignation officially announced 16 May.
17 May	Sweden unilaterally linked its currency to EMS, using bands of ± 1.5%.
19 May	*The Economist* reported that EMU negotiators, after five months of little progress, now appeared likely to accept compromises embodied in draft EMU treaty proposed by Luxembourg.
7 June	Finland unilaterally linked its currency to EMS.
9 June	UK and German leaders agreed they would try to slow the pace of EMU negotiations at forthcoming summit.
30 June	Luxembourg summit took no significant new steps toward EMU; key remaining decisions were apparently postponed until Maastricht summit.
15 November	Finland devalued by 12.3% against the ECU.
9–10 December	Maastricht summit.

1992

| 6 April | Portugal joined the ERM, using bands of ± 6%. |

Sources: The Economist, London; *Financial Times*, London; Giovannini (1990), Haberler (1990), Weber (1991).

REFERENCES

Artis, M. and M. Taylor (1990) 'Abolishing Exchange Control: The UK Experience', in Courakis, A. and Taylor, M. (eds), *Private Behaviour and Government Policy in Interdependent Economies*, Oxford: Clarendon Press, pp. 129–58.

Bertola, G. and L. Svensson (1991) 'Stochastic Devaluation Risk and Empirical Fit of Target Zone Models', Centre for Economic Policy Research Discussion Paper No. 513, London.

Chinn, M. and J. Frankel (1991) 'Exchange Rate Expectations and the Risk Premium: Tests for a Cross-Section of 17 Currencies', National Bureau of Economic Research Working Paper No. 3806, Cambridge, Mass.; forthcoming, *Review of International Economics*.

Cumby, R. and M. Obstfeld (1984) 'International Interest Rate and Price Level Linkages Under Flexible Exchange Rates: A Review of Recent Evidence', in John Bilson and Richard Marston (eds), *Exchange Rate Theory and Practice*, Chicago: University of Chicago Press.

Dooley, M. and P. Isard (1980) 'Capital Controls, Political Risk and Deviations from Interest-Rate Parity', *Journal of Political Economy*, **88**, 370–84.

Fama, Eugene (1984) 'Forward and Spot Exchange Rates', *Journal of Monetary Economics*, **14**, 319–38.

Flood, R., A. Rose and D. Mathieson (1990) 'An Empirical Exploration of Exchange Rate Target Zones', National Bureau of Economic Research Working Paper No. 3543, Cambridge, Mass.; forthcoming, *Carnegie-Rochester Series on Public Policy*.

Frankel, J. (1982) 'In Search of the Exchange Risk Premium: A Six-Currency Test Assuming Mean-Variance Optimization', *Journal of International Money and Finance*, **1**, 255–74. To be reprinted in R. Macdonald and M. Taylor (eds), *Exchange Rate Economics*, Cheltenham: Edward Elgar Publishing.

(1989) 'International Financial Integration, Relations among Interest Rates and Exchange Rates, and Monetary Indicators', in Charles Pigott (ed.), *International Financial Integration and the Conduct of U.S. Monetary Policy*, Colloquium sponsored by the Federal Reserve Bank of New York; New York, pp. 17–49.

(1991) 'Quantifying International Capital Mobility in the 1980s', in D. Bernheim and J. Shoven (eds), *National Saving and Economic Performance*, Chicago: University of Chicago Press, pp. 227–60. To be adapted in Dilip Das (ed.), *Current Issues in International Trade and International Finance*, Oxford: Oxford University Press.

Frankel, J. and S. Phillips (1991) 'The European Monetary System: Credible at Last?', National Bureau of Economic Research Working Paper No. 3819, Cambridge, Mass., and *Oxford Economic Papers*, Vol. 44, 1992.

Froot, K. and J. Frankel (1989) 'Forward Discount Bias: Is It an Exchange Risk Premium?', *Quarterly Journal of Economics*, **104**, pp. 139–61.

Giavazzi, F. and M. Pagano (1985) 'Capital Controls and the European Monetary System', in *Capital Controls and Foreign Exchange Legislation*, Occasional Paper, Milano: Euromobiliare.

Giavazzi, F. and L. Spaventa (1990) 'The "New" EMS', in Paul De Grauwe and Lucas Papademos (eds), *The European Monetary System in the 1990s*, London: Longman.

Giovannini, A. (1990) 'European Monetary Reform: Progress and Prospects', *Brookings Papers on Economic Activity*, **2**, Washington, pp. 217–91.

Giovannini, A. and P. Jorion (1988) 'The Time Variation of Risk and Return in the Foreign Exchange and Stock Markets', *Journal of Finance*, xliv, No. 2, pp. 307–25.

Hodrick, R. and S. Srivastava (1986) 'The Covariance of Risk Premium and Expected Future Spot Exchange Rates', *Journal of International Money and Finance*, 5, S5–S22.

Krugman, P. (1991) 'Target Zones and Exchange Rate Dynamics', *Quarterly Journal of Economics*, CVI, No. 3, pp. 669–82.

Macedo, J.B. and F. Torres (1989) 'Interest Differentials, Integration and EMS Shadowing: a Note on Portugal with a Comparison to Spain', in J. da Silva Lopes and L.M. Beleza (eds), *Portugal and the Internal Market of the EEC*, Lisbon: Banco do Portugal, pp. 173–80.

Rogoff, K. (1985) 'Can Exchange Rate Predictability be Achieved Without Monetary Convergence? Evidence From the EMS', *European Economic Review*, 28, pp. 93–115.

Rose, A. and L. Svensson (1991) 'Expected and Predicted Realignments: The FF/DM Exchange Rate During the EMS', Centre for Economic Policy Research Discussion Paper No. 552, London.

Svensson, L. (1991a) 'The Simplest Test of Target Zone Credibility', Centre for Economic Policy Research Discussion Paper No. 493 and *IMF Staff Papers*, 38, Washington, forthcoming.

(1991b) 'The Foreign Exchange Risk Premium in a Target Zone with Devaluation Risk', Centre for Economic Policy Research Discussion Paper No. 494, London.

(1991c) 'Assessing Target Zone Credibility: Mean Reversion and Devaluation Expectations in the EMS', Centre for Economic Policy Research Discussion Paper No. 580, London.

Weber, A. (1992) 'Time-Varying Devaluation Risk, Interest Rate Differentials and Exchange Rates in Target Zones: Empirical Evidence from the EMS', Centre for Economic Policy Research Discussion Paper No. 611, London.

Wyplosz C. (1986) 'Capital Flows Liberalization and the EMS: A French Perspective', INSEAD Working Papers No. 86/40 and *European Economy*, June 1988.

Discussion

RUDIGER DORNBUSCH

The Frankel–Phillips–Chinn study offers a sophisticated progress report on European currencies. Exploring the information content of interest differentials, much like a seer might inspect the entrails of a chicken, the authors conclude that progress has been accomplished:

currency parities in Europe have become more credible in the past few years compared with the late 1980s. That finding is, of course, a bit anti-climatic. In fact, does it take all the hard and careful work offered in this chapter to know that there has been some measure of convergence and, as a result, credibility in sustained exchange rate stability is strengthened.

D.9.1 Looking behind interest differentials

The FPC study offers a particularly clear view of what lies behind nominal interest rate differentials. Specifically, the nominal interest rate differential can be separated into two broad categories corresponding respectively to market segmentation (they call it 'country effects') and denomination premia ('currency effects'):

$$\text{Differential} = \text{segmentation premia} + \text{denomination premia} \quad (1)$$

The former arise because jurisdictions differ and these differences may find a reflection in the rates of return required to invest in particular locations. The tax regime, property rights or the reality of limitations on capital movements can give rise to a premium required by the world capital markets to lend in a particular market. Divergences between offshore and onshore rates in a particular denomination go some way in capturing these effects. Over time, these onshore/offshore differentials have narrowed as progress towards institutionalized capital mobility has helped to limit the scope for contrived segmentation or the prospect thereof. For major industrialized countries, going back on capital mobility is conceivable but not plausible.

The denomination premium captures factors that have to do with the fact that exchange rates may move. Here we have both the expected trend of a currency relative to the benchmark asset but also risk premia that would emerge from, say, a portfolio problem. This chapter ably seeks to use expectations data to help shed light on the risk premium. We now turn to further comments on each of these premia.

D.9.2 Hard monies and lemons

Consider first the denomination premia. Figure D.9.1 shows three-months nominal interest differentials, off-shore, for Belgium and Finland relative to Germany. In Belgium's case convergence to German inflation, the narrowing of the target zone and a fierce interest in monetary integration have basically eliminated interest rate spreads. Belgium's interest in a credible exchange rate regime is all the more significant in that the country has a huge domestic debt that can only be managed at low interest rates. There is no better way to get low nominal interest rates than by an iron commitment to the Deutschmark peg. In the case of Finland, by contrast, massive idiosyncratic shocks and a poorly defined exchange rate regime leave wide open the question of where the country's price level and exchange rate will ultimately end up. There is no evidence in this instance of convergence and credibility. In Finland, debt issues are not of major significance and the more critical question is how to adjust to the shocks coming from low pulp prices and the collapse of Russian trade. Because devaluation is clearly an option, probably preferred to deflation, interest rate differentials reflect that option.

In a case such as that of Finland, we see the worst possible scenario. A government and a country pay the interest rate premium corresponding to a devaluation option. Yet they may be fiercely determined not to exercise the option; if they cannot make credible arrangements, however, they cannot escape high interest rates. To use the parlance of Akerlof, the Finmark is a 'lemon'.

D.9.3 Market segmentation

The authors measure the segmentation premium by the onshore interest differential adjusted by the forward premium, i.e. deviations from an arbitrage equation. This is a good first approximation, but it really does not go far enough to indicate the extent to which markets are or are not integrated. The fact that in the wholesale market there is little deviation from arbitrage does not tell us about what is happening below the surface. The striking finding of Feldstein-Horioka (1982) that domestic saving in OECD countries strongly determines domestic investment suggests that there are important mechanisms of crowding in other than interest rates. And the same message emerges, of course, from modern credit theories based on information economics which emphasize asymmetric information and the resulting tendency towards credit rationing.

In terms of this approach, absence of segmentation at the level of prime commercial paper or government debt goes nowhere in satisfying us that capital markets are in fact thoroughly integrated. To conclude the latter we would not only want to rule out outright legal or institutional obstacles to cross-border lending, we would also want to have some criterion by which to judge how much of a correlation of credit growth and loan premia across loan qualities corresponds to an integrated as opposed to a segmented retail market. By definition, retail means segmented, but just how much. And has the segmentation at the retail level been changing? Large firms enjoy financial service competition across regional and national borders, small firms and households do not. Have changes in national saving rates (private or public) led to substantial changes in credit availability and terms? That question is still open; work on an answer is only starting to be done, overly slowly because the data are not easily available.

D.9.4 Realignment

The authors use skilfully the information contained in expectations surveys and actual data to separate two aspects of exchange rates under target zones: on one hand there is the regression towards the mean that Krugman (1992) highlighted:

$$\dot{e} = f(e), \quad f'' < 0 \tag{2}$$

But there is also the possibility of a realignment. Hence a high price of the Deutschmark in terms of Irish punts will contain some of each: some possibility of appreciation toward par and some possibility of a realignment. Filtering out the mean reversion component, the authors identify a reduced but still notable expectation of realignment – more, but not full, credibility. There is some question of how much these estimates can be trusted. Two reasons are important. First, in a multi-currency system the level of a particular currency relative to the Deutschmark may not be enough to extract the likelihood of a bilateral realignment. There may also be information in other exchange rates.

Second, if narrowing of bands has an effect on the relationship between the level of the rate and the mean reversion, then filtering must take into account the narrowing of bands that has in fact taken place. Specifically, Belgium in 1990 narrowed its band formally. The result has been a narrowing of interest differentials: do these reflect the more limited room given the hypothesis of no realignment, the reduced likelihood of a realignment or both? Also, the Basle–Nyborg agreement of September 1987 limits the scope for any realignment, should one occur. The assumption of an invariant target zone regime (except for realignments) passes over these details and hence some accuracy is sacrificed.

D.9.5 How much can interest rate data tell us?

In concluding, we ask how much can be learnt from interest rate data. A first approximation is given in Figure D.9.1. There is an unambiguous narrowing of the differential and it is appropriate to ascribe it to a sharply reduced denomination premium. But there is a second approximation when the data is used with a very fine comb. That

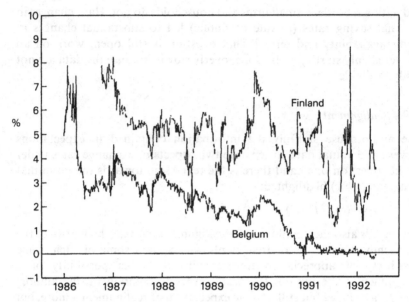

Figure D.9.1 Three-months interest differential (Finland and Belgium relative to Germany)
Source: DR1/McGraw-Hill data base

Table D.9.1. *Euro-interest differentials relative to Germany, January 1987 (% per annum)*

	Italy		France	
	1 mth	12 mths	1 mth	12 mths
6–10 days before re-alignment	5.3	5.9	5.3	4.5
1–5 days before re-alignment	9.7	6.5	5.2	5.2
1–5 days after re-alignment	6.7	6.1	5.0	4.5

Source: DRI/McGraw-Hill data base.

approach may not be so good. First, bid-ask spreads are very substantial. Even in the offshore market, differentials between bid and ask rates are as much as 5–10% of the average of the bid and ask rates. Second, it is not clear how sharply they are driven by expectations of exchange rate changes.

Specifically, consider the behaviour of rates around the January 1987 realignment (Table D.9.1). Any plausible model of the realignment process would suggest that one realignment is unlikely to be followed by another one very soon. Accordingly, the short term interest differential would be expected to decline sharply, while for longer maturities a realignment is likely to be reflected in some premium.

Such changes in the term structure simply did not take place. The term structures are too flat for a world where the size and timing of realignments represent all of the action.

REFERENCES

Feldstein, M. and C. Horioka (1982) 'Domestic Savings and International Capital Flows', *Economic Journal*, Vol. 92, June.
Krugman, P. (1992) 'Exchange Rates in a Currency Band: a Sketch of the New Approach' in P. Krugman and M. Miller (eds), *Exchange Rate Targets and Currency Bands*, Cambridge: Cambridge University Press.

Discussion

PAOLO ONOFRI

Frankel, Phillips and Chinn have written a very useful chapter indeed. In a few pages they give a full documentation of the nominal convergence among the EMS economies. Their goal is very ambitious: to try to measure such an immaterial thing as credibility. Others have already tried, but the authors of this chapter have done it by measuring another immaterial thing: the expected but not materialized re-alignment of the central parities.

Of course, they can work only on clues; nonetheless the results they get are quite reasonable: the fears of realignment have declined in the very recent past, hence the credibility of the exchange rate mechanism (ERM) has increased.

This statement allows the authors to draw the following two conclusions:

(a) differentials in interest rates among the EMS countries mainly depend on the degree of currency integration, and only to a smaller extent on the integration of financial markets;

(b) as the ERM approaches full credibility, predictions of Paul Krugman's target zone model (Krugman, 1991), which seemed to have failed empirical confirmation, can be tested more consistently.

As far as point (b) is concerned, the chapter documents a statistical and econometric procedure which shows that the target zone model predictions are not rejected by actual behaviour. The general analytical design of such an empirical analysis is presented in another publication by the first two authors – Frankel and Phillips (1991) – to which the reader should refer for possible criticism.

In this discussion I shall make a specific note on what can be guessed from the present chapter about the procedure the authors followed, and raise a more general question about where to go from nominal convergence.

Nobody would deny that interest rate differentials *vis-à-vis* Germany have declined in recent years for the European countries; the authors present statistical evidence as to the behaviour of the single components of the differentials. They show that the covered interest differentials are on declining trends; that the exchange risk premium might be interpreted as declining, even though statistical results do not point so sharply in a single direction; and finally, that the expected change in the exchange rate seems to have been declining during the period 1988–91. Moreover, spot exchange rate levels and exchange rate changes show a negative correlation, and the expected mean reversion coefficient always proves negative and higher over a longer horizon. All this does not contradict the predictions of the target zone model.

These are the main contributions of the chapter; they confirm the intuition that everybody shares: the nature of the EMS has been changing in recent years and credibility has been growing.

From the point of view of the procedure, they take the expected change of the exchange rate of individual currencies *vis-à-vis* the Deutschmark (measured either by the appropriate interest rate differentials or by a survey of agents forecasts) and then subtract the expected change of the exchange rates within the band in order to get the expected change of the parities.

The basic econometric contribution of the chapter is the estimation of the relationship between the observed position of the individual exchange rate within the band and the observed change of the exchange rate. The estimation of the relationship in a period of no exchange rate realignment (1988–91) allows the authors to get an expected mean-reversion coefficient for each exchange rate to be used to estimate the expected change of the exchange rate within the band. They can do this under the assumption that such a mean-reversion coefficient is the 'true' coefficient that investors already had in mind, at least, since 1988. This assumption is very innocent, on one side, and rather intriguing, on the other.

The intriguing side of the assumption is due to the combination of both rational expectations and incomplete information. Agents are rational and know that a target zone implies an 'objective' process of mean reversion, and they can guess the values of the parameters of such a process independently of their incomplete information about the features (hence the behaviour) of the government. Actually, they do not know whether they are facing either a tough government or a weak one which will not stick to the determination not to change the central parity. As time goes by, they revise upward the subjective probability that the government is a tough one.

In the real world this could be expressed also by saying that an increasing credibility (a better word might be reputation) means an increase in the number of people who choose to believe that the government is tough. We cannot exclude that the possible mental reservation of the authorities in favour of a cheating solution is a decreasing function of the number of people who believe the policies they are enacting. In other words, monetary authorities would be more convinced of their policies as they are given greater credit for those policies. Under strategic externalities of this kind is it really innocent to assume that the 'technology' of mean-reversion that the economy shows is independent of the changing features of the monetary authorities?

Here, the more general remarks come in. The thrust of the chapter is to try to convince, on an empirical basis, that as we move towards a fully credible target zone, we could exploit the positive effect of the target zones (see Krugman, 1991); in other words, slow and steady wins the race of credibility. The pre-commitment to an exchange rate agreement has been useful in getting rid of the temptation to avoid difficulties through an inflation tax. We cannot detect whether the effect of the pre-commitment has worked through the impact on private agents' expectations or through the economic policy moves required to stick to the pre-committed stable exchange rate. The uniformity of the positive results that the single countries have reached, however, is not useful evidence of the different paths that they have followed. Anecdotal observations still leave an impression of fragility.

As soon as the race of credibility was won, another race started: that of sustainability of the costs of a credible nominal target zone for the real sector.

In the target-zone model the authors refer to, the fundamentals are exogenously given; in the sample period on which they focus, fundamentals have been disturbed both exogenously and endogenously. Let us take those two types of disturbances separately.

(i) *Exogenous shocks*. The fundamentals that rule the exchange rates among the EMS currencies have been changed by German unification. It cannot be ignored that the authors' measure of credibility reaches its highest range right when the unification announcement was made together with the 1:1 exchange rate between the east and west mark. The potentially inflationary terms of the unification seem to have increased the credibility of the individual policy targets of other European countries. This would amount to saying that it is relative credibility that matters.

Recent months have shown that both Deutschmark/dollar relationships and the Maastricht announcement about the deadlines for EMU are other exogenous factors which can influence the measure of credibility proposed. For instance, Italy emerged as a country with a strong improvement in credibility as long as the dates for the final stage of EMU were unknown; once they were fixed the question of real sustainability of the exchange rate came to the surface. On the other side France, a well disciplined country, had a lower improvement of credibility, but has been affected less by recent events.

The impression of irreversible progressiveness in credibility which emerges from the chapter seems to be weakened by the impact of these shocks, and by the fact that credibility is not independent either of fundamentals or of institutional factors.

(ii) *Endogenous feedback*. The true challenge of the credibility of the nominal target zone will be the real exchange rate misalignment that the new EMS produced in some currencies [for a theoretical analysis of the problem, see Miller–Weller (1991)]. The main one is the Italian lira. I would like to bring a piece of evidence to show how the behaviour of either the budget authorities or the private agents that is inconsistent with the increasing reputation of the Bank of Italy, can undermine a well improved credibility. I shall use the behaviour of the French economy as a standard of reference and I shall draw from Onofri–Tomasini (1992).

During the final years of the 1980s, as the new EMS matured, the performance of Italian inflation worsened and budgetary policy seemed to slow further its improving path. Froot–Rogoff (1991) explain the real appreciation of the lira during this period in terms of the larger demand effect that they assume to be exerted by public expenditure, on non-tradable goods.

There is also a line of argument which attributes some weight to private agents' behaviour. I shall focus on this. In the second half of the 1980s two shocks hit symmetrically both France and Italy: the drop in the price of oil and of other raw materials and the growing credibility of the new EMS.

Both countries acted to reduce the price of tradable goods relative to non-tradable goods. The terms of trade effect was stronger in Italy owing to the higher degree of imported energy and raw materials. Given the higher wage inertia in Italy (longer overlapping labour contracts and backward-looking indexation compared with forward looking indexation in France) and also the stronger target real wage growth in Italy (this growth declined from the 1970s to the 1980s more rapidly in Italy, but it is still at a definitely higher level – i.e. 3.4% compared with 1.2% in France), the impact of the full stabilization of the nominal exchange rate must also have been stronger in Italy than in France. On the whole, there seem to be reasons to assume that the relative price of tradables declined more in Italy than in France. The change in relative prices might have produced excess demand for tradables (thus leading to a deterioration in the trade balance) and an incentive to increase the supply of non-tradables.

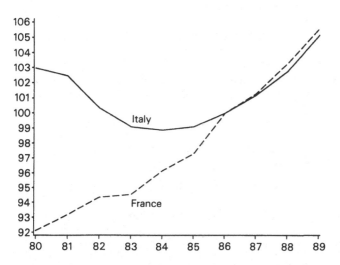

Figure D.9.2 Italy and France: value added per head in the service sector, 1980–9

Let us assume that the non-tradable sector can be approximated by service sector behaviour. The service sector in France experienced a steady growth of value added per head, whereas in Italy, service sector productivity was stagnating. As a result, the ratio of the value added at constant prices in the services sector to value added in industry increased in France and remained constant in Italy. In other words, the country (France) with a more elastic service sector supplied relatively more non-tradables, thus correcting the shock to relative prices and producing an almost stable ratio of tradables to non-tradable prices. Italy came out with an appreciated real exchange rate, which is the other side of the coin of an increasing ratio of non-tradables to tradables prices.

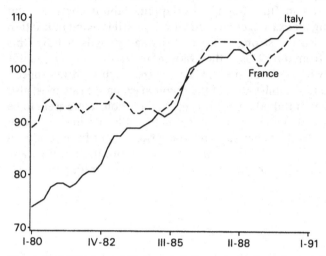

Figure D.9.3 Italy and France: relative prices of services and industrial goods, 1980–91

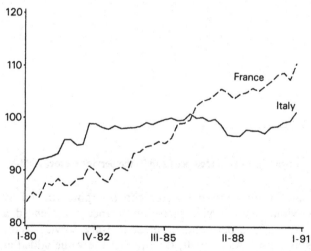

Figure D.9.4 Italy and France: relative value added of service sector and industrial sector, 1980–91

This inconsistent behaviour of the private sector does not exclude inconsistent behaviour on the side of the public sector, or that the latter is of stronger importance. The emphasis I put on the private sector is simply aimed at remarking how variegated the endogenous feedback from nominal target zones can be.

REFERENCES

Frankel, J. and S. Phillips (1991) 'The European Monetary System: Credible at Last?', National Bureau of Economic Research Working Paper No. 3819, Cambridge, Mass. and *Oxford Economic Papers*, Vol. 44, 1992.
Froot–Rogoff (1991) 'The EMS, The EMU, and The Transition to a Common Currency', National Bureau of Economic Research Working Paper No. 3684, Cambridge, Mass.
Krugman, P. (1991) 'Target Zones and Exchange Rate Dynamics', *Quarterly Journal of Economics*, CVI, No. 3, pp. 669–82.
Miller, M. and Weller, P. (1991) 'Exchange Rate Bands with Price Inertia', *Economic Journal*, November, pp. 1380–99.
Onofri, P. and Tomasini, S. (1992) *France and Italy: A Tale of Two Adjustments*, forthcoming.

10 Currency substitution: from the policy questions to the theory and back

MATTHEW CANZONERI, BEHZAD DIBA
and ALBERTO GIOVANNINI

1 Introduction: from the policy questions to the theory

In Europe the issue of currency substitution has surfaced in the debate on monetary policy and economic and monetary union (EMU). The main concern is that the liberalization of financial and goods markets can bring about instabilities in money demand with undesirable side effects.

The removal of capital controls has eliminated restrictions on holdings of liquid assets in foreign currency by the residents of countries in the European Community (EC). A noticeable increase in cross-border deposits, documented for example by Angeloni, Cottarelli and Levy (1991), has accompanied the financial liberalization.

The increase in cross-border deposits raises two separate questions. The first, discussed especially by Angeloni et al., concerns the statistical definition of monetary aggregates. If monetary aggregates used by central banks for policy design and implementation do not include a large and growing stock of cross-border deposits, the control problem of the monetary authorities can be made more difficult. Suppose, for example, that a stable demand relationship exists between the 'true' monetary aggregates (which include, in some appropriate way, cross-border deposits) and observable variables. But suppose central banks, in their day-to-day management, use monetary aggregates that do not include cross-border deposits. Then the stability of the aggregate used by central bankers depends on the stability of the stock of cross-border deposits.

The second question raised by the increase in cross-border deposits – largely separate from the first – concerns the stability of the 'true' aggregates. If agents can freely determine the composition of their currency portfolio, what determines the demand for each separate currency? Is that demand function going to be stable and predictable? In this chapter we concentrate on this last question.

Following Girton and Roper (1981), several theoretical studies have

318

analysed the instabilities associated with currency substitution within the context of *ad hoc* money-demand models. The object of these studies has been to specify money demand equations which account for the substitutability of different currencies. This procedure, however, has a basic problem: since it is not known where the postulated demand equations originate from, it is not possible to state unambiguously what constitutes currency substitution. In the absence of a clear definition of currency substitution, there are no certain predictions of its effects. Canzoneri, Diba and Giovannini (1991), show that currency substitution can be defined in alternative ways, and that for every definition an increase in currency substitution can have different effects on exchange-rate volatility – both qualitatively and quantitatively.

Given the ambiguities of *ad hoc* money demand models, we feel it is necessary to study in greater depth what are the possible sources of currency substitution, by specifying explicitly how a money-demand function arises from the organization of markets and transactions imperfections. Once markets and transactions are specified fully, we can deal with the questions arising from the experience in Europe: what are the likely effects of the increased integration of markets and of financial liberalization?

The rest of this chapter is organized as follows. Section 2 presents a model of money demand in the tradition of Baumol and Tobin. The model highlights the role of the interest elasticity of money demand but, for the purpose of exposition has only one good and one money. Section 3 provides the extension to a multi-currency world, and highlights the effects of differences in opportunity costs of holding money. Section 4 discusses the main results of the analysis and relates them to the rest of the literature. Section 5 discusses the implications of this analysis for policy, with special reference to the policy questions currently facing Western European countries.

2   The case of a single currency

To illustrate our model of money demand, we consider first the case of a single currency. The model is one of an endowment economy, where output is produced by a stock of productive capital that does not depreciate and that cannot be reproduced. Claims to the productive capital stock are traded. There is a single, representative consumer in this economy. The fiction of the representative consumer is equivalent to the assumption that financial markets are complete. Even in the case of multiple currencies, we assume a stand-in representative consumer since we concentrate on money demand, and are not interested in the pattern of international distribution of wealth arising under the different assumptions we explore.

The consumer's utility function is:

$$E_0 \sum_{t=0}^{\infty} \beta^t [U(C_t) + V(l_t)] \tag{1}$$

where β represents the utility discount factor, C is consumption and l is leisure. We assume that utility is separable across leisure and consumption to simplify the algebra.

To introduce the budget constraints that the consumer's maximization problem is subject to, it is useful to describe the organization of markets. At the beginning of each period, the consumer enters asset markets, where he (or she) trades shares to the productive capital, money, and bonds. Specifically, at beginning of each period, the consumer receives any remaining dividends from the previous period, a transfer of new money, interest and principal on any bonds held in the previous period. He decides now much money and other assets to hold, and how much to consume. The holdings of money are determined by a binding cash-in-advance constraint, so that goods can only be purchased with money.

Consumption purchases occur at an even rate during the period, while actual consumption occurs at the end of the period. Money balances required for consumption are acquired through a series of transactions which occur directly with the firm. In these transactions, the consumer essentially withdraws cash from the firm. These transactions are evenly spaced within the period. Their frequency is chosen optimally by the consumer, and determines his initial and average money holdings.

Figure 10.1 contains an illustration of the model. Period t is divided into N_t equal sub-periods. At the beginning of the first sub-period, the consumer trades in asset markets and, among other things, acquires initial money holdings, just sufficient to finance his planned consumption purchases during the first sub-period. During this time, the consumer exchanges with the firm his money holdings for the consumption good. At the end of the first sub-period, the agent walks to the firm and withdraws all cash earnings of the firm: these are dividend payments – that is profits – from the sale of output during the first sub-period. Given that consumption occurs at an even rate and trips to the firm are equally distanced in time, the cash withdrawal at the end of the first sub-period is exactly identical to the nominal value of planned purchases in the second sub-period, and so on. As the figure shows, the consumer takes $N_t - 1$ trips to the firm. At the end of the last sub-period (the end of period t in the figure) he has no idle cash balances. These are still held by the firm, and are turned over to the consumer in the asset market at the beginning of period $t + 1$.

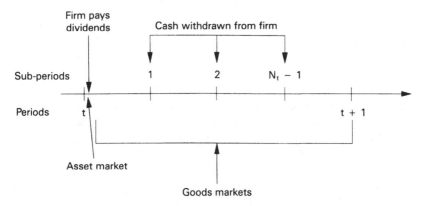

Figure 10.1 Organization and timing of markets and transactions

Given this sequence of transactions, the budget constraint is written as follows:

$$[z_{t-1}P_{t-1}d_{t-1} - (N_{t-1} - 1)M_{t-1}]\frac{1}{P_t} + q_t z_{t-1} + (1 + i_{t-1})\frac{b_{t-1}}{P_t}$$

$$+ \left[h_t + (\omega_t - 1)\frac{\bar{M}_{t-1}}{P_t} \right] x_{t-1} = \frac{M_t}{P_t} + \frac{b_t}{P_t} + q_t z_t + h_t x_t \quad (2)$$

The first term on the left-hand side of equation (2) represents the real value, in terms of the consumption good, of the cash receipts of the last sub-period of the previous period (see Figure 10.1). $P_{t-1}d_{t-1}$ are total nominal sales in period $t-1$, while z_{t-1} pro-rates that amount by the proportional share of the firm held by the consumer-investor. From the value of total nominal sales we subtract the value of all withdrawals during the last period. This leaves the amount left to the consumer at the end of the last period. q is the price of shares, and z represents holdings of shares, b nominal 1-period bonds, and x claims to monetary transfers, which we assume are tradable in the assets market at price h. $\bar{M}$ is the exogenous total supply of money, while ω is the stochastic gross rate of growth of the money stock. The money supply process is thus:

$$\bar{M}_t = \omega_t \bar{M}_{t-1} \quad (3)$$

Hence $(\omega_{t-1})(\bar{M}/P_t)$ is the 'dividend' from the claims to monetary transfers.

Every period, the consumer is endowed with one unit of time, which he allocates to leisure and the effort of providing cash balances needed to consume. Such effort, measured in units of time, is equal to k for every trip to the firm. Hence the time constraint at time t is:

$$1 - l_t - k(N_t - 1) = 0 \tag{4}$$

Finally, the cash-in-advance constraint is:

$$\left(\frac{M_t}{P_t}\right) N_t = C_t \tag{5}$$

Equation (2) shows that, at the beginning of time t, the consumer acquires M, to finance his purchases during the first $1/N_t$ fraction of the period. He then takes $N_t - 1$ trips to the firm to acquire, in each trip, the same quantity of money M, which is, of course, the sub-period revenue of the firm.

Let λ_t, μ_t and η_t be the multipliers associated, respectively, with the constraints (2), (4) and (5). The first-order conditions for the consumer's maximization problem are:

- with respect to C_t:

$$U'(C_t) = \eta_t \tag{6}$$

- with respect to b_t:

$$\beta E_t\left(\frac{\lambda_{t+1}}{P_{t+1}}\right) \Big/ \left(\frac{\lambda_t}{P_t}\right) = \frac{1}{1 + i_t} \tag{7}$$

- with respect to l_t:

$$V'(l_t) = \mu_t \tag{8}$$

- with respect to M_t:

$$\frac{\lambda_t}{P_t} + \beta(N_t - 1)E_t\left(\frac{\lambda_{t+1}}{P_{t+1}}\right) = \frac{\eta_t N_t}{P_t} \tag{9}$$

- with respect to N_t:

$$k\mu_t = \eta_t\left(\frac{M_t}{P_t}\right) - \beta M_t E_t\left(\frac{\lambda_{t+1}}{P_{t+1}}\right) \tag{10}$$

We omit here the asset-pricing equations (the first-order conditions with respect to z and x), which are not necessary for the discussion of money demand. Equation (6) says that the value of the cash-in-advance constraint equals the marginal utility of consumption. Equation (8) says that the value of the time constraint equals the marginal utility of leisure. Equation (7) is a dynamic equation for the marginal utility of wealth. It relates the expected increase of the marginal utility of wealth to the expected real interest rate, net of the utility discount factor. Equation (9) says that the marginal cost of an extra unit of money that the agent accumulates at the start of each of the N_t sub-periods of t equals the marginal utility of wealth λ, plus the expected utility value of the extra cash carried over to the next period. The total marginal cost should equal the marginal benefit, represented by a unit release of the cash-in-advance constraint, for each of the N_t sub-periods. Finally, equation (10) reports the costs and benefits of increasing the frequency of cash collections. On the cost side, the increase in the frequency of trips to gather cash leaves less time for leisure, at a cost $k\mu$. More frequent trips also mean that there will be fewer cash balances left at the beginning of period $t + 1$. On the benefits side, an increase in the frequency of trips implies, for a given unit size of withdrawals, a release in the cash-in-advance constraint (the term $\eta(M/P)$).

Equilibrium conditions for this model are:

$$z_t = 1 \tag{11}$$

$$x_t = 1 \tag{12}$$

$$C_t = d_t \tag{13}$$

$$\bar{M}_t = M_t \tag{14}$$

$$b_t = 0 \tag{15}$$

Substituting these equilibrium conditions into the budget constraint it is easy to verify equation (3). To obtain the 'money demand equation' implied by this model, we manipulate equations (9) and (10), and use the expressions for the two Lagrange multipliers μ and η, to get:

$$\frac{M_t}{P_t} = \frac{kV'(l_t)}{U'(d_t)}\left(1 + \frac{N_t}{i_t}\right) \tag{16}$$

The main difficulty in interpreting the effects of changes in output and interest rates on money demand is that, in this model, N_t depends on i_t and d, and l_t depends on N_t and d_t. In general, we are unable to sign the partial derivative of interest. It is possible to prove, however, that with a significantly linear V function, and more precisely, when $V'(l)/V''(l)$ is 'big enough', then an increase in i decreases N/i and leaves $V'(l)$ substantially unaffected, thus lowering the demand for money. Similarly, an increase in output and consumption leads to an increase in money demand.

To conclude this section, and before the model is extended to a multi-currency economy, it is useful to highlight some of its characteristics. This model, unlike the standard cash-in-advance models, yields a variable velocity equation, and a money demand equation that could resemble those used in standard empirical models, with velocity positively correlated with the nominal interest rate and negatively correlated with output.

Intuitively, this result is straightforward. An increase in the nominal interest rate decreases the value of cash balances left at the firm in the last sub-period. For this reason, the consumer takes more frequent trips to the firm, and correspondingly needs to withdraw less in each trip. The positive correlation of money demanded with output is essentially due to the requirement that goods be always purchased with each.

In summary, the model displays the typical features of the Baumol (1952) and Tobin (1956) models of money demand. The difference is that in the Baumol–Tobin models the agent receives interest on his average deposit holdings during each sub-period, while in this instance, interest is paid on initial bond holdings. If cash withdrawals in each sub-period are smaller, initial bond holdings can be larger. Hence the correct measure of the opportunity cost of holding money remains the interest rate. In our model the interest rate represents, in equilibrium, the correct shadow value of money, despite the fact that financial intermediaries are absent. Alternatively, our model is consistent with the presence of a competitive banking system, which faces no cost of managing payments and holding deposits and is subject to a 100% reserve requirement, so that it cannot pay any interest on intra-period deposits.

3   A two-currency economy

Having studied the implication of the model for money demand, we now extend it to a two-currency economy. This extension allows us to face the issue of currency substitution in the most direct way: by forcing us to specify the conditions under which trading in the two currencies occurs, and how such trading is linked to goods market trading. The demand for the two currencies is then derived endogenously from utility maximization and market clearing conditions.

We start from the case of a two-good, two-currencies economy, and only later discuss what happens in the single-good case. The objective function is:

$$E_0 \sum_{t=0}^{\infty} \beta^t \left[U(C_t, C_t^*) + V(l_t) \right] \tag{17}$$

Where C^* is consumption of the foreign good, produced by a foreign firm. Purchases of the foreign good require the foreign currency. Trading in the two currencies occurs as in the above section. The consumer decides on the number of trips to each firm independently. While these trips are evenly distributed in each period, they may occur at different frequencies for the two currencies.

The budget constraint becomes:

$$\frac{z_{t-1}P_{t-1}d_{t-1}}{P_t} - \frac{M_{t-1}}{P_t}(N_{t-1}-1)$$

$$+\frac{e_t z_{t-1}^* P_{t-1}^* d_{t-1}^*}{P_t} - \frac{e_t M_{t-1}^*}{P_t}(N_{t-1}^*-1)$$

$$+ q_t z_{t-1} + q_{t-1}^* z_{t-1}^* + (1+i_{t-1})\frac{b_{t-1}}{P_t} + (1+i_{t-1}^*)\frac{e_t b_{t-1}^*}{P_t}$$

$$+\left[h_t + (\omega_t - 1)\frac{\bar{M}_{t-1}}{P_t}\right]x_{t-1} + \left[h_t^* + e_t(\omega_t^* - 1)\frac{\bar{M}_{t-1}^*}{P_t}\right]x_{t-1}^*$$

$$= \frac{M_t}{P_t} + \frac{b_t}{P_t} + q_t z_t + h_t x_t + \frac{e_t M_t^*}{P_t} + \frac{e_t b_t^*}{P_t} + q_t^* z_t^* + h_t^* x_t^* \quad (18)$$

The notation is straightforward. Notice that output d is sold for the domestic, numeraire currency (to be precise, the currency in which the prices used in the deflator are expressed), while d^* is sold for the foreign currency. e represents the price of the foreign currency in terms of the domestic currency. Nominal 1-period bonds and claims to cash transfers are traded for both currencies. Prices of claims to the foreign currency cash transfers, as well as claims to the foreign firm's profits, are denominated in terms of the domestic consumption good.

The time constraint at time t becomes:

$$1 - l_t - k(N_t + N_t^* - 2) = 0 \quad (19)$$

Finally, the cash-in-advance constraints are:

$$\left(\frac{M_t}{P_t}\right) N_t = C_t \quad (20)$$

$$\left(\frac{M_t^*}{P_t^*}\right) N_t^* = C_t^* \quad (21)$$

Let λ_t, μ_t, η_t and δ_t be the multipliers associated, respectively, with the constraints (18), (19), (20), and (21). The first order conditions for the consumer's maximization problem are:

- with respect to C_t

$$U_1(C_t, C_t^*) = \eta_t \quad (22)$$

- with respect to C_t^*:

$$U_2(C_t, C_t^*) = \delta_t \quad (23)$$

- with respect to b_t:

$$\beta E_t \left(\frac{\lambda_{t+1}}{P_{t+1}} \right) \Big/ \left(\frac{\lambda_t}{P_t} \right) = \frac{1}{1+i_t} \tag{24}$$

- with respect to b_t^*:

$$\beta E_t \left(\frac{e_{t+1}\lambda_{t+1}}{P_{t+1}} \right) \Big/ \left(\frac{e_t\lambda_t}{P_t} \right) = \frac{1}{1+i_t^*} \tag{25}$$

- with respect to l_t:

$$V'(l_t) = \mu_t \tag{26}$$

- with respect to M_t:

$$\frac{\lambda_t}{P_t} + \beta(N_t - 1)E_t \left(\frac{\lambda_{t+1}}{P_{t+1}} \right) = \frac{\eta_t N_t}{P_t} \tag{27}$$

- with respect to M_t^*:

$$\frac{e_t\lambda_t}{P_t}\beta(N_t^* - 1)E_t \left(\frac{e_{t+1}\lambda_{t+1}}{P_{t+1}} \right) = \frac{\delta_t N_t^*}{P_t^*} \tag{28}$$

- with respect to N_t:

$$k\mu_t = \beta M_t E_t \left(\frac{\lambda_{t+1}}{P_{t+1}} \right) = \eta_t \left(\frac{M_t}{P_t} \right) \tag{29}$$

- with respect to N_t^*:

$$k\mu_t = \beta M_t^* E_t \left(\frac{e_{t+1}\lambda_{t+1}}{P_{t+1}} \right) = \delta_t \left(\frac{M_t^*}{P_t^*} \right) \tag{30}$$

Equilibrium conditions are:

$$z_t = z_t^* = 1 \tag{31}$$

$$x_t = x_t^* = 1 \tag{32}$$

$$C_t = d_t \tag{33}$$

$$C_t^* = d_t^* \tag{34}$$

$$\bar{M}_t = M_t \tag{35}$$

$$\bar{M}_t^* = M_t^* \tag{36}$$

$$b_t = b_t^* = 0 \tag{37}$$

To highlight the relation between interest rates, we combine equations (24) and (25):

$$\frac{1 + i_t}{1 + i_t^*} = E_t\left(\frac{e_{t+1}}{e_t}\right) + COV_t\left(\frac{\lambda_{t+1}}{P_{t+1}}, \frac{e_{t+1}}{e_t}\right) \Big/ E_t\left(\frac{\lambda_{t+1}}{P_{t+1}}\right) \tag{38}$$

Equation (38) shows that the risk premium depends on the conditional covariance between the exchange rate and the marginal utility of nominal wealth.

Money demand equations are derived following the steps outlined in Section 2. They are:

$$\frac{M_t}{P_t} = \frac{kV'(l_t)}{U_1(d_t, d_t^*)}\left(1 + \frac{N_t}{i_t}\right) \tag{39}$$

$$\frac{M_t^*}{P_t^*} = \frac{kV'(l_t)}{U_2(d_t, d_t^*)}\left(1 + \frac{N_t^*}{i_t^*}\right) \tag{40}$$

From equations (39) and (40) and the cash-in-advance constraints we get:

$$\frac{N_t}{N_t^*} = \frac{d_t U_1(d_t, d_t^*)}{d_t^* U_2(d_t, d_t^*)} \frac{1 + N^*/i_t^*}{1 + N_t/i_t} \tag{41}$$

This equation can be used to determine the equilibrium relative frequency of trips in the two countries, which – as can be verified – are quadratic functions of the other variables.

We now turn to the real effects of the postulated monetary regime. Equation (27) and (28) imply:

$$\frac{e_t P_t^*}{P_t} = \frac{\delta_t}{\eta_t}\left(\frac{N_t^*}{N_t}\right)\left[\frac{1 + \left(\frac{N_t - 1}{1 + i_t}\right)}{1 + \left(\frac{N_t^* - 1}{1 + i_t^*}\right)}\right] \tag{42}$$

The left hand side of the equation above is the marginal rate of transformation between domestic and foreign goods, while the first fraction on the right hand side is the marginal rate of substitution. The equation indicates that in this model there is a distortion, represented by a wedge between the marginal rate of substitution and the marginal rate of transformation. The equation suggests the condition for the distortion to disappear:

$$\left(\frac{N_t}{N_t^*}\right) = \left[\frac{1 + \left(\frac{N_t - 1}{1 + i_t}\right)}{1 + \left(\frac{N_t^* - 1}{1 + i_t^*}\right)}\right] \tag{43}$$

This amounts to a restriction on the stochastic processes of forcing variables which unfortunately we cannot write out in closed form. The rationale for this result is as follows. If the consumer faces a high opportunity cost from holding, for example, the domestic currency because, say, the domestic rate of inflation is higher than the foreign rate of inflation, he will try to economize in the use of domestic cash balances by taking more frequent trips to the domestic firm. Since these trips have a cost in terms of utility, they will affect the relative price of domestic goods. Since the cost of acquiring money for the purchase of a given supply of domestic goods has increased, for the available supplies of the two goods to be consumed the relative price of domestic goods has to be less than the ratio of the marginal utility of consumption of the domestic good and the marginal utility of consumption of the foreign good.

Hence, there is an optimal *relative* rate of inflation in this economy, that eliminates any wedges between the marginal rate of transformation and the marginal rate of substitution between the two goods. Ever larger deviations from that optimum imply larger relative price distortions.

Equations (42) and (43) imply the following relationship:

$$\frac{N_t}{N_t^*} = \sqrt{\frac{d_t}{d_t^*} \left(\frac{P_t}{e_t P_t^*}\right) \frac{i_t/(1 + i_t)}{i_t^*/(1 + i_t^*)}} \tag{44}$$

A conventionally-looking exchange-rate equation is obtained combining the above and the cash-in-advance constraints:

$$e_t = \frac{M_t}{M_t^*} \sqrt{\frac{d_t^*}{d_t} \left(\frac{e_t P_t^*}{P_t}\right) \frac{i_t/(1 + i_t)}{i_t^*/(1 + i_t^*)}} \tag{45}$$

which implies that the exchange rate is obtained by inverting the money demand equations, and accounts for the fluctuations of relative prices.

We now turn to the question of currency substitution. For the purpose of this discussion we begin with the case of a credibly fixed exchange rate regime, whereby the domestic and the foreign interest rates are equal. The first problem we need to tackle is: which structural parameter in the model can be associated with the concept of currency substitution? That is, can we think of an experiment amounting to a change in a parameter as representing the increase in currency substitution coming from increased market integration? Notice that equation (45) suggests that very few parameters can be manipulated to describe the effects of increased currency substitution. In particular, the view expressed in *ad hoc* money demand models that increased currency substitution implies a higher elasticity of money demand with respect to relative interest rates is clearly not applicable here, where such elasticity equals $1/2$. In our setting, a natural parameter is the substitutability between the two goods. It is arguable that increased economic integration brings about increased stability of real exchange rates, which is associated with increased goods market integration and increased factor mobility (recall that financial markets are already perfectly integrated in the model we consider).

Consider the limiting case of perfect substitutability. In this case equation (43) follows directly from (42), since the real exchange rate has to be equal to 1 by arbitrage, and the marginal utilities are equalized. With credibly fixed exchange rates, the only potential solution to (43) is $N = N^*$. Equation (44), however, says that with equal interest rates and the law of one price the equality of N and N^* implies the equality of d and d^*, a result that is clearly not guaranteed in general. If the latter condition does not hold, the model does not have an equilibrium.

This result (the general absence of an equilibrium with perfect goods substitutability) extends to the case of floating exchange rates. To illustrate the argument under floating exchange rates take interest rates to be the exogenous forcing variables, instead of money supplies. This change in forcing variables can be accomplished without any loss of generality, since the domestic and foreign money stocks can be determined to produce any domestic and foreign interest rates given exogenous output shocks. In this case, it is straightforward to show that with perfect goods substitutability an equilibrium does not exist in one trivial case: when the domestic and foreign interest rates happen to be equal. Even when interest rates are not equal, however, the levels of N and N^* implied by equation (43) are not necessarily those that satisfy (44). Hence with perfect substitutability of goods an equilibrium does not exist, unless the monetary authorities follow fine-tuned policies aimed at equalizing the costs of carrying out transactions in each of the different currencies.

4   Relationship with previous results

The recent theoretical literature on currency substitution has provided a number of results pointing to instabilities associated with higher currency substitutability in general equilibrium monetary models. The first important result can be found in Kareken and Wallace (1981) who showed that, if the distribution of currency holdings is not tied down by transactions constraints, the nominal exchange rate in a floating exchange-rate regime is indeterminate. Their result is not specific to the overlapping generations model they use, where money is the only asset and is valued for its store-of-value function. It can be reproduced in a cash-in-advance model, as long as the cash-in-advance constraint is not specified for each currency separately, but applies to the sum of domestic and foreign currency (see, for example, Sargent 1987). The multiple equilibrium exchange rates in Kareken and Wallace (1981), however, do not give rise to different welfare levels. Therefore they raise the question of whether such potential extreme volatility has any undesirable effect, or is just the result of the irrelevance of exchange-rate fluctuations in the presence of well-operating financial markets.

King, Wallace and Weber (1991) provide an example where the Kareken–Wallace indeterminacy has important real effects. In their model agents are heterogeneous. While some agents are indifferent about the distribution of their currency holdings, others are not. They show that exchange-rate fluctuations can be due to what they call non-fundamental (or extrinsic) uncertainty, for the Kareken–Wallace type of reasons. They show, however, that such exchange rate fluctuations have real effects, since they affect the distribution of wealth across the different agents.

Another analysis of the effects of currency substitutability on monetary equilibria can be found in Woodford (1991) and Weil (1991). These authors show that high currency substitutability can give rise to multiple rational expectations equilibria in which the price level and the exchange rate vary stochastically in response to 'sunspots', and that multiple steady state equilibria can arise in the case of perfect substitutability. They also show that the likelihood of hyper-inflationary equilibria is enhanced by higher currency substitutability. We adopt in this chapter Woodford's device of likening currency substitutability to the substitutability of the goods to which the cash-in-advance constraint applies. By considering the option of economizing in the use of cash balances within each trading period we produce money demand equations that are interest-elastic in the traditional Baumol–Tobin sense.

Our result extends the range of effects associated with high currency substitutability in a direction that, to our knowledge, was previously unexplored. The basic intuition of our result is that divergences in money supply processes give rise to goods markets distortions. In the extreme case where the domestic and foreign goods are perfectly substitutability, these distortions cannot be absorbed in the goods markets. Hence, in this extreme case, if money supply processes are not 'in line' in a well specified way, an equilibrium where both currencies are held does not exist.

5   Back to the policy questions

It is always difficult to translate the predictions produced by stylized general equilibrium models into prescriptions for macroeconomic policy, even though the results obtained in this chapter can be easily explained. In other words, the state of monetary economics nowadays is such that the trip from the policy questions to the theory and back tends to leave the traveller too tired at the end of it. This is clearly a problem we could not solve in this chapter. Yet, it is important, in our view, to make the effort to identify the usable lessons from the models which have been discussed. Only a careful assessment of these models can help to clarify the remaining issues which need to be tackled.

The main characteristic of the model we have presented is the presence of cash-in-advance constraints in both national goods markets: a very strong assumption that has been traditionaly adopted to pin down money demand unambiguously. We have shown that, despite this strong local element in money demand, monetary equilibria may not exist if domestic and foreign goods are perfectly substitutable. That happens when the cost of carrying the domestic and foreign currency – and as a result the costs of transactions through the domestic and foreign currency – are not equal, despite the fact that the utility from consuming the domestic good and the foreign good is the same.

Can this result be expressed in terms applicable to Europe? We think so. Our result says that if economic union succeeds in integrating goods and factor markets, it will not be possible to run different monetary policies without the disappearance of financial intermediaries and the use of the currencies which are more costly to hold. This interpretation of our result is very similar to the basic premise of the original proposal on currency competition put forward by the Treasury in the United Kingdom, that economic agents may be expected to shy away from those currencies that are more costly to hold. In our model there is no equilibrium since agents will not want to buy the output of the firm whose currency is costly to hold. In other words, the model highlights to the maximum the real effects of currency substitution: the firm whose currency is costly to hold does not sell its output.

We also believe that other effects, not captured by our model, should be taken into consideration when trying to foresee the consequences of economic and financial integration on the demand for European currencies. These effects are those studied by King, Wallace and Weber (1991) and are associated with the fact that payments for a large and growing fraction of transactions will not be constrained to the use of specific currencies. As these authors show, this will induce additional financial and exchange-rate instability with undesirable real effects.

What are the policy implications of these models? They bear on the debate concerning the desirability of maintaining the status quo, within the European monetary system, with full capital market integration but separate currencies and adjustable exchange rates. Our model, as well as all the others we mentioned, show that this state of affairs is likely to be unstable and that in many cases such instability will induce welfare losses. The normative implications, therefore, are two-fold. First, full market integration might be inconsistent with separate currencies. And second, if a currency union cannot be achieved suddenly but has to be preceded by a transition period of unspecified length, such transition period should be characterized by measures aimed at maximizing the convergence of monetary policies. Whether measures that effectively offset the potential instabilities in foreign exchange and money markets can be identified remains, in our opinion, an open question.

REFERENCES

Angeloni, I., C. Cottarelli and A. Levy (1991) 'Cross-Border Deposits and Monetary Aggregates in the Transition to EMU', mimeo, Bank of Italy.

Baumol, W.J. (1952) 'The Transactions Demand for Cash: An Inventory Theoretic Approach', *Quarterly Journal of Economics*, 66, November, pp. 454–556.

Canzoneri, M., B. Diba and A. Giovannini (1991) 'Two Concepts of Currency Substitution and Their Implications for Exchange Rate Volatility, mimeo, Columbia University and Georgetown University, presented at the conference *Monetary Policy in Stage Two of EMU*, CEPR and Bocconi University, Milan.

Girton, L. and D. Roper (1981) 'Theory and Implications of Currency Substitution', *Journal of Money, Credit and Banking*, 13, February, pp. 12–30.

Kareken, J. and N. Wallace (1981) 'On the Indeterminacy of Equilibrium Exchange Rates', *Quarterly Journal of Economics*, 96, pp. 207–22.

King, R.G., N. Wallace and W.E. Weber (1991) 'Nonfundamental Uncertainty and Exchange Rates', Working Paper 307, Research Department, Federal Reserve Bank of Minneapolis, February.

Sargent, T.J. (1987) *Dynamic Macroeconomic Theory*, Cambridge, Mass.: Harvard University Press.

Tobin J. (1956) 'The Interest Elasticity of Transactions Demand for Cash', *Review of Economics and Statistics*, 38, pp. 241–7.

Weil, P. (1991) 'Currency Competition and the Evolution of Multi-Currency Regions', in A. Giovannini and C. Mayer (eds), *European Financial Integration*, Cambridge: Cambridge University Press.

Woodford, M. (1991) 'Does Competition Between Currencies Lead to Price Level and Exchange-Rate Stability?', in A. Giovannini and C. Mayer (eds), *European Financial Integration*, Cambridge: Cambridge University Press.

Discussion

LUCAS PAPADEMOS

This stimulating and thought-provoking paper is of interest to both theoretical economists and policy-makers. It is motivated by important policy issues, which have been at the centre of the debate on the effectiveness of monetary policy in the European Community during the transition to economic and monetary union (EMU). The authors' final aim is to assess the validity of a number of propositions advanced in this debate on the basis of rigorous theoretical analysis. The full liberalization of capital movements and the integration of European money markets and payment systems will have significant implications for monetary policy. Increased currency substitution and cross-border deposits will affect the stability of the demand for each national currency, the predictability of national money-income relationships and the volatility of exchange rates. Such effects would, of course, have implications for the choice of monetary aggregates as intermediate targets and policy indicators, and, more generally, for the conduct and effectiveness of monetary policy within the European monetary system.

My comments will focus first on the theoretical contribution to money demand theory and to our understanding of the effects of increased currency substitution on exchange rate determination. I will then discuss the implications of the theoretical analysis for financial stability and monetary policy.

The core of the chapter is a theoretical analysis of the determinants of money demand and the exchange rate in a multiple-currency economy, and of the consequences of currency substitution for monetary stability and exchange-rate volatility. Most previous analyses of the effects of currency substitution have been based on plausible but *ad hoc* specifications of the demand for different currencies and have yielded ambiguous results. Canzoneri, Diba and Giovannini present a theoretical framework which allows for a precise definition of the concept of currency substitution and an examination of its implications. In this framework, the demand for domestic and foreign currency is derived from utility maximization by a representative consumer subject to three constraints: one restricts the allocation of wealth among assets, the other the amount of time allotted to leisure and the effort to acquire the money balances necessary for consumption, while the third is a 'cash-in-advance' constraint requiring that goods shall always be purchased with money. A key feature of the model is that it explicitly specifies the organization of trading in financial and goods markets and the frequency of the monetary transactions required for the purchase of goods. The formulation is along lines similar to those of the Baumol–Tobin models, but with some differences. In this model there are no financial intermediaries and the money balances needed for the purchase of goods are acquired directly through transactions with the producers. The frequency of such transactions is chosen optimally and this determines the average money balances of the representative consumer.

To highlight some basic features of the model and its implications for money demand, the authors examine first a single-good, single-currency economy. The main result is that, unlike other models incorporating a cash-in-advance constraint, in this model the demand for money is influenced by the nominal interest rate on bonds, both directly and indirectly through the effects of the interest rate on the equilibrium levels of leisure and the frequency of transactions. This result reflects the effects of the nominal interest rate on the value of money balances at the firm in the last trading period. It is interesting to note, however, that the relationship between money demand and the interest rate is not unambiguous. To obtain the conventional negative association of money demand and interest rate, it is necessary to assume that the consumer's utility from leisure can be expressed as a 'significantly linear' function.

The implications of currency substitution are examined by extending the model to a two-good, two-currency economy. Trading in the two currencies takes place as in the single-good, single-currency case. The analysis, however, of this more general case depends crucially on some additional assumptions. One is that purchases of the foreign (domestic) good require the use of foreign (domestic) currency. A second and related assumption is that the consumer makes independent trips to the domestic and foreign firms to obtain the necessary amounts of the two currencies, and that these trips may occur at different frequencies for each of the two currencies. With financial markets fully integrated, as assumed in the model, an increase in currency substitution reflects an increase in the substitution between domestic and foreign goods.

When domestic and foreign goods are imperfect substitutes, utility maximization and market equilibrium conditions yield the following results. First, the real demand for each currency depends directly on the quantities of the domestic and foreign goods consumed, the frequency of trips to acquire the respective currency, and the respective interest rate, but not on the interest rate differential. There are, however, indirect effects. The interest rate differential may influence the demand for each currency by affecting the quantities of the two goods purchased and the relative frequency of trips to acquire the two currencies. Second, an interesting result is that the real exchange rate, that is the marginal rate of transformation between domestic and foreign goods, is not in general equal to the marginal rate of substitution between the two goods. This 'distortion' originates from divergences in the money supply process and depends on the frequencies of transactions in the two currencies. Third, the nominal exchange rate is determined by a rather conventional specification: it depends on the relative supplies of money, the relative levels of output and interest rates, and the equilibrium real exchange rate, which is partly influenced by monetary factors.

The effects of increased currency substitution are examined by associating the extent of currency substitution with the degree of substitution between domestic and foreign goods. Thus, unlike other money demand models, an increase in currency substitution in this model does not imply a higher elasticity of money demand with respect to relative interest rates. Given the stocks of domestic and foreign money, an increase in the substitutability between the two goods influences the nominal exchange rate by affecting the equilibrium relative frequencies of transactions in the two currencies.

An important result of the theoretical analysis is that, in the case of perfect substitution, equilibrium does not in general exist under either a fixed or a floating exchange rate regime. The reasoning is straightforward. When exchange rates are credibly fixed and domestic and foreign goods are perfect substitutes, the real exchange rate must be equal to unity, the marginal utilities of consumption equal, and domestic and foreign interest rates also equal, which implies the equality of the frequencies of transactions in the two currencies. Consequently, equilibrium can exist only if the quantities of the two goods consumed are the same, which need not always be the case. The non-existence of equilibrium in the case of perfect substitution relates to the distortion in the goods markets which can be caused by divergent monetary policies. When domestic and foreign goods are perfect substitutes, monetary policies must be pursued so as to eliminate this distortion, otherwise there is no equilibrium with both currencies being held. These strong conclusions may be consistent with the structure and hypotheses of the model but do not seem consistent with reality. Linking currency substitution to substitutability between domestic and foreign goods is a helpful but over-simplifying hypothesis. In highly integrated economies where both domestic and foreign goods are consumed, the public does not normally hold different currencies for transactions purposes, although it may do so for speculative or investment purposes. A limitation of this model is that it does not adequately capture the explicit and implicit transactions costs associated with holding different currencies solely for the purpose of acquiring domestic and foreign goods.

The theory presented in this chapter was motivated by the desire to address certain issues concerning financial stability in an integrated economic area and the efficacy of monetary policy during the transition to EMU. Canzoneri, Diba and Giovannini draw from their analysis two major lessons for policy. The first is that in an economic union, in which financial markets as well as goods and factor markets are fully integrated, it is impossible to conduct independent national monetary policies. The implementation of divergent national monetary policies would lead to the disappearance of financial intermediaries and of the currencies that are more costly to hold. This last conclusion echoes arguments used in the British proposal on the hard ECU and currency competition. The second major policy implication of the theory concerns the stability of the European monetary system (EMS), after the completion of the single European market. According to the authors, their model suggests that the EMS is likely to be unstable. They also conclude that full market integration might be inconsistent with the existence of separate currencies and that the transition to EMU requires measures aimed at maximizing the convergence of monetary policies.

Two questions should be raised about the above conclusions: (i) are they valid in general? and (ii) to what extent do they follow from the theory presented? With regard to the infeasibility of conducting independent monetary policies in an economic union, I have several comments. First, the authors are obviously correct when economic union is complemented by monetary union. In a union where markets – both financial and real – are fully integrated and exchange rate are irrevocably fixed, independent and incompatible national monetary polcies would lead to instability and the breakdown of the exchange rate system. The model presented focuses on one mechanism which can cause instability, but there are other and more important sources of instability associated with the behaviour of asset holders, the inconsistency between national economic and monetary policies, as well as differences in the economic structures and adjustment mechanisms of the members of the union. Second, the theory explaining the non-existence of equilibrium in an economic union with fixed exchange rates is based on the presumption that the integration of goods markets results in increased substitutability between domestic and foreign goods. This is a questionable proposition. The creation of the single European market is likely to encourage specialization, at least in certain sectors, thus reducing substitutability between the goods produced in different nations. Finally, economic union *per se* does not necessarily imply that it is not possible to pursue independent monetary policies.

With flexible exchange rates the possibility exists, although there may be questions concerning the economic efficiency and financial stability of such a system. The authors have argued that when goods are perfectly substitutable the non-existence of equilibrium extends to the case of floating exchange rates. But the reason given for such a result is not sufficient for rejecting the view that an economic union with flexible exchange rates and independent monetary policies is both feasible and desirable. The case for the adoption of a single currency and a single monetary policy in an economic union must be made on the basis of other theoretical arguments, such as the potential for financial instability and exchange-rate volatility from speculative portfolio adjustments in response to expected changes in yields of assets denominated in different currencies, rather than in response to attempts to economise money balances held for transactions purposes; it should also be made by examining the effects of exchange-rate and interest-rate volatility on trade and growth.

The conclusion that the EMS is likely to be unstable after the completion of the single European market is a valid one, but again for reasons other than those suggested by the model. The stability of the EMS will be affected much more by the complete liberalization of capital movements and financial integration rather than by the creation of a single market for highly substitutable goods. Moreover, the stability of the system will be affected adversely not so much by the divergence and incompatibility of national monetary policies, which is not significant, but by the inadequate convergence of national budgetary policies. An inappropriate policy mix in member states will impair the functioning of the EMS exchange rate mechanism. If market participants become convinced that national fiscal policies are unsustainable and inconsistent with the monetary policies pursued within the EMS, the credibility of the EMS exchange-rate structure will be undermined and its stability will be jeopardised. Moreover, in such circumstances the EMS will be more vulnerable to shocks which affect asymmetrically the economies of member states. It is unlikely that central banks will succeed in offsetting the resulting market pressures in an environment of perfect capital mobility. National currencies will not gradually disappear, as implied by the model, but their relative values will change. These arguments suggest that a smooth passage to EMU cannot be secured by relying solely on increased convergence of monetary policies. Improving the policy mix in some member state and strengthening economic policy coordination will be vital for the stability of the EMS and a successful transition to EMU.

Canzoneri, Diba and Giovannini have taken us along on an interesting round trip from policy issues to theory and back. The analysis presented at the theoretical destination was valuable and elegant, and the findings useful and suggestive. The return part of the trip, however, was not as satisfactory because the connections from theory to policy were somewhat loose and uncertain, and, in some cases, non-existent. Nevertheless, the trip was enjoyable overall. It offered us useful insights and it whetted our appetite for more theoretical explorations, along the lines suggested above, which can provide a solid theoretical basis for addressing challenging policy problems on the road to economic and monetary union.

Discussion

ANTÓNIO S. MELLO

In this chapter, Canzoneri, Diba and Giovannini analyse the effects of goods markets and capital markets integration in the demand for money balances expressed in different currencies. It is a stylized analysis of competition between, and the survival of, different currencies. In a model of the type first developed by Baumol and Tobin, people hold money to purchase goods for consumption, from which utility is derived. In order to get the cash balances needed, people must travel to a firm (bank) and this costs them time that could be used for leisure: leisure can include the time spent shopping (the pleasure of choosing and buying goods) but not that spent going to the bank. Since leisure enters the utility function and is separable from consumption, this explicit substitutability enables the authors to derive endogenously an optimal number of times the representative agent goes to the bank to withdraw the amount of cash needed for his expenditures in consumption, which are known with complete certainty.

When there is more than one numeraire, the authors ask whether it is reasonable for all of them to co-exist simultaneously. The answer is no, for obvious reasons: markets are complete, there is a single representative agent who buys a single good (although there are two goods, these are perfect substitutes). In this set-up, it is said that the good money dominates the redundant currency that has bad properties. It is conjectured, because no formal proof is given, that a higher opportunity cost of holding money is, in general, associated with a lower demand for money. The bad properties arise, in this model, from a higher inflation rate, due to a larger growth rate in the supply of one money relative to the other. In a more complete model the proper comparison would also take into account the relative growth rates of the stock of productive capital. Of course, the bad properties could be related not to monetary sources but to real sources, such as transaction frictions affecting differently the efforts k, etc. It is important to mention the real sources because the story is only artifically a monetary one: everything (i.e. the relative equilibrium costs and prices) is, indeed, derived from differences in the goods markets: the exchange rate, for example, results entirely from the equilibrium in the goods market (i.e. substitution of currencies is homothetic to substitution of goods).

The work presented here represents an advance in the topic of currency substitution, because the authors provide a specification of how a money demand function arises out of the economic set-up. Although the theoretical analysis is quite interesting – ignoring some complications not really needed such as bonds, and some requirements of the model which are hard to accept, such as the so-called claims to monetary transfers – I have some reservations about the policy implications. Integration of goods markets and liberalization of financial markets are by no means sufficient conditions for agents to become alike or goods to become perfect substitutes, or markets to be more complete, or life to become less uncertain (recall that uncertainty was totally ignored in the present formulation). And as long as there are differences in individuals' preferences, as long as there are different baskets of consumption goods there will be different clientèles holding different currencies. Indeed, goods markets integration may even reinforce the argument of alternative currencies, by means of a more specialized and clearer spatial allocation of productive resources affecting the relative efforts of providing cash balances needed for consumption purposes. Also, the conclusions depend on the static and certain nature of the analysis: in a true dynamic framework, the consumer must take into account that sometimes one currency is more costly to hold, while at other times it is cheaper, and therefore there is no reason to believe that at any point in time there is an absorption barrier.

I think that the authors are well aware of these qualifications, but have chosen to make a point by means of stylized and somewhat extreme case. The fact that they have used a corner solution should not make their point irrelevant for policy decision-makers: the dominance argument is still important, although in a less radical way than that prescribed in the model used by the authors. Indeed, I frequently ask myself what can explain such intense financial innovation, even in contracts that are perfect substitutes: why do we have N stock-index futures contracts trading simultaneously in the same country? Economic theory must find answers to the problem of asset substitutability, be it in the form of money or other assets. I welcome the work of the authors as a useful contribution in this area of research.

11 Coordination of capital income taxes in the economic and monetary union: what needs to be done?

PETER B. SØRENSEN

1 The issues

A major part of the economic benefits from the internal market and the economic and monetary union in the European Community (EC) is expected to stem from the integration of EC capital markets. The idea is that capital market liberalization and the ensuing pressure of competition will eliminated monopoly rents and X-inefficiency in the financial services sector, allow more scope for economies of scale in that sector, and channel the supply of capital to those parts of Europe where it can be most productively invested.

From the perspective of a tax economist, this scenario may be too optimistic. The reason is that the present national systems of capital income taxation in Europe are not very well coordinated. Liberalization will cause capital to flow to those countries which offer the highest private rate of return, but these may not be the countries providing the highest social rate of return, given the wide divergences in effective tax rates on income from capital. Moreover, financial services may not come to be provided by least-cost producers, but rather by producers in countries offering the most favourable tax climate for investors and financial institutions.

In this chapter some of the most important tax obstacles to an efficient allocation of capital within the EC will be discussed; consideration will also be given to the way in which these obstacles may be removed.[1] Among other things, the following questions will be addressed. In what sense do present tax systems distort intra-European investment patterns? How large are the existing tax distortions of cross-border investments, and what are the major sources of distortion? Can intensified tax competition among governments be expected to ensure the desired degree of convergence of national capital income tax systems, or is there a need for more tax coordination at the Community level? If such a need exists, should coordination take the form of partial or even full harmonization of capital income taxes, and if so, what is the likely size and distribution of the efficiency gains from harmonization?

Since investor behaviour must be assumed to depend on the total tax burden on capital, the analysis will cover personal as well as corporate taxation. Further, whenever relevant, we shall distinguish between international portfolio investment and international direct investment, because the two investment categories are motivated by different factors and subject to different tax rules.

Following a discussion of criteria for a neutral tax treatment of international investment, Section 2 of this chapter will provide a brief overview of capital income taxation in the EC and its main competitors, the United States and Japan. Against this background, the issue of tax competition versus tax harmonization in Europe will be discussed in Section 3. In Section 4 the recent efforts to coordate capital income taxes in the Community will be considered together with reviews of some proposals for further 'piecemeal' reforms of the European systems of capital income taxation. Some recent estimates of the size and distribution of the efficiency gains from corporate tax harmonization are considered in Part 5, and our main conclusions are summarized in Part 6.

2 The taxation of income from capital in the European Community

In this section, three issues will be considered (i) efficiency and equity in international taxation; (ii) the main elements of taxation of income from capital in the EC; and (iii) the importance of existing tax distortions.

2.1 Requirements for efficiency and equity in capital income taxation

Before describing capital income tax rules in the EC, it is useful to define some efficiency and equity criteria which can be used to evaluate these rules.

From a Community-wide viewpoint, there are two main conditions for efficiency in the EC capital market. The first one is that the value of the marginal product of capital should be the same in all member countries, since it would otherwise be possible to increase Community output by reallocating investment from member countries with low marginal products to those with high marginal products.

The second efficiency criterion requires that consumers' marginal rate of substitution between present and future consumption be equated across member countries. Otherwise it would be possible to obtain a Pareto-improvement by reallocating the Community's savings from member countries with a higher preference for present consumption to countries where consumers require a lower premium to postpone consumption.

An equalization of marginal products across member states will obtain if firms are competitive, if capital mobility is perfect, and if investors are taxed at the same effective rate on domestic and foreign investment. Equality of effective tax rates on investments at home and abroad may in turn be achieved if countries of residence tax investors on their accrued world-wide income – applying the same accounting rules in the calculation of domestic and foreign-source income – and provide full credit for taxes paid abroad against the domestic tax liability.[2] In these circumstances, investors will obtain the same after-tax return on investment at home and abroad when the pre-tax rates of return are the same. Capital mobility will therefore tend to equate the rates of return before tax which, under competitive conditions, are given by the marginal products of capital. A tax regime like this is said to possess the property of capital export neutrality (CEN), because it provides no incentive to invest in one jurisdication rather than another.

By contrast, a cross country equalization of the marginal rates of substitution between present and future consumption can be achieved through a tax regime ensuring cross-country equality of the after-tax rates of return to saving. With perfect capital mobility, the after-tax rates of return would tend to equality if capital income taxation were based on a pure source principle. Thus, if foreign investment income were exempt from domestic tax, and if source-countries were to tax foreign and domestic investors investing in their jurisdiction at the same effective rate, efficiency in the Community-wide allocation of savings would obtain. The tax system is then said to display capital import neutrality (CIN), because foreign and domestic suppliers of capital to any given national market are given the same tax treatment.

Unless effective capital income tax rates are the same in all countries, it will be impossible to achieve CEN and CIN simultaneously. In the theoretical literature it is usually argued that CEN should take precedence over CIN. There are at least two theoretical reasons for preferring CEN to CIN:[3]

First, under the assumptions outlined above, capital export neutrality would guarantee 'production efficiency' in the Community by equating marginal products of capital across member countries. According to the theory of optimal taxation, such production efficiency will be desirable even when consumption patterns are distorted, given the popular assumption of constant returns to scale.[4] In contrast, it is not obvious that capital import neutrality is desirable under second-best conditions where capital income taxes inevitably distort consumer choices between present and future consumption. For instance, if savings were highly elastic in some countries and very inelastic in others, it might be worthwhile to violate CIN and have higher after-tax rates of return in the former group of countries and lower net rates of return in the latter, in order to reduce the overall tax distortion of the inter-temporal consumption pattern.

Second, a regime of capital export neutrality would be consistent with the generally accepted norm of horizontal equity in taxation, since investment income from foreign and domestic sources would be taxed according to the same tax schedule. Thus, two taxpayers with the same worldwide income would pay the same amount of tax, regardless of the division of their income between domestic and foreign sources. This would not be the case under a regime of capital import neutrality.

For these reasons deviations from CEN seem a more serious matter than do deviations from CIN. In the sections below we shall therefore evaluate the present EC tax system mainly against the criterion of capital export neutrality.

2.2   A brief overview of capital income taxation in the EC

Existing capital income tax systems are notoriously complex. Capital income may take many forms such as business profits, interest, dividends, and capital gains. Taxes on such income may be levied both at the business level and at the personal level, and income from cross-border investments may be taxed both in the country of source (where the income originates) and in the country of residence (where the investor resides). An evaluation of the incentive and distribution effects of the tax system must account for the interaction of all of these taxes.[5] In the subsequent discussion of current EC tax rules, we shall abstract initially from foreign direct investment, assuming that cross-border flows of capital take the form of portfolio investment. Further, we shall start by focusing on investment financed by debt instruments. Following this, we shall address the complexities relating to equity-financed investments and direct investments by multinational enterprises.

2.2.1 The tax treatment of debt-financed investment

Consider first the tax treatment of business investment financed by debt, where the (marginal) return is channelled to savers in the form of interest payments. At least in theory, the taxation of interest income in the EC (and in the Organisation for Economic Cooperation and Development – OECD) is based on the residence principle. Savers are liable to domestic tax on interest income from foreign as well as domestic sources. If interest income from abroad has already been subject to a foreign withholding tax, the country of residence usually grants a credit for this tax, up to a limit given by the domestic tax liability. If tax enforcement is effective, savers will therefore normally end up paying the domestic tax rates indicated in the last two columns of Table 11.1 on all of their interest income.

In principle, the taxation of interest in the EC is thus characterized by capital export neutrality. In the absence of expected exchange rate changes, free capital mobility should therefore imply a tendency for pre-tax rates of interest to be equated across member countries. If taxable business profits correspond to true economic profits after deductions for interest, and if debt is the marginal source of business finance, firms will find it profitable to carry their real investment to the point where the marginal rate of return before tax equals the rate of interest before tax. Hence, with identical pre-tax interest rates across the Community, there should be a tendency for the marginal product of capital to be equated across member countries, as required for production efficiency.[6]

The assumptions underlying this argument, however, are unlikely to hold in practice. First of all, the residence principle of interest income taxation is difficult to enforce. If tax authorities cannot monitor interest income from foreign sources, such income may escape personal tax in the country of residence and will then only be subject to source-country withholding tax rates which typically range from zero to 15%. The tax regime for interest income may thus in practice favour investment in other member countries at the expense of investment at home.

On the other hand, it has been claimed that a large part of the interest income from domestic sources escapes personal tax in several member countries. At present, only four EC member countries (Denmark, France, the Netherlands, and the United Kingdom) operate a reporting system whereby financial institutions are required to notify the tax authorities of their interest payments to domestic residents. In countries without a reporting system, it is likely that substantial amounts of domestic-source interest income are subject only to domestic withholding taxes which are usually lower than the marginal personal tax rate on interest. On balance, it is therefore not clear whether the present EC tax regime for interest income is favourable or unfavourable to investment in other member countries compared with investment at home. Presumably, the situation differs somewhat from one member state to another.

Apart from a cross-country equalization of pre-tax interest rates, we noted above that an equalization of the required rate of return on debt-financed business investment throughout the Community also requires coincidence between taxable business profits and true economic profits. Such coincidence is very hard (if not impossible) to achieve.

Among other things, it would require equality between depreciation for tax purposes and true economic depreciation, and it would call for full taxation of all accrued capital gains.

In Table 11.3 the typical depreciation rates allowed for machinery and buildings in the EC in 1991 are given. According to the estimates of Hulten and Wykoff (1981), a typical exponential rate of true economic depreciation for machinery would be 12–13%, while a typical exponential rate of economic depreciation for industrial buildings would be 3–4%. Since these are real rates of depreciation, they are not directly comparable to the rates indicated in Table 11.3 if the inflation rate is positive, because the rates in the table are applied on a historical cost basis. In a future monetary union, however, where the inflation rate should be (close to) zero, the depreciation rates stated in Table 11.3 would generally be rather favourable compared to true economic depreciation, especially in member countries which also offer general investment allowances.

Apparently it is widely believed that a great step towards tax neutrality would be taken if all EC member countries adopted the same corporate tax base. This belief is not necessarily correct. For instance, suppose depreciation rates were harmonized at a level substantially above the true rates of economic depreciation. For the individual firm, this would imply a tax subsidy to investment the value of which would be higher, the higher the rate of profits tax.[7] Given the existing differences in corporate tax rates across the Community (see Table 11.2), a harmonization of the corporate income tax base would thus fail to eliminate differences in investment incentives within the Community, unless such harmonization succeeded in ensuring (rough) equality between taxable profits and true economic profits.

In summary, it seems fairly clear that the present tax regime for debt-financed investment in the EC deviates from the norms of capital export neutrality and production efficiency. Given the cross-country differences in personal tax rates and withholding tax rates on interest, it also seems safe to conclude that savers in various parts of the Community typically end up with different after-tax returns, so that capital import neutrality is likewise violated.

2.2.2 Equity-financed investment: the tax treatment of portfolio investors

Equity-financed business investment in the corporate sector is subject to tax at the corporate as well as the shareholder level. The corporate income tax rates prevailing in the EC in 1991 are shown in Table 11.2, while personal tax rates on dividends and estimated effective tax rates on accrued capital gains on shares are given in Table 11.1.

Table 11.1. *Personal tax rates (all levels of government) on capital income in the European Community, 1991*

	Tax rate on dividends[a] (per cent)		Tax rate on interest (per cent)		Estimated effective tax rate on accrued capital gains on shares (per cent)
	Top rate	Average marginal rate	Top rate	Average marginal rate	
EC countries					
Belgium[b]	25	25	10	10	0
Denmark	45	37.6	57.8	51.1	18.1
France[c]	57.9	45	18.1[d]	5.6	10.4
Germany	53	39.1	53	39.1	0
Greece	50	n.a.	0	0	0
Ireland	53[e]	27	53	38.4	26.0[i]
Italy	50	39.4	12.5	12.5	7.8
Luxembourg	51.3	25.6	51.3	25.6	0
Netherlands	60	49[f]	60	42	0
Portugal	25[g]	25	25	25	0
Spain[h]	56	28.4	56	31.5	27.9[j]
United Kingdom	40	32	40	24	25.8[j]
Major trading partners					
USA	36	31	36	28	22.7
Japan	35[i]	35	20	20	11.6

Notes:

[a] Based on statutory rates prior to any grossing-up and dividend tax credits.

[b] The 25% withholding tax on dividends and the 10% withholding tax on interest is the final tax paid.

[c] Including an additional tax of 1.1% introduced in 1991 (cotisation sociale généralisée).

[d] Different withholding tax rates are applied to different sorts of interest income; the figure used reflects that on State bonds.

[e] The personal tax rate on the first IR£7000 of dividends from firms paying the 10% corporate tax rate is half the statutory rate.

[f] The dividend and interest exemptions have not been taken into account.

[g] A withholding tax of 25% is levied on 80% of the value of dividends from shares quoted on the Portuguese Stock Exchange. Individuals may elect withholding taxes as the final tax they pay on the dividends.

[h] Spanish interest income is taxed as ordinary income, 10% of dividends received can be deducted from the personal income tax.

[i] Japanese shareholders have a choice between a final withholding tax and personal tax. The figures reflect the withholding tax.

[j] Tax is levied only on capital gains in excess of the general inflation rate.

Source: OECD (1991) – Table 3.19 and Annex 1.

Table 11.2. *Corporate tax rates and methods of double taxation relief in the European Community, 1991*

	Corporate tax rate (per cent) all levels of government	Relationship to personal income tax	Degree of mitigation of double taxation of dividends[a]	Dividend tax credit extended to foreign portfolio shareholders	Taxation of dividend from foreign subsidiaries in treaty countries
EC countries					
Belgium	39	Classical	0	—	Exemption of 90% of gross dividend
Denmark	38	Shareholder reflief	0.5		Exemption
France	34/42[b]	Imputation	0.69	Yes, on treaty basis	Exemption of 95% of gross dividend
Germany	57/44[b]	Imputation	0.81	No	Exemption
Greece	46(40)[c]	Dividend deduction	1.0		Credit
Ireland	10/40[d]	Imputation	0.5	No (except UK)	Exemption
Italy	48	Imputation	1.0	No (except UK)	Exemption of 60%, deduction on rest
Luxembourg	39	Classical	0		Exemption
Netherlands	35	Classical	0		Exemption
Portugal	40	Shareholder relief	0.32		Credit
Spain	35	Partial dividend deduction and shareholder relief	0.42		Credit
United Kingdom	34	Imputation	0.65	Yes, on treaty basis	Credit
Major trading partners					
United States	38	Classical	0	—	Credit
Japan	50	Shareholder relief	0.12	—	Credit

Notes:

[a] The figures indicate the value of a fraction defined in the following way: (total dividend tax under no mitigation – actual total dividend tax)/(total dividend tax under no mitigation – dividend tax under full mitigation).

[b] The first-figure is the rate for retained profits; the second figure is the rate for distributed profits.

[c] Varies with activity, status, and nature of investment.

[d] The first-figure is the rate for the manufacturing sector; the second figure is the rate for other sectors.

Source: OECD (1991).

Table 11.3. Depreciation allowances and general investment reliefs in the European Community, 1991

	Depreciation allowances[a] (per cent)		General investment reliefs	
	Machinery	Buildings	General investment allowance available	General investment credit available
EC countries				
Belgium	DB(40) with switchover to SL(20)	DB(10) with switchover to SL(5)	Yes, minimum 3%, maximum 10%	No
Denmark	DB(30)	First 10 years: SL(6) Subsequent years: SL(2)	No	No
France	DB(36) with switchover to SL(6)	SL(5)	No	No
Germany	DB(30) with switchover to SL(10)	First 4 years: SL(10) Next 3 years: SL(5) Subsequent years: SL(3.5)	No	No
Greece	SL(20)	SL(8)	Yes, 40–70% of investment cost	No
Ireland	First year: 50 Subsequent years: DB(13)	First year: 50 Subsequent years: SL(4)	No	No
Italy	First 3 years: SL(18) Subsequent years: SL(10)	DB(5)	No	No
Luxembourg	DB(30) with switchover to SL(20)	SL(4)	No	Yes, if investment exceeds average of last 5 years

			Yes, between 2–18% of investment costs (with ceiling)	
Netherlands	DB(25) with switchover to SL(12.5)	DB(6.6)	Yes, between 2–18% of investment costs (with ceiling)	No
Portugal	DB(31)	SL(5)	No	No
Spain	DB(20)	DB(7.5)	No	Yes, new fixed assets
United Kingdom	DB(25)	SL(4)	No	No
Major trading partners				
United States	First 3 years: DB(29) Subsequent years: SL(9)	SL(3.2)	No	No
Japan	DB(30) with switchover to SL(10)	SB(6.6) with switchover to SL(2.2)	No	No

Notes:
[a] Typical depreciation rates for manufacturing sector.
DB = declining balance. SL = straight line.
Source: OECD (1991).

Under a so-called 'classical' corporate tax system, there is no attempt to alleviate the double taxation of corporate equity income resulting from the coexistence of corporate and personal income taxes. Such a system currently prevails in the Benelux countries. As indicated in Table 11.2, however, most EC countries mitigate the double taxation of dividends through some form of integration of corporate and personal income taxes. Under the 'shareholder relief' schemes in Spain and Portugal, shareholders receive a tax credit amounting to a fixed percentage of the dividends received, whereas the shareholder relief scheme in Denmark takes the form of a reduced personal tax rate on dividends. Under the 'dividend deduction' scheme in Greece, distributed profits are fully deductible from the corporate income tax base, while Spain allows a partial deduction for distributions. Finally, under the 'imputation systems' operating in France, Germany, Ireland, Italy, and the United Kingdom, resident shareholders receive a credit for part or all of the corporation tax underlying the dividends received.

The third column in Table 11.2 quantifies the degree to which the double taxation of dividends is mitigated for domestic portfolio shareholders. Full mitigation is defined as a situation in which the total tax burden on distributed profits equals the shareholder's personal tax rate times the amount distributed. In that case, the degree of mitigation is 1.0. It is seen that Italy and Greece are the only EC countries offering full mitigation. Germany also offers her resident shareholders a full credit for the central government corporation tax, but since no credit is granted for the local 'Gewerbesteuer' on corporations, the overall degree of mitigation is less than unity. In the 'classical' Benelux countries, the degree of mitigation is zero by definition. The remaining member countries are seen to offer degrees of mitigation somewhere between zero and unity.

It should be mentioned that the combination of the corporate income tax and the personal tax on capital gains on shares may also imply some amount of double taxation of retained corporate profits, compared with the tax burden on interest income. Since several EC countries exempt capital gains from personal tax, however, and because the other member countries only tax realized gains, the estimated effective tax rates on accrued capital gains shown in Table 11.1 are rather low. As a consequence, the total tax burden on retained corporate profits is usually lower than that on distributed profits.

Because of the interaction of corporate and personal income taxes, the requirements for capital export neutrality towards portfolio investment in shares are quite complex.[8] CEN requires that shareholders be subject to the same total corporate and personal tax burden, whether they purchase a share in a domestic or in a foreign corporation. In principle, corporate portfolio investors acquiring shares in a foreign corporation should thus be subject to domestic corporation tax on their *pro rata* share of the profits of the foreign firm, and they should be given full domestic credit for the foreign corporation and withholding taxes which have already been levied on their imputed profit share. Further, when the corporate investor distributes income from foreign sources to the ultimate domestic shareholders, the latter should be given the same amount of dividend tax relief as that granted when domestic-source profits are distributed.

As far as foreign portfolio investment by household investors is concerned, full capital export neutrality would require an adjustment of each investor's personal income tax to eliminate the differential between the foreign and the domestic corporation tax. More precisely, it would be necessary to impute to each investor his or her *pro rata* share of foreign corporate profits, and to impose a surtax or to grant a refund equal to the difference between the domestic and the foreign corporation tax on these profits. Further, the foreign withholding tax on dividends would have to be fully credited against domestic personal income tax. Finally, in so far as relief of the economic double taxation of dividends is granted in the domestic sphere, a similar relief for the adjusted corporation tax would have to be granted when dividends are received from abroad.

Given the obvious administrative difficulties of administering the tax rules sketched here, it is no surprise that EC countries have never attempted to impute *pro rata* shares of the profits of foreign corporations to domestic owners of foreign shares (just as countries do not impute the retained profits of domestic corporations to domestic shareholders). At the corporate level, portfolio investors are thus exposed to the foreign corporation tax when they invest abroad and to the domestic corporate income tax when they invest at home.

Further, with the few modifications indicated in the fourth column of Table 11.2, EC countries mitigating the economic double taxation of dividends do not extend their dividend tax reliefs to non-resident shareholders, and they normally do not offer reliefs to resident holders of foreign shares for the foreign corporation tax underlying foreign-source dividend income. Roughly speaking, existing systems of dividend tax relief in the EC benefit only domestic holders of domestic shares.

For these reasons, the present tax treatment of portfolio shareholders in the Community violates the principle of capital export neutrality. In particular, the current methods of alleviating the economic double taxation of dividends tend to favour domestic investment at the expense of investment in other member countries.

2.2.3 The taxation of foreign direct investment

Although international capital flows still tend to be dominated by short term deposits, bank loans, and portfolio investment in debt instruments, foreign direct investment by multinational enterprises has gained increased importance during the last decade and is expected to grow even further in the future economic and monetary union.

The preceding discussion immediately suggests what it would take to ensure capital export neutrality towards foreign direct investment. First, the profits of the foreign subsidiaries and branches of EC multinationals would have to be taxed according to the corporate tax rules prevailing in the country of residence of the parent company, and the country of residence would have to grant an unlimited credit for corporation and withholding taxes levied by the foreign source countries. This would ensure that EC multinationals would face the same effective corporate tax rate on domestic and foreign operations. Second, distributions to the ultimate shareholders of profits from foreign sources should be subject to the same amount of dividend tax relief as distributions on profits from domestic sources.

The present EC tax regime for foreign direct investment is a far cry from these neutrality requirements. As made clear in the last column of Table 11.2, a majority of member countries alleviate international double taxation simply by exempting from domestic corporation tax the dividends of foreign subsidiaries. The exemption method of international double taxation relief obviously implies that foreign investment income is subject only to the foreign corporate income tax (and possibly foreign withholding taxes), which will generally deviate from the domestic corporation tax, on a similar amount of profits.

Furthermore, while four EC countries do in fact tax the worldwide income of their resident multinationals, these countries only grant a credit for taxes paid abroad up to a limit given by the amount of domestic tax on the foreign-source income.[9] When the effective foreign corporate income tax rate (plus the foreign withholding tax) exceeds the effective domestic corporate tax rate, the multinational thus ends up paying the higher foreign tax rate on its foreign operations.

In addition, in countries practising 'world-wide' corporate income taxation with a foreign tax credit, domestic tax on the profits from foreign subsidiaries is normally deferred until the time when these profits are repatriated in the form of dividends. Consequently, profits retained abroad bear only the foreign corporation tax.

Finally, in countries mitigating the economic double taxation of dividends, dividend tax relief is usually granted only to the extent that the underlying corporate income tax has accrued to the domestic exchequer, and not if the corporation tax has been paid to a foreign country. Thus, while the specific rules in individual member countries differ slightly, there is generally discrimination against direct investment income from foreign sources, in so far as this income is passed on to the ultimate domestic shareholders.[10]

As this brief description indicates, the achievement of capital export neutrality in foreign direct investment would require substantial changes in current EC practices. First, all member countries would have to switch to a system of world-wide corporate income taxation and adopt the credit system of international double taxation relief. From an administrative viewpoint, this would be a disadvantage, since the exemption method of double taxation relief is considerabely simpler to operate.

Second, the limitations on foreign tax credits would have to be abolished and, if necessary, countries of residence would have to grant a refund for corporate taxes paid abroad. This would cause some loss of revenue. It might also induce source countries to set their corporate tax rates at an inefficiently high level, since foreign investors would not be deterred by a high source-country tax rate, if they could always get a refund for the foreign tax from their home government.

Third, EC countries would have to abandon the practice of deferring home country tax on foreign-source profits until the time of repatriation. In other words, member countries would have to tax all of the Community-wide profits of their resident multinationals on a current basis. This would have some controversial implications. For instance, neutrality would require that investment incentives offered by the home country (such as accelerated depreciation, investment grants, etc.) should also apply to investment in foreign affiliates and not just to domestic capital formation, which is the usual current practice. It is also problematic that the home-country tax authorities would have to rely on accounts submitted by foreign subsidiaries without being able to check this information through proper field audits. Effective tax enforcement would thus require increased cooperation between national tax administrations in the Community. If the current differences in the national definitions of taxable profits persist, such cooperation may be very difficult to achieve.

Finally, distributions of foreign-source profits to domestic shareholders should qualify for the same amount of dividend tax relief as distributions of profits earned domestically. While this should cause no serious technical difficulties, it would impose a revenue loss on those member countries which currently mitigate the economic double taxation of dividends. This might be seen as unfair, since countries with a 'classical' corporate tax system would not need to undertake any adjustments and hence would suffer no loss of revenue.

From the viewpoint of individual member countries, the advantage of a tax regime of capital export neutrality is that it would in principle enable each country to choose its own preferred corporate tax rate without distorting the location of investment within the Community. As we have just seen, however, the practical and political obstacles to the achievement of full capital export neutrality in foreign direct investment are quite impressive.

Moreover, even if these obstacles could be overcome, it would probably be hard to retain substantial differentials of effective corporate tax rates across member countries. The reason is that, with an unlimited foreign tax credit, EC multinationals would have an incentive to shift their place of legal 'residence' to the member state applying the lowest effective corporate tax rate. In this way, multinationals could minimize the total tax liability on their Community-wide income. Such a concentration of parent companies in 'tax haven' countries could inflict revenue losses not only on higher-tax jurisdictions, but also on the low-tax countries which would have to grant unlimited credits for the foreign taxes paid by their 'resident' multinationals. Both groups of countries might thus be induced to harmonize their corporate tax rates to prevent the shifting of legal residence.

2.3   How large are the existing tax distortions?

As the preceding sections should have made clear, the present EC tax systems tend to distort the Community-wide allocation of investment and savings. Our discussion also revealed that the implementation of full tax neutrality would meet with formidable practical difficulties. For policy-makers, the interesting question is whether the existing tax distortions are so large that they should be a matter of serious concern?

One way of answering this question is to calculate the required pre-tax rate of return – i.e. the cost of capital – on domestic and cross-border investments in the Community, allowing for the current differences in the national systems of capital income taxation. Such calculations can be carried out on an internationally comparable basis by means of a model constructed by Michael Devereux and Mark Pearson of the Institute for Fiscal Studies in London. The model is based on the methodology developed by King and Fullerton (1984) and is described in detail in OECD (1991).

Some results produced by the model are shown in Table 11.4; they relate to the EC and its main trading partners. The calculations in the table assume a common pre-tax real rate of interest of 5% and a common inflation rate of 3.1%. Such assumptions of common rates of interest and

Table 11.4. *The cost of capital in domestic and transnational direct investment in the European Community, 1991*

	Domestic cost (per cent)	Transnational cost of capital (per cent)		Standard deviation of transnational cost of capital	
		Residence	Source	Residence	Source
EC countries					
Belgium	5.1	5.9	3.7	0.7	1.8
Denmark	2.8	2.5	4.2	0.3	2.0
France	5.9	6.4	4.2	0.7	2.0
Germany	1.7	2.3	4.1	0.3	2.1
Greece	5.8	7.5	3.5	0.6	1.7
Ireland	2.6	2.7	3.8	0.3	1.7
Italy	6.6	6.3	4.5	0.6	2.3
Luxembourg	3.2	2.6	4.6	0.3	2.0
Netherlands	2.4	2.0	4.4	0.3	2.0
Portugal	4.3	5.6	4.1	0.9	2.2
Spain	2.8	2.2	4.9	0.3	2.1
United Kingdom	3.9	3.9	4.1	0.3	1.9
EC average	3.9	4.2	4.2	0.5	2.0
Major trading partners					
USA	4.9	5.9	4.6	0.3	1.8
Japan	6.2	7.0	5.3	0.4	1.6

Notes: The assumptions behind the calculations in this table are: real interest rate of 5%; inflation rate of 3.1%; top personal tax rates. Investment is in a weighted average of buildings, machinery and inventories. Transnational investment is financed equally from retentions by the foreign subsidiary, new equity from the domestic parent, and loans from the parent. The parent company raises finance through a weighted average of debt, retentions and new equity. Figures for EC countries are for intra-EC investments. For non-EC countries, they are for investment only into the EC and from the EC.
Source: Calculations by Michael Devereux and Mark Pearson of the Institute for Fiscal Studies, London.

inflation seem appropriate for a future economic and monetary union, and they enable us to isolate the effects of tax rules on the cost of capital. The figures in the table also presume that shareholders face the top marginal personal tax rates in their country of residence. The numbers should be interpreted as risk-adjusted real rates of return, since they do not include the necessary risk premia stemming from uncertainty.

The first column in Table 11.4 shows the average required rate of return on real investment in the domestic corporate sector, allowing for the relevant parameters of the corporate and personal tax systems. The figures represent a weighted average of investment in buildings, machinery, and inventories, assumed to be financed by a weighted average of debt, new equity, and retained profits. These weights are common to all countries, and are chosen so as to reflect conditions in a 'typical' country.[11] The calculations also rely on estimates of true economic depreciation rates produced by Hulten and Wykoff (1981).

The second column (residence) in Table 11.4 shows the average required rate of return on outward foreign direct investment from the country in question into all other EC countries, while the third column (source) indicates the average required rate of return on inward foreign direct investment from all other EC countries into the named country. Foreign direct investment is a weighted average of buildings, machinery and inventories and is assumed to be financed equally by retentions by the foreign subsidiary, injections of new equity from the parent company, and loans from the parents. The parent is supposed to raise its finance in the same way as purely domestic corporations, i.e. through a weighted average of debt, retentions, and new share issues.

The fourth column in the table reports the standard deviation of the required rates of return on outward foreign direct investment from the named home country into the other EC countries, and the fifth column measures the standard deviation of the rate of return required by investors from other EC countries when they undertake foreign direct investment into the source country indicated.

To give an example, the first row of figures in Table 11.4 show that, when the real rate of interest before tax is 5% and the inflation rate is 3.1%, the average required pre-tax return on domestic corporate investment in Belgium is 5.1%. At the same time, Belgian-based multinationals on average require a 5.9% return on their direct investments in other EC countries, but since Belgian-owned companies are subject to different tax rules in different EC countries, there is a standard deviation of 0.7 percentage points of this required return on outward investment from Belgium. Further, the required return on direct investments from other member countries into Belgium is only 3.7% on average, but there is a substantial 1.8% standard deviation around this average, indicating that the return required on inward investment in Belgium depends very much on the particular EC country supplying the capital.

Given this interpretation of Table 11.4, we may now restate the conditions for tax neutrality. First, all the figures in the first column, indicating the cost of capital in domestic investment, would have to be identical and equal to the 5% real rate of interest before tax. Second, capital export neutrality would require that the costs of capital in the first and second columns of the table should be identical for each country, and that the standard deviations in the fourth column should all be zero. Finally, capital import neutrality would call for the rate-of-return figures in the first and third columns to be identical, and for all the standard deviations in the fifth column to be zero.

The actual figures in Table 11.4 obviously do not meet these neutrality requirements. For the EC as a whole, the cost of capital in domestic corporate investment is 1.1 percentage points lower than the assumed 5% real interest rate, so on average EC tax systems tend to subsidize domestic investment. This subsidization is mainly due to two factors. First, the present tax systems allow a full deduction for all nominal interest payments, and not just for the real interest expenses of corporations. Second, although depreciation for tax purposes is calculated on a historical rather than a replacement cost basis, the present value of current depreciation allowances nevertheless tends to exceed the present value of the true economic depreciation of physical corporate assets. As a consequence of these general features of the current EC tax systems, corporations are typically allowed deductions in excess of their true economic costs of doing business, and this drives their cost of capital in domestic investment below the market rate of interest.

It can also be seen from Table 11.4 that the required pre-tax rate of return on outward as well as inward foreign direct investment in the EC is on average 0.3 percentage points higher than the cost of capital in domestic investment. Thus, the current tax systems tend to discriminate against transnational investment, although not on a dramatic scale. The reasons for this discrimination have already been suggested in the previous section. They include withholding taxes on cross-border dividend payments,[12] limitations on foreign tax credits, and the lack of dividend tax relief for distributions of foreign-source profits.

The absence of CEN and CIN is further revealed by the positive standard deviations in the fourth and fifth columns of Table 11.4. In particular, the relatively high standard deviations for inward foreign investment (the last column) indicate that the different foreign suppliers of capital to the typical EC country are subject to substantial differences in their total tax burden, implying large departures from the norm of capital import neutrality.

It is worth noting from the last three rows in Table 11.4 that the typical EC corporation seems to face a lower cost of capital in domestic investment than companies in the United States or Japan. Moreover, as a result of current tax rules, US and Japanese multinationals investing in Europe appear to require a higher return than the rate of return required by

European multinationals investing in the US or Japan. The tax factors reflected in the figures in Table 11.4, however, may be offset by the non-tax determinants of the cost of capital.

Finally, it should be stressed that the figures in Table 11.4 may well over-estimate the (risk-adjusted) cost of capital. The figures conceal a substantial amount of variation in the cost of capital across different asset types and different modes of finance. In so far as corporations tend to concentrate their investments on the assets enjoying the most favourable tax treatment, and in so far as they tend to rely on the most 'tax-efficient' modes of finance, the actual cost of capital will be lower than indicated in Table 11.4, because common asset and financing weights have been assumed for all countries, despite the cross-country differences in tax rules.

In particular, Table 11.4 may exaggerate the cost of capital in transnational investment. Only the simplest form of multinational group relations, i.e., the relation between a parent and a 100% owned foreign subsidiary is considered. It is also assumed that the parent raises all its finance in the domestic economy. In reality, multinationals may use more complex financial arrangements and more complicated group structures in order to minimize tax burdens. Moreover, it is assumed in Table 11.4 that goods, services and assets are transferred between members of the same group of companies at their true economic values. In other words, the possibility that multinationals may engage in transfer pricing in order to shift profits to low-tax jurisdictions is neglected.

Nevertheless, Table 11.4 does at least indicate the potential for tax distortions of intra-Community investment patterns, and since the tax planning activities just mentioned are not costless, a large part of these potential distortions are likely to materialize as actual distortions.

3   Tax competition versus tax harmonization

As already demonstrated, current tax systems cause the cost of corporate capital to vary from one EC country to another. The magnitude of the resulting investment distortions will depend on the elasticity of investment with respect to the cost of capital. A comprehensive review of existing empirical research on tax effects on international investment is provided in Sørensen (1991a). According to that survey, changes in capital income tax rules often have important effects on transnational flows of portfolio capital. The survey also showed that, although taxes are rarely the dominant determinant of international direct investment, there is nevertheless substantial evidence of non-negligible tax effects on the international location of business investment.

Nevertheless, it is a matter of opinion whether the non-neutralites indicated in Table 11.4 are unacceptably large. Most European-minded observers appear to agree that the tax distortions described above should not be tolerated in a future economic and monetary union. On the other hand, some observers believe that the forces of tax competition among European governments will automatically tend to ensure the desired degree of convergence of national tax systems, and that there will be no need for tax coordination or tax harmonization through political intervention by Community institutions. To evaluate this proposition, it is useful to review some recent research on the effects of international tax competition.[13]

3.1 The theory of international tax competition

In its broadest sense, the term 'tax competition' describes a process in which governments design their tax rules so as to maximize their own country's welfare, given the (tax) policies pursued by other governments.

From the national viewpoint of a small country in an integrated world economy, the optimal system of capital income taxation will depend crucially on the ability of the authorities to enforce taxes on foreign-source investment income. Suppose first that such income can in fact be monitored. Suppose further that countries of residence offer no credits to international investors for taxes levied by source countries. Under these assumptions, it has been shown to be non-optimal for a small economy faced with perfect capital mobility to levy any source-based taxes on capital income. Instead, a small economy striving to maximize the welfare of its citizens should adopt a pure residence principle of capital income taxation, i.e. it should implement a regime of full capital export neutrality and abstain from the use of source-based taxes.[14] Given perfect capital mobility and the absence of foreign tax credits, the introduction of a source tax would just drive up the domestic cost of capital above the exogenous world rate of interest, thereby distorting domestic investment decisions without enabling the government to shift any part of the domestic tax burden on to non-resident investors.

According to this analysis, the only necessary form of international tax coordination is an international exchange of information to enable governments to enforce world-wide capital income taxation. Apart from that, national governments should be left free to choose their own preferred absolute and relative tax rates on income from capital and labour, balancing the tax distortions of savings decisions against the tax distortions of the labour/leisure choice. With structural differences between national economies, the optimal capital income tax rate would differ from one country to another, and attempts to harmonize effective capital income tax rates at a common international level would therefore imply a welfare loss for all countries.[15]

Consider next a situation in which it is impossible for home countries to enforce taxes on capital income from at least some foreign source countries. In that case, any domestic capital income tax would essentially work like a source-based tax, since it could always be avoided through investment in the foreign 'tax haven' countries. Since it would still be non-optimal for the government of a small economy faced with perfect capital mobility to levy any source tax, the process of tax competition would then lead to the complete elimination of capital income taxes! Tax burdens would instead come to be concentrated on internationally immobile factors such as labour and land.[16]

It is worth noting the strength of the proposition that tax competition will cause capital income taxes to vanish in an integrated world economy with tax havens. The proposition applies as long as some tax havens exist, even if a sub-group of countries were willing to engage in international exchange of information among tax authorities.

It should also be stressed that effective monitoring of foreign source income will in principle enable governments to attain a higher level of welfare for their citizens. When world-wide capital income taxation can be enforced, governments can control the net return to saving through their choice of the capital income tax rate, just as they can control the net reward to labour via their choice of the tax rate on labour income. Hence policy-makers can trade off tax distortions in the capital market against tax distortions in the labour market. When taxes on foreign-source capital income cannot be enforced, the net return to savings is equal to the exogenous foreign rate of return which escapes domestic tax. Thus the domestic government has one fewer policy instruments at its disposal, and will therefore generally not be able to ensure the same level of consumer welfare as would be attainable under world-wide capital income taxation.

3.2   Will capital income taxes actually vanish under tax competition

While theoretically interesting, the prediction of vanishing capital income taxation would clearly have to be modified when some of the underlying simplifying assumptions are relaxed.

First of all, a large debtor country with a noticeable influence on the international capital market might find it optimal to impose a positive source-based capital income tax, since this would cause an outflow of capital which would drive down the world rate of interest that the country would have to pay on its debt.

At the more practical level, it is necessary to distinguish between the taxation of international portfolio investment and international direct investment. Casual empiricism suggests that international portfolio capital – in particular capital invested in debt instruments – is indeed highly mobile and very responsive to tax factors. The prediction that the forces of tax competition will make it increasingly difficult for governments to maintain significant taxes on interest income may therefore not be too far off the mark.

The situation is different for international direct investment by multinational corporations. There are several reasons why source-based corporation taxes on the income from such investments are unlikely to vanish even under unfettered tax competition.

First, the international mobility of direct business investments is unlikely to become perfect. A reallocation of production activities and physical capital across countries usually involves considerable adjustment costs. As a consequence, it will often be unprofitable for multinationals to relocate their activities in response to (modest) tax differentials.

Second, multinationals will sometimes be able to earn above-normal profits by investing in a particular country. This may be because of local factors such as easy access to markets or raw materials, the presence of a qualified labour force with special skills, a high quality of the local infrastructure, and so on. Whenever multinationals enjoy such 'location-specific rents', the governments of source countries will be able to tax them via the corporation tax without distorting investment and without deterring foreign investors.

Third, as international economic integration proceeds, the international 'cross-hauling' of foreign direct investment will increase. In each country, a growing proportion of the stock of business capital is therefore likely to become owned by foreigners. Thus, while economic integration may increase capital mobility and thereby make it more difficult to impose taxes on capital income, integration will also imply that a growing proportion of the domestic corporation tax will fall on non-residents. If governments care only about the welfare of their own citizens, this will make the corporation tax a more attractive policy instrument.[17]

Fourth, the practice of some home countries of alleviating international double taxation through a foreign tax credit obviously enables source countries to shift some of the burden of corporation tax on to foreign governments without deterring foreign private investors.

For all of these reasons, it is not to be expected that source-based corporation taxes will vanish in the future economic and monetary union, even in the absence of any attempts by Community institutions to coordinate or harmonize corporate income taxes. Of course, this is not to deny that corporation tax rates might end up at a sub-optimal level under unfettered tax competition.

3.3   What is the evidence on international tax competition?

Anecdotal evidence from recent years seems to confirm the hypothesis of the preceding section that the forces of international tax competition are stronger in the field of international portfolio investment than in the area of direct investment. For instance, in 1984 the US government repealed the 30% withholding tax on most interest payments from US debtors to non-residents.[18] As another example, in early 1989 Germany introduced a modest 10% domestic withholding tax on interest income. This resulted in a substantial flight of assets to financial intermediaries (many of which were branches of German banks) based in Luxembourg, where no withholding taxes are imposed. Faced with these pressures from the capital market, the German government had to abolish withholding tax after a few months.

By contrast, there is no evidence that the source-based corporation tax is waning. According to the OECD revenue statistics, the revenue from corporate income tax in the EC and its main trading partners has not declined during the last decade, either as a proportion of gross domestic product or as a proportion of total tax revenues. Thus, while the average statutory corporate tax rate in the EC indeed fell from 46.0% to 39.7% between 1980 and 1988,[19] this fall was accompanied by measures to broaden the corporate tax base so that revenues were more or less maintained over the decade.

In so far as EC governments compete for the taxable 'paper profits' which can to some extent be shifted from one jurisdiction to another through the transfer-pricing practices of multinationals, the fall in the average statutory corporate income tax rate can be seen as evidence of a form of tax competition. This is because the incentives for multinationals to engage in transfer pricing depends on statutory tax rate differentials rather than on differentials in effective tax rates.

Apart from this, there is little evidence that tax competition exerts a strong downward pressure on corporate income tax in the EC. If governments are concerned about revenue losses and about the possibility of retaining the taxation of income from capital, there seems to be a greater need for a neutralization of tax competition in the field of intra-Community portfolio investment, for example, through a more effective exchange of information and a liberalization of bank secrecy laws.

4   Some proposals for coordination of capital income taxes in the EC

While some observers continue to subscribe to unfettered tax competition, there is a widespread belief that such competition will not automatically reduce the existing tax distortions in the allocation of investment and savings in the EC. Consequently, the recent years have witnessed a number of proposals for improved coordination of capital income taxes in the Community. Before reviewing some of these proposals, a brief overview is given of the amount of coordination which has already been achieved.

4.1   What has been achieved so far?

Until recently, almost no progress had been made in coordinating direct taxation in the EC. In the summer of 1990, however, the Council of Ministers adopted three directives which were aimed at reducing or eliminating tax obstacles to cross-border activities by European multinational enterprises.

The so-called parent-subsidiary directive is intended to eliminate the double taxation of cross-border dividend payments within the Community. The directive calls for the abolition of withholding taxes on dividends paid from a subsidiary in one member country to a parent company in another member country. As far as corporate income tax is concerned, the directive requires all member states to relieve the international double taxation of intra-Community dividend payments from subsidiaries to parents through the method of exemption or credit. While the directive has generally been welcomed by the business community, there have also been complaints that it does not require the abolition of withholding taxes on dividends from one subsidiary to another within a group of related companies.

The 'mergers' directive provides for any capital gains arising from a merger of firms in different member countries to be taxed only upon realization. Finally, the 'arbitration procedure' convention establishes a procedure to prevent double taxation when the tax authorities in a member country decide to adjust the internal transfer prices applied to transactions between related firms in a multinational group. More specifically, the convention seeks to ensure that an upward adjustment of taxable profits in one member country is followed by a corresponding downward adjustment of taxable income in another member country.

These three directives were supposed to be implemented by 1st January,

1992. In November 1990, the European Commission adopted two additional draft directives: The 'interest and royalty' directive, involving the abolition of withholding taxes on such payments within European groups of companies; and the 'foreign losses' directive, allowing parent companies to set against their profits any losses made by their branches or subsidiaries in other member countries. The aim was to implement these two directives before 1st January, 1993.

Although the five directives mentioned here should remove some of the existing tax discrimination against cross-border investment within the Community, they are felt by many to be insufficient to guarantee a reasonably efficient allocation of capital. In the following sections we shall consider some proposals for further coordination of capital income taxes. To limit the scope of the chapter, we shall confine ourselves to the reform proposals which have been most vividly discussed among EC policy-makers. We shall thus have to disregard the more radical reforms advocated by academic writers such as Sinn (1990) who argues for a pure source-based tax system with immediate writing-off of all business investment; Giovannini and Hines (1990), who favour a residence-based tax system; and Keen (1991) who would like to see the current corporate income tax replaced by a corporate cash flow tax. Nor will we be able to discuss the proposal for a 'unitary' EC corporation tax which would solve the problem of transfer pricing by allocating the total taxable profits of EC multinational corporations among member states according to a common fixed formula (see Weiner, 1991). All of these interesting proposals certainly deserve to be scrutinized, but they are probably too sweeping to be politically acceptable in the near future.[20]

4.2   Towards a common system of corporate-personal tax integration?

In 1975 the European Commission proposed a directive calling for all member countries to adopt an imputation system of dividend taxation with approximately the same degree of relief in each country. The directive was never approved by the Council of Ministers and has recently been withdrawn by the Commission. Because, however, of the widely varying degrees of corporate-personal tax integration across the Community (see Table 11.2), the need for some harmonization in this field is still under debate.

The size of the cross-country investment distortions stemming from the different degrees of dividend tax relief depends very much on whether the so-called 'new view' of dividend taxation is correct, or whether the traditional 'old' view is a more accurate description of reality.[21]

To clarify the different implications of the two views for the cost of corporate capital, some simple algebra will be useful. Suppose for simplicity that depreciation for tax purposes coincides with true economic depreciation. The required pre-tax rate of return c on an equity-financed corporate investment will then be given by

$$c(1 - t) = a \tag{1}$$

where t is the corporate income tax rate, and a is the shareholders' required rate of return before personal tax. The old view is based on the hypothesis that – for various reasons which are not yet very well understood – shareholders will *ceteris paribus* have a preference for dividends over capital gains on their shares. To keep down their cost of equity finance, corporations therefore feel a need to pay out a considerable proportion of profits in the form of dividends. Suppose that the dividend payout ratio is a, and consider a 'classical' corporate tax system where no dividend tax relief is granted. If the marginal personal tax rate on dividends and interest is m, if the effective personal tax rate on accrued capital gains is g, and if the market rate of interest is r, the required rate of return on shares, a, will then be given by the arbitrage condition

$$a[a(1 - m) + (1 - a)(1 - g)] = r(1 - m) \tag{2}$$

Equation (2) may be explained as follows. A fraction a of the shareholder's return takes the form of a dividend which is taxed at the rate m. The remaining fraction $1 - a$ of the post-corporate-tax profit is retained by the corporation, resulting in a capital gain for the shareholder which is taxed at the effective rate g. Hence the left-hand side of (2) is the total return on shares after payment of personal taxes on dividends and capital gains. In equilibrium (and in the absence of uncertainty), this net return must equal the after-tax interest rate, which appears on the right-hand side of (2).

Consider next the new view. Supporters of this view see no reason why shareholders should prefer dividends to capital gains. They claim that, because the total tax burden on retained profits is usually lower than the total burden on distributed profits, shareholders would want corporations to use retentions as the marginal source of equity finance. In that case the personal tax on dividends will not reduce the incentive to invest. If the corporation retains an extra unit of profits today, reinvests it at a post-corporate-tax return of X, and increases its distributions tomorrow by $1 + X$ units, the shareholder will forego a net dividend of $(1 - m)$ today, but will receive an additional net dividend of $(1 - m)(1 + X)$ tomorrow. Obviously, the shareholder's relative rate of return on the net income foregone today will then be independent of the personal tax on dividends. The retention of profits, however, will cause an appreciation of share values which will be subject to personal capital gains tax. Under the new view, the shareholder's required rate of return will therefore be determined by the arbitrage condition

$$a(1 - g) = r(1 - m) \tag{3}$$

stating that the percentage after-tax return on shares must equal the shareholder's opportunity cost of capital, i.e. the after-tax interest rate.

The implications of the new view are quite striking. For 'mature' corporations which are able to meet their need for equity finance through their own retentions, the taxation of dividends is irrelevant for the cost of capital. Instead, the new view focuses on the disincentive effects of the double taxation of retained earnings resulting from the coexistence of corporate income taxes and personal taxes on capital gains. The new view does not deny that double taxation of dividends will discourage investment in new and immature firms which have to rely on new share issues for their marginal source of equity finance. Adherents of the new view, however, point out that only a small fraction of total corporate investment is financed by new share issues, suggesting that double taxation of dividends will only have a minor effect on aggregate corporate investment.

To get a feeling for the quantitative implications of the two conflicting views of dividend taxation, consider the following stylized parameters for an 'average' EC country:

$$a = 0.5, t = 0.4, m = 0.3, g = 0.1, r = 0.05 \tag{4}$$

where r should be interpreted as a real rate of interest. With these parameters, the reader may easily verify from equations (1)–(3) that the cost of corporate equity capital, c, under the new view would be 6.5%, whereas it would be 7.3% under the old view, given the assumption of a classical corporate tax system.

Moreover, while relief of the double taxation of dividends would have a negligible effect on the cost of capital under the new view, such dividend tax relief would clearly encourage investment under the old view. For instance, suppose a country were to move from a classical corporate tax system to a system of full imputation. Under a full imputation system, the dividends paid out would be 'grossed up' by a dividend tax credit equal to the underlying corporation tax. The shareholder would therefore receive a total cash income of $1/(1 - t)$ for every unit of dividend paid out from the corporation. Since this total income would be subject to the personal tax rate m, the old view would imply that the arbitrage condition (2) would change to

$$a\left[a\left(\frac{1-m}{1-t}\right) + (1-a)(1-g)\right] = r(1-m) \qquad (5)$$

where the left-hand side represents the after-tax dividend received under full imputation. Equations (1) and (5) yield a cost of corporate equity capital equal to 5.6%, which is considerably lower than the 7.3% cost of capital implied by the old view under a classical corporate tax system. If the old view is correct, the present variations in the degree of dividend tax relief reported in Table 11.2 would thus seem to cause substantial variations in the cost of capital across EC member countries.

Unfortunately, the empirical evidence on the relevance of the two conflicting views of dividend taxation is mixed. For instance, the new view is consistent with the observed fact that retained earnings typically account for the major share of corporate equity finance in OECD countries. On the other hand, the old view is consistent with the fact that corporations often try to maintain a fairly steady stream of dividend payments, despite the volatility of corporate profits and investment expenditures.[22]

At any rate, if a substantial part of marginal investment expenditures are financed by debt, the disincentive effect of dividend taxes will be limited, even if the old view is correct. For example, if half of the marginal investment is financed by debt, the parameters in (4) can be shown to imply a cost of capital of 5.8% under the new view, and a required return to 6.1% under the old view, given a classical corporate tax system. With a full imputation system, the cost of capital under the old view would drop to 5.3%. In this particular example, the maximum cross-country variation in the cost of capital due to differences in the degree of dividend tax relief would thus be $6.1 - 5.3 = 0.8$ percentage points. Although this difference is not negligible, our numerical exercise nevertheless suggests that the potential efficiency gains from an EC harmonization of systems and degrees of dividend tax relief would hardly be dramatic.

Against this background, the case for a sweeping harmonization of systems of dividend taxation in the near future does not seem very strong. There does seem to be a need, however, to eliminate the systematic discrimination, embodied in most existing systems of dividend tax relief, against transnational investment in shares. In other words, if domestic shareholders benefit from relief of the taxation of dividends from domestic corporations, a similar benefit should be granted to all other EC taxpayers investing in those same corporations. Otherwise the national stock markets will remain segmented, because domestic investors benefiting from dividend tax relief will be willing to pay higher prices for domestic shares than investors from other EC countries who do not obtain relief. Such stock market segmentation will imply an inefficient allocation of risks in the Community, because the possibilities for portfolio diversification in the European capital market will not be fully exploited.

The tax discrimination against foreign shareholders could be removed if the countries which currently mitigate the double taxation of dividends extended their dividend tax credits, etc. to all EC residents, and not just to domestic residents. The revenue costs of such a procedure, however, should be fairly shared among EC governments. Hence the 'classical' countries offering no dividend tax relief should be obliged to bear part of the revenue cost, for example, through a clearing house mechanism.

4.3   Should member countries adopt a common system of international double taxation relief?

If full capital export neutrality within the EC is to be achieved, all member states would have to adopt a pure credit system of international double taxation relief. In Section 2.2 we saw that the implementation of a pure credit system would involve a number of practical and political difficulties relating to the abolition of limits on foreign tax credits, the repeal of 'deferral' in the field of transnational direct investment, and last, but not least, the integration of the foreign corporation tax with the domestic personal income tax in the field of transnational portfolio investment.

If these obstacles cannot be overcome, a Community-wide move towards a common foreign tax credit system of the present 'impure' type would hardly yield efficiency gains of a magnitude which could justify the transnational problems and the additional administrative complexity of a credit system compared with an exemption system in the area of foreign direct investment.

In the short term, it seems most natural to concentrate efforts on the removal of tax discrimination against the distribution of foreign source profits to domestic shareholders. As will be recalled from Section 2.2, such distributions generally do not obtain the same amount of dividend tax relief as distributions of domestic source profits. In countries such as Britain and France which use the imputation system, this situation could be rectified by allowing the foreign corporation tax on the foreign income to be credited against the domestic advance corporation tax which is payable when the domestic parent distributes profits to domestic shareholders.[23] Again, the revenue loss resulting from this crediting ought to be shared fairly between source countries and residence countries through a clearing mechanism.

4.4 Must the corporate tax base be harmonized?

In 1988 the European Commission circulated a draft directive calling for partial harmonization of the corporate income tax base. Since the draft met with scepticism from several member states, it was later withdrawn.

Many economists have argued that a harmonization of the corporate income tax base should take precedence over a harmonization of corporate tax rates. The rationale for this position was explained in Section 2.2 which mentioned that, for debt-financed investment, capital export neutrality can be obtained in the presence of cross-country differences in tax rates, as long as taxable profits correspond to true economic profits in all countries.

In practice, however, it is extremely difficult to ensure coincidence of taxable profits and true profits. Differences between the two profit measures will almost inevitably exist under any harmonized income tax base. In that case, we saw in Section 2.2 that tax base harmonization will not achieve capital export neutrality when national corporate income tax rates differ. Therefore, it would probably be too optimistic to expect significant efficiency gains from base harmonization.

Base harmonization might nevertheless entail some benefits by making the Community tax system more transparent, and by reducing the tax compliance costs for European multinationals. It might also help to neutralize beggar-thy-neighbour practices whereby member countries try to divert capital from each others' jurisdictions by offering favourable depreciation allowances and so on.

Member countries would probably be reluctant to give up their right to stimulate particular types of investment through such incentives. Still, it can be argued that incentives should be given in the form of grants (subject to Community approval) and be recorded in a separate budget so as to make them more visible. This might help the Community to do away with distorting subsidies which serve no legitimate social purpose.

4.5 A minimum corporate tax rate?

Some observers have advocated the adoption of a required minimum statutory corporate income tax rate to limit the scope for tax competition (see, for example, Cnossen (1991, p. 29)). There is indeed a case for such a provision. Even though we argued in Section 3.2 that the corporation tax would hardly vanish under unfettered tax competition, there are still reasons to believe that corporate tax rates would end up at a level which is inefficiently low from a Community viewpoint.[24] The reason is simple. If one member country diverts capital from other member countries by lowering its corporate tax rate, the outflow of capital from the other members will generally impose a loss of output, employment and tax revenue on them.

Still, in the absence of base harmonization, a minimum statutory corporate tax rate would not prevent member states from lowering their effective tax rates by offering generous deductions from taxable profits. Hence it would be natural to combine a minimum statutory tax rate with some amount of harmonization or approximation of corporate tax bases.

4.6　Can enforcement of taxes on interest be improved?

One potential objection to the adoption of a minimum (effective) corporate tax rate is that this could exacerbate the current tax discrimination against equity finance.[25] In Section 3 it was pointed out that taxes on interest income may become increasingly difficult to enforce in an economic and monetary union with high mobility of portfolio investment. With a strong downward pressure on taxes on interest combined with a minimum tax on corporate equity income, the current tax preference for debt over equity may become even stronger. This could induce corporations to accept high gearing ratios which would make them undesirably vulnerable to downturns of the business cycle and other negative shocks.[26]

The obvious solution to this problem would be improved enforcement of taxes on interest income through the introduction of reporting systems, Community-wide exchange of information, and relaxation of bank secrecy laws. To be effective, however, such measures of coordination might have to involve several non-EC countries (e.g. Switzerland and even the United States) where international tax evaders could otherwise seek refuge.

5　The size and distribution of efficiency gains from tax harmonization

A programme of (partial) capital income tax harmonization in the EC would involve a loss of sovereignty for the makers of national tax policies. Before deciding whether to accept this loss, policy-makers would wish to have at least a rough idea of the likely size and distribution of the economic gains from harmonization.

The aggregate efficiency gain from an equalization of effective tax rates on capital income would stem from the resulting cross-country equalization of marginal products of capital. This total efficiency gain, however, would be unevenly distributed across countries and across socio-economic groups within individual countries. Generally speaking EC member countries experiencing an outflow of capital as a result of harmonization would suffer a loss of national income[27] whereas countries faced with an inflow of capital from abroad would see their national income levels go up.

The national gain to the countries receiving an increase of investment from abroad would mainly accrue to wage earners (and possibly land owners) in those countries. For the owners of capital in the previous high-tax countries, the gain from a lower tax burden would gradually be eroded, because the inflow of additional investment from abroad would tend to drive down the pre-tax rate of return on investment in the country. Conversely, in the low-tax countries which experienced an outflow of capital, the national loss would mainly be felt by wage earners who would be faced with a lower demand for labour resulting from a falling investment level. For the owners of capital in these countries, the higher tax burden would gradually be compensated by a rise in the pre-tax rate of return stemming from a lower supply of capital to the country.

If the total economic gain from tax harmonization is positive, the gainers from harmonization should in principle be able to compensate the losers, so as to leave all the parties involved better off than before. In practice, such a scenario may be very difficult to implement, since it would require that a programme of tax harmonization be supplemented by policy measures to redistribute income across and within EC member countries.

An estimate of the effects of corporate income tax harmonization within the EC has recently been offered by Fuente and Gardner (1990). They base their calculations on a simplified computable general equilibrium model of a 'world' economy consisting of the EC, the United States and Japan. Estimates of marginal effective corporate tax wedges[28] are incorporated into the model to capture the (dis)incentives for investment implied by the corporate tax system. Foreign direct investment is excluded, so all transnational flows of capital are assumed to take the form of portfolio investment. The model is calibrated so as to be able to reproduce a data set on the capital stocks invested in the various countries in 1985. It is then used to simulate the reallocation of these capital stocks and the ensuing changes in net domestic products resulting from various hypothetical EC tax harmonization programmes. Because savings and labour supplies are assumed to be inelastic, the changes in output levels also reflect welfare changes.

Fuente and Gardner consider three alternative harmonization scenarios. In scenario 1, they assume that statutory corporate income tax rates are allowed to stay at their 1990 levels, but that the corporate income tax bases are partially harmonized in accordance with the Commission's 1988 draft proposal. This scenario still leaves room for a standard deviation of

Table 11.5. *Estimated effects[a] on output levels of corporate tax harmonization into the European Community*

	Output level in an integrated market without harmonization (1985 = 100)	Harmonization scenario		
		(1)	(2)	(3)
		(Index, first column = 100)		
Belgium	98.9	99.3	98.7	99.9
Denmark	100.9	98.9	98.5	99.8
France	94.7	101.4	101.4	101.2
Germany[b]	90.7	101.2	103.0	105.4
Greece	118.4	101.6	101.0	102.2
Ireland	120.5	99.8	97.3	98.1
Italy	99.8	99.5	100.0	103.2
Luxembourg	96.6	99.0	99.1	98.6
Netherlands	95.9	101.2	100.0	102.3
Portugal	128.5	101.6	101.2	102.2
Spain	111.1	100.4	98.9	101.1
United Kingdom	115.9	101.0	101.0	99.9
European Community	101.9	100.7	100.9	102.1
United States	100.0	99.5	99.4	98.5
Japan	100.0	99.5	99.4	98.5
World	100.0	100.0	100.0	100.1

Notes:
[a] The estimates assume a common inflation rate of 2%. Output levels are measured by net domestic products. See the text for an explanation of the three alternative harmonization scenarios.
[b] Figures are for the Federal Republic of Germany before unification.
Source: Fuente and Gardner (1990, Table 10).

1.1 percentage points in marginal effective corporate tax wedges across EC member countries. Scenario 2 includes scenario 1 plus an equalization of the statutory income tax rates of individual countries around the 1990 weighted EC average of 43%. The scenario further assumes the elimination of local income taxes on corporations, but it retains the existing differences in the degree of dividend tax relief, the existing taxes on the value of corporate assets or corporate net worth, and differences in depreciation rates[29] and investment grants. The harmonization of statutory tax rates in scenario 2 only reduces the standard deviation of marginal effective corporate tax wedges within the EC by 0.3 percentage points relative to scenario 1, leaving a 0.8 percentage point standard deviation of effective tax wedges. Scenario 3 assumes complete equalization of company tax systems in the EC. In particular, this implies abolition of capital based (wealth) taxes and investment grants and the introduction of a common imputation system involving a credit on dividends equivalent to 50% of the underlying corporation tax, with this credit being extended to all EC residents. By construction, scenario 3 reduces the standard deviation of marginal effective corporate tax wedges within the EC to zero.

In Table 11.5 the estimated effects on net domestic products of these alternative harmonization scenarios are shown; perfect mobility of portfolio capital is assumed between the EC and the 'rest' of the world, consisting of the US and Japan. The figures in the three last columns are index numbers which are measured relative to the first column. The numbers in the first column indicate the output levels which would prevail if after-tax returns to corporate investment were completely equalized within the Community. These output levels of an 'integrated' Europe with non-harmonized tax systems are measured relative to the 1985 output levels calculated by the model. For example, Table 11.5 shows that Portugal can expect an increase in potential output of about 28.5% relative to 1985 as a result of EC capital market integration, if the 1990 tax rules are maintained. Further, relative to the output level associated with an integrated European capital market, Portugal would experience an additional output gain of 2.2% in the case of complete EC corporate tax harmonization, as indicated in the last column of Table 11.5.

It will be seen from the first column of the table that countries like Portugal, Ireland, Greece, the UK and Spain will be the major beneficiaries of European capital market integration under the 1990 tax rules, whereas Germany will be the major loser from the integration process. These estimates simply reflect the hypothesis that in a unified EC capital market, capital will flow from countries like Germany with a high effective corporate tax wedge to the countries just mentioned where effective tax wedges are relatively low.

The figures shown in Table 11.5 also suggest that the changes in potential output levels which would follow from corporate tax harmonization would be fairly modest compared to the changes that would seem to follow from the process of capital market integration. Thus, it can be predicted from this table that no country would experience an additional change in potential output in excess of 1.6% if the European Commission's 1988 draft proposal for partial harmonization of the corporate tax base were implemented. If such base harmonization were supplemented by harmonization of statutory corporate tax rates, Germany would apparently experience a noticeable output gain of 3%, while Ireland would suffer an output loss of 2.7%, but for most other countries the output changes would be small. For the EC as a whole, the two harmonization scenarios would imply an output gain of less than 1%.

On the other hand, the Fuente-Gardner simulation model implies that a complete harmonization of corporate tax systems (scenario 3) would yield an increase in total Community output of about 2%. Germany and Italy would be the major beneficiaries, while countries like Ireland and Luxembourg would lose. The total EC output gain of 2% may be compared to the expected gains from the completion of the internal market, which have been estimated by the Commission to be in the order of 4.5–6.5% of EC output.

It is important to note that most of the EC gain from corporate tax harmonization would come at the expense of the rest of the world. The specific harmonization, scenario 3, considered by Fuente and Gardner implies a reduction of the average value of the marginal effective corporate tax wedge in Europe. This leads to an increase in the demand for capital in the EC area which in turn drives up European interest rates, thereby attracting capital from the US and Japan and reducing the output and income levels of those countries. According to the simulation model, which embodies a variant of the 'old view' of dividend taxation, a major reason for the fall in the effective tax wedge on European corporate capital in scenario 3 is that this scenario involves an increase in the average degree of dividend tax relief in the EC. As recognized by Fuente and Gardner (1990, p. 31), however, and as borne out by our previous discussion of the 'new' view versus the 'old' view, the quantative effects of dividend tax relief on the cost of corporate capital is rather uncertain. At any rate, the main point is that the level around which effective corporate tax rates are harmonized will be crucial for the magnitude and even the sign of the gains from harmonization. If tax rates are harmonized at a high level, capital will be driven out of Europe, and the Community as a whole could then suffer a loss of output and income.

It should also be stressed that from the Fuente-Gardner model, it can be predicted that corporate tax harmonization would induce a substantial reallocation of capital stock, both within the Community, and between the Community and the rest of the world. In other words, the short and medium term effects on international investment flows could be sizeable. The reason why the longer term effects on potential output levels are nevertheless modest is that the elasticity of net aggregate output with respect to capital inputs is only around 0.2–0.3.

Of course, the quantitative estimates of Fuente and Gardner should not be taken too literally, because of the underlying simplifying assumptions. In particular, their model considers only the static effects of the reallocation of the existing world capital stock induced by tax harmonization.

The dynamic effects of tax harmonization on savings, capital accumulation and economic growth are not incoporated into the model. Again, the sign and magnitude of these effects would depend crucially on the level around which effective tax rates were harmonized. Harmonization at a low level could spur savings and growth, whereas equalization of tax rates at a high level would be likely to have the opposite effect.

6 Conclusions

It is time now to summarize the main conclusions from this lengthy journey through the European tax jungle.

While certainly not negligible, the magnitude of the intra-Community tax distortions of capital costs reported in Section 2.3 are not dramatic. Although the study reviewed in Section 4 found considerable tax distortion in the allocation of capital in the EC, the resulting loss of economic welfare seems to be modest. Moreover, the potential gains from harmonization of capital income taxes will be unevenly distributed and may to a large extent come at the expense of the rest of the world.

On this basis, it can be conjectured that it should be possible to reap the major part of the benefits from economic and monetary integration in Europe without harmonizing capital income taxes. To be sure, we have identified a need to remove certain tax obstacles to transnational investment in the Community. The removal of one of these obstacles has already been ensured by the agreement to abolish withholding taxes on dividends from a subsidiary in one member country to a parent company in another member country. The discrimination against transnational investment embodied in existing systems of domestic and international double taxation relief, however, also needs to be abolished before EC capital markets can become truly integrated. Further, it was seen that increasing capital mobility in Europe may exacerbate the existing tax discrimination against equity finance, by making it ever more difficult for governments to collect taxes on interest income. This suggests a need for improved intra-Community cooperation to enforce these taxes.

The last observation leads immediately to the most important political question raised by the analysis in this chapter. Governments in the EC should soon consider seriously whether they wish to retain personal taxes on income from capital in reality and not just on paper. If the answer is affirmative, they must soon take steps to ensure that such taxes can actually be enforced in an integrated European (and indeed global) capital market. This will be a very difficult task, involving sensitive issues such as bank secrecy laws, and requiring a cooperative attitude from non-EC countries.

If EC governments refuse to face this challenge directly, the days of the personal income tax as we know it may be numbered. Personally, I believe that significant gains in efficiency, equity, and administrative simplicity could be made by exempting capital income from tax (and abolishing the deductibility of interest) at the personal level, and by taxing the rents accruing in the business sector through a cash-flow tax on businesses.[30] A tax system like this, however, should be introduced in a civilized and orderly way as a result of informed, democratic decision-making. It should not be forced upon governments and citizens in an erratic manner by the forces of reckless and self-interested tax competition!

NOTES

I have benefited from discussions with numerous colleagues, in particular Michael Daly and Michael Devereux in preparing this chapter. Constructive comments and criticisms from the two discussants of the conference, Alberto Giovannini and Vitor Constâncio, are also gratefully acknowledged. Parts of the chapter drew on my work as a consultant for the committee of independent experts examining business taxation in the European Community. The views expressed in the chapter are purely personal, however, and have not been endorsed by the committee.

1. The chapter supplements recent contributions by Cnossen (1991), Daly (1991), Devereux and Pearson (1989, 1991), Fuente and Gardner (1990), Giovannini (1989 and 1990), Gros (1990), Hermann et al. (1991), Isard (1991), Keen (1991), Sinn (1990), Sørensen (1990a), Tanzi and Bovenberg (1990), and Vanheukelen (1991).
2. If taxes paid abroad exceed the domestic tax liability, it will be necessary for the country of residence to grant a refund of the excess foreign tax bill.
3. For a thorough discussion of the choice between the two neutrality criteria, see OECD (1991, Ch. 2).
4. See, for example, the survey of optimal tax theory by Auerbach (1985).
5. This chapter can only sketch the main features of the present EC tax systems. A more detailed description of the tax rules prevailing on 1 January 1991 can be found in OECD (1991).
6. This point has previously been stressed by Sinn (1990).
7. Accelerated depreciation implies deductions in excess of true costs in the first years following an investment outlay, and the tax saving from this deduction is clearly higher, the higher the tax rate.
8. The following discussion draws on Sørensen (1991c, section C.7).
9. It is only fair to add that this limitation on the foreign tax credit is a common OECD practice.
10. In the UK, the discrimination stems from the fact that foreign taxes cannot be credited against the so-called advance corporation tax payable at the time of distribution. In France, where foreign-source income is exempt from domestic tax, discrimination is caused by the fact that advance corporation tax is likewise levied at the time of distribution, even though corporate and withholding taxes have already been paid abroad.
11. The asset weights are 27% for buildings, 50% for machinery, and 23% for

inventories; while the financing weights are 35% for debt, 10% for new equity, and 55% for retentions.

12. The calculations in Table 11.4 may exaggerate the disincentive effects of withholding taxes, because multinationals can often circumvent these taxes by channelling dividends through third countries with low or zero withholding taxes. For a description of such 'treaty shopping' practices, see Giovannini (1989). Further, as will be noted below, withholding taxes on intra-Community dividend payments from subsidiaries to parent companies are in fact about to be dismantled as a result of the so-called parent-subsidiary directive.

13. The following three sub-sections draw on current joint work with Michael Devereux.

14. See Razin and Sadka (1989). A similar result was found by Sørensen (1988).

15. Giovannini (1989) essentially arrives at the same conclusion, albeit via a slightly different route.

16. Again, see Razin and Sadka (1989, 1991) or Sørensen (1988, 1990b).

17. This point is due to Mintz (1991).

18. For a description of the events culminating in the repeal, see, for example, Sørensen (1991a, p. 20).

19. These averages exclude Greece where information for 1980 was not available.

20. In Sørensen (1990a) I have discussed the Sinn-proposal and the proposal for unitary taxation in some detail.

21. A non-technical exposition of the two 'views', with references to the literature, can be found in OECD (1991, Ch. 2).

22. In an oft-quoted study, Poterba and Summers (1985) found that the British post-war experience tended to confirm the old rather than the new view. On the other hand, Auerbach (1984) found empirical support for the new view in US data.

23. If the foreign tax exceeds the domestic advance tax, the difference could be set against other domestic tax liabilities or refunded, if necessary.

24. For a theoretical analysis supporting this conclusion, see, for example, Sørensen (1991b).

25. As demonstrated in OECD (1991), the cost of capital for debt-financed investment is systematically lower than the required return on equity-financed investment throughout the OECD area. This is mainly because of the full deductibility of nominal interest payments and the fact that interest income is taxed at rates below the corporate tax rate in many countries.

26. In addition, growing debt ratios and corporate interest expenses would erode the revenue from the corporate income tax, and this would not be offset by a higher revenue from interest income taxes, if the latter taxes cannot be enforced.

27. In some extreme cases this may not be true. If a country offers very generous tax incentives, implying a large negative marginal effective tax rate on foreign investment into the country, a reduction of capital imports may actually raise the national income of the country by reducing the amount of tax subsidies transferred to foreigners. Note, however, that such a scenario presumes that the capital-importing country is initially pursuing a tax policy which is not in its own best interest.

28. The marginal effective corporate tax wedge is defined as the difference between the required pre-tax rate of return on a marginal corporate invest-

ment and the pre-tax market rate of interest, with both rates being measured in real terms.
29. The Commission's 1988 draft proposal did not require an equalization of depreciation rates.
30. The cash flow tax I have in mind is the so-called 'R-base' tax described by the Meade Committee (Meade *et al.*, 1978). For a lucid discussion of the international implications of such a tax, see McLure (1991).

REFERENCES

Auerbach, A. (1985) 'The theory of excess burden and optimal taxation', in A. Auerbach and M. Feldstein (eds), *Handbook of Public Economics*, Vol. I, Amsterdam: North-Holland, 1985.
Auerbach, A. (1984) 'Taxes, firm financial policy, and the cost of capital: An empirical analysis', *Journal of Public Economics*, 23, 27–57.
Cnossen, S. (1991) 'Must the corporation tax be harmonized?' Paper prepared for the 1991 Annual Meeting of the Confederation of European Economic Associations, Amsterdam.
Daly, M. (1991) 'Problems of taxation in the European Community'. Paper prepared for the 1991 National Bureau of Economic Research Summer Institute.
Devereux, M. and Pearson, M. (1989) 'Corporate tax harmonisation and economic efficiency'. Institute for Fiscal Studies, Report Series No 35, London.
    (1991) 'Capital export neutrality, capital import neutrality and European tax harmonisation: An empirical assessment'. Paper prepared for the 1991 National Bureau of Economic Research Summer Institute.
Fuente, A. and Gardner, E. (1990) 'Corporate income tax harmonization and capital allocation in the European Community', International Monetary Fund Working Paper 90/103, Washington DC.
Giovannini, A. (1989) 'National tax systems versus the European capital market', *Economic Policy*, 9, 346–71.
    (1990) 'International capital mobility and capital income taxation – Theory and policy', *European Economic Review*, 34, 480–8.
Giovannini, A. and Hines, J. (1990) 'Capital flight and tax competition: Are there viable solutions to both problems?', Centre for Economic Policy Research Discussion Papers 5/90, London.
Gros, D. (1990) 'Capital-market liberalisation and the taxation of savings', Working Party Report No. 2, Centre for European Policy Studies, Bruxelles.
Hermann, A., Leibfritz, W., Woon Nam, C. and Sørensen, P.B. (1991) 'Scope and limits of fiscal policy coordination in the EC', *Tokyo Club Papers*, No. 4, Part 1, Tokyo Club Foundation for Global Studies.
Hulten, C. and Wykoff, F. (1981) 'The measurement of economic depreciation', in C. Hulten (ed.), *Depreciation, inflation and the taxation of income from capital*, Washington DC, The Urban Institute Press.
Isard, P. (1991) 'Corporate tax harmonization and European monetary integration', *Kyklos*, 43, 3–24.
Keen, M. (1991) 'Corporation tax, foreign direct investment and the single

market', in L. Winters and A. Venables (eds), *The impact of 1992 on European trade and industry*, Cambridge: Cambridge University Press.

King, M. and Fullerton, D. (1984) *The taxation of income from capital: A comparative study of the U.S., U.K., Sweden and West Germany*, Chicago: Chicago University Press.

McLure, C. (1991) 'Replacing income taxes with direct consumption taxes as the international norm', Paper presented at the 1991 International Seminar in Public Economics on Taxation in Open Economies, CORE, Belgium, June 15–16.

Meade, J. *et al.* (1978) 'The structure and reform of direct taxation', London: Institute for Fiscal Studies.

Mintz, J. (1991) 'Is there a future for capital income taxation?: A theoretical analysis', Paper prepared for the Organisation for Economic Cooperation and Development.

Organisation for Economic Cooperation and Development (1991), *Taxing profits in a global economy: The experience of OECD countries*, Paris: OECD.

Poterba, J. and Summers, L. (1985) 'The economic effects of dividend taxation', in E. Altman and M. Subrahmanyem (eds), *Recent advances in corporate finance*, Homewood, Illinois: Irwin.

Razin, A. and Sadka, E. (1989) 'International tax competition and gains from tax harmonization', National Bureau of Economic Research Working Paper No. 352, Cambridge, Mass.

Razin, A. and Sadka, E. (1991) 'International fiscal policy coordination and competition', Paper presented at the 1991 International Seminar in Public Economics on Taxation in Open Economies, CORE, Belgium, June 15–16.

Sinn, H.-W. (1990) 'Tax harmonization and tax competition in Europe', *European Economic Review*, **34**, 489–504.

Sørensen, P.B. (1988) 'Optimal taxation of capital and labor in a small open economy', Paper presented at the international conference on Tax Reform for Tax Neutrality at the University of Bielefeld, Germany, May 30–June 2.

(1990a) 'Tax harmonization in the European Community: Problems and Prospects', Bank of Finland Discussion Papers no. 3/90.

(1990b) 'Optimal capital taxation in a small capital-importing economy', in V. Tanzi (ed.), *Public finance, trade and development*, Detroit: Wayne State University Press.

(1991a) 'The effects of taxation on international investment and economic efficiency'. To be published as an annex to the forthcoming report from the committee of independent experts examining business taxation in the EC.

(1991b) 'Welfare gains from international fiscal coordination', in Rémy Prud'homme (ed.), *Public Finance with Several Levels of Government*, Proceedings of the 46th Congress of the International Institute of Public Finance, Brussels. The Hague: Foundation Journal Public Finance.

(1991c) 'The corporate income tax: Main policy issues', Working Paper from the Institute of Economics, Copenhagen Business School.

Tanzi, V. and Bovenberg, L. (1989) 'Is there a need for harmonizing capital income taxes within EC countries?', Paper presented at the conference on Reforming capital income taxation at the Kiel Institute of World Economics, Germany, December 7–8.

Vanheukelen, M. (1991) 'Corporate tax harmonization in the European Community', in Rémy Prud'homme (ed.), *Public Finance with Several Levels of*

Government, Proceedings of the 46th Congress of the International Institute of Public Finance, Brussels. The Hague: Foundation Journal Public Finance.

Weiner, J. (1991) 'Formula apportionment and the European Community: Evidence from the U.S. states on the effects of an apportioned tax on business investment', Discussion Paper no. 9102 from the Centre d'Economie Mathématique et d'Econometrie, Université Libre de Bruxelles.

Discussion

ALBERTO GIOVANNINI

The chapter by Peter Sørensen provides an admirably clear synthesis of the research on the policy questions surrounding capital income taxation in the presence of international capital mobility, and of some of the problems facing European countries. Like the literature it surveys, the chapter does not take a stand on the welfare effects of alternative regimes of capital income taxation, and therefore it does not answer the biggest question currently facing European countries: what are the efficiency losses of the current regime, and can governments afford to leave it unchanged, despite substantial integration of goods and factor markets?

The purpose of my comments is to highlight the reasons why, in the current state of the art, a reliable answer to this question is not available. Yet I believe that an analysis of the current regime and of its problems does help to evaluate alternative reform proposals.

Interest in the field of international taxation began when capital controls were liberalized by a number of industrial and developing countries during the 1980s. This interest is at an all-time high in Europe, as EC countries embark on economic and monetary union. International taxation, however, like other areas of public finance, does not always rest on firm analytical grounds: hence the proliferation of terms like 'criteria' and 'views'. Criteria and views should not provide the foundation for sound policy decisions, but often in public finance they do.

Sørensen starts, traditionally, with the definition of capital import neutrality (CIN) and capital export neutrality (CEN), and argues, convincingly, that the latter is the most reliable criterion. (The debate on the relative desirability of CIN versus CEN is a good illustration of a tendency to move away from fully specified general equilibrium models to study the effects of alternative tax regimes: the author brings us back on track with his own discussion). Having argued for the superiority of CEN, Sørensen sensibly reminds us that the current regime of capital income taxation in European countries does not satisfy CEN. He also points out that a move to full CEN requires some very sweeping reforms, including the abandonment of credit limitation on foreign taxes and the full harmonization of tax rules.

The biggest problem that international tax reformers are encountering in Europe is not, as some observers suspect, the rule requiring unanimity rather than qualified majority in EC decisions on tax matters. It is instead the territoriality of tax enforcement: European countries can force the obedience to their own laws only within their own territories. Because authorities in any one country cannot send their police force abroad to pursue tax evaders, all sorts of beggar-thy-neighbour policies become attractive in a world of high international capital mobility.

The question is thus whether, in the present imperfect world, differences in the level of capital income taxation across EC countries are significant. Sørensen provides some evidence to answer this question by reporting results from models of the cost of capital to international firms. These models incorporate all relevant features of tax systems, including the different regimes of corporate-personal income tax integration, and are used to estimate the cost of capital under alternative transnational investment patterns. The results of these estimates are reported in Sørensen's Table 11.4. The table shows a remarkable variation in the cost of capital across the countries of residence of the original investors, as well as across the countries of location of the productive investments. How could such large differences be realistic? Two observations need to be made here. First, the numbers in the tables are not computed on the assumption that agents or corporations are optimizing. For example, the capital structure of the multinationals in Table 11.4 is arbitrary – one-third of the investment is financed by retentions, one-third by new equity, and the rest by debt. It is almost certain that an alternative capital structure would be more desirable as a way of minimizing taxes. The second observation is that it is not clear that an investor willing to increase his holdings in, say, a Belgian company should directly bring his own funds from his country of residence to Belgium. Funding a venture capital company in Luxembourg with the purpose of investing in Belgian corporations might prove to be a more desirable strategy from a tax viewpoint. Hence, the geograhic pattern of investment is also arbitrary.

This discussion provides two explanations for the evidence given in Table 11.4. The first is that the table is not useful, because investment does not actually take place at the rate shown in the table. The alternative is that investment does take place, but that the rates in Table 11.4 do not represent the actual shadow values of capital in European countries.

I can think of two main reasons why the calculations in Table 11.4 might not represent the actual incentives to move capital across European countries. These reasons provide, in my opinion, potential areas for research in international taxation, since Table 11.4 represents a genuine and important puzzle, which needs an explanation. The first potential explanation is that information is asymmetric. It appears that the shadow cost of alternative means of financing might change significantly as it is associated with a different distribution of information on the value of the activities being financed, and different patterns of control. Problems of asymmetric information are likely to be magnified in an international setting. The second potential explanation has to do with adjustment costs. In the presence of uncertainty, companies might be reluctant to move capital around, when they know they can be stuck with unproductive investments, either at home or overseas. In a world where tax rules are non-neutral, and where there is still exchange-rate uncertainty, it is possible that the cost of capital will have to deviate a long way from what it would be in conditions of certainty if productive investment is to move across borders.

In sum, while we see a lot of tax arbitrage opportunities, and we suspect that accountants and bankers are busy advising their clients on many more of them, we are not quite sure why such opportunities are not fully arbitraged away. This ignorance, however, should not, in my opinion, prevent us from addressing the problems of European corporate tax harmonization.

It is clear that the regimes of corporate income taxation presently in existence in Europe were constructed at times when governments did not have much to fear from international capital flows. It is also clear that the creation of the single European market provides a unique opportunity to make the system more rational and efficient in all European countries. Sørensen reminds us, however, the theoretical optimum may not be a feasible reform in the short term. Given these observations, I would like to conclude that the Commission's strategy, to harmonize corporate tax bases to the maximum extent while at the same time imposing floors on corporate tax rates, is eminently reasonable.

Index

absolute interest differential 271, 273
absolute risk premium 276
adjustable exchange rates 331
adjustment
  costs 133
  exchange rate 194
  problems in monetary unions 267
  speed of 194, 197, 209, 217–221, 223, 224, 231
  to permanent shocks 198
  to region-specific shocks 199
aggregate demand disturbance 194, 200, 215, 221, 223
  correlation of EC countries Figure 7.4
  correlation of Mid East region with USA as a whole Figure 7.4
  in European Community and USA Figure 7.3
aggregate demand shocks 194, 195, 207, 209, 212, 223, 255
aggregate-supply-aggregate-demand models 202, 207, 209
aggregate supply disturbance 194, 200, 215, 221, 223, 230
  correlation of, EC countries Figure 7.4
  correlation of Mid-East region with USA as a whole Figure 7.4
  in European Community and USA Figure 7.3

balanced budget rule 47, 48, 50, 71, 72, 73, 77, 83, 87
balanced budget targets 75
Basle-Norborg agreement 309
Baumol-Tobin models 334, 338
Bayesian learning 111, 113
Bretton Woods period/system 121, 122, 207
budget deficits 38, 70–71, 193

Calvo contracts 94, 103–107

capital controls 11, 128, 130
capital export neutrality (CEN) 342, 344, 345, 352, 353, 354, 355, 356, 358, 359, 370, 382
capital import neutrality (CIN) 342, 359, 382
capital flows 196, 273
capital mobility 42, 136, 141, 144, 145, 190, 193, 196
cash flow tax 378
cash-in-advance requirements 151
  models 323, 329
Chow tests 207
classical corporate tax 352, 355, 370
Cobb-Douglas production function 134, 136, 155
convergence criteria 1, 2, 3, 11, 16, 41, 43–45, 90, 232, 332
coordination of capital income taxes 365
core countries 3, 160, 190, 205, 212, 214, 216, 221, 223, 224, 231, 234, 236, 237
Council of Finance Ministers ECOFIN 9, 10, 12, 13, 15, 19, 20, 39
country barriers 272, 297
covered interest rate differential 272, 273, 276, 313
crawling peg system 232
cross-border investment 7, 340
  payments 14
  deposits 30, 318, 333
  labour mobility 239
Currency Forecasters' Digest 281, 287, 288, 289, 290, 295
currency substitution 7, 30, 319, 324, 328, 329, 333, 334, 335, 339

data generating process (DGP) 53, 54, 83, 84, 87
debt to gdp ratio 12, 15, 17, 18, 39, 40, 46, 47, 50, 51, 56, 57, 61, 62, 68, 84

385

deficits-excessive 2, 25, 38, 47
Delors Report 11, 12, 21, 23, 27, 41, 42, 46,
    47, 48
    committee 20, 21
demand disturbances 207, 212
demand shocks 202, 214
    regional 212
Deutschmark 5, 29, 93, 119, 128, 130, 283,
    294, 303
    area 76
    target zone 286
dividend deduction scheme 352
double taxation 352, 353, 354, 355, 368,
    370

ECOFIN 9, 10, 12, 13, 15, 19, 20, 39
economic and monetary union (EMU) 1, 4,
    9, 10, 11, 20, 25, 26, 28, 34, 37, 44, 45,
    46, 73, 190, 193, 230, 241, 266, 333, 340
ECU 14, 15, 23, 24, 25, 26, 27, 34, 232, 336
    currency composition of 14
    effective tax rates 340
employment growth 253–256
endogenous growth
    models 160, 164, 165, 179, 180, 189, 190,
    191, 192, 258
ERM bands 7, 292, 293, 314
European central banks 12, 28
European Monetary Institute 8, 10, 11, 12,
    13, 14, 15, 18, 21, 22, 25, 26, 27,
    28–29, 33, 34, 42
European monetary system (EMS) 1, 46,
    93, 116, 122, 128, 145, 149, 154, 193,
    230, 231, 232, 234, 235, 239, 241, 243,
    259, 260, 266, 267, 270, 272, 279, 312,
    313, 336, 337
European system of central banks (ESCB)
    12, 13, 23, 27, 31, 42, 44
excessive government deficits 2, 11, 15, 17,
    47, 50, 75
exchange rate
    adjustment 44, 125, 195
    credibility of 123, 128, 142, 153
    instability 6, 29, 30, 331
    mechanism (ERM) 1, 5, 94, 126, 239,
    304, 313
    nominal 123, 127, 153, 335, Figure D.4.8
    peg 94, 153, 156
    real 119, 196, 197, 269, 315, 335, Figure
    D.45, D.4.6 and D.4.7
    stability 29, 270, 279, 281, 328
exchange risk premium 273, 281, 313
external economies 245, 247

Factor mobility 161, 176, 190, 194, 223,
    224, 230, 243, 247, 254, 255, 258

fiscal balances 74, 84
fiscal convergence 90, 92
fiscal deficits 47, 75
fiscal guidelines 50, 75, 90
fiscal policies
    independent 46
    of EC countries 49
    primacy of 255–256
fiscal rules 2, 47, 48, 71, 72
fiscal stabilization 239
Fischer contracts 99–103, 121, 122, Figure
    4.2
flexible exchange rates 337
floating exchange rates 329, 335, 337

geographic concentration 245, 246, 259
    linkages 176, 180
    spillovers 169
growth rate differentials Figures D.6.1 and
    D.6.2
    correlation of Figures D.6.3 and D.6.4

harmonization
    of capital taxes 7, 341, 345, 361, 377
    of corporate tax base 371
    of dividend taxation 369
    distribution of efficiency gains 372–377
    size of efficiency gains 372–377

imputation systems 352, 368, 369, 370
impulse response function 139, 207, 209,
    221, 223
    to demand shocks Figure 7.7
    EC and USA Figure 7.2
    supply shocks Figure 7.6
increasing returns to scale 159, 160, 164,
    190
industrial specialization 238
inflation convergence 5, 93, 95, 111, 116,
    128, 130, 138, 144, 145, 153, 155, 233,
    270
    differentials 4, 6, 94, 119, 121, 144, 270,
    272, 281, 294, 297, 307, 313; Finland
    and Belgium in relation to Germany
    Figure D.9.1
    sluggishness 111
inflation rates
    Germany, Italy, Portugal Figure D.4.4
    Germany, Netherlands, France Figure
    D.4.1
    Portugal Figure 5.1
    USA and Canada Figure D.4.3
    US cities Figure D.4.2
instruments of economic policy 269
interest rate
    real 5, 38, 135

nominal 124, 126, 127, 128, 143, 144, 151, Figure 5.1
intergovernmental conference 1, 9, 10, 12, 28

knowledge spillovers 165

labour mobility 4, 167, 169, 170, 171, 190, 191, 192, 198, 239, 263, 264, 266, 268
learning spillovers 165
liberalization
of capital flows 141, 144, 168, 333
of goods 168
linkages 161, 167, 170, 176, 245, 247, 259
Lucas critique 83, 87
Lucas type endogenous growth 192

Maastricht Treaty 1, 8, 12, 18, 25, 26, 27, 28, 38, 41, 43, 44, 47, 50, 52, 270
money demand equation 323
money demand function 319
monetary policy 14, 21, 24, 28, 29, 30, 31, 38, 42, 143, 233, 236
monetary policy instruments 22, 28, 31, 33, Table D.2.1
monetary union 2, 224, 230, 255, 266, 269, 270, 307

national monetary authority 24, 25
non-tradables
relative price of 5, 120, 149, 153, Figure 5.1
goods 128, 129, 130, 133, 134, 136–140, 141, 143–145, 150, 233, 316
neutral tax treatment 341
New England 241, 242, 243, 244
nominal exchange rates 123, 127, 153, 335
and prices Figure D.4.8

optimum currency area 44, 194, 195, 197, 236, 237, 266
optimum taxation 342
Organisation for Economic Cooperation and Development (OECD) 49, 56, 71, 80, 155, 202, 203, 207, 308
overlapping contracts 93, 94, 123, 124

payments systems 33, 34
peripheral countries 3, 188, 206, 212, 214, 216, 217, 221, 230, 231, 234, 236, 237
policy instruments 23, 42, Table D.2.1
political business cycle models 66–67
political instability models 64–65
pooling of operations, central banks 22, 23
primary balances 75, 90
primary deficits 52, 61, 62, 63

surpluses 53, 63, 76, 84, 90
public choice models 63–64
purchasing power parities 119, 122, 149

rational expectations 6, 93, 94, 107, 111
realignment 4, 26, 27, 271, 279, 281, 309, 310, 313, 314
expected rate against the Deutschmark Figures 9.9 and 9.10
term, estimation of, 292–294
real exchange rates 119, 196, 197, 269, 315, 335
Canada Figure D.4.7
Italy and Portugal Figure D.4.6
Netherlands and France Figure D.4.5
regional concentration 267
regional demand disturbances 212, 217
regional growth rates 243, 248, 266, 267
regional specialization 224, 242, 244, 247, 249–252, 254, 258, 262
regional stabilization policies 255, 256, 257
region-specific shocks 196, 248, 252, 255, 260
reputational mechanisms 50, 74
reserve requirements 23, 24, 33
residence principle of taxation 343, 344
Romer-Lucas model 188
Route 128 244, 251

Schwartz-Bayesian information criterion 207
shareholder relief schemes 352
Silicon Valley 244, 251
size of shocks 215–217
Solow-Cass-Loopmans neoclassical model 137, 192
source-based taxation 362, 363, 364
speed of adjustment 194, 197, 209, 217–221, 223, 224, 231
spillovers 165, 169, 177, 180, 191
strategic debt models 65, 66
supply disturbances 207, 215
supply shocks 202, 211, 214, 215

target zone model 281, 286–292, 294, 313, 314
target zones 6, 279, 283, 292, 307, 309, 314
Taylor contracts 95–99, 112, 121, 122, Figure 4.1
tax arbitrage opportunities 383
tax competition 7, 340, 361, 362, 363, 364, 371
tax discrimination 370, 377
tax distortions 341, 356, 360, 361, 377
tax harmonization 361, 372–377

tax haven countries 356, 362
tax neutrality 345
tax smoothing 48, 49, 50, 67, 71, 72, 73, 75,
  83, 87, 89, 90
time-varying credibility 281, 297
time-varying risk premium 276
tradable goods 128, 133, 134, 136–140, 142,
  143–145, 150, 233, 316
tradables, relative price of 5, 129, 149, 153
transfer pricing 364, 366

two-speed EMU 50, 76, 223, 224, 230
uncovered interest parity 281, 283, 294

wage contracts 121, 123
wage setters 94, 123, 125, 126
wage setting 93, 124
Walters critique 144–145
Werner plan 1, 2
withholding taxes 345, 353, 354, 359, 364,
  366